Who's Who in Early Hanoverian Britain

1714–1789

Who's Who in Early Hanoverian Britain

1714–1789

GEOFFREY TREASURE

STACKPOLE
BOOKS

First published in North America in 2002 by
STACKPOLE BOOKS
5067 Ritter Road
Mechanicsburg, PA 17055
www.stackpolebooks.com

Originally published in Great Britain in 1991 by Shepheard-Walwyn
(Publishers) Ltd.

Printed in the United States of America

10 9 8 7 6 5 4 3 2 1

FIRST EDITION

Library of Congress Cataloging-in-Publication Data

Treasure, G. R. R. (Geoffrey Russell Richards)
    Who's who in early Hanoverian Britain, 1714–1789 / Geoffrey
Treasure.— 1st ed.
        p. cm. — (Who's who in British history)
    Originally published: London : Shepheard-Walwyn, 1992.
    Includes bibliographical references and index.
    ISBN 0-8117-1643-0
    1. Great Britain—History—18th century—Biography. 2. Great
Britain—History—George I, 1714–1727—Biography. 3. Great Britain—
History—George II, 1727–1760—Biography. 4. Great Britain—
History—George III, 1760–1820—Biography. 5. Hanover, House of.
I. Title. II. Series

DA483.A1 T74 2002
941.07—dc21
                                            2002017015

To my brother Ronald

Contents

General Introduction

The original volumes in the series *Who's Who in British History* were well received by readers who responded favorably to the claim of the late C. R. N. Routh, general editor of the series, that there was a need for a work of reference which should present the latest findings of scholarship in the form of short biographical essays. Published by Basil Blackwell in five volumes, the series covered British history from the earliest times to 1837. It was designed to please several kinds of reader: the "general reader," the browser who might find it hard to resist the temptation to go from one character to another, and, of course, the student of all ages. Each author sought in his own way to convey more than the bare facts of his subject's life, to place him in the context of his age, and to evoke what was distinctive in his character and achievement. At the same time, by using a broadly chronological rather than alphabetical sequence, and by grouping together similar classes of people, each volume provided a portrait of the age. Presenting history in biographical form, it complemented the conventional textbook.

Since the publication of the first volumes of the series in the early sixties, the continuing work of research has brought new facts to light and has led to some important revaluations. In particular, the late medieval period, a hitherto somewhat neglected field, has been thoroughly studied. There has also been intense controversy about certain aspects of Tudor and Stuart history. There is plainly a need for fuller treatment of the medieval period than was allowed for in the original series, in which the late W. O. Hassall's volume covered the years 55 B.C. to 1485 A.D. The time seems also to be ripe for a reassessment of some Tudor and Stuart figures. Meanwhile, the continued requests of teachers and students for the series to be reprinted encourages the authors of the new series to think that there will be a warm response to a fuller and more comprehensive *Who's Who* which will eventually include the nineteenth and early twentieth centuries. They are therefore grateful to Shepheard-Walwyn for the opportunity to present the new, enlarged *Who's Who.*

Following Volume I, devoted to the Roman and Anglo-Saxon period, two further books cover the Middle Ages. The Tudor volume, by the late C. R. Routh, has been extensively revised by Dr. Peter Holmes. Peter Hill and I have revised for republication our own volumes on the Stuart and Georgian periods. Between Edward I's conquest of Wales and the Act of Union which joined England and Scotland in 1707, the authors' primary concern has been England, with Scotsmen and Irishmen figuring only if they happened in any way to be prominent in English history. In the eighteenth century, Scotsmen come into the picture, in the nineteenth Irishmen, in their own right, as inhabitants of Great Britain. It is hoped that full justice will be done to Scotsmen and Irishmen—and indeed to some early Welshmen—in subsequent volumes devoted to the history of those countries. When the series is complete, we believe that it will provide a comprehensive work of reference which will stand the test of time. Nowadays, when so much historical writing is necessarily becoming more technical, more abstract, or simply more specialized, when textbooks seem so often to have little room to spare for the men and women who are the life and soul of the past, there is a place for a history of our country which is composed of the lives of those who helped make it what it was, and is. In contributing to this history the authors can be said to have taken heed of the stern warning of Trevor H. Roper's inaugural lecture at Oxford in 1957 against "the removal of humane studies into a specialization so remote that they cease to have that lay interest which is their sole ultimate justification."

The hard-pressed examinee often needs an essay which puts an important life into perspective. From necessarily brief accounts he may learn valuable lessons in proportion, concision, and relevance. We hope that he will be tempted to find out more and so have added, wherever possible, the titles of books for further reading. Mindful of his needs, we have not, however, confined our attention to those who have left their mark on church and state. The man who invented the umbrella, the archbishop who shot a gamekeeper, a successful highwayman, and an unsuccessful admiral find their place among the great and good. Nor have we eschewed anecdote or turned a blind eye to folly or foible: it is not the authors' view that history which is instructive cannot also be entertaining.

With the development of a secure and civilized society, the range of characters becomes richer, their achievements more diverse. Besides the soldiers, politicians, and churchmen who dominate the medieval scene there are merchants, inventors, industrialists; more scholars, lawyers, artists; explorers and colonial pioneers. More is known about more people and the task of selection becomes ever harder. Throughout, whether looking at the medieval warrior, the Elizabethan seaman, the Stuart radical, or the eighteenth-century entrepreneur, the authors have been guided by the criterion of excellence. To record the achievements of those few who have had the chance to excel and who have left a name behind them is not to denigrate the unremarkable or unremarked for whom there was no opportunity to shine or chronicler at hand to describe what they made or did. It is not to deny that a Neville or a Pelham might have died obscure if he had not been born to high estate. It is to offer, for the instruction and inspiration of a generation which has been led too often to believe that individuals count for little in the face of the forces which shape economy and society, the conviction that a country is as remarkable as the individuals of which it is composed. In these pages there will be found examples of heroism, genius, and altruism; of self-seeking and squalor. There will be little that is ordinary. It is therefore the hope of the authors that there will be little that is dull.

GEOFFREY TREASURE
Harrow

Preface

Anybody who reads about the eighteenth century will be struck by a quality of originality in its foremost men and women. Amid those contrasts which are puzzling, yet so revealing—the reverence for law with the lack of means and will to enforce it, the concern for salvation with the heedless, earthly gusto of everyday life, the freedom and color of individual lives with the restraint and formality of style in buildings and pictures, prose and poetry—one is left with an idea, above all, of confidence expressed in the arts and in the manner of living at all levels of society. In some this took the form of a pleasing serenity and sense of proportion, in others an outgoing, arrogant belief in achievement and a contempt for the mediocre. Historians have seen an element of complacency in the thinking of the time. "Rejoice in our matchless constitution" was Blackstone's message to his contemporaries. Walpole governed with success upon the principle of inertia, and lesser men sought to imitate him. The Church acquiesced too calmly in abuses which interrupted the operation of its divine mission. Indeed one does not have to look far to find examples that fit the popular idea of the eighteenth century: bucolic squires, pluralist parsons, politicians well endowed with rotten boroughs and sinecures, aged admirals and generals who fought by the book. More characteristic, however, is an energy of spirit which foreigners noted in this country and contrasted favorablly with what they found in their own. Voltaire told his readers that "the English nation is the only one on earth which has managed to regulate the power of its kings while resisting them; where the lords are great without insolence and without vassals, and where the people takes part in the government without confusion. In England it is common to think; and literature has more honor with them than with us French." He saw the secret of success in free institutions and the rule of law. Other reasons suggest themselves. I would place emphasis upon the absence of formal education for the mass of people, and on the relatively free upbringing of the upper and middle classes. This was a mobile society, with opportunities for fame and fortune for adventurous men, a Clive, a Cook, a Hogarth, or an Arkwright. Or one might stress the superlative craftsmanship of the age, when techniques had advanced to their furthest point, before the machine took over. Men could create beautiful objects, as well as appreciate them. Whatever the reasons there can be no doubt that it was an age of great achievements. The eighteenth century saw the first effective application of the lessons of physical science to industry, and the beginnings of that intensive and devoted study of natural history which means so much to Englishmen. To mention Reynolds and Gainsborough, Fielding and Jane Austen, is only to touch the peaks of a vast artistic experience; English painting came of age and the English novel was born. Some will look for the spirit of the time in the heroic exploits of seamen like Hawke and Anson, and others will go to the circle of Doctor Johnson and his friends of "the club." Wherever one is in these supposed "pudding times" one encounters the eager spirit of self-help which is associated more usually with the Victorians. The eighteenth-century monument, with its grinning skull mocking the elegance of lettering and phrase, is an apt image of an age when men lived close to the knowledge of disease and sudden death. At a time when it seems that only the strong and lucky lived to maturity, it may be that there was something of the gambler's edge on life, an obligation upon the survivors to live fully, without thought for the morrow. The age of "sophisters, calculators, and economists," to borrow from Burke's splendid diatribe, had not yet dawned.

The field of the biographer is indeed a rich one and poses awkward problems of selection. This collection of biographical essays is meant to be a guide and introduction to the student, a consecutive history, as it unfolds in the lives of the men who made it, and a picture of the age in so far as it can be pieced together from miscellaneous facts. Trying to balance these objectives, I have become keenly aware of omissions. There are fifty more at least who should be here, and hundreds of candidates for a volume of minor characters. Faced with the choice between comprehensiveness and pursuit of what I have found most interesting, I have taken a middle road, and it has been strewn with casualties. As the centuries proceed, the field of study opens up and the period of time has to be reduced. This century begins with the union with Scotland and contains such important themes as the creation of an overseas empire, the central phase of the industrial revolution, the romantic movement, and the growth of radicalism, which all carry one also beyond this century. To be complete, the book should have gone to the Reform Bill or beyond. To preserve some unity of subject matter, and to keep the length of the book within bounds, I have made the French Revolution my terminus, leaving the great figures of the age of Pitt and the Regency to be covered in a second and companion volume. I am afraid that there are therefore some loose ends, though the French Revolution marks a greater break in English history than any single domestic event. As an example of the inconsistencies,which I have been unable to avoid, Burke appears in this book, Pitt and Fox do not; Tom Paine and Christopher Wyvill are in this one, most of the other radicals in the next. As in the previous volumes, the order is roughly that of dates of birth; within this scheme however, the subjects are grouped together for convenience of reference. I have listed only the books which I have found specially useful or interesting. I have also appended a short list of books of general interest which may enable the reader to discover more about the society and culture of the period.

A second edition has provided the opportunity to make changes and additions. Over the past twenty years historians like Linda Colley and Jonathan Clark have opened up new fields of inquiry, compelled reassessment, or revived old issues. Toryism and Jacobitism, for example, wear a different face while a bold review of the dominance in church and state of the traditional upper class has lent a sharp edge to debate about society and politics. How revolutionary was the "industrial revolution"? Teased by such questions and affected in a number of cases by recent biographical writing, my main purpose has been, as before, to provide the facts to enable the reader to make his own judgments. In the spheres of painting, sculpture, and architecture, where my limitations would otherwise have been exposed, I am again grateful to Francis Pearson for his perceptive essays; likewise, to my wife, Melisa, for the musicians and for all her loving help over years of authorship. My colleague Howard Shaw has guided me through some of the current controversy. To Anthony Werner of Shepheard-Walwyn I am indebted for his faith in the series now gaining momentum as it passes the halfway mark.

GEOFFREY TREASURE
Harrow

Who's Who in
Early Hanoverian Britain

GEORGE I (1660–1727) became heir to the English throne upon the death, in June 1714, of his mother, Sophia, granddaughter of James I and queen-designate by Act of Parliament. The death of Queen Anne on August 1st had found the Whigs ready to act. Bolingbroke and his followers were unable to put to the test their plans for a Jacobite succession. The politicians and courtiers who thronged to Greenwich to make their court saw a burly figure, of medium height, with dark hair under a brown wig, a pointed nose, and the prominent china-blue eyes of the Guelfs. They may have noted a certain dull immobility of countenance, and missed the watchful, shrewd expression which is caught in Kneller's portrait. Lady Mary Wortley Montagu thought George a blockhead, but those who knew him privately found a ready wit. Ministers came to respect his judgment. Meanwhile, he had reason to be on his guard, for he knew that he was accepted as a political convenience by men who might turn against him if he overstepped the limits of his power. He was entering a circle of ruthless politicians, adept in a game which included impeachment and the Tower among its penalties. One of his ministers, Sunderland, had been an avowed republican. Marlborough, the renowned soldier, had once shown James II that his loyalty could not be relied upon; Shrewsbury, as Lord Treasurer, had done as much as any to bring George to the throne; both thought it worth their while, during the Jacobite crisis of 1715, to reinsure by sending money to James Edward.

George was too experienced a soldier to lose his nerve. He had served with distinction in the Turkish wars, then under Marlborough; as *Reichsfeldmarschal*, though the other allied commanders did little to help, he had shown resourceful generalship. Success in the Jacobite crisis of 1715 was gained, however, as much by the incompetence of his divided opponents as by his own calm response. After the collapse of the rising, Walpole, for one, would

1

have been fiercer, and it was against his advice that George pardoned four out of the seven captured at Preston. He could afford to be magnanimous, for the affair had consolidated his position. It also narrowed his range of choice, for, with the dismissal of Nottingham and Shrewsbury, he found himself more tightly constrained by obligation to the more extreme Whigs. In one combination or another they dominated the reign. Fortunately, in Stanhope he had a minister, an experienced general and European-minded, with whom he could work. The year 1715 also influenced the course of foreign policy. Since the Regent Orleans had been true to his word and declined to support the Jacobites, George was predisposed toward entente with France.

George shrank from the formalities and frivolities of court life. He liked to take his meals in private. When he visited the opera he preferred to avoid the royal box; when he wished to gamble he would slip off to a friend's house. He had not recovered easily from the ill-fated love affair of his wife, Sophia Dorothea, and Count Königsmark: until her death in 1726 she was kept confined in a castle in Germany. Her place in George's affections was taken principally by Melusine von Schulenberg, Duchess of Kendal, by whom he had three daughters, and by Charlotte Sophia Kielmansegge, Countess of Darlington: their English titles and interest in English politics did nothing to make them popular. They were the butt of satirists, but that did not prevent politicians from using their good offices to reach the king's ear. George's retreat from the ceremonious role of the sovereign may seem to have reflected a shift in the balance of power from the king to the magnates: the style of rule should not, however, be mistaken for the substance. Stanhope, Sunderland, Walpole, and Townshend thought at times that they were manipulating the king, but they also served his purposes: he remained in control. Of course he made no bones about relying on German advisers, especially Bernstoff, Bothmar, and the Huguenot Robethon, for advice about appointments and policy. He liked to visit his comfortable electorate, now strengthened by the acquisition from Sweden of Bremen and Verden: the Hanoverians accepted his benevolent rule without question and he spent much of his reign there, at Herrenhausen, or the pleasant summer retreat of Göhrde.

In England the limits of his power were set as much by practice and habit as by law. He had to be a Protestant. He was forbidden to

give office, title, or estate to a foreigner without Parliament's consent. He could appoint, but not dismiss a judge. He leaned heavily
on his ministers' knowledge of the close world of politics but could
make his will effective in a number of ways. He appointed and dismissed ministers; to keep their place they had to please him as well
as command Parliament. The intense struggle for office of the
leading Whigs did not in itself weaken the Crown. A vast amount of
patronage stemmed from the king: used intelligently, as after 1721
by Walpole and Newcastle, this helped to secure the dynasty even
while it lowered the standing of the king. George had sufficient English for understanding, though not for easy conversation. He
spoke French fluently as did most of his ministers. Disinclination to
the more tiresome parts of business, rather than any language bar-
rier, accounts for the decline in the day-to-day influence of the
king. At first he attended meetings of the cabinet; after 1718 he
stayed away. This facilitated the development of the inner cabinet
of leading ministers which, by the middle of the century, had superseded the full cabinet council on all but formal occasions. Individual ministers had often to take their cue from the king,
especially in foreign affairs. George dismissed Townshend in 1716
because he felt that the safety of Hanover was jeopardized by delays
in the signing of the Anglo-French alliance. He was always attended
by one Secretary of State on his visits to Hanover. In 1723, such was
the mutual jealousy and fear of dismissal of Carteret and Townshend that they both accompanied him abroad.

George was of course primarily interested in Northern Europe.
He came to the throne in the later part of the Great Northern War,
and his grasp of the situation and concern for Hanover's interests
were important factors in Stanhope's active and effective policy. He
had a large share in the return of Britain to the main theatre of
diplomacy which enabled the country to share in the evolution of
the congress system: with interlocking guarantees European conflicts could be resolved with minimum recourse to military action.
He was neither sensitive nor subtle, yet he was far from the graceless boor of Tory propaganda. Music stirred his German soul: he
enjoyed Handel's operas and it was for the royal river fete that the
great composer wrote the *Water Music*. His apparently unfeeling
conduct toward his son can be explained partly by the constitutional problem arising out of the king's visits to Hanover. George
wished to arrange that only minor matters should be settled in

London; the more important were to be referred to him. This allowed room for intrigues and accentuated the already awkward position of the Prince of Wales. He was officially Lieutenant of the Realm, but in practice denied full powers of regency. His father even had him imprisoned briefly for an alleged insult to the Duke of Newcastle. The royal martinet's lesson was but too well learned: the future George II was to behave toward his own son in equally hurtful fashion. George I showed tenderness toward his daughter Sophia, Queen of Prussia, but the mean streak in him remains a strong impression. When he died suddenly, from a stroke, near Osnabrück, he was mourned mainly by those whose jobs depended on his life.

Ragnhild Hatton, *George I, Elector and King*, 1978.
J. F. Chance, *George I and the Northern War*, 1909.
J. J. Murray, *George I, the Baltic and the Whig Split of 1717*, 1969.

JAMES, 1st EARL STANHOPE (1673–1721) was one of the most talented statesmen of the early Georgian period. He came late to the center of politics after a strenuous career in the army. In seven years he made his mark, vigorous in foreign policy, liberal and imaginative at home. He died at the height of his powers in the middle of a political scandal for which he was in no way to blame.

His father was a diplomat and he was born in Paris. He spent much of his early life abroad, but he was sent to school at Eton, where he became an accomplished classic. An impatient, active man, he was also scholarly in his tastes, and a bibliophile who left a fine library behind him. Dubois called him "un philosophe," and Speaker Onslow once referred to him as "the best scholar perhaps of any gentleman of his time." After a spell at Trinity College, Oxford, he served as a volunteer in Flanders. At the start of the Spanish Succession War he was a colonel in the Guards. In these days he was "a young man that did not mind anything divine or human when it came into competition with his own humor." He was a heavy drinker and a boon companion, among others, of Henry St. John, later his political foe. He saw his principal service in Spain where he was second in command under the eccentric Peterborough, who captured Barcelona in 1705 and Madrid in 1706. He was not present at the battle of Almanza in 1707, but was sent home soon afterward to represent the view of the Archduke Charles that the war should be pursued to the bitter end. Unfortunately the English and Austrian troops found themselves confronted by a patriotic movement in favor of the Bourbon Philip V; he was sent back by the government with orders to "enlarge the bounds" of the operations, but with so small a force that he could only play a minor role. With the imperial General Stahrenberg, he was unable to regain the initiative. In July 1710, however, he distinguished himself in the small action of Almenara, meeting and killing the enemy cavalry commander. The general advance on Madrid that followed represented his policy of offensive action at all costs, but the skillful generalship of Vendôme, divisions between him and Stahrenberg, and his own rashness brought disaster. At Brihuega, in December, with an army of 4,000, he was trapped, battered, and forced to surrender. By then the Whig government had been ousted and with it their policy of "no peace without Spain." The Tories were in no hurry to effect Stanhope's release; he came home only to face indictment, in the House of Lords, at the hands of his old commander, Peterborough, and his successor in Spain, Argyll.

Stanhope had good cause to be an ardent Whig. First elected in 1701, he had been defeated, in his absence in Spain, in a raucous Westminster contest, by the Tory General Webb. Like Marlborough, he was now hounded by Tory politicians and pamphleteers. The peace of Utrecht, repudiating Whig commitments to the Archduke Charles, touched him personally. He disapproved too of the Tory religious policy, their Occasional Conformity and Schism Acts. His energy, honesty, and tolerance won the respect of the Whig leaders. In the last days of Queen Anne, when Bolingbroke was trying to engineer a Jacobite succession, Stanhope directed the tactics of his party. At the fateful dinner party, assembled by Bolingbroke on July 28 to test Whig views, it was he who delivered the ultimatum to the Tory leader: "Harry, you have only two ways of escaping the gallows. The first is to join the honest party of the Whigs; the other to give yourself up entirely to the French King and seek his help for the Pretender." George I succeeded without trouble, and Stanhope received his reward, on the prompting, perhaps, of his friend, George's secretary, Robethon, in the shape of the office of Secretary of State.

It was his object to restore the prestige which he considered England to have lost by the Treaty of Utrecht. He was one of the few ministers who could approach George I in his grasp of European affairs, and he was often by his side in his stays in Germany. This separation of the ministers, as much as differences of personality and policy, was responsible for the Whig schism when Walpole and Townshend left the ministry. Along with Sunderland, Stanhope, who became First Lord of the Treasury in 1717, Secretary of State again in 1718, enjoyed until his death the confidence of the king. He brought England into the center of a European coalition designed to thwart the ambitious plans of Elizabeth Farnese, wife of Philip of Spain, and her minister Alberoni. The base of his system was the alliance with France, made possible by the Treaty of Utrecht and the moderation of the Regent Orleans. Round this novel entente were grouped, by the Triple and Quadruple Alliances of 1717 and 1718, Holland and the Empire. In 1718 the British fleet was used to crush the pretensions of Spain when Byng won the battle of Cape Passaro. Alberoni's Northern Alliance dissolved when Charles XII of Sweden died, in the same year. Stanhope had been prepared to wage war on him too, when he was discovered to be involved in a plot to restore the Pretender, and the English Baltic fleet was given orders to "burn, sink, and destroy" Swedish men-of-war. Stanhope was not afraid to be belligerent, but he could also be constructive, even tactful. Working through his ambassador Carteret, he patched up the differences between Hanover and Prussia which touched England closely in the person of her Hanoverian king. He was less successful in his attempts to buttress Sweden against the demands of Russia, and the Northern War ended with the peace of Nystadt giving control of the Baltic to Russia. It is surprising to find that Stanhope was ready, on one occasion, to cede Gibraltar to Spain, and was only prevented from doing so by parliamentary outcry. His judgment was not infallible, his actions like his temper sometimes rash, and his policies involved expensive subsidies; on balance, however, he left England stronger and more respected than in 1714.

At home his record is checkered. Secure in the king's support, he trod somewhat heavily through the political maze, more interested in the uses of power than in the means by which it was got. His realistic appraisal of the cause of recent political turbulence led him and his colleagues to pass the Septennial Act (1716), which doubled the life of Parliament and the value of patronage, and did more than anything else to secure the Whig supremacy.

His religious liberalism was reflected in the repeal of the Schism and Occasional Conformity Acts. He wished to do the same with the Corporation Act and Test Act, to restore civil rights to dissenters and ease the position of the Catholics, but was thwarted by the opposition of the Church, led by Archbishop Wake. His impetuosity, too, disturbed some of his supporters who feared that violent change might bring violent reaction. Walpole was his constant critic and led the opposition which killed Stanhope's ill-conceived project, the Peerage Bill (1719), to restrict the king's prerogative of creating new peers. He himself had been created viscount in 1717, earl in 1718.

The government's scheme to liquidate the National Debt that led to the speculative mania of the South Sea Bubble was not Stanhope's work, but Sunderland's. Nor was Stanhope involved financially, as were several of the ministers. But it was while defending the government's policy in the House of Lords, in February 1721, that he suffered a stroke and died. None of the odium for the financial debacle clung to him. In his lifetime he was respected for his integrity. After his death, during the long peace of Walpole's ministry, his countrymen reaped the benefit of his diplomatic efforts. He had made England, for a few years, the arbiter of Europe.

J. J. Murray, *George I, the Baltic and the Whig Split of 1717*, 1969.
Basil Williams, *Stanhope*, 1932.
Paul Langford, *Modern British Foreign Policy. The Eighteenth Century*, 1976.

CHARLES TOWNSHEND, 2nd VISCOUNT TOWNSHEND (1674–1738), statesman, inherited a considerable position in Norfolk. His father, Sir Horatio, had been rewarded with a peerage for the part he played in the restoration of Charles II. After Eton and King's, Charles entered politics an ardent Whig, like his neighbor Robert Walpole, whose sister Dorothy he married in 1713. He was given the task of conducting the negotiations of Gertrudenberg with the French and Dutch in 1709. The Anglo-Dutch treaty of that year, which provided for Dutch military help if the Hanoverian cause seemed in danger, greatly pleased the future George I. Townshend was marked for promotion and it came with his appointment in 1714 to be Secretary of State for the north. At first he was held to be the leading man in the administration, but the less experienced

Stanhope soon emerged as the dominant influence. The aims of the two men did not differ widely; to undo any ill effects of the peace of Utrecht abroad and to consolidate the dynasty at home was their common purpose. In 1715 Townshend showed himself to be both zealous and thorough. His measures, the arrest, for example, of Sir William Wyndham, helped to keep the country calm. He never lacked moral courage nor shrank from decisions. His faults were rather overhastiness at times and obstinacy. He lacked subtlety; once set on a course he would not easily be deflected.

Townshend shared in the achievement of the Triple Alliance, but delays in the completion of the treaty with France were the ostensible cause of his dismissal, in the polite form of preferment to Ireland, in December 1716. The breach was the predictable consequence of power shared between two men of strong will, before the notion of a prime minister had come to be accepted. It was exacerbated by the long absence of George I in Hanover and his inability to distinguish, as it seemed to Townshend and Walpole, between his duty as King of England and inclination as Elector of Hanover. Townshend was concerned about the rise of Russia and wanted the maritime powers and the Emperor to agree on terms to end the protracted Northern War and reestablish a balance between Sweden and Russia, George was bent on securing Bremen and Verden and regarded Townshend's advice as unrealistic. The slowness of communications between Germany and London gave rise to misunderstandings on both sides. Townshend was only three months in Ireland before he joined Walpole in the stimulating business of opposition. This was effective enough, especially in the matter of the Peerage Bill, to convince Stanhope that there must be reconciliation. In 1720 the brothers-in-law returned to minor office, Townshend as President of the Council. Early in 1721 he took his former office as Secretary of State, vacated by the death of Stanhope. For the rest of the decade his was the guiding spirit in foreign affairs. Till 1724 he worked with Carteret, then virtually on his own.

During this period he had to deal with the stresses which arose, despite the existence of the Quadruple Alliance, over the claims of France, Spain, and the Emperor. Spain sought to recover Gibraltar and to assert her claims in Italy, the Emperor to maintain himself in Italy and to promote the activities of the Ostend Company which was so unpopular with English merchants. After 1726, when Cardinal Fleury replaced Bourbon as first minister, Fleury sought rapprochement with Spain and started to wriggle away from his commitments to England. Townshend stood firm on the French alliance and backed English trading and strategic interest wherever he saw them threatened. In 1725 the Spanish minister Ripperda came to terms with the Emperor Charles VI in the Treaty of Vienna; secret clauses promised mutual support in the matter of the Ostend Company and Gibraltar. Townshend's principal concern was to destroy the former and keep the latter. By the Alliance of Hanover, Prussia was detached from the Emperor and brought into line with England and France. In 1727 the Spanish embarked on the siege of Gibraltar. War was not declared but Townshend moved confidently toward it: Parliament voted the taxes and Holland was sympathetic, attracted by Townshend's proposal for a partition of the Austrian Netherlands between Holland and France. Charles VI drew back and accepted a seven-year suspension of the Ostend Company. Negotiations for a permanent settlement began in 1728 at Soissons; while Townshend fretted at the formalities and delays, Walpole and Newcastle undermined his position. In 1729 the Treaty of Seville was signed. It was essentially Walpole's treaty, through the agency of Newcastle in his capacity as Secretary of State for the south. In return for support of Spain's claims in the Italian Duchies, the privileges of the *Asiento* were to be restored. The prospect of war receded, but the rift between Walpole and Townshend had opened too wide. The land tax had risen to 4s. in the £. Walpole was alarmed by the cost of Townshend's subsidies, by Hessian troops, and the mobilized fleets. He scented political danger at home; Townshend had become a liability. He could also see that Townshend was playing into the deceptively gentle hands of Fleury by his tough line with Austria. The disgruntled minister resigned in May 1730 when he found that the king preferred Newcastle's dispatch to his. Significantly no colleague went with him. Walpole marked the change of direction by signing the second Treaty of Vienna with the Emperor. So the Stanhope-Townshend policy of entente with France gave way to the older Whig conception of alliance with Austria and Holland.

To his credit Townshend left office no richer than he entered it. After his dismissal he had no further dealings with Walpole but left politics to return to his estates in Norfolk. His largeness of mind may seem admirable—but it has to be said that he had little choice. George II did not respect him as his father had done. He had neither taste nor patience for the political game; it is noteworthy that he had served no apprenticeship in the Commons. He had no party, little electoral interest. Newcastle had it in abundance and had used it to isolate Townshend. Walpole is open to the charge of ingratitude, but he had personal as well as political reasons for his actions. Dorothy's death in 1726 had removed the last personal tie between the two men. Walpole, relishing power, did not brook rivals easily. Townshend, who has still found no biographer, could be both peremptory and patronizing: Walpole was a squire, he a peer. Honest himself, restrained in his private life, he could not fail to disapprove of the blatant style of Walpole, whose great palace at Houghton, only a few miles away, outshone even his own stately Raynham. Ultimately, however, it came down to politics. There could be no real sharing of responsibility with Walpole. It was less surprising that the breach occurred than that it had not happened earlier.

"All Townshend's turnips and all Grosvenor's mines." Pope's line recalls the source of Townshend's latter fame. Both the planting of turnips and the marling of light soils were established farming practices in the eastern counties, and "Turnip" Townshend's contribution to Norfolk agriculture was less as innovator than as advertisement for the four-course rotation of wheat, barley, clover, and turnips. With so distinguished an advocate for the root crops that cleaned the ground and kept sheep and cattle in good winter condition, it can still be said that farming was improved by the enforced retirement of this energetic statesman.

F. S. Oliver, *The Endless Adventure, 1710–35,* 3 vols., 1930–5.
Paul Langford, *Modern British Foreign Policy. The Eighteenth Century,* 1976.
J. Black, *British Foreign Policy in the Age of Walpole,* 1985.

CHARLES SPENCER, 3rd EARL OF SUNDERLAND (1674–1722), politician, unlike his father, the 2nd earl, who made himself indispensable to William III within months of deserting James II, was a man of fixed principles, the embodiment of the stiff Whiggery of the Glorious Revolution. With this went, however, a restless ambition and capacity for intrigue that made him distrusted by many of his colleagues. Few great political figures have inspired less affection than he.

His father's fame and knowledge of the business of politics ensured the intelligent son a good start. He entered Parliament for Tiverton in 1695. By his first marriage he entered the Newcastle circle. It was his second marriage, however, to Anne Churchill, that did most to promote him. Although a member of the junto and one of the inner group of Whigs, he might not have become Secretary of State if he had not been Marlborough's son-in-law. In 1705 he had done good service as envoy at Vienna with the task of mediating between the Emperor and the Hungarian insurgents; in the following year the Churchills, who wished to be assured of solid support at home, pressed Anne to accept him. She had reason to dislike him for his avowed republicanism and frigid manners, and feared that she was "throwing herself into the hands of a party." Sunderland, awkward and proud, did not even try to please Marlborough: as Vryberg said, "he does not hesitate even to gainsay his father-in-law's opinions when he thinks they are not right." His dismissal in June 1710 was the prelude to the defeat of the Whigs in the general election of that year. He was rightly thought to be associated with the policy of all-out war and "no peace without Spain," and the more extreme Tories wanted to prosecute him. He trimmed his sails a little and even voted for the Occasional Conformity Bill (1711), which he was only too pleased to see repealed in the next reign. He could afford to wait, however, for the accession of George I, upon whom his prospects depended. When George formed his first ministry he thought himself slighted by the office of Lord Lieutenant of Ireland. In August 1715 he slipped into Wharton's office of Lord Privy Seal, on the latter's death, and addressed himself to the interests of the king and Stanhope. During the crisis of George I's relations with Townshend he was conveniently in Hanover and able to misrepresent the actions of the ministers at home. Townshend was dismissed in December 1716. In April 1717 the ministry was reconstituted with Stanhope, First Lord of the Treasury, and Sunderland, Secretary of State. In the following year he exchanged offices with Stanhope. He made little effort to dispute Stanhope's primacy, accepting the fact that he directed foreign affairs. He had plenty of scope, however, and enjoyed the confidence of the king, who had earlier mistrusted him as a covert republican, but came to appreciate his *savoir-faire*, fluent French, and the attention to the king's interests. The Peerage Bill of 1719, which sought to limit new creations—and failed—reflected his oligarchic attitude. He welcomed the scheme of the South Sea Company to take over, on favorable terms, the greater part of the National Debt, and shared therefore the odium which fell upon ministers when the speculative bubble collapsed in August 1720. Though he received an allocation of company stock, there is no evidence that he was particularly corrupt in his dealings with the company, but he fell with those who were. Aislabie, Chancellor of the Exchequer, was expelled from the House of Commons in March 1721; Sunderland resigned office in the same month and Walpole replaced him. Sunderland still had the ability and will to come back, though Walpole earned the gratitude of the king by the stout way in which he defended the court and screened the ministers (Sunderland himself was acquitted by 233 votes to 172).

Had Sunderland lived he, not Walpole, might have dominated the next twenty years; at least there would have been a battle of giants. But in April 1722 he suddenly died, of pleurisy, leaving behind the superb library that he had amassed at Althorp and an heir to carry on the titles of the Churchill family. He was not widely mourned for most thought him selfish and arrogant. His habitual expression was, in later years, glum and sour. Yet he was capable of deep feeling. He loved his wives passionately; he wrote to Anne, his second wife, wherever he was, by every post. Foreign diplomats, says Ranke, trusted him. He was a man of cultivated tastes, fastidious by the side of a Walpole or a Townshend. Of his talent there is little doubt. Hardwicke wrote later of his ability to "remove from one office to another still retaining the character and influence of prime minister." But he lacked that warmth of personality which makes political friendships live. To contemporaries he was remote, Jesuitical. To us there is something objectionable in his patrician insolence. He is the least appealing of the Venetian oligarchs.

W. S. Churchill, *Marlborough: His Life and Times*, Vols. III and IV, 1933–8.
J. J. Murray, *George I, the Baltic and the Whig Split of 1717*, 1969.
J. H. Plumb, *The Growth of Political Stability in England, 1675–1725*, 1967.

JAMES BUTLER, 2nd DUKE OF ORMONDE (1665–1745), Irish landowner and grandson of Charles I's Lord-Lieutenant, Tory general and politician, Jacobite adventurer, is buried in Westminster

Abbey, though the latter part of his life was spent abroad intriguing against the British Crown.

He was educated in France but went to Oxford in 1679. From 1680 to 1682 he lived in Ireland, but thereafter was mostly an absentee landlord, except during his spells as Lord-Lieutenant. In 1682 he came close to the court circle by his marriage with Lady Anne Hyde; she died in 1684 and he married Lady Mary Somerset. He served as a volunteer with the French army, and against Monmouth in 1685. In 1688 he inherited his grandfather's dukedom and in the same year became Chancellor of Oxford University. He joined the cause of William belatedly, but was Lord High Constable at his coronation. He fought at the Boyne and at Steinkirke; at Neerwhinden in 1693 he was captured but exchanged. In Anne's reign he was for several years Lord-Lieutenant. In 1712 he was sent to replace Marlborough as captain-general of the allied army. Bolingbroke was engaged in peace talks with the French and he had secret orders not to fight. His inactivity, much resented by Marlborough's troops, contributed to the defeat of the Dutch at Denain. At Anne's death he was a recognized leader of the Jacobites, but his ineffectual conduct in the year that followed damaged rather than aided the cause. Although the evidence is naturally unsatisfactory, it seems probable that there were scattered but strong Jacobite interests in the country, ready to respond to a strong call to arms. In June 1715, when a rising looked imminent to the government, Ormonde was threatened with impeachment. He retired to Richmond and planned a revolt in the west, but, hearing that troops were being sent to arrest him, he left hurriedly for France, leaving no instructions behind him. His presence could have been a rallying point for the Western Jacobites. As it was, the ministers acted promptly, detaining leading suspects and dismissing Tory magistrates. Then Louis XIV died and with him hope of French support; Mar embarked upon the Scottish rising which could not be effective, Bolingbroke thought, without some corresponding effort in England. Ormonde appeared off the west coast in the autumn but was told that there was then no chance of a rising. By the following spring all was over in Scotland too. Berwick was one of many Jacobites who blamed Ormonde for the débâcle. Thereafter he was consistently unlucky. Alberoni's squadron, which he led to invade England in 1718, was scattered by a storm. A plot in which he was active was stillborn when its details were revealed to the

British ministers in 1722. In 1740 he visited Madrid to suggest an invasion of England, but the opportunity, missed so badly in 1715, was not to recur again until 1745, the year of Charles Edward's adventure and of Ormonde's death.

D. Szechi, *Jacobitism and Tory Politics, 1710–1714,* 1984.
B. P. Lenman, *The Jacobite Risings in Britain, 1689–1745,* 1980.

SIMON FRASER, 12th BARON LOVAT (1667?–1747) was executed for his part in the '45 rebellion after a life of intrigue and treachery. Two facts add interest to the end of his disreputable career: he was the last peer executed for high treason and he was painted by Hogarth on the eve of his death—his leering visage is not easily forgotten.

His father was Thomas Fraser, a younger son of the eighth Lord Lovat; his mother was a MacLeod. At Aberdeen he received a good classical education. When the tenth Lord died without male heir and his lands were claimed by his daughter, Simon carried her off; the legality of the marriage was in doubt and the coup seemed to have failed. But toward the end of King William's life he got a pardon and took the title of twelfth Lord Lovat (his father, "eleventh Lord," having died in 1699). He shuttled between St. Germains and London, playing the succession game with almost pathological eagerness and complete lack of shame. In 1702 he claimed to be a convert to Roman Catholicism and promised to assist Louis XIV in invading Scotland; he returned to Scotland with a letter from Mary of Modena (James II's widow) and tried to persuade Atholl and others to join the cause. But he was suspect to the Highlanders as a double agent and was arrested when he returned to France. He spent Queen Anne's reign under surveillance there; his reluctant wife, meanwhile, had successfully secured the Fraser land and married a Mackenzie. But the clan resented this and persisted in loyalty to their unsatisfactory chief. He escaped from France in 1713 and was arrested; on his release he raised the clan for George I in the 1715 rising, captured Inverness, and was rewarded with a full pardon and life rent of the estates, which stretched from Inverness to the hills around the river Beauly. About the time of the futile 1719 attempt Lovat was again flirting with the Jacobite cause and had to explain his conduct in London. To show his loyalty he proposed the raising of companies of clansmen, the "sidier dhu" or black troops, to act as auxiliaries to the redcoats. In 1732 he helped his friend Lord Grange in the violent restraint of Lady Grange. In 1733 he obtained full recognition of his title, but soon, for the promise of a dukedom, he began to mobilize support for the Young Pretender.

In 1745, when Lovat's professions were put to the test, he dithered. By now he was old and fat. His son by his second marriage, the eighteen-year-old Master of Lovat, brought out the Frasers, but too late to join the march south. They fought at Falkirk and Culloden. Simon himself was taken as hostage by the Whig governor of Inverness, but escaped. After Culloden he saw the prince and urged him to make a last stand. He then went into hiding, carried around by his loyal clansmen until he was taken, his legs sticking out from under a hollow tree on an island in Loch Morar. Tried in the spring of 1747 he defended himself coolly, and he died, avowing himself to be a good Catholic, with salty jokes and a line of Horace on his lips. His estates were spoiled and Castle Dounie was burnt to the ground, but his son was pardoned in 1750 and raised a Highland regiment for the Crown in 1757.

B. P. Lenman, *The Jacobite Risings in Britain, 1689–1745*, 1980.
F. McLynn, *The Jacobites*, 1985.

JOHN ERSKINE, 11th EARL OF MAR (1675–1732), called Bobbing John because of his frequent changes of allegiance, is known best for his fumbling leadership of the Scottish Jacobite rising in 1715. The regime of George I was barely established and political temper in England was uncertain; in Scotland the Union was unpopular. The Highlanders in arms were more numerous and hopeful than in 1745, and skill and nerve in leadership might have restored James Edward to the throne. Mar's role was crucial.

He succeeded to his father's title and estates in 1688 and attached himself to the court party in 1696. He supported Queensberry and the Union, and was made Secretary for Scotland and Keeper of the Signet. In 1713, however, he supported a motion in the House of Lords, where he sat as a representative peer, for the repeal of the Union. In 1714 he professed loyalty to George I but was soon in Scotland, almost blatantly preparing for revolt. On September 6, 1715 he raised the standard of James III at Braemar and marched on Perth. His numbers rose rapidly to about 12,000, while

Argyll had only 3,300 men, and he controlled the coastline—which invited French aid. The size of the army suggests that he had a large following and some capacity for organization. But when he marched south and fought Argyll at Sheriffmuir on November 13th, the result was indecisive. On the same day at Preston, Forster was defeated by Mills and Carpenter. Ormonde's descents upon the Devonshire coast had raised no support. But Mar could still have posed a serious threat in Scotland had he advanced resolutely. As it was, he was uncertain, and James pessimistic. The Pretender landed at Peterhead in December, joined Mar at Perth, and made him Duke. By now Argyll had been reinforced by some Dutch troops, so Mar fell back toward Montrose, burning the villages of Strathearn as he went. On February 4 he took ship back to France with the prince. Cadogan superseded Argyll and hunted down the remnants of the Highland force. James was loyal to Mar who, he thought, had lost everything for his cause. In fact Mar was soon trying to insure his future by intriguing against James with Lord Stair. He sent a memorial to the Regent Orleans proposing the dismemberment of the British Empire. His keen sense of changing opinion had degenerated into mere opportunism. He betrayed Atterbury into a correspondence and then revealed the letters to the British Government, who gave him a pension of £3,500; in his last years he was taken seriously by neither side, but allowed to live out his days undisturbed at Paris and then at Aix-la-Chapelle.

B. P. Lenman, *The Jacobite Risings in Britain, 1689–1745*, 1980.

FRANCIS ATTERBURY (1662–1732), Bishop of Rochester, leading High Churchman and Tory, came of a family of small gentry in Northamptonshire; his father was rector of Milton Keynes in Buckinghamshire. He was sent to Westminster School, then enjoying its golden age under Dr. Busby, and Christ Church. In 1686 he made some stir by his defense of the Church against the Roman Catholic dons, whom James II was using to infiltrate certain colleges. His scholarship and his taste for controversy were formed in the fervent air of Oxford. He took orders in 1687, was a "Queen Mary's man" at the Revolution, and was made royal chaplain. He then attached himself to the Princess Anne, thumped the latitudinarians in pamphlet and pulpit, and spoke stoutly for the independence of Convocation. In these years the mood and politics of leading churchmen like Tenison, Burnet, and Wake was "Broad Church" and Erastian. To Atterbury the Church was not a department of state or a form of spiritual and social insurance, but divinely ordained, organic, and self-governing. In Feiling's phrase, it was, too, "the ark of those causes which has made seventeenth century royalism." With sufficient right on his side, with energy, scholarship, and unfailing polemical zest, Atterbury inspired the Lower House of Convocation to challenge the bishops and their Whig patrons. To him the Church owed the revival of synodical government in Queen Anne's reign. In turbulent meetings of Convocation he pressed the view that Convocation, not Parliament, was sovereign of the Church.

He was hot against toleration but he had, too, a more positive, attractive faith. In a sermon before Queen Mary in 1702 he looked forward "to the reestablishment of the beauty of praise in our sanctuary." Preferred to the deanery of Carlisle in 1704, more congenially to Christ Church in 1709, and then to Westminster, finally Bishop of Rochester in 1713, Atterbury spent much of his talents in controversy. He relished the Sacheverell affair and at his impeachment is said to have composed the Tory doctor's stirring speech of defense. He was also a zealous administrator, in the Laudian style. Strict requirements for ordination and careful directions about confirmation witness his concern for high standards. Moreover, his numerous friends saw a person very different from the embattled public figure. "How pleasing Atterbury's softer hour," wrote Pope. William King put his conversation in the same class as Dr. Johnson's. He helped to perfect the polished style of controversialists of his time. Self-assertive, hasty in debate, he was generous and loyal to party, creed, and friends. He found much to anger him before the succession of George I; thereafter the Whig paradise was his hell. He gave his services increasingly to political opposition: the priest was near lost in the partisan.

In 1710 he had begun to contribute to the Tory journal, *The Examiner*. In 1714 he was the probable author of an outspoken pamphlet: *English Advice to the Freeholders*. He was at first anti-Whig, rather than anti-Hanoverian, a Platonic Jacobite. Disappointment rankled, however: in 1714 he was to have had the Privy Seal under Bolingbroke, but Anne died, he was snubbed by George I, and took the oath with reluctance. He was appalled by the executions which followed the 1715 rising. After 1716 he was in the Jacobite secrets. In 1717 he opposed the Septennial Bill. In the same year the Lower House of Convocation was suspended after an attack upon Hoadley; Atterbury became more outspoken as he became more isolated in the episcopal hierarchy. With Oxford clerics and country Tories it was a different matter. Intelligent but impulsive, uncompromising in his attitude and strong in the pulpit, Atterbury was a symbol of protest. Especially he detested Walpole, "A bold, bad, blundering, blustering booby," and it was Walpole, ever vigilant toward Jacobite plots, who brought him to book. In December 1721 a group of Jacobites including Atterbury invited the Pretender to take advantage of the collapse of the South Sea Bubble and mount an invasion. The plot was exposed but the evidence that Atterbury had treasonable plans was not strong enough to secure condemnation by the usual processes of law. The ministry brought a bill of pains and penalties against him. He conducted his own defense with spirit, but the Whig bishops were solid against him and the bold and clever arguments of the young Duke of Wharton could not save him; he was sentenced to deprivation and banishment.

When Atterbury had gone to the Tower the friendly mob surged about his carriage; he was prayed for by the London clergy. In June 1723, however, he was escorted to a waiting man-of-war without disturbance; the time was gone when the cry "The Church in danger" could rock a ministry. Atterbury went to France and Bolingbroke came back to England. "So we are exchanged," said the bishop. Atterbury's fretfulness and deteriorating health, the intrigues and jealousies of the Jacobite camarilla, and the frustrations of exile, meant that his talents were wasted. Mar was probably treacherous, James indifferent, the cause waning. Walpole continued vindictive, and spies tracked the bishop's movements. When he died the ministry allowed his body to be interred in Westminster Abbey, where the restored north front and a fine new dormitory for the King's Scholars commemorated his stewardship. After the service, government agents broke into his coffin to look for documents which might incriminate his friends.

G. V. Bennett, *The Tory Crisis in Church and State 1688–1730: The Career of Francis Atterbury, Bishop of Rochester*, 1975.
L. Colley, *In Defiance of Oligarchy, The Tory Party 1714–60*, 1982.

THOMAS BRAY (1656–1730), born at Marton in Shropshire, was the founder both of the Society for Promoting Christian Knowledge and of the Society for the Propagation of the Gospel. The author of the popular catechetical lectures, he was chosen by the Bishop of London to be his commissary in Maryland. He arrived there in 1700 but soon returned, thinking he could better serve the church at home. His mission was to supply knowledge, in the shape of books and missionaries, to counteract the ignorance of the mass of Christians. In 1699 the SPCK began the work of Christian propaganda which it is still doing. The SPG, a regularly incorporated society whose charter was given by William III in 1701, provided for both "our own people" and the "poor natives" who were to be converted "from that state of barbarity and idolatry in which they now live, and be brought into the sheepfold of our blessed Saviour." These words, from the Dean of Lincoln's first annual sermon to the society, epitomize its aims then. In its long history the society has justified the hopes of its humane and charitable founder. Few men have influenced, though indirectly, so many people.

MATTHEW TINDAL (1657–1733) after a checkered career became one of the most influential of deists and the center of warm controversy. He was at Exeter College, Oxford, and then a Fellow of All Souls. During James II's reign he turned Catholic. Later he avowed that he found its absurdities intolerable and rebounded into rationalism. As was proper in an Oxford don, he made no haste. Not until 1706 did he attract notice by his published sermon, *The Rights of the Christian Church Established.* It was an attack upon the High Church position—and was ordered to be burnt, with Sacheverell's sermon, in 1710, by order of the House of Commons. He was an old man when he produced the first volume of *Christianity as Old as the Creation,* in 1730; the second volume never saw light as the manuscript came into the hands of Bishop Gibson, who decided that it would be unwise to add fuel to the flames. For Tindal, consolidating the position already reached by Tillotson, Hoadley, and Clarke, argued that since God was good, wise, and unchanging and since human nature was also constant in essentials, God's law was perfect, unalterable, and available to all. He denied any exclusive claims to Christian revelation: Why, he asked, should the American aborigine have been denied this special benefit by the creator? It follows that he was dubious, too, of the value of specifically Christian observances.

In Tindal's book the great debate came to a climax. Other deists began to question the evidence for the stories of the Bible; miracles had already received rough treatment; now the Resurrection itself was questioned, notably by Woolston. Leland and Foster, the Dissenters, tackled him; so did Law and, later, Warburton, amongst Anglicans. Tindal's conception was not ignoble, for at the heart of it lies the idea that God must have dealt equally with all men; doctrines not universally revealed cannot be imposed upon all by God; reason alone is the faculty granted to all and reason must therefore be the sole judge. Its tendency to further the well-being of mankind is the only test of any creed. Obedience to nature is the one sufficient principle of the religious life, which consists "in a constant disposition of mind to do all the good we can, and thereby render ourselves acceptable to God in answering the end of his creation." Rules, dogmas, and ways of worship must be judged by the degree to which they promote happiness. Asceticism has no more place than fanaticism in his system. We can see in his writing not only the lofty rationalism of Voltaire, who admired him as "the intrepid defender of natural religion," but also the more mundane arguments of the utilitarians. An important result of his work, because it was superficially formidable, was to make theologians examine the evidence in a more critical spirit. Would Butler or Law, for instance, have written so well had it not been for the deist challenge?

R. N. Stromberg, *Religious Liberalism in Eighteenth Century England*, 1954.
L. Stephen, *History of English Thought in the Eighteenth Century*, Vol. 1, 1876.

WILLIAM WAKE (1657–1737) was an Archbishop of Canterbury whose ecumenical labors displayed a generous and scholarly spirit typical of the eighteenth-century Church at its best. The son of a Dorset landowner of ancient family, he was educated at Blandford Grammar School and Christ Church, Oxford, before going to Paris as chaplain to the embassy in 1682. There he made friends among leading French churchmen at a time when the Gallican movement was at its height and when there was much talk of reunion. He acquired a sympathy with moderate Church leaders such as Bossuet and a lasting interest in projects of reunion between the churches. He returned in 1685, the year in which the Revocation of the Edict of Nantes dealt a mortal blow to such projects and the accession of James II sharpened religious animosities in England. From 1688 to 1696 he was preacher at Gray's Inn. Another influential pulpit was opened to him when he became rector of St. James, Westminster, in 1693. He was already Doctor of Divinity and Canon of Christ Church. In 1703 he became Dean of Exeter, in 1705 Bishop of Lincoln, where he was conscientious in his pastoral oversight of the huge diocese. In 1716, like Tenison before him, he was translated from Lincoln to Canterbury. His primacy is disappointing only by contrast with the high hopes that attended him, and with what he wanted to achieve.

In his reply to Bossuet's *Exposition* of the Roman Catholic faith, Wake established principles which he held to all his life: a distinction should be made between fundamental and secondary articles of faith; individual churches should enjoy a measure of liberty; churches might differ, even as much as the Anglican and Gallican Churches, yet be in intercommunion. In a correspondence with du Pin (1717), a moderate French theologian with Jansenist leanings, Wake again displayed a reasonable irenism, and it was in this spirit that he took up the remains of a project for the unification of Reformed and Lutheran Churches in Prussia, upon an episcopal basis, and the union of the resulting body with the Church of England. This scheme, promoted by Daniel Jablonski, a bishop of the Unitas Fratrum, the old Reformed Church of Bohemia, was a promising one; there was a current of opinion in Germany, typified by Leibnitz, toward reunion; England's influence, because of her new connection with Hanover, was potentially great. In complexities as much political as theological the scheme faded away, and the only permanent result was the translation (1704), in German, of the *Book of Common Prayer*. Nor was any greater progress made with the Swiss churches, despite Wake's friendly contacts with prominent Swiss divines.

Wake believed ardently in episcopacy. He makes this clear in his picture of the Anglican Church, "Catholic in regimen, preserving the episcopal polity, duly moderated and divorced from all unjust dominion." He encouraged foreign students to receive episcopal ordination before leaving the country. He defended the Church at home alike against "the new notions of libertinism" which he saw in Hoadly and others like him who wanted to minimize the authority of Church and creed. He fell out of favor with the Whig ministers, as he did with some historians, because of his firm opposition to the Repeal of the Occasional Conformity Act. He wished the Church to be comprehensive but not to the point of negation. He may more justly be criticized for his failure to reform those aspects of Church government and life which mar the eighteenth-century Church: the passive role of Convocation, pluralism, and absenteeism of the clergy. But he could do little in the face of a deliberate policy of using Church patronage for political ends.

The record at the end is a sound but modest one. His scholarship was preserved in many solid works of theology and history. He maintained a proper state; indeed, he is supposed to have been the last archbishop to have used his barge to travel in state from Lambeth to the Houses of Parliament. He married the daughter of a Norfolk knight, Etheldreda Hovell, produced a large family, and left an ample fortune. He was also, however, a generous man who gave much to the restoration of buildings in his dioceses. He cannot be better summed up than in his own words: he hoped that when he came to judgment, "tho' I have been an unprofitable servant, nevertheless I have ever sought, counseled, and with all my zeal and effort pursued those things which belong to the peace of Jerusalem."

N. Sykes, *William Wake*, 2 vols., 1957.
N. Sykes, *From Sheldon to Secker*, 1959.

BENJAMIN HOADLY (1675–1761) was an able controversialist but a scandalous bishop. A Tory print of the time of the Sacheverell affair shows six horses drawing the carriage of the Commonwealth, with Cromwell sitting inside: "slavery," "republican tyranny," "presbytery," "rebellion," "moderation," and "occasional conformity" canter over the recumbent bodies of "monarchy" (Charles I), "liberty of the subject" (Magna Carta), "loyalty" (Strafford), and "episcopacy" (Laud). The postilion, trumpeting the cause of the Low Church, is Benjamin Hoadly. The print epitomizes the religious issues of the day; it also represents fairly, if not the exact views of Hoadley, at least the reason for his swift preferment after the accession of George I. He was a man of much political skill, who devoted himself to the public advocacy of the Low Church principles that pleased Whig politicians and fitted his comfortable, mundane view of life.

The son of a schoolmaster and clergyman of no repute, he became Fellow of Catherine Hall, Cambridge, where his excellent portrait by Hogarth hangs today, was ordained in 1701, and took a living in London. Soon he was one of the leaders of the Low Church party; indeed, Lecky, who had a high view of his ability as a controversialist, compares his position with that of Burnet in the reign of William. Against Atterbury and Blackall he put forward a view of the Church which was to receive its clearest definition after he had become a bishop. He made a vigorous attack in 1716, upon the nonjurors, seeking to show that the Church had no right to an independent position outside the State. In the following year his sermon before the king precipitated the Bangorian controversy in which 53 writers produced some 200 pamphlets, of which 12 came from Hoadly himself. In order to avert the embarrassment of a direct attack by the Lower House of Convocation upon the Bishop of Bangor, the house was suspended, not to meet again until the middle of the nineteenth century. Hoadly won the political battle, but he was strongly attacked in the weak points of his doctrinal argument. He believed that the Church had no right to exercise authority in doctrine or discipline since the laws of Christ were not subject to interpretation by any earthly body, and that the rule of God was infringed by those priests who set themselves up as his mediators or interpreters. Law, the nonjuror, and Sherlock, the future Bishop of London, answered properly: his arguments nullified all obligations to any particular Communion and led inevitably to deism.

How was it that Hoadly was content, not merely to be a bishop but to receive steady preferment, from Bangor to Hereford, Hereford to Salisbury, and, in 1734, at the behest of Queen Caroline, Salisbury to Winchester? Only because he accepted the convenient view that the Church was an instrument of State. Even here he was inconsistent, for if he denied the existence of a visible Church, he was denying by implication the Royal Supremacy from which was derived the whole system of ecclesiastical appointments. He was in fact an unblushing careerist and a glutton. Caroline, who enjoyed the acrimony of debate and accepted Hoadly in her inner circle of keen-minded ecclesiastics, made the appropriate comment when she said that there was only one objection to making this good Whig an Archbishop of Canterbury, namely that he "was not a Christian." He showed so little concern for the sacerdotal part of his calling that he visited his see of Bangor but once, Hereford not at all. He was a cripple, so that he was unable to ride and had to preach from a kneeling position. His "Plain Account of the nature and end of the Sacrament" (1735) suggests that it would not have disturbed him to see an end of the practice of episcopal confirmation. Most bishops were more conscientious than Hoadly, but those who wish to see what was amiss behind the picturesque externals of Georgian churchmanship, the box pews, and the cobwebbed chancels, cannot do better than to study the life of this complacent cleric.

N. Sykes, *Church and State in the Eighteenth Century,* 1934.

EDMUND GIBSON (1669–1748), Bishop of London, was an imposing churchman whose career illustrates both what far-reaching reforms could be envisaged by an energetic and ambitious prelate and what obstacles were created by the political dependence of the Church. He had no significant patronage but rose by his ability. Fellow of Queen's College, Oxford, he became chaplain to Archbishop Tenison and librarian at Lambeth, and there he began the cataloging of the great library. He became prominent in debate with the High Churchman Atterbury, and was successively preferred to the archdeaconry of Surrey and, in 1716, after Wake, to the bishopric of Lincoln. In 1720 he was consecrated Bishop of London. Already he had commended himself to Walpole by his staunch support of the administration. After 1723 he was the minister's adviser on ecclesiastical patronage. Canterbury was bypassed. He was, in Walpole's words, "Pope," and he did not abuse his trust.

Gibson's standards were those of his time. He had no doubt that the bishops should all be Whigs. He made no bones about it. "All slanders cast upon the Ministry, do really end in the dishonor of the prince." Political dissent implied resistance to the Lord Anointed. But he insisted, too, that they should be sound churchmen. Because of the feebleness of the archbishops (Wake was now a spent force) and the thoroughness of Gibson, Walpole and Townshend secured a firm control over the hierarchy. On occasion he crossed swords with Queen Caroline, who was also interested in

Church matters and had a leaning toward unorthodoxy. With Walpole relations grew strained in the thirties until their break in 1736 over the Quaker's Relief Bill, which Gibson opposed. Up to that time he had been in a position to make his views felt in no uncertain way. That there were not more prelates of the type of Hoadly may be put to his credit. But his reputation should rest upon his radical proposals for the reform of the Church. They show an awareness of its shortcomings in organization and pastoral provision which is startlingly modern. His own experience as bishop of the vast diocese of Lincoln, stretching from Humber to Thames, as well as the notorious differences in the income of the various sees, convinced him that boundaries must be redrawn. The prevailing social conditions, and the difficulty of financing them, put suffragan bishops out of the question (though we may still wonder why). He therefore proposed a wholesale redistribution of diocesan areas. Besides the truncation of Lincoln (to consist only of that county), Chester (to the enlargement of Carlisle), and Norwich (most of Suffolk to go to Ely), new bishoprics of Eton (Huntingdon, Bedford, Buckinghamshire, and Hertfordshire), Brecknock, and Southwell were to be made. Nearly every diocese was affected to some degree; careful plans were laid to finance the new arrangements. If they had been implemented, three of the greater scandals of the Church would have been modified: inefficent oversight of large dioceses, neglect of the poorer ones, and competitive pressure among bishops for promotion.

Gibson also put forward proposals for the stricter control of archdeacons (their office to become void if they were nonresident), for the establishment of rural deaneries, the suppression or regular visitation of peculiars, and at least the mitigation of the abuse of pluralism. Few areas of Church life escaped his notice. His project of reform swept up many ideas that were being canvassed at the time: compiling new *terriers*, authorizing new forms of service— for visiting of prisoners, consecrating new churches, receiving a convert from the Roman Church, preparing one book of visitation articles for the whole country, reforming Church music. No suggestion was carried into effect, the failure was complete. Yet Gibson was a determined man, ambitious but an idealist. In another age he might have been a creative statesman of the Church. He was defeated by the social and political framework within which he worked. The Whigs with whom he allied were virulently anticlerical. Even the unobjectionable scheme, which Gibson among others championed, for providing bishops to the colonies was blocked by those who professed to believe that they would undermine the authority of the civil governors. The result was a notable confusion and wasted opportunity. If the whole body of bishops in England could not prevail upon successive ministers to make this logical move, it is not surprising that isolated bishops like Gibson could not carry projects of reform. Ministers who maintained themselves by use of patronage had a vested interest in the abuses of the Church. Gibson was no martyr and he came to terms, as he grew older, with a philosophy of inaction. In 1747 he was offered the archbishopric of Canterbury. He had long been in indifferent health; he refused the offer and died the following year.

N. Sykes, *Edmund Gibson*, 1926.

THOMAS CORAM (1668–1751), shipwright, seaman, and philanthropist, provided Hogarth with the subject of one of his finest paintings. The painter seems to have recognized in him a man of dignity and plain virtue; no wig and ruffles, an old rusty coat, but a hero in his own simple way. He was born in Lyme Regis and while still young emigrated to Massachusetts, where he settled to work as a shipbuilder. He took to the sea and captained merchantmen. In 1719 he returned to England and set up as merchant in Rotherhithe, but he continued to be interested in American affairs. In the opinion of Horace Walpole he was "the honestest, most disinterested, and most knowing person about the plantations, I ever talked with." He was a trustee for Oglethorpe's colony in Georgia, and he projected a scheme for settling Nova Scotia with unemployed workpeople, which was later adopted.

Coram was appalled by the conditions he found in London, especially by the callous disregard of the fate of unwanted infants. To his lasting honor he fought a campaign for many years to rouse the conscience of the well-to-do until finally in 1737 he was able to present a petition to the king, headed by Lord Derby and twenty-one ladies "of Quality and Distinction," in which he proposed the erection of a hospital "after the example of France, Holland and other Christian Countrys . . . for the Reception, Maintenance and proper Education of such abandoned helpless Infants." Inevitably his plan was pilloried by journalists as an invitation to loose living and "Joyful news to Batchelors and Maids." There were delays before the bill for his Foundling Hospital was granted a Royal Charter (1739), but subscriptions were plentiful, led by the king, who contributed £2,000 and then another £1,000 to endowing a preacher. Handel gave an organ and the score of *The Messiah* and directed performances in aid of the hospital. Parliament voted grants of up to £500,000 in all, and between 1756 and 1760 nearly 15,000 children were admitted. This in itself is evidence of the problem and the need, but indiscriminate acceptance, overcrowding, and disease defeated good intentions. It is sad to record that only 4,400 lived to be apprenticed. Parliament's grants ceased, the hospital became again a private charity and was better managed.

D. Marshall, *The English Poor in the Eighteenth Century*, 1926.
R. K. McClure, *Coram's Children: The London Foundling Hospital in the Eighteenth Century*, 1981.

JETHRO TULL (1674–1741), writer and pioneer in agricultural matters, was an original and significant figure. Though it is no longer the fashion to see the agricultural revolution of the eighteenth century in terms of a few heroic leaders and developers, and though Tull's role remains controversial, his inventive career deserves notice. An Oxford man and a barrister who became a bencher of Gray's Inn in 1724, he became interested in seed drills when he was farming at Howberry near Wallingford. About 1701 he produced his horse-drawn drill, an improvement on the earlier model of Worldidge sixty years before. In his advocacy of sowing in drills rather than broadcast, and of hoeing regularly between the rows to produce a fine tilth and destroy weeds, he was rather a popularizer than an innovator. He was attacked for plagiarism. But he traveled extensively abroad, noting foreign methods, and produced a series of treatises, notably *Horse-hoeing Husbandry* in 1733, which were influential. He could be quite wrong, as when he said that his pulverizing method would remove the need to practice crop rotation. But he was far from being a mere crank. The natural conservatism of farmers was leavened by enquiring spirits such as his. It remains to add, however, that he made more money by his books than by his husbandry at his own "Prosperous Farm."

JONATHAN WILD (1683–1725), master criminal, was more than any man responsible for the growth of crime in London at the start of the eighteenth century. A less attractive and less heroic figure than he appears in the largely fictitious pages of Fielding, he was perhaps more significant than even that student of the underworld may have realized. He realized that, in a big and crowded city, crime may be organized as a business; he has some claim, therefore, to be called the first of the racketeers.

His father was a poor carpenter of Wolverhampton, and he was apprenticed to a buckle maker. While still an apprentice he married and had a son. Bored with making buckles after about ten years, he came to London. His career there followed a pattern on which the moralist may dwell. It was when he was in prison for debt that he met a prostitute, Mary Milliner, and became her ponce; soon he owned two brothels. He learned how to make money as a "fence"—a receiver of stolen property—and by acting as broker for the return of such property. His arrangements benefited alike thieves who had easy money and victims who were otherwise unlikely to recover their goods. His career brought home to men like Fielding the pitiful inadequacy of law enforcement. Wild actually set up an office in Cock Alley where those who had been robbed might apply to him. He grew rich, bought a country house, employed a manager and clerks. His private sloop conveyed stolen goods to a warehouse in Holland and brought back contraband. A special Act of Parliament made his reward technique a felony, but he merely changed his method. Eventually he was brought to trial when it emerged that he was organizing gangs over the whole country, some specializing in certain sorts of crime such as blackmail, others following the assizes or the country fairs. The evidence may have been exaggerated but, since Wild's life coincided with a great increase in robbery and violence and the roads, even in towns, were alarming to travelers, the charges were generally believed. The young Attorney-General Yorke prosecuted for the Crown. Wild was found guilty of receiving reward for the return of stolen property and hanged at Tyburn. It may seem surprising that Wild escaped for so long the only remedy which Hanoverian England knew and applied to about 160 different offenses, from murder to impersonating a Chelsea pensioner or damaging London Bridge—the rope. So it should be added that it was from the city marshal himself, Charles Hitchen, that Wild received his first lessons in the business of receiving.

Henry Fielding, *Jonathan Wild* (a novel).

RICHARD TURPIN (1706–39), highwayman, is the subject of plentiful romance, but the facts of his life are sordid. The cult of the criminal, so strong then in England, as in France, made a hero out of unpromising material. Turpin was the son of an innkeeper at Hempstead in Essex. He became a butcher who found meat for his shop by stealing sheep. He then joined a gang of thieves who did not hesitate to treat their victims with violence: an old woman was put on a fire, a maid raped in the dairy where she hid. Turpin graduated to highwayman. Upon this lucrative trade the imagination of posterity has dwelt; even at the time, men like Duval and McLean were treated as heroes by sentimental ladies. In truth the insecurity of the roads was a social menace. Turpin's career did not last long. He shot, by accident, his partner Tom King. He was eventually arrested for horse stealing, but not before he had shot one of his captors. He was cheered as he went to the gallows at York, dressed in a new frock coat and followed by five hired mourners. The *Newgate Calendar* records that the spectators "seemed much affected by the fate of a man distinguished by the comeliness of his appearance."

GEORGE II (1683–1760) was the subject of the acid attentions of both Hervey and Horace Walpole; much therefore is known about his private failings; less about the public virtues of a king who still lacks a scholarly biography. His position was an awkward one. There was no written constitution but only a few statutory limitations, with a large, debatable field of maneuver. After the fall of Walpole he had to deal with the situation caused by the fragmentation of the Whigs into cliques and clans, so to some extent he was ruled by the Pelhams. It is to his credit that there were not more collisions with the ministers who used his name in Parliament while they lectured him "in the closet." He yielded much, but he was no puppet.

His youth was bedeviled by the ructions which became tradition in this ungracious family. After the disgrace of his mother, whom he believed at first to be innocent, he lived with his grand-parents. George I's threats of disinheritance may have contributed to his son's sense of insecurity. As Prince of Wales he was tactless and ostentatious in his dealings with politicians out of office. They, notably Walpole, between 1717 and the reconciliation of father and son in 1720, did not scruple to exploit the breach. When he came to the throne in 1727 he received a humiliating lesson in the realities of power, for Spencer Compton, his nominee, was unable to form an administration in place of Walpole. Not surprisingly he continued to prefer the advice of Carteret "behind the curtain." He learned to value the ministers whose policies were so evidently successful. At the same time he learned the limits of his compe-tence through a series of checks: notably the concerted resignation in February 1746 of the Pelham group, which compelled him to accept Pitt.

George's irritable temper and obsessive dislikes should be set against the frustrating confinement of his political existence. He brought the style of a drill sergeant to a situation which would have tried the patience of a diplomat. Just as his quarrels with his father came to a head when George I had forced him to accept Newcastle as godfather to his son Frederick, so that son in turn made the birth of his first child the occasion for a more serious and permanent breach. In July 1737 Frederick withdrew Princess Caroline in her birth pains from Hampton Court to ensure that she would not give birth in a palace where the king was resident. Father and son were proclaimed enemies. Even allowing for the perversity of "poor Fred," his father's virulence is astonishing: Frederick was "a monster and the greatest villain that ever was born." His main offence was that he followed his father's example in setting up at Leicester House as the head of a factious opposi-tion to the Crown. The prince seemed to be waiting eagerly for his father's death and the chance to gratify his friends; when he died first the king was not visibly upset.

For a king who reigned for more than thirty years, George II has received remarkably little attention from historians. He can in-deed be presented as boring, callous, mean-spirited, fussy, even a buffoon. He should also be remembered as a zealous sovereign who worked hard at his dispatches; his comments, in points of de-tail, were often shrewd. He was methodical even in his relation-ships with his mistresses; at nine prompt he would be in his apartment, watch in hand, waiting for Mrs. Howard. Behind the huffing and puffing there was a watchful eye. He neglected books but loved music. That Handel made his home in England was largely due to his patronage—and did he not rise to his feet enraptured at the Hallelujah chorus? He was indifferent to paintings but made a noisy scene when Queen Caroline had some pictures changed in the drawing room of Kensington Palace. He had a passion for uniforms and parades; he was also a brave soldier. He had distinguished himself at Oudenarde, and at Dettingen, in 1743, he was the last English king to lead his soldiers in battle. Indeed he led the Pragmatic Army into a trap, but the French were unable to exploit their advantage. At a violent point George got off his horse and marched at the head of his infantry, sword in hand. Handel celebrated the victory with a famous anthem. George basked in the patriotic warmth of the Dettingen summer. It was short-lived. The British expected peace but heard rather of new alliances. He was surely happier than ever at court, where intrigue and gossip fretted his nerves. St. James was certainly dull, but it was a blessing to his subjects that George had no ambition to build a second Versailles.

For the first ten years of his reign he was frequently overborne by Walpole and the queen, who was artful enough to suggest that her ideas were his. After her death, in 1737, he showed more independence. The conflict of interests caused by the union of Britain and Hanover resulted in strains throughout the period. George preferred Hanover, where his word was law, over England, where there were already "kings enough," the Whig magnates. His long stays there, twelve in all, made him unpopular. It is arguable, however, that Britain was well served by Carteret and George II in their nearly three years of partnership (1742–44); also that George had a more realistic grasp of British interests in the war of 1740–48 than either Walpole, or the Pelhams who compelled him, in November 1744, to dismiss Carteret. Subsequently, after the concerted resignation of the ministry, though he "made obstacles in the closet," he had to accept the objectionable Pitt as paymaster. In the initial crisis of the Seven Years War the need to have a strong minister persuaded him to accept the once "terrible cornet of horse" as Secretary of State. Pitt had been scathing about Carteret and had derided Hanover as "a despicable electorate." But George's stand against him was not just arrant prejudice. Pitt had shown himself to be unsound in some of his wilder orations and later events were to show how thin was the line between inspiration and mania. There is irony, however, in the way in which Pitt brought glory to the Crown. The great war minister made personal amends too. When comparing George II with George III, he said that "the good old king possessed justice, truth and sincerity in an eminent degree; so that it was possible to know if he liked you or disliked you."

George could be both affectionate and loyal in his own fashion: to friends like Carteret, in whom he saw "the greatest abilities that this country ever bred"; to successive ministers whom he first mistrusted, then, like Henry Pelham, came to rely on; to his mistresses, discreet Mrs. Howard, the Countess Walmoden. Especially he loved his wife; courtiers were amused by the way in which he would rush unceremoniously into her arms when he returned from a stay abroad. He asked in his will that his coffin should be laid beside Caroline's and a side removed from each so that their dust should mingle in death. A certain clumsy spontaneity was a pleasant trait. There was an element of the absurd, a touch of the strutting prince of comic opera. Yet the reign which saw less of a diminution of the royal authority than historians used to think was also one in which Britons enjoyed growing prosperity and a large measure of religious and political liberty. It ended at the climax of a victorious war when the king died, of a stroke, in his water closet.

J. D. Griffith Davies, *A King in Toils*, 1938.
J. B. Owen, "George II Reconsidered," in *Statesmen, Scholars and Merchants*, A. Whiteman et al., eds., 1973.

CAROLINE OF ANSPACH (1683–1737), wife of George II, was Queen Consort for only ten years before her death. She made a mark, however, upon the first decade of George's reign which cannot be accounted for only by her political alliance with Walpole or by the devotion of her chamberlain, Lord Hervey. The latter repaid her confidences with a literary portrait of unusual warmth and sensitivity. It is not entirely flattering, but it reveals a woman of courage and good sense, one who loved power but did not abuse it. There is nothing in the facts of her life to suggest that the portrait, in essentials, is false.

As Princess of Wales, Caroline found herself in the difficult position of wife to the heir to a Hanoverian: between the distrust of the father and the silly conceit of the son. She made her own life, therefore, creating around her a court of intellectuals and aspiring clerics. She does not seem to have had any literary talent herself; her letters are clumsy and reveal no clarity or originality of mind. It is, however, typical of her that she should have caused her sergeant-surgeon to inoculate two of her children, Princess Amelia and Princess Caroline, before this method of insuring against smallpox had become either fashionable or safe. She enjoyed the discussion of philosophical and religious topics, especially when these inclined to the unorthodox. She prided herself, too, upon her theological discernment and had regular meetings with churchmen like Clarke, Butler, Berkeley, and Hoadley—all men of a speculative cast of mind. In her friendship with Leibnitz, up to his death in 1716, she anticipated the royal fashion of the Enlightenment; indeed it is not hard to see her as a contemporary of Catherine the Great and Joseph II. Instead, she was compelled to inhabit a narrower stage. Unable to find any common interest with her husband, who despised "all that lettered nonsense . . . called her a pedant and said she loved to spend her time more like a schoolmistress than a queen" (Hervey), she directed her energies to the pursuit of power. She endured the company of George, irritable though he was and incapable of sustained conversation upon any general theme, in order to rule him: "for all the tedious hours that she spent there watching him while he slept, or the heavier task of entertaining him while he was awake, her single consolation was that she had power, and that people in coffee houses and *ruelles* were saying she governed the country without knowing how dear the government of it cost her."

She was a fine-looking woman in a German way, fair and buxom, and she knew that she could hold the king's affections whatever his temporary aberrations. When he returned from his visits to Hanover he would always rush straight to her chamber; he relied upon her, but he was exasperated by her calm detachment. She endured his snubs and perversities and the physical pain of an umbilical rupture which she concealed for fear of his turning from her.

She ruled George but could not rule the country, although she was four times "Guardian of the Realm." Her relationship with Walpole has often been described: how she would suggest to the king ideas that came from Walpole in such a way as to make the king think, the next morning, that they were his own. Walpole cultivated her friendship with cynical care. As he boasted later, he paid no heed to Mrs. Howard, but took "the right sow by the ear." She was invaluable to Walpole in the years after the king's accession, but after her death there was little change in his relationship with the king. It is possible too that her influence in ecclesiastical appointments has been exaggerated. It is to her credit that she secured the promotion of two of the best bishops of the century, Berkeley and Butler, but their talents might have secured recognition anyway. She also enjoyed the company of Hoadly who, though an assiduous courtier, was one of the worst bishops of the time.

A constant theme of Hervey's memoirs is the bitter feud between her son, Frederick, Prince of Wales, and his parents. This must remain a mystery. Even if Frederick was as silly and heartless as his father, even if his opposition was constitutionally dangerous, and allowing also for Hervey's interest in fomenting the quarrel, Caroline's attitude was unnatural. The prince showed his mettle by removing his wife, in the pains of childbirth, from Hampton Court to St. James's, in order to prevent his first-born being born under his parents' roof. His mother said that she would give it under hand that "my dear first-born is the greatest ass, and the greatest liar, and the greatest canaille, and the greatest beast in the whole world, and that I heartily wish he was out of it." On another occasion she told Walpole that he did not "know my filthy beast of a son as well as I do." It may be that normal affection had turned sour in the strained atmosphere of the court; anyway, Caroline, usually humane and reasonable, claims our sympathy again by the manner of her dying, after days of agony. She urged George to marry again; tears streaming down his face, he said, "Non, j'aurai des maîtresses." "Ah!" she said, "Cela non empêche pas." Broadminded by nature, she never sank to the fashionable cynicism of the day. Essentially an authoritarian, she had the sense to use, rather than to abuse, such power as she could conjure out of the political system of her adopted country.

P. Quennell, *Caroline of England*, 1939.

SIR ROBERT WALPOLE, 1st EARL OF ORFORD (1676–1745), principal minister of the Crown from 1721 to 1742, was born at the old manor house at Houghton in North Norfolk, the third son of nineteen children. His father had broken away from the cavalier tradition of this old county family and sat as a Whig in William III's Parliaments. His early death in 1700 left Robert, because of the death of his elder brothers, to manage the family estates. He was educated at Eton, where he was a colleger, and at King's. He loved Eton and missed no opportunity later to advance the fortunes of his school friends. But his intellectual interests did not last, for he became entirely absorbed in political business; relaxation he found in the talk of friends, in lavish entertainment, and hunting. In 1700 he married Catherine Shorter, heiress to a timber merchant; her extravagance matched Walpole's own taste for good living and added to his debts.

He entered Parliament for the pocket borough of Castle Rising in 1701, but in the following year, he transferred to King's Lynn, in order to provide a safe seat for his uncle Horace. Lynn was then a thriving port and Walpole grew familiar with problems of trade. Within a few years he had come to be regarded as the leader of the Norfolk members. He lost no chance to cultivate the interests of friends and relations, notably his cousin and brother-in-law, Lord Townshend, and Charles Turner, a leading citizen of Lynn. From his earliest years Walpole exhibited a capacity for taking pains over people as well as over material concerns. In Parliament he soon showed also that he could be formidable in debate. His friendship with Townshend provided an entry into Whig society, where he was valued for his direct manner and jovial temper. In the Commons he was fortunate in that most of the Whig leaders sat in the Upper House; in town, at the weekly meetings of the Kit-Cat Club, he learned about politics from such experienced hands as Somers, Halifax, and Wharton.

In June 1705 Walpole was made a member of the naval council of Prince George, Lord High Admiral. In February 1708 he succeeded his Tory rival, St. John, as Secretary at War: this gave him control, at the height of the war, of all aspects of military life in England and Scotland. In January 1710 he became Treasurer of the Navy. Thus he was associated intimately with the conduct of the war—a Whig war since the Whigs had eased the Tories out of office and stood firm for the succession of the Archduke Charles to the Spanish throne. After the Tory victory of 1710 Walpole was marked for destruction, and in 1711 he was committed to the Tower after accusations of corruption in the negotiation of contracts. They were political charges, although evidence for them was not lacking, and Walpole's "martyrdom," coming at the same time as Marlborough's disgrace, only enhanced his position with the Whigs.

The failure of Bolingbroke's plans for the accession of James Edward in 1714 found Walpole strongly placed among the Whigs who looked for places under George I. He was made first paymaster, then, in 1715, First Lord of the Treasury and Chancellor of the Exchequer. Now he could indulge his love of building and display, and fortify himself by solid investment. Even by contemporary standards he was careless of the distinction between public and private money, as some remarked when they saw the great house of Orford rise in the grounds of Chelsea Hospital. The major part of the sums which passed through his hands in three years of office seems to have been the surplus which paymasters were entitled to use for their own benefit; some may have been Chelsea Hospital funds which Walpole used to speculate with in transit. But the country benefited too from Walpole's financial sense. The measures which he took for the redemption of debt, the consolidation of rates of interest. and the establishment of a sinking fund were models for subsequent work in this field. The precarious harmony of the Whig ministers was, however, destroyed by Townshend's misfortune in crossing the king in foreign affairs, and by the constitutional difficulties created by the king's absences in Germany. After Townshend was dismissed, Walpole followed his friend into opposition, along with a significant group, Pulteney, Methuen, Orford, and his devoted friend, Devonshire. From April 1717 until June 1720, when he became paymaster again, Walpole enjoyed the pleasures of faction. On at least one point, his opposition was farsighted. He helped to destroy the Peerage Bill which, if it had been passed in 1719, would have turned the House of Lords into a closed oligarchy.

Walpole speculated rashly and lost heavily on the rise and fall of the South Sea Company stock in the summer of 1720. But his political gain was vast. He was not so closely involved as the principal ministers, Sunderland, Stanhope, Aislabie, and Craggs, father and son. The suicide of the elder Craggs, the disgrace of Aislabie and the younger Craggs and death by smallpox of the latter, the death of Stanhope in 1721 and of Sunderland the following year, cleared the way for his ascendancy. The way in which he set to work to reestablish public credit was typical of him: pragmatic and calm. What he did was less important than what he appeared to be doing. His scheme (proposed by his banker, Jacombe) for incorporating South Sea stock in that of the bank was not adopted, but it helped to restore confidence and persuade men to invest again. To contemporaries Walpole was not a financial wizard but the "skreen-master general." Defending directors and ministers against bitter attacks, he showed political courage; if he did not endear himself to the House, he made influential friends.

From 1721 to 1742 Walpole was First Lord of the Treasury. During this time he obtained a mastery over Parliament and an initiative in the conduct of affairs which transformed the office he held. He was not the first to be called "prime minister": Godolphin and Harley had enjoyed sufficient influence at Queen Anne's court, command of patronage, and standing in Parliament to earn the title, and the odium that went with it. After Walpole there were to be other First Lords who were not "prime" ministers; the elder Pitt, who was a Secretary of State. In the government of the Pelhams there was no distinct head. Walpole's long tenure of office nevertheless proved decisive. The office of "prime minister" evolved logically from the Crown's retreat from the active center of government. It would not have been surprising in the emergencies of war; it was Walpole's special achievement that it happened during the "pudding times" of a long peace. He was relentless in the pursuit of power, tenacious in his grasp. He was committed to no program or timetable. It may be that principle was prominent only when wedded to political advantage. That does not mean, however, that there are no steady notions to be deducted from his acts and speeches.

Walpole held by the House of Hanover. His opposition to Toryism was as stern as it was shrewd. It was not his doing that Toryism was tainted with Jacobitism, but he made capital out of Bolingbroke's past errors and, till convinced, by 1726, that he was harmless, would not countenance his return from exile. Blooded in faction, he valued stability above all. He became supreme master of a system which "was flexible enough to contain the competing demands of different interests and rival pressure groups" (Dickinson). At its heart was the parliamentary forum where the powerful and wealthy were sufficiently well represented to assume that they could work through the system: even when temporarily it did not favor them they could always hope to effect change. Parliament was open to external pressures through lobby, petition, and the voices strident or seductive, of a free press. It also provided a well-publicized arena for debate. Walpole there maintained his dominance by unremitting vigilance, by noting what would appeal to that impressionable assembly, not least the lucid presentation of facts and figures; above all by his handling of the Crown patronage. This gave rise to the complaint that he reduced corruption to a system but it must be remembered that he had to contend with a press persistently hostile, often scurrilous, which he did little to propitiate. More elevated writers might stand on principle; Grub Street noted the wealth that enabled him to play Maecaenas—and employed its talents to denounce the means by which he apparently achieved it. Yet the judgment of a later master of the practice of politics should count for something: Burke wrote that "he governed by party attachments. The charge of systematic corruption is less applicable to him, perhaps, than to any minister who ever served the crown for so great a length of time." Certainly the means of such "corruption" did not increase during his ministry. Nor did Walpole monopolize patronage. Ecclesiastical preferment was only partly in his hands; both kings retained control over military and naval appointments.

Walpole had "bottom," as contemporaries described those qualities of sound judgment and staying power, that even rivals had to recognize. One after another they were elbowed into eccentric corners, society's "insiders" left to brood on the frustrations of being permanently "out": Pulteney and Carteret, Wilmington after hopes briefly raised by the accession of George II, Chesterfield, and in 1730, his old ally Townshend. Memory of the Schism, the menace of Jacobitism, the cost of ambitious foreign policies, and the violence of domestic mobs were all arguments which could weigh with king or Parliament. In a country virtually unpoliced, when it was necessary to send for the troops when riot threatened, there was evidence to frighten the most fervent admirers of English liberty: the destruction of toll-gates in Herefordshire in 1734, attacks on Irish laborers in the Rag Fair riots of 1736, and most alarming, in the same year, the lynching of Captain Porteous in Edinburgh for acting against the ever-popular trade of smuggling. Pleas for tough action were all the stronger for being presented in the bluff language of the country squire, skeptical of fine talk "that buttered no parsnips." Cultivated image or natural style, the lolling figure of the Commons chamber, stout and ruddy, munching his Norfolk russets, the dashing horseman who would hunt in Richmond Park if he could not get down to Houghton, provided cover for the shrewdest political mind of his generation. London laughed when it heard that Walpole had landed face down in the Richmond mud: in the political saddle he had a surer seat. In consideration of his managerial skills style must find a place; in the end, however, it was policies that counted. In Parliament the squire predominated: many (though less than might be thought from their professions of disgust) spurned the places and jobs that would bind them to "Robinocracy." Alienated, these men of the "country party" could endanger the dynasty. Walpole wooed them, supporting the stern Game Laws, notably the comprehensive "Black Act" of 1723, furthering private bills for enclosures and turnpikes. Above all he reduced the Land Tax which, when levied at 4s, placed a large share of the state's expenditure on the backs of the squirearchy. An essential part of the strategy behind his ill-fated Excise Bill of 1733, extending the duties already imposed on tea and coffee (1723) to wine and tobacco, was that it would enable him to perpetuate the low rate of 1s.

Clearly Walpole cannot be called a free trader; nor was he a rigid mercantilist. Always the pragmatist, he studied the needs and sentiment of city merchants and bankers. The lowest interest rates in Europe, down to 3 percent by the late thirties, reflected their confidence in his financial management and consequent willingness to invest. His Sinking Fund was responsible for a significant reduction in the capital of the National Debt. So far was he from being a purist in financial matters that he periodically raided it in order to keep expenditure down, and therefore taxation. In his re vision of the customs rates, he removed all duties on the export of agricultural produce and on over a hundred articles manufactured in England that found a market overseas. He abolished certain import duties on raw silk, flax, and dyes. He laid down regulations of quality to maintain the standard of British products; to secure low wages, acts were passed requiring justices to fix wages. But to protect home industry Walpole retained high duties on the import of foreign goods which competed with English manufacturers. In his view of the colonies, Walpole was insular; inert, except when there was trouble. The colonies were looked on as a source of valuable raw materials, a market for English products, and they were forbidden, for the most part, to trade directly outside the mother-country. When the West Indian planters complained that the colonies were buying their sugar more cheaply from the French West Indies, Walpole produced the Molasses Act (1733), placing duties upon foreign sugar, placating the English planters—but alienating the colonists, though the duties were easily evaded. Ministerial action was for emergencies, or when there was an evident consensus.

Broadly speaking, two foreign policies were open to English statesmen in the eighteenth century: involvement in the dynastic wrangles of Europe with the commitments that this required, in the William-Marlborough-Stanhope tradition, or isolation, with some insurance in the shape of a close understanding with one country. The latter was the Tory idea as expressed in the peace of Utrecht and in essentials it was Walpole's. In 1730 he parted company with Townshend, who seemed to him to be precipitate in his engagements and to be endangering peace. After 1730 he was in control, with Newcastle and Harrington, Secretaries of State, at his service. In 1731 the Treaty of Vienna was signed: England guaranteed the Pragmatic Sanction while the Emperor admitted Don Carlos to the Italian duchies that had been for so long a cause of strife. This treaty marked the end of the Stanhope-Townshend idea of cooperation with France and the return to the earlier system of alliance with the Emperor. Unfortunately Walpole, an isolationist at heart, did not foster this alliance. England's influence was seen to dwindle when two years later, France and Spain made the first of the Family Compacts. When Fleury led France into the Polish Succession War, Walpole refused to commit England to support of the Emperor; he rejoiced that he thus saved English lives and shillings in a meaningless dispute, but he found too, as other English statesmen have found after him, that influence has to be paid for. He was edged out of the peace negotiations by Fleury. The Austrians were sore at what they regarded as his desertion. A year after another Treaty of Vienna of 1738, by which France gained Lorraine and the Emperor nothing but a French guarantee of the Pragmatic Sanction, Walpole was driven into war with Spain without an ally in Europe.

Between the outbreak of war in 1739 and his fall from power in January 1742, Walpole fought to hold his position. His conduct of the war was uncertain, but he remained master of Parliament to the end. His survival in these years indicates the strength of the position he had built for himself. The death of Queen Caroline, his friend and confidante, in 1737 was a blow to him, although the king remained loyal. An opposition had built up over the years composed of the hard core of Tories, the deprived Whigs led by men like Pulteney and Chesterfield whom Walpole had ousted, and those groups of aspiring politicians who saw the old minister as an obstacle to their advancement: the Leicester House faction who clustered round the Prince of Wales, embarrassing opponent of both king and minister; the Cobham cousinhood, among whom was the ardent young Pitt. The opposition had already shown its teeth over the Excise Bill, withdrawn by Walpole after a country-wide campaign of unparalleled ferocity. It triumphed when it drove Walpole reluctantly into war with Spain in 1739, ostensibly for the rights of Jenkins, the sailor who lost his ear, so he claimed, at the hands of *gardacostas* but really for freedom of trade in Spanish colonial waters. Walpole secured the Convention of Pardo and a small money compensation and urged that this be made the grounds of honorable treatment. But Pitt caught the mood of Parliament and country when he championed the "despairing merchants" and denounced the convention. The war that followed was first popular but fruitless, after Admiral Vernon's seizure of Porto Bello. Walpole was unable to rise to the scale of the European war that this became when Frederick of Prussia seized Silesia from Austria in 1740. It would have mattered less had Newcastle been moderately competent. In the election of 1741 Walpole's majority was diminished, but he held on until February 1742; then he was defeated on an election petition—but he had already decided to resign. He had lost the support of the House of Commons without which no minister could long survive in the eighteenth century. He knew it. "I have lived long enough in the world, Sir," he said in debate in 1739, "to know that the safety of a minister lies in his having the approbation of this House . . . I have always made it my first study to obtain it, and therefore I hope to stand." When he met Pulteney in the House of Lords, soon after both men had accepted peerages, he is supposed to have remarked: "You and I, My Lord, are now two as insignificant men as any in England." This could not have been said in the reign of Queen Anne, when the Whig junto ruled the country from the House of Lords. Walpole had raised the House of Commons to a unique sense of authority. Even if, in his management of the House, he relied principally upon the "old gang," the body of about 150 placemen who could be relied upon to support government in all weathers, he never became insensitive to the needs of the more independent members.

He explained and defended his policies with clear reasoning and the plain words that won respect; he approached debate with an open mind and he could always be converted by good arguments. During the *Pax Walpoleana* there were few great public issues, but there was plenty of good debate.

He did not live long enough to enjoy his earldom or the treasures of his great house at Houghton. The king still consulted him "in the closet" and the danger of impeachment in Parliament for peculation receded after committees had sat to collect evidence against him. The pain of gout and the stone tormented his last years, but he was game to the end. It is hard to admire Walpole without reservation. His ministry was fairly called the Robinocracy, since his relatives and dependents enjoyed place at every level. He professed no idealism: "I am no Saint, no Spartan, no reformer." He was a man of coarse fiber. "I have the right sow by the ear," he said of his relationship with Queen Caroline. Even the pictures which form today the center of the great Russian gallery of the Hermitage he bought with a sort of materialist gusto. Caricaturists dwelt upon the homely features and his vast bulk (he weighed twenty stone); historians have analyzed the election lists, the petitions, and his vast correspondence. The picture that emerges is a complex one, but certain qualities stand beyond dispute. He was endowed with a prodigious capacity for work and he devoted himself to the interests of his country as he saw them. He was a man of great physical and moral courage. Finally there was a certain humanity about him; he worked, not in vain, for peace abroad and toleration at home.

J. H. Plumb, *Sir Robert Walpole*, Vols. I and II, 1956, 1960.
H. T. Dickinson, *Walpole and the Whig Supremacy*, 1973.
J. H. Black, *Robert Walpole and the Nature of Politics in Early Eighteenth Century England*, 1990.
J. H. Black, ed., *Britain in the Age of Walpole*, 1984.

WILLIAM PULTENEY, 1st EARL OF BATH (1684–1764), possessed talents enough to make him a great Parliamentarian. It has sometimes been assumed that he would also have been a statesman if it had not been for the implacable opposition of Robert Walpole; for this, however, there is little evidence.

His education at Westminster and Christ Church left him with an abiding love for the classics and a facility in the sort of oratory that was specially admired by his contemporaries. In Lecky's view he was "probably the most graceful and brilliant speaker in the Commons in the interval between the withdrawal of St. John and the appearance of Pitt." He entered Parliament an ardent Whig, upheld Walpole in debate, and visited him in prison after his disgrace in 1712. After the Hanover Succession he was rewarded by Walpole's former office of Secretary at War; with Walpole and Townshend he resigned his office in the Schism of April 1717. He did not, however, return to greatness with his allies in 1721; in 1723 he was fobbed off with the small but lucrative office of Cofferer of the Household. Walpole may have hoped that his well-known "instinct for accumulation" might prove stronger than his political ambition. But he was not so easily assuaged and he lost the office in 1725 after vehement attacks on Walpole's financial arrangements.

Pulteney had been left the borough of Hedon and a fortune by an early patron, Henry Guy, Secretary of Treasury under William III—and he married another. He was therefore as independent as he was ambitious; not the man whom Walpole would choose for running partner in the administration—he preferred Newcastle. But it is not certain that Pulteney would have made the better minister. He had a large share of the "spirit of faction" that characterizes the years of the Whig supremacy. Hervey had good reason to emphasize his nuisance value, for he had been gratuitously offensive to this "delicate Hermaphrodite" as he called him and they subsequently fought a bloodless duel. He was not, however, rancorous in his references to Pulteney and his opinion is revealing: "a man of parts but not to be depended upon; one capable of serving a minister, but more capable of hurting him from desiring to serve himself." Pulteney's talents were not limited to oratory. He had an excellent head for figures and a clear understanding of the problems of foreign and domestic policy. He proved himself, too, an adept political journalist. With Bolingbroke he inspired *The Craftsman* and from 1726 to 1736 he was one of its most effective contributors. In its pages may be seen the attitudes of the Old Whiggery which Pulteney came to represent: it was the tradition of the country party, not so very different from the new Toryism which Bolingbroke fostered after his return from exile, opposition to the court, the financiers, and to the corruption which was thought to fester in the seats of power. To this was added the notion of the patriot: in Walpole's view, a man who has been refused a favor, but in Pulteney's, one who stands apart from the court, who opposes "arbitrary power" (as in the case of the Excise) and stands for a robust foreign policy. It was the latter, expressed in the clamor over Jenkins's Ear and the demand for war with Spain in 1739, that provided the occasion for one of the parliamentary scenes in which Pulteney excelled and was the long-term cause of Walpole's fall. But when that happened in January 1742, Pulteney declined to form the "broad bottom" ministry which Argyll and the Prince of Wales wanted: "The heads of parties, like the heads of snakes, are urged on by their tails." Morley speaks of "the sense of shame that made him hesitate at turning courtier after having acted the patriot for so long." If true, then enough is said of the failings of the attitude and of the man. It may, however, be merely a sign of the weariness that he referred to in a letter to George Berkeley after "the struggle against universal corruption." He had no wish "to be the Whig who undermined Hanoverian Whiggism" (Langford).

He accepted a peerage in this year, along with Walpole, to be greeted by his rival with the words: "You and I, My Lord, are now two as insignificant men as any in England." In 1746 he did make an abortive attempt to form a ministry with Granville; perhaps at that juncture it was well that he failed. Without the largeness of spirit of a Pitt, or the application of a Henry Pelham, it may be that he had fulfilled the role for which he was best qualified, that of leader of opposition. It was an important one in an age when oligarchic government could easily have declined into a conspiracy to defraud the nation. He challenged the unhealthier aspects of Walpole's monopoly, even if he seemed at times, in his animosity against Walpole, to be narrowing political life to the petty conditions of the duel. By the manner in which he fought the duel he quickened the sluggish pulse of Parliament and earned the tribute of Shelburne: "the greatest House of Commons orator that had ever appeared."

L. Colley, *In Defiance of Oligarchy*, 1982.

WILLIAM SHIPPEN (1673–1743), Tory and Jacobite, was the son of the rector of Stockport in Cheshire and was educated at Stockport Grammar School and at Trinity College, Cambridge. After practicing law he entered Parliament for Bramber, a borough of Lord Plymouth, but was then unseated on petition. In 1710, however, he returned upon the High Church cry "Huzzah for Queen and Church." He was prominent in the October Club, strong for Anglican measures and for the charges against Marlborough. After 1714, the débâcle of the Tories and the exile of Bolingbroke, he emerged as a leading spokesman for a loose grouping of some fifty independent-minded members, united only in their detestation of court and palace. Shippen's own position was precarious: he was an avowed Jacobite but committed to working by constitutional ways. He spent a few months in the Tower for his speech at the opening of Parliament in 1717, when he said that "twas a great misfortune that the King was stranger to our language and constitution," but thereafter he enjoyed a certain immunity, as the ministry grew more stable and the Jacobite threat receded. From Walpole he got a gruff appreciation; politics apart, they were friends. "Whoever is corrupt," said Walpole, "Shippen is not." When the vote of the Tories could have been fatal to Walpole in 1741, Shippen and his friends abstained, for he preferred Walpole to any conceivable alternative.

Sometimes Shippen's opposition was more effective. In 1716 he made a stout resistance to the Septennial Bill, declaring that "Long Parliaments would grow either formidable or contemptible," and he was prominent in the attack upon the Excise Scheme of 1733 which Walpole was eventually forced to withdraw. He was predictably hot about the South Sea Company and was attacking ministerial participation in the affairs of the company several years before the crash. The Civil List and the king's frequent journeys to Hanover were regular targets, and for "the bottomless pit of the secret service" he had an exaggerated horror. Shippen was not a great orator; indeed Horace Walpole tells us that he habitually spoke with his glove in his mouth. But the disinterested and bold critic who is known to have no ambitions for himself, who can speak to the minds and moods of the independent gentleman, has seldom wanted a hearing in the House. Shippen's wife reflected his prejudice admirably: she would never attend the court of the Hanoverian king. Shippen's own outlook was limited. But his character and actions may have had more effect than the bibulous toasts of stay-at-home Jacobite squires. In an age of placemen and faction Shippen helped to preserve, if not greatly to enrich, the Tory tradition.

K. G. Feiling, *The Second Tory Party, 1742–1832*, 1938.
J. Biggs-Davison, *Tory Lives*, 1952.

SIR WILLIAM WYNDHAM, 3rd BARONET (1687–1740), Tory politician, was born at Orchard Wyndham in Somerset. His family cherished a tradition of stubborn loyalty to the Crown and his father had opposed the election of William of Orange and Mary. Wyndham was educated at Eton and Christ Church and entered Parliament in 1710 as member for Somerset. He became master of the queen's buckhounds and, in 1712, Secretary at War. He was a member of the right-wing October Club and a founder of the Brothers Club of which Swift was a member. He introduced the Schism Bill which made reception of the sacrament the test of teaching in a school, a measure which, though it passed the House by a majority of a hundred, reflected an old-fashioned view of the relationship of Church and State and was repealed soon after the accession of George I.

When Bolingbroke left the country in 1715, Wyndham stayed. At the start of the Jacobite risings his father-in-law, the Duke of Somerset, secured the king's promise that Wyndham would not be arrested; but the ministry did not think that he could be trusted. A thousand pounds was put on his head, he surrendered himself and was put in the Tower, and the Duke of Somerset resigned all his offices in a fury. When he was a boy, Wyndham had been warned by two different fortune-tellers to "beware of the white horse"; as he passed beneath the gate of the Tower a painter was busy adding the arms of the Elector of Hanover to the royal crest: the White Horse. He spent eight months in the Tower before release, but he was never brought to trial. Gradually Wyndham came to accept the new dynasty, recognizing like Bolingbroke that loyalty to James Edward Stuart was futile. He was devoted to Bolingbroke, but to us Wyndham may appear the better man, less brilliant but more constant. His perspectives were broader than those of Shippen, leader of the Jacobite Tories. His group, supported by the admirable Lord

Gower, a byword for integrity, made up in constancy what it lacked in numbers. Wyndham may have lacked the ruthlessness of a successful party leader, but he was a fine speaker. He had a slight stammer, but a presence and a power of developing argument that compelled attention. Walpole respected him as a man who spoke a language above that of mere party interest. From his impartial place Speaker Onslow was well-qualified to judge him and in his opinion he was "the most made for a great man of any that I have known in this age." Pope wrote, admittedly with a Tory bias, of

> Wyndham, just to freedom and the throne,
> The master of our passions, and his own.

Thanks partly to Wyndham, the Tory party kept their ideological character and their ability to act in concert. It cannot, however, be said that the Tories were able to make much impact upon Walpole's administration. There was a divergence of policy between Wyndham and Shippen, and despite Bolingbroke's hard work and *The Craftsman*'s propaganda, no strong base for action in the alliance of Wyndham and Pulteney, "the two consuls." At heart Wyndham was more the country squire than the dedicated leader of party. Aided, perhaps, by his second marriage to the Whiggish Lady Blandford, he gravitated toward a philosophical central position. The incapacity of the Tories was revealed when they solemnly seceded from Parliament in 1739. Yet Walpole feared him and was mightily relieved by his death. Wyndham was out hunting and was thrown when jumping a ditch. He was riding a white horse.

Linda Colley, *In Defiance of Oligarchy*, 1982.

GEORGE WADE (1673–1748), Field Marshal, was a good and steady soldier who is now best remembered as the builder of the military roads which helped to improve the economy of the Highlands and to subject the region to efficient government. He was first commissioned in the "Tenth" in 1690, served in Flanders in William III's reign and at the start of the Spanish Succession War as adjutant-general in Galway's expedition to the peninsula; in 1707 he fought bravely at Almanza, where the English were defeated. He was present at the capture of Minorca in 1708 and in command of a brigade at Saragossa in 1710. In England in 1715 he was stationed in the west of England where the expected insurrection did not materialize. He captured Vigo in the short Spanish War of 1719.

In 1725, he was sent to Scotland with orders to execute, with Lord President Duncan Forbes, the provisions of the Act for Disarming the Highland Clans. He at once raised six companies of Highlanders, recruited from Whig clans, notably the Campbells; the number was later raised to ten and formed into the Black Watch, who were blooded on the field of Fontenoy. With this went the disarmament of Jacobite clans: easier to enact than to execute. Anyone who has tramped over General Wade's roads, that which crosses the Coryairack pass for instance, reaching 2,500 feet and saving a journey of 60 miles, will appreciate Wade's achievement as road-builder. In 1731 one of the Macleods, who crossed the pass, saw six great fires at which six oxen were being roasted whole as a treat for the five hundred soldiers who had just completed "the great road for wheel-carriages between Fort Augustus and Ruthven, it being October 30th, His Majesty's Birthday." Wade's roads were usually made 14 or 15 feet wide (many a modern Highland road is only 10!). Some of his bridges still stand; a particularly fine one is that which crosses the Spey beside the old barracks at Garvamore. By his work Perth was linked to Inverness, Fort Augustus, and Fort William. In the '45, however, these places were so lightly garrisoned that improved communications were of more use to the Jacobites than to the defenders.

Wade was by then in Flanders. Promoted Field Marshal in 1743, he was made commander-in-chief in succession to Stair. His army being smaller than that of Marshal Saxe, a formidable man to oppose, the septuagenarian may be forgiven for slow and cautious tactics designed to avoid action. He was recalled to face the threat of invasion in England. His task was to concentrate what British regiments could be found in England or recalled from Flanders; he also called out the militia. In the autumn of 1745 he moved slowly northeast to Newcastle, marched across in response to Murray's feint move only to find that the Jacobites had slipped past him, taken Carlisle, and were apparently bound for London. The capital was covered, and Charles Edward turned back, but Wade made no attempt to intercept his return journey but stood on the border "with his feet in the snow." That was the end of a career in which he was respected by his troops for his personal qualities rather than for any genius for training or tactics. A strict disciplinarian, he seems also to have been a fair and considerate man.

J. B. Salmond, *Wade in Scotland*, 1934.

JEAN-LOUIS LIGONIER (1680–1770), general, was born at Castres, the son of Huguenot parents of good stock. In 1698 he followed into exile others of his family who had left after the Revocation of the Edict of Nantes. From Holland he went to Ireland, whence, after four years of obscurity, he turned up in England, became a naturalized Englishman, and joined, as a volunteer, the army of the Duke of Marlborough. He showed courage and discretion in the campaigns of Flanders and Germany. He was the first man through the breach into Liège in 1702 and was allowed to buy himself a company in the Tenth Foot. In 1706, for dashing leadership of assault troops in the attack on Menin, he was promoted major. At Malplaquet he showed once more the courage for which he became renowned; after the battle he counted twenty bullet holes in his clothing. After the Peace of Utrecht, in 1713, he was given the governorship of Fort St. Philip in Minorca. He was adjutant-general to the force which captured Vigo in 1719 and in 1720 acquired his own regiment, the Eighth Horse. Thus, without favor or private income, he made his mark. Stationed in Ireland from 1720 to 1724, the Black Guards, as they were called, became known as an elite force, so that men paid for the privilege of being a trooper and later distinguished themselves in the Flanders campaigns of 1742–45. Ligonier did not marry, but kept a mistress in Southwark, by whom he had several children. He had, nevertheless, some standing in Irish society; he seems to have been a man of much charm, generous, vivacious, and hospitable.

Circumstances favored him in the War of the Austrian Succession. In the small army allowed by peacetime economies there was a shortage of good regimental officers who had taken pains to study their craft, or had much fighting experience. That the supreme command in Flanders went, after the resignation of Stair in 1743, first to the septuagenarian Wade, then, in 1745, to the Duke of Cumberland, twenty-five years old, speaks for itself. Again Ligonier, as a relative outsider, was by necessity a professional whose prospects were unprejudiced by political affiliations. He knew, too, how to make himself agreeable to George II and accompanied him as a personal staff officer, liaising between the king, the cabinet, and Lord Stair. At Dettingen, in 1743, George II was so taken with his conduct that he wished to make him a Knight Banneret on the field; he was subsequently made a Knight of the Bath. In 1744, because of Wade's indisposition, he was for long periods virtually commander-in-chief. By contrast with his fellow-general Hawley, he was humane: "it is with the greatest reluctancy I set my name to a death warrant." At Fontenoy in 1745, under Cumberland, he was in command of the British infantry who were praised throughout Europe for their gallant advance and disciplined retreat. Their training, and their handling on the field, saved the army from the effects of Cumberland's careless reconnaissance and rash orders.

Ligonier preceded Cumberland home after the Jacobite landing later in the year but, after organizing the army which was to have confronted Charles Edward if he had marched upon London, he played no part in the subsequent Scottish campaign. It is typical of Ligonier that he should have provided for an issue of blankets for his troops against the hazards of winter in the Highlands—the first time that this was done. Earlier he had paid out of his own pocket for an extra doctor for his regiment, got Treasury approval for the issue of wheat instead of rye for soldiers' bread, and instituted regimental hospitals in Flanders. At Roucoux in 1746 it was his handling of a much smaller force that saved the allies from a severe defeat. He was captured at Laffeldt in the following year, ironically, after his greatest feat of arms. By his advice to Cumberland to hold the village of Laffeldt—which inflicted heavy casualties on Saxe—and by his superb use of the cavalry, he enabled the infantry to extricate themselves from a tricky situation. The devotion of young Lord Henry Campbell, who met his death scouring the battlefield for his chief, is a tribute to Ligonier's power to inspire young officers. Saxe, who had lost about 10,000 men, far more than the allies, is said to have presented him to Louis XV as "a man who has defeated all my plans by a single glorious action," to which Louis replied, "The English have not only paid all but fought all." Ligonier was subsequently released on exchange.

Peace, in 1748, brought recognition of his services. He entered Parliament for Bath. He seems to have taken some interest in the affairs of the growing town and was a close friend of Ralph Wood, after Nash the principal organizer of Bath society, but never spoke in Parliament. Another unsolicited honor was election to the Royal Society, a remarkable honor for a Frenchman and a soldier, although he had cultivated tastes and an extensive library. In the same year he became lieutenant-general of the Ordnance, the highest professional military position in the peacetime army. It was of this period of his life that Horace Walpole wrote: "He had all the gallant gaiety of his nation. Polished from foppery by age and by living in a more thinking country, he was universally beloved and respected." He was also very busy. As President of the Board of Officers, he was concerned during these years with the standardization of dress, drill, and tactics. During this period, the Ordnance Survey was begun and the Corps of Engineers developed as a military body. When war broke out again in 1756, and after the severe economies of the Pelham administration and the mistakes of men on the spot, Byng and Braddock among them, the ministry found itself faced with a crisis of nerve and resources; it was lucky that Pitt had as adviser a man of Ligonier's caliber.

It is difficult to apportion credit for the remarkable victories of 1758–62 between the politician Pitt and the soldier Ligonier, who was the equivalent of a modern chief of general staff. Ligonier left very few papers; advice taken over the dinner table leaves no mark in history. But both Corbett, naval historian of the period, and his own biographer Whitworth, make large claims for him. In two ways particularly he was of service. The precise and ambitious plans for the reconquest of North America were his work, and the appointment to independent commands of relatively junior officers such as Forbes, Wolfe, and Amherst reflects his own knowledge of the service. Amherst had been on his staff; he was a brilliant success in Canada. He was also largely behind the policy of diversionary attacks on the French coast. Tactically, they can be criticized for waste of precious resources, but they helped to relieve the pressure on Frederick the Great. More effective in this way were the Continental campaigns of Ferdinand of Brunswick. Again Ligonier pressed for full support in these operations, against a sometimes reluctant Pitt. Brunswick had under him, at one point, more redcoats than ever Marlborough did. The glory of the battle of Minden has to some extent obscured the success of later actions, but the brilliant performances of the Marquis of Granby, and Brunswick's victories, proved the wisdom of Ligonier and the quality of English troops. Again and again the French were defeated; after 1758, Frederick had no French troops to face. The year after

Pitt's retirement, 1762, brought victories as fine, in their way, as 1759. The achievement of a man of his age, at a time when staffs and secretariats were minimal, in planning a global war effort, places him among the few great chiefs of staff. The success of the British in this war was owed largely to the fact that there was an overall strategic direction from a soldier, familiar both with the problems of the soldier in the line and the commissariat at home.

When Ligonier became a baron, he was dismissed as Master of the Ordnance by Bute's government in 1763 (one of the charges of the *North Briton*): he had been an Irish peer since 1757. In 1766, when he was superseded by Granby as commander-in-chief, he was raised to an earldom. He lived four more years, single to the end, although he nearly made a match with a widow before she discovered that he was over eighty at the time. His reputation for gallantry received unpleasant twists from a scurrilous satire which suggested that he employed a valet to procure girls for him. He may have been licentious. He could also be hard: in 1759 he ordered the court-martial sentence upon Sackville, dismissed the service for disobedience to orders at Minden, to be read out to all regiments as an example, "so that officers may be convinced that neither high birth nor great employment can shelter offenses of such a nature." But his name was secure with the British soldier whose interests he had always made his first concern. An obituary notice said of him: "In him the soldier has lost a real friend: one who in public and private life did honor to humanity."

R. Whitworth, *Field Marshal Lord Ligonier*, 1958.

EDWARD VERNON (1684–1757), admiral, was a greater man than the bare record of his life would suggest: it was his misfortune that most of his service was performed at a time when there was limited scope for distinction, but his humanity and practical sense contributed much to the well-being of the navy.

Edward Vernon's father was a Whig politician, Secretary of State from 1697 to 1700. He entered the navy in 1701, one of the earliest from his class to make a career at sea. He was also a more active politician than most naval officers, becoming a member of Parliament in 1722, for Ipswich. Toward the end of the long peace of Walpole's administration, which was as irksome to the keen naval officer as it was to opposition politicians, Vernon stressed in speech after speech the weakness of the Spanish in the West Indies. He declared that he could take Porto Bello, haunt of the *gardacostas* who tried to stop the English trading in that area, with six ships. He was loud in his denunciation of the Convention of Pardo by which Walpole tried to patch up a settlement with Spain. When war came, in 1739, Vernon was promoted vice-admiral and dispatched to Porto Bello with eight ships. His orders were merely to burn the shipping in the harbor. Its defenses looked formidable, but Vernon prepared an assault worthy of Drake. After two days of fighting, on November 22, he captured the place. The manner of the assault, besides the value of Porto Bello, particularly in the eyes of city and plantation men, made Vernon a public hero, as mugs and public houses bearing his effigy, roads and farmhouses named after him, testify to this day. But the early advantage was dissipated. Vernon believed that the ministry would be better to keep a large fleet in West Indian waters, "by which means, let who will possess the country, our Royal Master may possess the wealth of it," than to mount expensive operations to capture the islands. Not only did they send out such an expedition but they delayed fatally in the process. Not until January 1741 did the fleet, thirty ships and 10,000 men, assemble; then the military commander, General Wentworth, carried out a pedantic assault by slow stages while his men were reduced by disease. In the end, Vernon had to reembark the 2,500 survivors of the force. Similar attempts upon Santiago and Panama also failed dismally. At the end of 1742 Vernon was recalled to England, where the threat of French invasion and Jacobitism were causing alarm.

Vernon was a man of independent views and never afraid to speak his mind. He was bold enough to tell George II, in the year before the battle of Dettingen, that "his Security lay in being master of the sea, and that when he ceased so to be, his land army could not preserve him." He was a constant advocate of the seamen, whose conditions were indeed brutal and degrading. "Our fleets," he said, "which are defrauded by injustice, are first manned by violence and maintained by cruelty." They were, in effect, "condemned to death, since they are never allowed again to set foot on shore, but turned over from ship to ship." The abuse of the press gang was made worse by the vast expansion that became necessary when war was declared. Three times this occurred in this century—in 1739, 1755, and 1775, after years of peacetime neglect and contraction. It is surprising that battles could be won by raw crews lashed into subservience, that there was no serious general mutiny to the end of the century—and men could still feel devotion for their officers. One reason is that men such as Vernon understood their plight. Vernon is justly famous for his introduction of "grog" (so called after his conspicuous grogram cloak), a quart of water mixed with a half-pint of rum, though this in itself was no cure for the plague of scurvy. But he was more remarkable in condemning in Parliament the distribution of prize-money, "the sailors' part having no proportion to that of the officers." After he had been unjustly dismissed from the navy, Vernon displayed a characteristic interest in social problems. On similar lines to Fielding's *Proposal for the Poor*, he and other local landowners started a House of Industry at Nacton in Suffolk. It was far in advance of its time, with its separate apartments for married couples, single men, and single women, and was copied elsewhere. His fine tomb at Nacton commemorates a man who cared for ordinary people more than seems to have been usual amongst the upper classes of his day.

Douglas Ford, *Admiral Vernon*, 1907.

RICHARD NASH (1674–1762) was king of Bath at a time when this city was the "queen of spas." The eighteenth century in England was an age of watering places where the affluent went to purge themselves, to ease their gout, and to enjoy the diversions of social life with their fellow sufferers. The oldest of the spas was Bath, and at Bath for many years the presiding genius was "Beau" Nash. Carmarthen Grammar School and Jesus College, Oxford, nurtured this supple Welshman. He studied law at the Middle Temple after a brief period in the army, made a name as a dandy, and paid his bills by lucky gambling. Early in the century he fixed on Bath which had been visited by Queen Anne and was frequented by invalids and quack doctors but was still a shabby place; the waters were dirty and the amenities few. An easy and negligent manner concealed in Nash a talent for planning and persuasion, and within a few years a new city rose round the "reaking steam" of the baths. There was a new pump room and a theatre; roundabout villas sprang up. The key to the success of the spa was easy transport, so Nash raised money to improve the Bath Road and others leading to the town.

For forty years Nash reigned unchallenged. Street lighting and a night watch were among the improvements ordered by the town council under his instructions. He assisted in the foundation of a hospital, opened in 1742. His insistence upon order, space, and elegance, together with the genius of the Woods, father and son, architects of the North and South Parades, Queen's Square, and the Circus, made a complete and beautiful town. He had the gift of being able to make himself agreeable to the visiting gentry and indispensable to the town council. As Master of Ceremonies he assumed the role of enlightened despot. The insulting behavior of the chairmen was corrected. His code of dress and deportment dealt with such matters as requests to dance and the summoning of footmen. One may be quoted to show their flavor: "That no gentleman gives his tickets for the Balls to any but Gentlemen. N.B. Unless he has none of his acquaintance." He did not hesitate to enforce his rules. When the Duchess of Queensberry appeared in a white lace apron of which he was known to disapprove, he tore it from her and threw it into the back benches where the ladies' maids were sitting. He waged a campaign against the wearing of boots in the Assembly Rooms; if any person erred in this way, Beau Nash would ask him, in the most public way, where he had hidden his horse. He grew more tyrannical with age, and would embarrass young ladies by inquiring why they were not dancing, or press dowagers to subscribe to some new charity.

As a shareholder in the gaming tables, and in other ways which he did not reveal, Beau Nash made a splendid living out of his private empire. But he did not want Bath to become a mere gambling den and he intervened personally on occasion to save young gamblers from ruin. The same mixture of good nature and business sense led him to ban dueling in Bath. About this time it became unfashionable for men to carry swords and the practice of duelling declined; a step toward civilization for which Nash must have some credit. A unique feature was that it was customary for visitors to attend daily morning service at the abbey, where now the marble tablets, row upon row, commemorate the fashionable worshippers who died in Bath. In his heyday Nash was a magnificent figure in his white hat and his extravagant clothes, preceded when he traveled in his post chariot by outriders, footmen, French horns, and similar pomps. The Gaming Act of 1739, which made illegal private lotteries and the games of Basset, Hazard, Faro, and the Ace of Hearts, was, however, a setback. Ultimately he lost his money and died poor.

Edith Sitwell, *Bath*, 1932.

SAMUEL RICHARDSON (1689–1761), novelist, has recently been revived in critical opinion; his important place in the development of his craft has always been beyond dispute. He was influential and respected in his day, in France and Germany as well as at home, but his personal life was insignificant; there are few details worth recording. He was the son of a carpenter who seems to have hoped that his son would enter the Church; but there was little money for his schooling, which was haphazard. Christ's Hospital and Charterhouse claim him, but there is no proof that he went to either school. He became a stationer's apprentice in 1716, set up as a printer in 1719, married in 1721. He prospered in business, becoming for a time printer to the House of Commons, but his private life brought the agony of successive bereavements. Of six children to his first marriage, five died in infancy. His wife died in 1730, but he married again in the following year: more deaths ensued. It was common enough in his day, but the effect upon a sensitive heart may be guessed. Critics who have commented on the obsession of Richardson with sex, the suggestiveness and even sadism of the protracted affairs described in his novels, have neglected this side of his life. In 1739 he took the lease of a pleasant house at Hammersmith; his books were not written under the pressure of financial need.

In November 1740, the first volumes of *Pamela* appeared and were an instant success. Richardson had been asked to compile some "letters written on such subjects as might be of use to those country readers who were unable to indite for themselves." One subject of these letters was the dangers that beset a young woman who was engaged as a family servant, especially if she were pretty. This was the genesis of *Pamela, or Virtue Rewarded*, a record, eventually in four volumes, in letters and then in journal form, of the resistance of the virtuous servant to the seductive advances of Mr. B.—and her subsequent happy marriage. Richardson seems to have written without difficulty; he said himself that he "almost slid into the writing of *Pamela*" and the novel took him only three months to write. The heroine, it has been said, is "precisely the sort to appeal to the bourgeoisie, then and now." Prudence, artfulness, a hypocritical strain in her seeming innocence, may account for the interest she aroused, both in her readers and in her lover, who described her as "an artful young baggage," more than the sentimental principles of virtue which the author sought to cultivate "in the minds of the youth of both sexes." Readers have variously found *Pamela* tedious, repulsive, or gripping. Doctor Johnson declared: "If you were to read Richardson for the story, your impatience would be so much fretted that you would hang yourself. But you must read him for the sentiment, and consider the story as only giving occasion to the sentiment." He also pronounced Richardson to be "the greatest genius that had shed its luster upon this path of literature." This may seem an exaggerated verdict, but *Pamela* did point toward a fruitful development in fiction, toward the novel of analysis of feeling. To this, for all his vulgarity and cynicism, he brought an almost feminine intuition and a gift for colloquial speech that makes his characters of the middle and servant class live in their own right.

Clarissa Harlow, which followed in 1747 and 1748, had many of the faults of its predecessor, among them its inordinate length. The picture by Leech of a page boy staggering under the weight of its eight volumes (in the first edition there were seven) may be for some readers a suitable comment on a pretentious work. Again his purpose was ostensibly moral: to show that a reformed rake does not necessarily make the best husband. In a time when arranged marriages were common, the refusal of Clarissa to accept her parents' choice of husband touched upon a live issue. She was tricked into putting herself under the protection of Lovelace, a more complex villain than Mr. B., but designed primarily to bring out the essential nobility of the heroine. After piling on the agony of her deception and humiliation, Richardson achieves the difficult feat of presenting her death as a relief and a sort of triumph. *Sir Charles Grandison* is supposed to have been Jane Austen's favorite among the novels, which influenced her own art. But because Richardson is unable to infuse the same life into an upper class hero as into a woman of his own class, the novel is hampered from the start. Sir Charles, impeccable in his own disinterested conduct, amounts to an embodiment of eighteenth-century notions of virtue, but feeling is little roused because there is no vital conflict in the book. So the reader has to content himself with the social portraiture and a pleasing delicacy of style, with a tendency toward epigram, which go far to explain Jane Austen's preference.

On the publication of *Pamela*, Richardson became a figure of consequence, at least as large in his own ideas as in those of his admirers. Fashionable ladies made a point of being seen with the book; it was recommended from the pulpit and paid the compliment of satires, the most notable being *Joseph Andrews*. In France, where he was fortunate in his translator, Prévost, he was received with rapture. Diderot was unrestrained in his eulogy: "You shall remain on the same shelf as Moses, Euripides and Sophocles and I shall read you by turns." De Laclos, the author of *Les Liaisons Dangereuses*, acknowledged his debt; more important for the world was the reaction of the young Rousseau, whose *Nouvelle Heloise* was suggested by *Clarissa*. The same appeal of Richardson to those who were beginning to swim in the currents of Romanticism can be seen in his popularity in Germany, where the market was soon full of imitations. It is disappointing to turn from the almost prophetic status of the work, largely dependent though it was upon the contemporary fashion in literature, to the personality of the man. Easily flattered himself, he was absurdly sensitive to criticism. He himself criticized the works of Fielding in a way which showed as much jealousy as lack of comprehension of that virile talent. He told Fielding's sister that he was concerned for his continued lowness! He continued, however, to edify his admirers with his letters and reflections, in which moral issues loomed large. In his last years he was increasingly subject to nervous disorders and insomnia. In July 1761 he died of a paralytic stroke.

John Carroll, ed., *Selected Letters of Samuel Richardson*, 1964.
T. C. D. Evans and B. D. Kimpel, *Samuel Richardson*, 1971.

LADY MARY WORTLEY MONTAGU (1689–1762), was the daughter of Evelyn Pierrepont, afterwards Duke of Kingston, and of Mary Fielding, daughter of Lord Denbigh. She was largely self-educated which, as so often in the case of well-bred girls brought up amid beautiful objects and good libraries, produced the happiest effect. She later studied Latin surreptitiously, but she thought scholarship was for professional men and advised women to conceal their learning as they would a physical defect. So much for her name as a "blue-stocking." Her critical intelligence and sensibility made an impact upon Mr. Wortley Montagu; the letters which Mary addressed to his sister were undoubtedly intended for his eye, the answers dictated by him. When her father planned marriage for her with another man, in 1712, she eloped with Montagu.

The grandson of Pepys's friend the Earl of Sandwich, and some years her elder, he was a man of ability and a scholar, the confidant of the Whig leaders and a Lord of the Treasury under George I. From 1716 to 1718 he was ambassador in Constantinople. Her letters from Vienna and Constantinople were the basis of her reputation in her own age. Indeed they are fascinating and no less so because they seem to be largely accurate. If she drew upon her imagination for her celebrated account of her visit to the *bagnio*, she also seems to have been well informed. These letters seem to have been prepared later for publication, from entries in her diaries. In Constantinople she learned of the smallpox inoculation which had been introduced by the Circassians and, when she returned, she had her children inoculated against the disease which had marred her own looks; she convinced some fashionable doctors of the utility of this treatment—and even the royal family, after she had induced George II to order the inoculation of three men and three women, convicts in Newgate jail.

For some years she was prominent in society. Her husband was a hot opponent of Walpole, which accounts for Horace Walpole's dislike of her, but she was always a controversial figure. At first the close friend of Alexander Pope, and his neighbor at Twickenham, she quarreled with him in 1721; thereafter there was mutual recrimination and abuse, venomous on his side. In 1739 she separated from her husband; he was growing notoriously mean and her fashionable activities may have irritated him, but some affection seems to have survived. She did not return from her self-imposed exile in Italy until after his death in 1761, and soon followed him to the grave. From Italy her letters continued to delight her friends. She was conscious of her powers and once compared her letters to those of Mme. de Sévigné: "very pretty they are, but I assert without the least vanity that mine will be full as entertaining forty years hence. I advise you therefore to put none of them to the use of waste paper." Her style was easy and unforced. But she was less feminine, less sentimental, less naive than Mme. de Sévigné. She admired Fielding and scoffed at Richardson; the latter is quite demolished in one caustic letter. With the interest of her sex in engagements, "conquests," and tattle of the fashionable world went intellectual interests as broad as they were unpretentious. Emancipated as she was in her views and comments, she was seldom coarse, and her comments on places, people, and books are often shrewd. From the letters of this unusual person we learn much, and most pleasantly, about the author and the century in which she lived.

R. Halsband, ed., *The Letters of Lady Mary Wortley Montagu*, 3 vols., 1965–67.

JOHN GAY (1685–1732) wrote light verse and ballads. He was, in Andrew Lang's phrase, "the spoiled improvident child of the group of wits" at the end of Anne's reign. Born at Barnstaple and left an orphan when he was ten, brought up by an uncle and apprenticed to a silk mercer in London, he showed little aptitude for business, but took pleasure in versifying, translating, and writing for the theatre. His *Tragical Comical Farce* is said to have been acted near the watch-house at Covent Garden. But he made more mark with *Rural Sports* (1713), dedicated to Pope and somewhat lamely imitative of Pope's own pastoral; ingenious and whimsical, this poem suggests, however, that the author had never closely observed the "feathered choirs" or "finny broods," and his attempt to compress the subtleties of fly-fishing into neat pentameters is merely ludicrous. Swift smiled, but Pope was encouraging, and Gay wrote the *Fan*; again it was thin stuff, but pleasing enough. In the *Shepherd's Week* (1714), however, he found a better vein. Written originally to cast ridicule upon "Namby-Pamby Phillips," another minor poet who had the misfortune to incur the cruel satire of Pope, this portraiture of "actual" country life became popular for its humor and served as model both for Alan Ramsay's *Gentle Shepherd* and later for Crabbe.

Gay was a sociable person, feckless, but happy with his friends and fortunate in his patrons. He was helped in turn by the Duchess of Monmouth, by Clarendon, Harcourt, and Pulteney; for the last twelve years of his life he was sustained by the sympathetic "Kitty," Duchess of Queensberry. He grumbled, but not very energetically;

anyway he received a "place" (a lottery commissionership) and a decent income from his writings, and enjoyed a modest fame. It was at least as much as he deserved. For the truth is that if he were not the author of *The Beggar's Opera* and *Polly*, for all the brittle charm and wit of his *Fables*, much loved in his day and later adorned with woodcuts by Bewick, he might not have merited this essay.

Produced in 1727 by John Rich, *The Beggar's Opera* "made Gay rich and Rich gay" and beat all records by running for sixty nights for two consecutive seasons. A frolicsome mockery of the heroic, a looking-glass picture of ordinary morality, and a burlesque of the sentimental drama and opera of the time, this "Newgate Pastoral," which Swift had suggested should be written to exploit the rich lives of the criminal population, is a graceful, enchantingly gay, and withal serious commentary on human failings. Sometimes the characters seem to be saying one thing while implying the opposite. There is, too, a piquant shockingness in the grimness of the theme, for Macheath, the highwayman, was not a gentle character. *The Beggar's Opera* has been revived recently with success; it has a fair claim, too, to be regarded as the ancestor of musical comedy. *Polly* was designed as a sequel, but it was prohibited by the Lord Chamberlain in the interests of the court and of Walpole, who had already winced at the stinging allusions to him in *The Beggar's Opera*. Gay's patrons, the Duke and Duchess of Queensberry, were forbidden the court, but the play sold merrily among opponents of the ministry.

Gay was lazy and he grew exceedingly fat. Incurious in money matters (he gained and lost a fortune in the South Sea Bubble), he died intestate. A fine monument by Rysbrach in Poets' Corner commemorates the man who, as Dr. Johnson observed, was regarded by the wits more as a playfellow than as a partner. He fully deserved, however, the valedictory phrase of Pope: "he died unpensioned with a hundred friends."

C. F. Burgess, ed., *The Letters of John Gay*, 1966.

JOHN ARBUTHNOT (1667–1735) was placed by Dr. Johnson at the head of all the wits and writers of Anne's reign as "the most universal genius, being an excellent physician, a man of deep learning and much humor." If today he has a more modest place in the shades cast by the literary giants, Pope, Addison, and Swift, it is because he was a modest man, an unassuming but generous friend, who took little care to preserve his own work or fame. In the acid and vindictive world of literary London he appears as a pleasantly good-natured person who bore his learning lightly. In the society of wits, politicians, and poetasters that made the coffee houses of London a humming exchange of ideas and letters, Arbuthnot played a central role. He did not dominate like Johnson, in his circle, but he contributed richly; he was the most learned of the wits, and not the least witty.

He was born at Arbuthnot in Kincardineshire, where his father was vicar; after the Revolution, however, his father was deprived, having refused to conform to the General Assembly. From the Marischal College at Aberdeen, he came to London to teach mathematics. He translated a book by Huygens on the laws of chance, went to University College, Oxford, as a commoner, and tutored for a time. In 1696 he adopted medicine, took a degree at St. Andrews, and returned to London to practice. He acquired a reputation for skill and learning, published a well-reasoned mathematical treatise, *On the Usefulness of Mathematical Learning*, and was elected a member of the Royal Society (1704). Lucky enough to be at hand when Prince George of Denmark was taken ill at Epsom, he soon became physician to his wife, Queen Anne. He moved in Tory circles, was intimate with Harley, and after the fall of the Whigs in the election of 1710 was "as much heard as any that give advice now." His friendship with Swift bore fruit in a series of pamphlets which urged the desirability of ending the war with France; in the best of these appears for the first time the figure of John Bull. The prototype of this much used—and abused—figure is a sensible, insular merchant, amenable to reason, when it comes from sound Tories and appeals to his purse. *Nicholas Frog, Lewis Baboon* (Bourbon), and *The Art of Political Lying* provide other examples of Arbuthnot's pungent satire. His level, genial character may partly be ascribed to the fact that he was still busy professionally. He attended Queen Anne in her last illnesses, and Gay, in his *Shepherd's Week*, referred to him as a skillful leech who had saved the queen's life. After her death, *Fuimus tories*, as Arbuthnot said, but he continued to write pamphlets on political or medical subjects. The *Memoirs of Scriblerus* were not published until 1741, but the Scriblerus Club, devoted among other things to ridiculing "all the false tastes in learning," had been founded in 1713: with Pope,

Swift, Gay, Parnell, Congreve, Lord Oxford, and Atterbury, Arbuthnot was a prominent member. At least part of *Gulliver's Travels* was contributed and inspired by him. When Arbuthnot was ill in 1725, Swift wrote, "If the world had but a dozen Arbuthnots I would burn my Travels." Perhaps none of his friends meant so much to the eccentric Dean of St. Patrick's. When he returned to his deanery, Arbuthnot, who was very musical, recommended singers for his choir.

Atbuthnot's wife died in 1730; his own health was poor but he remained, in Pope's words, unalterable in friendship and quadrille. Neither a move to Hampstead nor the solicitude of his friends could long delay his death. Because it is so hard to attribute precisely his share in many pamphlets, in numbers of *The Craftsman* or the *Variorum Dunciad* (1729), his reputation must rest primarily on his *History of John Bull*, which deserves to be better known and to stand alongside Addison's *Sir Roger de Coverley*, and upon the opinion of the friends who valued him so highly. "You every day give us better hints than all of us together could do in a twelvemonth," wrote Swift. It is no less remarkable that in his last few years he wrote two medical works, *An Essay concerning the Nature of Ailments* and *An Essay concerning the Effect of Air on Human Bodies*, which show him to have been ahead of his time in medical science, alert and fertile to the end.

L. M. Beatty, *John Arbuthnot*, 1935.

ALEXANDER POPE (1688–1744), greatest of the Augustan poets, was the son of a linen draper who retired to the country at the age of forty-two with a modest fortune and a newly married wife, a witty, gracious woman in her midforties and, like her husband, a pious Roman Catholic. Alexander was the only son of this contented late marriage and she was passionately fond of him. Alas, he grew up a stunted, meager cripple, about four foot six high, suffering from a tubercular infection which led to curvature of the spine. Ultrasensitive, driven in on himself by self-consciousness, he found relief in intense absorbed reading and in the conversation of a few sympathetic adults. After unsatisfactory experiences at several private schools he was largely self-educated, but his creative urge was all the stronger for this, and he was writing poems by the age of twelve and planning for himself the life of a poet.

He came to London in 1704, the year of Blenheim, and was soon taken up by William Wycherley, who gave him his tired lyrics "to mend," and by other literary men who were pleased by his fragile precocity. So he was drawn into a world of coffee houses and cultivated talk, where literature was respected and genius could flourish. "Knowing" Walsh, a busy poetaster, declared portentously that "there was but one way left of excelling: for though we had several good poets, we never had one great one that was correct," and he desired Pope to make that his study and aim. This correctness has the wrong meaning for us, as it may have had for Walsh. Pope was indeed to be the most "correct" of poets, but his ideal was not the cold, inhuman compression of feeling and image into a conventional frame that much of eighteenth-century poetry may seem to be. Pope was "correct only in that he was a laborious perfectionist, acutely, even agonizingly, sensitive in ear and eye to the form, texture, and rhythm of verse. His search for the right and the best informed his life and affected his relationships and his attitudes to people and things. The suffering dwarf with his lustrous eyes and fine-drawn features, constantly in pain from the headaches and rheumatism that affected his "little crazy carcass," so thin-skinned that everything that was not a compliment seemed to be a slight, should be judged in the light of this search. His art was his life.

When he was twenty-one his *Pastorals* appeared in Tonson's *Miscellanies:* they foreshadowed the delicacy and musicality of his mature work. Here indeed was the born poet who, however he might borrow from other writers, such as Dryden, could not but "lisp in numbers." In 1711 came the *Essay on Criticism*, an ambitious attempt to distill in 750 lines the essence of critical thought since Aristotle. There was little that was original, but this was no mere academic dissertation: with a felicity of phrase that has given many lines to dictionaries of quotations, Pope put warmth and even, sometimes, lyrical feeling into commonplace ideas. His own couplet expresses exactly the brilliance and the limitations of the essay:

> True wit is Nature to advantage dress'd,
> What oft' was thought, but ne'er so well expressed.

That he was perfectly master of his craft he demonstrated with *The Rape of the Lock*, which was published in its first state in 1712.

His theme was magnificently trivial: an event in Roman Catholic society, the cutting of a lock of Miss Fermor's hair by Lord Petre. The poem was added to and polished by Pope as if he knew that it was a masterpiece, but in everything but Clarissa's speech it was complete by 1714. This poem can be enjoyed at several levels: as an occasional piece, a witty diversion, a satire of society's values, a criticism of the heroic manner, even a heartfelt lament for the ephemeral. "I am charmed," wrote Berkeley, "with all those images, allusions, and matters inexplicable, which you raise so surprisingly, and at the same time so naturally out of a trifle."

Pope was an amateur painter and for a time he studied under Jervas and made his home with that painter. *Windsor Forest*, which he published in 1713, is full of epithets of color which show the painter's eye. It is a complex and closely wrought "place" poem which drew upon Denham's *Cooper's Hill*, the Elizabethans Drayton and Spenser, besides being soaked in the feeling and imagery of Ovid and Virgil. This is not, as might be guessed from Pope's view (recorded by Warton) that a poem wholly of description would be as "absurd as a feast made up of sauces," a poem about nature alone: its allusions remind the reader of the work of man who was himself part of nature, and its climax, when Thames speaks of his glories and the historic pageant passes before him, expresses a glorious vision of the role of Great Britain, the bringer of peace and the gifts of civilization to all the world.

Pope's energies were long occupied with his translation of Homer's *Iliad*, which appeared between 1715 and 1720. "It's a very pretty poem, Mr. Pope, but you mustn't call it Homer," said the great Grecian Bentley. Modern readers would agree, but it was Pope's purpose to create a poem of his time. He discerned in Homer a "plentiful river" in which we "are borne away by a Tide of Verse, the most rapid, yet the most smooth imaginable." It is best now to treat Pope's *Iliad* as a poem in its own right, redolent of the ethos of the eighteenth century, neoclassical rather than classical in spirit. Pope was sufficiently encouraged by the reception of the poem to embark upon the *Odyssey*, with the aid of assistants. He grew rich enough to buy himself a villa at Twickenham, where he was to spend the rest of his life. But fame brought envy, and his own sharp pen drew cruel reprisals from rivals and victims. At times he seems to have lived in a perfect frenzy of controversy. It would be tedious to record the details of the feud; they are best left in the gutters of Grub Street. King in his world of letters he might be, but beyond the toil and stress of composition, the exacting search for the *mot juste*, we can see the taut nerves of a creative spirit, always ready to be hurt and always ready to hit back, even to anticipate the assailant's thrust. In his appalling attack upon Sporus (Lord Hervey) he expressed characteristic venom.

> Sporus, that mere white curd of Ass's milk!
> Satire or sense, alas! can Sporus feel?
> Who breaks a butterfly upon a wheel?
> Yet let me flap this bug with gilded wings,
> This painted child of dirt, that stinks and stings.

Pope could be servile too. He secured presentation at court; he ate at the table of Robert Walpole; but he parodied the royal family and joined in the throng of Walpole's enemies. He relished obscenity and he grew deceitful to the point of addiction. He was, however, no stranger to love; his passion for Martha Blount was at least returned in steady friendship: she became his constant companion. An early essay *Against Barbarity to Animals* expressed humane feelings unusual in his time: his Great Dane, Bounce, was one of the joys of his life. Then he was often kind to people in difficulties, Savage for instance. Among his close friends was Bolingbroke, whom he appreciated for his vitality and wit. "I never in my life," said Bolingbroke, "knew a man that had so tender a heart for his particular friends, or a more general friendship for mankind." Pope was brave above all, and to help a friend would do anything. His *Epistle to Lord Oxford* (1721) paid tribute to a man in disgrace and invited suspicion of Jacobite sentiments. He gave evidence for Bishop Atterbury at his trial for treasonable correspondence with the Pretender. He once wrote to Gay that it was his desire "to fix and preserve a few lasting dependable friendships," and to Swift: "I never aimed at any other fortune than friends."

For all the exuberance of fancy in the *Dunciad* (1728, but subsequently recast) we may regret that so much of Pope's energy was spent in personal satire. Some of its allusions foxed contemporaries; they are lost on us. But all but the obvious victims enjoyed it and so can the modern reader, for Pope is at his sprightliest even when he is being subtle in parody and riddle. The *Dunciad* enabled him to work off some of his rage. For a time he went around with a pistol in his pocket but soon, on the prompting of Bolingbroke, he was working in a calmer mood on the *Essay on Man*. It was an ambitious philosophical project, never completed. The first parts appeared in 1733–34: it summed up the popular philosophy of the day, in elegant pentameters which are often as forceful and lovely in form as they are trite in idea and sentiment. Let him who doubts it study the passage that begins: "Know then thyself, presume not God to scan." Throughout the poem there runs a cool vein of irony which, though Pope could sometimes still work up a white-hot blaze of contempt—as in his assault on Sporus—is typical of most of his later work, and notably the *Imitations of Horace* with which he was agreeably occupied in these years.

To the end Pope's life was strangely compounded of serenity, pleasant days with his friends and his garden at Twickenham, and frenzy. Paranoiac in suspicions, he embroiled himself in rows about the publication of his correspondence and a clash with Colley Cibber, which closed resoundingly with Pope's new version of the *Dunciad* (1743), in which Cibber was raised to the dubious status of principal dunce. His gnawing consciousness of inferiority gave him little rest: did he not falsify addresses, destroy some and rewrite others of his letters, to leave a better image of himself to posterity? He was often hurt, but he invited it in such a masochistic way that we may sympathize with Cibber's remark: "You seem in your *Dunciad* to have been angry with the rain for wetting you, why then would you go into it?"

In attack or defense, Pope used all the literary weapons: irony, caricature, even forgery. Much may be forgiven the man who was so preeminently the voice of his generation's culture, this fiery, quivering, indomitable spirit, whose poems have preserved for us "the feast of reason and the flow of soul" which above all things he epitomized and valued.

B. Dobrée, *Alexander Pope*, 1951.
E. Sitwell, *Alexander Pope*, 1930.
G. Sherburn, ed., *Correspondence of Pope*, 5 vols., 1956.

GEORGE FREDERICK HANDEL (1685–1759), along with his exact contemporary Johann Sebastian Bach, dominates early eighteenth-century music and represents the culmination of the baroque period. So great was their achievement as perfectors of existing forms and styles, rather than as inventors, that by necessity music followed an altogether new path after them.

Both men were born in Saxony in the same year and both ended their lives in blindness: Bach in 1750, Handel in 1759. Their music, taken as a whole, reflects a universality of styles and forms. Yet, surprisingly, they never met. Their lives and their music, when examined more particularly, are outstandingly unalike. Bach, descendant of so many musical ancestors that "a Bach" was German slang for any musician at the time, was relatively uneducated, being devoted only to God and to music. He fathered twenty children and lived a heavily domestic, overworked, and provincial life in dismal conditions and rarely ventured outside a forty-mile radius all his life. Therefore it has long been a matter of interesting speculation among critics of Bach as to where such a genius got his inspiration and how such a mind works. Bach's work remained virtually obscure until 1850, a hundred years after his death, when the Bach Gesellschaft was formed to gather and publish all his works, which were finally recognized as the finest and fullest technical, emotional, and aesthetic perfection of the musical idiom of the time. It is by virtue of their differences that Handel appears in this book, for Handel was a cosmopolitan, a traveler, a "character," and in 1726, by naturalization, an Englishman.

Handel was born on February 23, 1685, at Halle. He had more than his share of fortune's seesaw: again and again, by his own resourcefulness, adaptability, talent, and strength of character, he moved from disaster to triumph, from opposition to popularity, from insignificance to fame. His first obstacle was a father who disliked music and thought it an effeminate occupation for a boy, but with his mother's help he managed in secret to learn to play the spinet. At 7 he accompanied his father, in the course of his business as a barber-surgeon, to the ducal court at Saxe-Weissenfels. He managed somehow to play the organ for the duke, who was so impressed that he gave the boy money with which to pay for lessons and implored his father to let him study. The barber did not wish to offend his valuable client and, accordingly, young Handel was sent to study with F. W. Zachau, the organist of the Lutheran Church at Halle. He spent three years, during which time, by his teacher's admission, he mastered the organ, as well as achieving considerable proficiency on the clavier, violin, and oboe, and also began to compose religious music. At 11 he visited Berlin and impressed the court with his performance on the clavier and the organ. Money was provided by the Elector of Brandenburg to send him to Italy, but his father opposed him and he went instead as a law student to the University of Halle. During this time, having already acquired a reputation, he was offered the post of organist at the Cathedral of Moritzburg. He spent one brilliant year there; then, convinced that his future was in music, not law, he abandoned university and Moritzburg and went in 1703 to Hamburg, the center of German opera. He joined the opera house orchestra as a violinist, under Reinhard Keiser, and wrote two major works which were immediate successes: the *Passion According to St. John* and *Almira*. Keiser, in jealousy, now became his bitter antagonist and spared no effort to discredit and outdo him. Johann Mattheson, another excellent performer and composer at the opera, became involved in a dispute with Handel which ended in a duel: Mattheson's sword broke against one of Handel's buttons and thus Handel's life was spared!

In 1706, disgusted by petty jealousy and corruption, Handel left Hamburg for Florence. There he wrote *Rodrigo*, his first Italian opera, and then, to evade a papal ban on opera, turned to religious music. *La Resurrezione*, his first oratorio, was conducted in Rome by Arcangelo Corelli, and *Agrippina*, an opera, had its premiere in Venice: in their triumph Handel became known as "*Il Sassone*" (the Saxon).

In 1710 Handel returned to Germany to succeed Agostino Steffani as Kapellmeister at Hanover. Later that year, on leave of absence, he visited London, where he introduced another opera, *Rinaldo*. It played to full houses for a fortnight and established not only Handel's reputation in England, but also a new standard of Italian opera. Again, enemies came forward, namely Addison and Steele, who lambasted Handel as well as Italian opera in general in the *Spectator*, Pope and Hogarth, who did not wish to see traditional British drama injured, and professional singers who disliked imported artists, especially "the exotic and repulsive race of castrati," as Percy Young describes them. But these critics were far outnumbered by Handel's admirers, who lost no time in sweeping him into the artistic social life of the season.

Eventually he returned to Hanover, where he fulfilled his obligations dutifully as Kapellmeister, never, however, missing any opportunity to get away for a short time to other cities. Hanover no longer satisfied him. In 1712 he was granted another leave of absence and in the autumn he arrived in London. After several months he had written and seen performed two new operas, *Il Pastor Fido* and *Teseo*. Neither was a success, but his popularity continued and he was commissioned to write, for the first time in English, music for Queen Anne's birthday and for the completion of the Peace of Utrecht. Thus he became a court composer with a life pension of £200 a year. Apart from a few short visits, he never returned to Germany.

When Queen Anne died in 1714, the new king was, ironically, Handel's employer, the Elector of Hanover. George I had such high regard for his delinquent Kapellmeister's virtuosity as a performer and composer that he employed him as music master to the royal family, doubled his pension, and, in 1717, commissioned the *Water Music*. Also in 1717, while continuing as royal music master, Handel undertook the post of music master to the princely Duke of Chandos, who lived in baroque style at Canons, a magnificent estate near Edgware. During his three years there he also wrote many stage works, including the beautiful cantata *Acis and Galatea* and *Esther*, and for the king's children he wrote harpsichord suites, among them the most famous of all for reasonably competent pupils, the set of variations from the *E Major (No. 5) Suite* nicknamed *The Harmonious Blacksmith*.

In London the champions of Italian opera had founded the Royal Academy of Music, making Handel its artistic director. Handel's enthusiasm for this scheme was so great that he returned to London, installed himself for life at 57 Lower Brook Street, and began importing the finest singers he knew of from Germany. The premiere of *Radamisto* was a success and assured the future of the new opera house.

Once again Handel was faced with bitter opposition. The Earl of Burlington, advocating a purer form of Italian opera, gathered his supporters and imported from the academy Giovanni Battista Bononcini, a prolific Italian composer of opera. A good-natured match began between the two composers, each countering the other's operas with yet another of his own: *Floridante* and *Ottone* resulted from this rivalry. The latter opera restored Handel's position and Bononcini faded into obscurity. Unfortunately, in 1728, the academy went bankrupt through lavish spending and a waning of enthusiasm for Italian opera. Gay's satire on opera, *The Beggar's*

Opera, was enormously popular. In addition, the Prince of Wales had set up a rival company who drew away Handel's singers and his patronage as well; his virulent opposition to his father may have moved him as strongly as love of music. Handel made a few attempts to present operas in hired theatres: the result was financial and physical disaster. Ironically, while Handel suffered rheumatism, paralysis, and bankruptcy, a proud statue of him was erected in Vauxhall Gardens. Characteristically, Handel managed to come out on top. He realized that he must find a new medium of expression and experimented with the oratorio by converting *Esther* into a concert piece without scenery or costumes. It was a success, and in 1738, with *Saul* and *Israel in Egypt*, oratorio became an established form in English music. It was for Handel the greatest medium of all and his greatest contribution to music.

In 1741 the Duke of Devonshire, the Lord Lieutenant of Dublin, and three charitable trusts invited Handel to direct one of his works for a charity performance. In 25 days he produced *Messiah.* When he wrote the "Hallelujah Chorus" he thought he saw "Heaven opened and the great God himself." The intense feeling and energy that went into the composition of *Messiah* can be felt at every point. In this oratorio Handel was poet, prophet, and artist in one gigantic synthesis of inspiration. On March 23, 1743, it was performed in London in the presence of George II, who was so moved by the "Hallelujah Chorus" that he stood up and remained standing till its end. The audience followed him and this became an established tradition.

At this point Handel was at the peak of his creative period: *Samson, Semele, Belshazzar, Hercules, Judas Maccabaeus, Joshua, Solomon, Theodora,* and *Jephtha* all represent the greatest period in the history of oratorio. Handel produced other forms as well: the *Dettingen Te Deum* in 1743 to celebrate the English victory at Dettingen, the *Fireworks Music* in 1749 to mark the signing of the peace at Aix-la-Chapelle.

Another blow was dealt to Handel—by 1753 he was blind. The surgeon who failed to cure Bach also failed to cure Handel. Undaunted as usual, Handel revived his talents as a performer, giving organ concerts and conducting his oratorios until his death on April 14, 1759. He was buried in Westminster Abbey.

Handel wrote nearly fifty operas, twenty oratorios, an enormous amount of church, vocal, chamber, and harpsichord music, and orchestral pieces. A common criticism is that he only summed up the musical tendencies of his time, that "unlike Bach or Haydn, he lacked the power by which an artist is compelled to proceed beyond his contemporaries and to point the way to new methods which will preserve his art from stagnation." A more telling comment would be that he simply wrote too much. Could inventiveness thrive in such a busy workshop? In truth he was master of every form that he attempted; his polyphonic ingenuity has never been surpassed. There is a Shakespearean catholicity of ability and insight in Handel that defies any attempt to reduce his stature. Little is known about his private life—not surprisingly, for he was absorbed in his work. He was a sociable, unkempt bachelor who ate greedily and swore coarsely if he was put out, but usually he was placid. We have no private diary and only a few polite letters, but the likelihood is that he was that rarest of men, a creative artist who was largely content with what he found and saw in God and man. A broad common sense gave him stamina to persist. "What the English like is something they can beat time to, something that hits them straight on the drum of the ear," he said to Gluck. Standing before a painting of Handel, Gluck was later to say: "There, Sir, is the portrait of the inspired master of our art . . . the highest praise is due to your country for having distinguished and cherished his gigantic genius." Among the few who can be put in the same rank as Handel, Beethoven was the most generous in his praise: "He was the greatest composer that ever lived. I would uncover my head, and kneel before his tomb."

Christopher Hogwood, *Handel*, 1984.
N. Flowers, *George Frederick Handel: His Personality and Times*, 1959.
P. H. Láng, *George Frideric Handel*, 1967.

THOMAS AUGUSTINE ARNE (1710–78) was the greatest English composer after Handel. For a century or more he was known chiefly by his Shakespearean songs and by *Rule, Britannia*, but modern critics see in some of his operas and masques technical virtuosity and a distinctively English simplicity of expression.

Arne was the son of an upholsterer in Covent Garden, who sent him to Eton and intended him for the law. Music was, however, a passion and pursuit which could not be denied him: he would practice the spinet in his bedroom, muffling the strings with a handkerchief to escape detection, and he would sometimes borrow a livery in order to gain admission to the servants' gallery at the opera. He made progress with the violin, led an amateur chamber band, and was detected by his father, but forgiven for the sweetness of his playing. Meanwhile his sister Susanna was making her first appearances on the stage which, as Mrs. Cibber, she subsequently adorned. It was her success in 1732, in Lambe's opera *Amelia*, that induced her brother to try his hand at composition: he reset Addison's *Rosamond*. After several operas, his reputation was established firmly by the music he composed for Milton's *Comus* in 1740; its graceful and flowing melodies made a lasting impression. In the same year he composed *Alfred*, a masque with words by Thompson and Mallet; conceived to celebrate the accession of the House of Hanover, played in a temporary theatre in the garden of Cliveden, the Prince of Wales's private house, its finale *Rule, Britannia*, expressed suitably the patriotic emotion of the time, when war with Spain promised glory at sea and the imminent fall of the unpopular Walpole. This was a fruitful period for Arne who, in December 1740, adorned the neglected play *As You Like It* with beautiful settings for the songs: "Blow, blow, thou winter wind" and "When daisies pied."

Arne spent some years in Dublin in the fifties and sixties; he produced there, amongst other pieces, his important oratorio, *Abel*, notable for the beautiful *Hymn of Eve*. In 1756 he returned from his second visit without his wife Cecilia, an organist's daughter, whom he shamelessly neglected and slighted. Not unlike Handel, there was a coarse streak in this prolific composer, he was an unfaithful, perhaps also a cruel husband. His work remained, however, vital and resourceful. His opera *Thomas & Sally*, produced in 1759 at Covent Garden, soon after he had been made a Doctor of Music at Oxford, enjoyed a fair vogue and later formed the model for a number of plays. In 1762 Arne made the bold experiment of presenting to an English audience his translation of *Artaserse*, by Metastasio, in the Italian manner, with a recitative instead of a spoken dialogue: his *Artaxerxes* was a success; especially the part of Mandane, long considered the touchstone of the powers of a soprano singer. More surprisingly, to show what an English composer could do with Italian opera, he set Metastasio's *Olimpiade* in the original language: it was taken off after two performances. His last opera was *Caractacus* in 1775. Arne also wrote numerous glees, catches, and canons and various kinds of instrumental music. He was not a great composer, but he should not be lost sight of in the shadow of Handel. He was a considerable and interesting figure in his own right.

C. Hogwood and R. Luckett, eds., *Music in Eighteenth Century England*, 1983.

STEPHEN HALES (1677–1761) was one of the greatest of the amateur scientists who contributed so much to the advance of knowledge in his century. Academic honors came to him in profusion. Fellow of Corpus Christi, Cambridge, in 1702, Bachelor of Divinity in 1711, Doctor of Divinity at Oxford in 1733, he nonetheless chose to live for most of his life at Teddington, where he was perpetual curate. He seems to have been a dutiful parish priest and a simple, unworldly man. He was also endlessly inventive, a tireless inquirer into natural phenomena; a true product of the age of Newton. He wrote pamphlets on various questions of public concern such as dram drinking. His inventions included new ways of distilling water, preserving meat, and ventilating buildings. He advocated proper airing of ships and prisons and suggested new ways of cleaning harbors. In his *Vegetable Staticks* (1727) he recorded many experiments planned to estimate the physical forces involved in the growth of plants. Measuring the amounts of water absorbed by the roots and given off by the leaves, he estimated what has later been called "transpiration." He also measured the force of the upward sap current in the stems. His ingenious devices are illustrated in *Vegetable Staticks* by drawings which can be understood by anyone. In his general endeavor to show that the activities of living plants could be explained in mechanical terms with reference to their structure, he put botany on to a promising course. Moreover, his demonstration that air supplies something material to the substance of plants was pointing to what we now know to be carbon dioxide. In the same book appears his celebrated apparatus for collecting gases. From the retorts in which they were produced by heating they were led by a pipe to a balloon-shaped vessel filled with water and inverted over the "pneumatic trough," a bucket which also contained water. He measured thus the volumes of gases produced from weighed amounts of solids, but went no further since he supposed these gases to be "air," whose function was to hold together, as a sort of cement, the particles of the solids he had been heating. The product of this apparatus in other hands, however, was to be the discovery of many new gases and a consequent revolution in chemical theory.

Hales believed the pressure of blood in the body to be in some way analogous to that of sap in the plant. Here again his experiments, carrying on from where Harvey left off, were of seminal importance. He studied and measured blood pressure, showing that it varied according to location, whether in arteries or veins, according to the contraction or dilation of the heart, and to the size of the animal. By such experiments as those carried out on the rate of flow in the capillaries of the frog and on the carotid artery of the horse, he began a new phase in the science of animal physiology.

Friend and counsclor of such different people as Pope and Prince Frederick, chaplain to the future George III, and a founder and vice-president of the Society of Arts, a trustee for Georgia, and a Fellow of the Royal Society, Hales remained a quiet and unassuming person, who liked best to divide his life between his parishioners and his plants.

J. V. Sachs, *History of Botany 1530–1860*, translated by H. E. F. Garnsey, 1906.

GEORGE BERKELEY (1685–1753), philospher and divine, one of the most original minds of his time, was born and lived most of his life in Ireland. He was educated at Kilkenny School and then at Trinity College, Dublin, where, as student and then Fellow, he revealed an inventive and philosophical bent. It is recorded that, after witnessing a public execution, he experimented with hanging himself—with no worse effect than the ruffling of his bands. In 1705 he founded a philosophical society. Two years later he produced two mathematical tracts. Already by the evidence of his commonplace books, it appears that the new thought which was to be the mainspring of his philosophy had taken hold. In 1709 this was expounded in his *Essay toward a New Theory of Vision*. In 1710 followed the *Treatise concerning the Principles of Human Knowledge, Part I;* in 1713 the *Dialogues between Hylas and Philomores*, which has been described as "the finest specimen in the language of the conduct of argument by dialogue." "To print his new book" and "to make acquaintance with men of merit" he came to London, where he was befriended by some of the leading Augustans, Pope, Addison, Steele among others. Apart from his quality as a person, his writing had a "grace and irony" which Andrew Lang thought was "akin to the manner of Plato and Pascal." Upon Swift's recommendation, he accompanied Peterborough on a diplomatic mission to Italy, in the capacity of chaplain. He later made a longer stay there, writing a journal and collecting materials for a natural history of Sicily. He began work on the second part of the *Principles*, but lost the manuscript; the work was never resumed. On his way home, however, in 1720, he wrote a Latin treatise, *De Motu*.

Berkeley was a Platonist and an idealist at a time when the current fashion in theology was for logical reasoning in the Aristotelian manner, conducive toward deism. Berkeley attacked the deist notion of God—as being remote from a physical world which He had made but did not control—from a novel position. Ideas, he said, are the things that really exist and are all that we can really know. Material things only exist in so far as they are perceived: "the visible world has no absolute existence, being merely the sensible expression of supreme Intelligence and Will." Therefore "each man has the same kind of evidence that God exists—and in a much higher degree—which he has that a fellow man exists when he hears him speak." Human certainty about the permanence of an outside world is derived from the fact "that all objects are externally known by God, or, which is the same thing, have an eternal existence in His mind." The order of the existence of ideas is controlled by God; this is the meaning of the laws of nature. Deists, in his view, were obsessed with the idea that there was a rational principle in the universe: God was fitted into this materialistic scheme, but in a way which reduced Him to an irrelevance. In *Alciphron* he developed his attack, combating in turn the various sorts of infidelity from his own spiritual interpretation of reality.

Berkeley was alleged to have Jacobite sympathies; in the eyes of the Hanoverian ministers, the friendship of Swift was no recommendation. In 1721, however, he was preferred to the bishopric of Dromore and became involved in lawsuits with the bishop who claimed the right of this nomination. His fortune was secured by elevation to the deanery of Derry and by a fortuitous legacy of half her property from Swift's Vanessa, Hester Vanhomrigh. In 1725 he produced his plan for the advancement of religion and learning in America, where the English colonists, he thought, by the neglect of the mother church, were drifting away toward Rome or worse. He secured from Parliament a vote recommending a grant from the king, and sailed to America with private funds raised by interested friends and from the revenue of his deanery. Walpole himself subscribed, but made no effort to secure the promised grant. For three years Berkeley lived in Rhode Island, bought a farm, built himself a house. He wrote *Alciphron*, it is said, from a rock overlooking the sea. Indeed the book reflects his delight in this "distant retreat far beyond the verge of that great whirlpool of business, faction, and pleasure which is called the *world*" and the idyllic scenery of oak and walnut groves and limpid streams. His scheme for a college in Bermuda withered, however, for want of money, and in 1731 he gave his remaining funds to the existing Yale University and returned home. He had realized, ahead of his time though not alone, that American colonists must have their own priests; the failure to plant an indigenous church was to have important consequences, political as well as moral.

Thwarted by the indifference of English politicians and the inertia of leading churchmen, Berkeley, who had previously refused a bishopric, now accepted the meager see of Cloyne. Refusing offers of higher preferment, he settled to the life of a model bishop. Unusually sensitive to the needs of the poor, he gave money freely during the periods of famine and did not hesitate to oppose the penal laws which made it unlawful for the Irish to buy land. In a series of publications entitled *The Querist*, he made some proposals which anticipated the economic thought of Adam Smith and the physiocrats. Equally original was his campaign for tar water, a remedy which he had learned from his stay in America and which he believed to be a tonic for children and a cure for nearly all diseases. He went to live in Oxford and died six months later at a house in Holywell.

Berkeley was loved by the Irish for his charity and warmth of heart. Atterbury once declared his astonishment at finding in one man "so much understanding, so much knowledge, so much innocence, and such humility." In thought and outlook, though his ideas were much misunderstood, he seems to have had no enemies. He cut across the grain of his time, but with so much magnanimity, such sincerity of spirit, that there was no resentment. Lecky must have the last word upon "this most extraordinary man, who united the rarest and most intellectual gifts with a grace and purity of character and an enthusiasm of benevolence that fascinated all about him."

A. A. Luce, *The Life of Berkeley*, 1949.

ISAAC WATTS (1674–1748) has left a memorial in the shape of hymns which contain enough good poetry to ensure their survival, despite his strict Calvinist theology and natural archaisms of language. In the seventeenth century poets wrote for the accompaniment of some instrument, but their works were mostly intended for private use; there were some masterpieces, but only two attempts to compile a hymn book; neither Cosin nor Withers reached such a wide audience as Watts, with his *Hymns and Spiritual Songs in Three Books* (1707). With simple meters suitable for congregational singing, and poetry on nearly every page, Watts's collection had a large circulation from the start. "Jesus shall reign where'er the sun," "There is a land of pure delight"—such opening lines evoke at once the country congregation at evensong, candlelight reflective upon oak and deal, box pews and whitewashed walls, these enlivened perhaps by the texts and admonitions from scripture which he used to such good effect. Relevant, tidy, elevating but usually without the cloying sweetness, overadorned or precious notes of many later hymn writers, Watts's hymns are springy and cheerful, even when he handles grave themes. In their restraint and grace they are as expressive of Augustan culture as the urbane work of Addison or the measured irony of Swift. The most famous of his hymns, "O God, our help in ages past," has power still to emphasize the solemnity of a national occasion—or lend a reflective spirit to formal pomp.

Watts was a pioneer in his writing for children. In his preface to *Divine Songs Attempted in Easy Language for the Use of Children,* he addressed himself "to all that are concerned in the Education of Children" in the hope that his songs, learned by heart, "will be a constant furniture for the minds of children, that they may have something to think upon when alone, and sing over to themselves. This may sometimes give their thoughts a divine turn, and raise a young meditation." His picture of the child may be oversanguine, but it lacked the overbearing and fussy character of some later "edifying" works for children, and his lines reveal a tenderness and humor that contrast pleasantly with his stern beliefs. "Let dogs delight to bark and bite" and "How doth the little busy bee" became household sayings in Watts's lifetime.

Watts lived a gentle, retiring life. For some thirty-five years he lived at Stoke Newington, with Sir Thomas and Lady Abney. (He had been at school at the notable academy there.) From Stoke

Newington he would ride into London to preach at his dissenting chapel. He was not overworked for he had an assistant, and he was somewhat delicate. He found time to write doctrinal treatises, compile educational manuals, including *Logic* and *Scripture History*, both of which were successful. The admirable bust by Banks in Westminster Abbey shows an unusual face, sensitive, fine-drawn, and keen; a man, one would guess, capable of spiritual concentration and insight.

E. G. Rupp, *Religion in England, 1688–1791*, 1986.

WILLIAM LAW (1686–1761), mystic, nonjuror, wrote about Christianity in works both practical and controversial. He was a profound theologian, but his own saintly character was as good an argument for his faith as anything he wrote.

He was the son of a grocer in Kingscliffe in Northamptonshire. At Emmanuel College, Cambridge, Puritan in tradition, evangelical in spirit, he was ordained and elected Fellow. When he refused to take the oath of allegiance to George I he lost his Fellowship and chance of preferment in the Church. For a time he served as curate of Fotheringhay. In 1727 he was chosen to be tutor to Edward Gibbon, father of the historian; after his pupil had gone abroad he remained with the family at Putney, their cherished friend and spiritual director. He had already made a name as defender of nonjuring principles. In his *Three Letters to the Bishop of Bangor* (1717–19), Law demolished Hoadly's arguments for a church without authority for bishops or creeds. His *Remarks on the Fable of the Bees* (1724) was a caustic answer to Mandeville's poem and its moral—that "private vices are public benefits." *The Case of Reason* (1731) is a more profound work, and was an extended argument against deism as it was expressed in Matthew Tindal's *Christianity as Old as the Creation*. To the deist idea of God, standing apart from a universe which was governed by a fixed order of creation "both plain and perspicuous," Law opposed a living God who could only be understood by the intuitive, spiritual faculty.

Law was a mystic, but a man of his age too in his common sense. His *Christian Perfection* (1726) and the *Serious Call to a Devout and Holy Life* (1728) were concerned with the question of how to live in accord with the teaching of Christ. With wit and tender but cogent reasoning he expounded a way of Christian living based upon a new principle of life. In an age of tepid views Law's master-piece, the *Serious Call*, reached the hearts of thousands. John Wesley criticized it on the ground that, although he put a high ideal before men, he omitted to emphasize that the only means of attaining it was through the atonement of Christians. But he spoke of it as "a treatise which will hardly be excelled, if it be equaled, in the English tongue, either for beauty of expression or for justice of thought." The book had most appeal to the evangelical. But men of cooler temper were also captivated, for its appeal was as much intellectual as emotional. Dr. Johnson, who claimed that his reading it "was the first occasion of my thinking in earnest about religion," Gibbon the temperamentally skeptical, Lyttelton, all felt its power. "Though deep, yet clear his system," wrote the poet Byron. No other book, after the Bible itself, played such a part in molding the religious thought of the time.

In 1737 Law settled at Thrapston, subsequently at Kingscliffe again, with Mrs. Elizabeth Hutcheson and Mrs. Hester Gibbon, the historian's aunt. The trio resolved to live a religious life, to devote the ladies' wealth to charity, to put into practice the principles of the *Serious Call*. From a window in the manor house Law distributed charity to all comers. The quiet Northamptonshire countryside soon swarmed with beggars, the villagers protested, the vicar denounced indiscriminate giving from the pulpit. Law was, however, no sentimentalist. When he received £1,000 from an anonymous donor he used it to start a school for the village girls. Mrs. Hutcheson added a boys' school and an almshouse; there the old people still talk of Law as if he were alive. He founded a library used and visited by his devotees today, especially Americans. Tradition has it that he was plump and round-faced, but there is no certain record, for he would not allow himself to be painted. As he grew older his mystical preoccupations deepened. Boehme's writings appealed especially to his "hunger of the soul." When he first read the works of that shoemaker of Gorlitz (*c.* 1733) he was put into "a perfect sweat."

Law's own later works, *Appeal to All That Doubt* (1740), *The Spirit of Prayer* (1749–50), and *The Way to Divine Knowledge* (1752), were not widely popular or understood. They are based on the idea that nature and law are one; nature is God's book of revelation, His outward manifestation of what He inwardly is—and is able to do. Exceptional in its combination of lucidity and vision,

Law's mind is expressed in prose as fine as any of the century: explicit, rhythmic, and witty. Excelling in the use of simile and analogy, he could be severe or tender, homely or elevated, ironic or plain. If, as Leslie Stephen said of the *Serious Call*, its power could only be "adequately felt by readers who can study it on their knees," it is also true that his closely logical habit appealed to those who were unable to share his devout frame of mind. In an age that looked askance at enthusiasm he made religious feeling respectable and desirable. It was in character that he should have died, after a short illness, almost in the act of singing a hymn.

J. H. Overton, *Law, Non-juror and Mystic*, 1881.
A. K. Walker, *William Law, His Life and Thought*, 1973.

JOHN BYROM (1692–1763), a follower and friend of Law, was poet, mystic, and inventor. Much of our information about him (and Law) comes from his *Private Journal and Literary Remains*. After Cambridge, he traveled abroad and studied medicine; he never took a medical degree but was called Doctor by his friends. He was a Jacobite, but he was also a practical man, who invented a system of shorthand and made a fair income by teaching it. In 1740 he acquired a certain independence when he inherited a family property in Lancashire. Property did not spoil him. At a political dinner the conversation turned to the "subordination necessary to be amongst people." He wrote: "I contended for an equality, and for the poor people." Law, the saintly nonjuror, was his idol and in his verses Byrom sought to popularize his mystical ideas. Men as different in temper and outlook as Warburton and John Wesley approved of such poems as *Epistle to a Gentleman in the Temple* (1769). He wrote in a graceful and pleasing manner and could turn a neat epigram. His character seems to have been delightful: various in his interests, alive with fancies and foibles, essentially he was a simple and artless person.

R. Parkinson, ed., *The Private Journal and Literary Remains of John Byrom*, 1855.

JOSEPH BUTLER (1692–1752), the chief intellectual force in the Church of England in his time, was born the son of a Presbyterian draper of Wantage and educated until the age of twenty-three at dissenting schools. Under Mr. Samuel Jones at Tewkesbury he received a university education in miniature; before he left he was corresponding with the celebrated theologian Dr. Clarke, though this may not have been the cause of his decision to become ordained in the Church of England. At Oriel College he became a close friend of Edward Talbot, whose family's patronage assisted his early career in the Church. On going down from Oxford he was appointed preacher in the Rolls Chapel, where he preached the course of sermons which set out the principles of his moral philosophy. In 1725 he proceeded to the ample living of Stanhope in Weardale, resigned his preachership, and settled down to a pastoral life. In 1732 Queen Caroline asked Archbishop Blackburne whether Dr. Butler was dead. He replied, "Not dead, Ma'am, but buried." He was a careful vicar, but it is not for this that he is remembered. He used these years for reflection upon the being of God and the nature of man; the result, published in 1736, was the *Analogy of Religion, Natural and Revealed, to the Constitution and Course of Nature.*

As a moralist he was concerned to refute the notions of Hobbes and his followers, who held that every action is necessarily selfish. At the same time he sought to correct the facile optimism of Shaftesbury and other deists. He is always acutely aware of the misery of the human lot in this world, the imminence of judgment in the next. Conscience is not an aesthetic perception of the harmony of the universe but the sense of shame which makes our moral nature "tremble like a guilty thing surprised" in the presence of its creator. It is the supreme force in human life, because it represents the will of God. He maintained that "self-love though confined to the interest of the present world, does in general perfectly coincide with virtue, and leads us to one and the same course of life" and that, even for those who are deaf to conscience, the means of happiness will lie "in the exercise of charity, in the love of their neighbor, in endeavoring to promote the happiness of all they have to do with, and in the pursuit of what is just." The proof of this doctrine he derived from examination of "the inward frame of man." In an age when it was possible to write good sense about human thoughts and feelings without resort to the technical terminology of an exact science, his writing is notable for shrewd psychological understanding. His ethical teaching does not rely upon acceptance of a supernatural being, nor did he analyze ethical notions in terms of God's will, but it was molded by a belief in God which assures us that the world is morally ordered; without it his moral theory may be seen to be incomplete.

The *Analogy* was designed to refute the deists by showing that their natural arguments for the all-powerful creator were beset with greater difficulties than were the arguments for a God revealed in man. "You admit difficulties in the Laws of Nature, yet you believe that God created the Natural World; why then do you allow similar difficulties in the history of revealed religion to keep you from accepting it reverently? All evidence is imperfect, everything is extremely imperfect in this world." He grounds his reasoning upon the supremacy of the "inner light" or conscience of man; he insists that the revelation of God to man is visible by this light. Each man, in his view, is a kingdom in himself, with "a constitution of divine origin"; duty consists in "obeying the laws of this kingdom, though we may not know why they exist or were ordained." His method is magisterial in its fairness and he is scrupulous in his acceptance of awkward facts. Indeed, his gentle pessimism, his awareness of an irrational element in a God who is something more than deified reason, and his idea of life as a state of probation for a higher life, all appeal now as then to those who cannot accept all his arguments.

Queen Caroline was delighted by the *Analogy* and made him, in 1736, Clerk of the Closet. His chief duty was to be present at her evening gatherings of savants and divines. After her death he was appointed to the bishopric of Bristol; it was typical of his scrupulous conduct in these matters that he resigned the prebend of Rochester on receiving the deanery of St. Paul's: if it had to be, then he would be a pluralist in moderation. He was translated to Durham by the Duke of Newcastle; again he stood by his principles by refusing to accept any of the priorities which the minister wished to attach to his appointment. At Bishop Auckland he indulged his taste for building and planting. But that he did not neglect his pastoral duties may be seen in his charge of 1750, a thoughtful commentary upon the problems of the parish priest. He had never enjoyed robust health, and he died the following year. The story is often told of Butler that on Wesley's talking to him about the source of his inspiration, the bishop retorted, "Sir, the pretending to extraordinary revelations and gifts of the Holy Ghost is a horrid thing, a very horrid thing." He meant a thing that shocked; he was reasoning with a man who defied ecclesiastical discipline by preaching without authority and who believed himself to be divinely inspired. Yet the remark may stand as typical of Butler's approach: it is typical of his period's mistrust of enthusiasm, of his own reserved, sensitive spirit—his habits were retiring, his manner despondent. But Butler was no tepid churchman. He cared for reverent ceremonial in churches and for missionary work outside them. He urged, in vain, the appointment of bishops in North America. He wanted provision for the sick, whom he visited assiduously, and for the education of the poor.

About his character as about his writing there was a rare integrity. "Things and actions," he said, "are what they are, and the consequences of them will be what they will be; why then should we desire to be deceived?"

Rev. Thomas Bartlett, *Memoirs of the Life, Character and Writings of Joseph Butler*, 1839.
A. Duncan Jones, *Butler's Moral Philosophy*, 1952.

LORD JOHN CARTERET, EARL GRANVILLE (1690–1763) was one of the statesman of the eighteenth century to whom the word "genius" does not seem misapplied. Yet his achievement is not so considerable as his talents would suggest, and his main period of office ended in apparent failure and sharp abuse.

In social position Carteret, a peer at the age of six, was second to none, for there was Norman blood in both sides of his family. The Carterets came from Jersey, where eight of them, father and seven sons, had been knighted in one day by Edward III. His mother, the daughter of the Earl of Bath, was Countess of Granville in her own right, and from her Carteret inherited his second title in 1744. To pride of blood was added pride of intellect. At Westminster, in the golden age which produced Prior, Pulteney, Newcastle, Atterbury, and Murray, Carteret became a superb classical scholar. He was a friend of the great Bentley and his intellectual peer, perhaps the best Grecian of his time. He is said to have been able to recount the whole of the Greek Testament by heart, and he would gladly break off the discussion of politics to talk of some point of Homeric lore. He was also versed in modern languages; his command of German and French gave him special advantages in his diplomatic contacts and commended him to

George II. His first essay in diplomacy, in 1719, when he was ambassador in Stockholm, gave proof of his talent. He fulfilled the intentions of his patron Stanhope by the way in which he obtained freedom of the Baltic for British vessels and negotiated the peace between the northern powers. In 1721 he was a natural choice for Secretary of State to succeed Craggs after the Bubble.

Carteret enjoyed the favor of the King and promoted with vigor his Hanoverian interests, but he found himself, as the heir to Stanhope, consistently thwarted by the partnership of Townshend and Walpole. After the untimely death of Dubois, with whom he enjoyed some rapport, he was humiliated over his failure in an involved domestic intrigue in France and the consequent replacement of Sir Luke Schaub, the ambassador and his agent, by Horatio Walpole. Like Townshend before him, he was transferred to Ireland, ostensibly to deal with the crisis that had arisen there over Wood's halfpence. Wood had bought from the Duchess of Kendal her grant of the royal prerogative of coining in Ireland. His copper halfpence were needed by Ireland, which especially lacked coin of small denominations, but they were minted in England and could justly be represented as a further example of the exploitation of Ireland. There, Lord Middleton, the Lord Chancellor, was opposed to Walpole, while Swift, Dean of Clontyre, seized upon the hated halfpennies to make propaganda for his Tory views in the satirical *Drapier's Letters*. Carteret, who had opposed the issue of the halfpence, now found himself trying to justify the government's policy. Walpole, who soon appreciated that it would be politic to abandon it, could congratulate himself upon a stroke which had removed his most talented rival and placed Ireland under his intelligent and amiable rule. Carteret remained in Dublin until 1730, in hope of recall to favor, while Walpole ensured that Ireland would be quiet through the agency of his client, Hugh Boulter, Archbishop of Armagh.

From 1730 to 1742, Carteret contributed to the talented opposition which harried Walpole and finally destroyed him. He was detached from the grubbier aspects of the struggle in the Commons and the constituencies, but denounced Walpole's conduct of the War of the Austrian Succession with the Olympian confidence of a man who knew that he could do better. In 1742, with the fall of the great minister, his opportunity came. From then until the end of 1744, in the war which he understood, and among the kings and statesmen whom alone he regarded as his equals, he was virtually the "sole minister" that Pitt decried.

Carteret gave a firm direction to English policy, nerveless in the last days of Walpole. He had an unrivaled knowledge of the constitution and politics of the German Empire. He realized that France was the real enemy, although Frederick had begun the war by violating the Pragmatic Sanction through the invasion of Silesia and although England and France were not officially at war until 1744. His object therefore was to isolate France by diplomacy supported by subsidies, to build up a coalition against her, and to revive the glories of Marlborough's war. He therefore raised Maria Theresa's subsidy to half a million pounds, recruited Hanoverians to join the usual Hessians in English pay, thus committing Hanover to the war, and maneuvered Prussia out by the Treaty of Berlin, in July 1742. He would have liked to involve the Dutch as well, and Savoy to counterbalance the Spanish in Italy, but in these objects he failed. Nevertheless, the peripatetic minister enjoyed some success in 1743 and had the satisfaction of watching, from the safety of his coach, George II lead the troops of the Pragmatic Army to the muddled victory of Dettingen. Since in the same year the French were driven out of Prague, and the Bavarian Emperor Charles VII out of his own country, Carteret's policy seems to have been vindicated. But he was hampered both by his allies and by his fellow ministers at home. Maria Theresa was reluctant to give up Bavaria as the price of peace, and Frederick the Great took the initiative once more, in 1744, with a second attack upon Austria. At home, Pitt thundered invective against "the Hanoverian troopminister" who had thus taken affairs into his own hands, and the Pelhams, offended by his "obstinate and offensive silence" about the German negotiations, pinched his plans at the source by refusing to pay the subsidies that he promised. Newcastle had special reason to be hurt, for Carteret secured the alliance of Charles Emmanuel of Savoy, at the Treaty of Worms, heedless of the fact that Savoy and Italy came into the department of Newcastle as Secretary of State for the South. Hervey once wrote of him that he had "many admirers but not one adherent."

Against the complaints of the Pelhams and the invective of Pitt, he could now no longer argue success. In February 1744 Mathews and Lestock failed ignominiously to defeat the French and Spanish fleet when it emerged from Toulon, and in the same month there was an invasion scare which was no less alarming for the plan being known by the government. In Flanders, the Pragmatic Army, suffering from disunity and an uninspired commander in the septuagenarian Marshal Wade, was lucky to avoid defeat by Marshal Saxe; Maria Theresa lost Alsace and Prague and was forced to abandon Bavaria. In November 1744, at the instigation of the Pelhams, Carteret was dismissed. His system of alliances was in ruins because of the reckless ambition of Frederick the Great and the failure of the English to produce a great commander by land or sea. It is a measure of the limitations of royal power that George II had to abandon the minister whose capacities and policies he so admired. It is also the key to Carteret's failure that he believed that, with the Crown on his side, he could "defy everything," and ignore the views of Parliament. He fancied that he could act like a statesman without needing to be a politician. He enraged his supporters by refusing to meet them at the Feathers tavern, saying that he never dined at taverns. He was contemptuous, too, of the small change of patronage in which the Pelhams accumulated their balance of power: "What is it to me who is a judge or who is a bishop? It is my business to make Kings and Emperors." As he trundled between the capitals of Europe, talked bluntly to kings, supervised in person the making of treaties and committed his government to them without so much as a warning of his intentions, it may have seemed that he was, as Pitt suggested, drunk with power. Even foreign rulers he treated with disdain, as Frederick observed: "en petits garçons." In methods and outlook Carteret was indeed something of an anachronism. Furthermore, for all his grand abilities, he had serious personal faults. Lord Rosebery, who wrote with an insight that might have come from thinking of his own career, said that "his energy came in gusts, he could scarcely bring himself to bend, and he was incapable of that self-contained patience, amounting to long-suffering, which is a necessary condition of the highest success in official life." He saw the issues plainly; it may be urged too plainly. His notion of England's part as being to knock the heads of the kings of Europe together and jumble something out of it which might be of service to his country, lacked finesse, wisdom too perhaps.

Granville, as he became in 1744, was never again to enjoy executive responsibility though he was to retain, for some time, influence with the king as "the minister behind the curtain." He found solace in Homer, Burgundy, and a romantic second marriage to Sophia Fermor, thirty years his junior; it caused a stir in society—alas, she died within a year. He had by this time lost all ambition and much of his old fire, at least before he had taken to his bottle, but his swift and pithy judgment remained and he could still be alarming, to Newcastle for one. He was ready to serve again if the opportunity should come. In 1746 he tried to form a ministry when the Pelhams threw up their offices, but found no support. A minister could not govern if he could not command the allegiance of a sizeable group in the Commons, and the king could not resist the pressure of the dominant group of ministers so long as they held together, as the Old Whigs did against Granville, and so long as they, and not the king, had the patronage at their disposal. In 1751 he finally returned as President of the Council, but did not bestir himself to help Newcastle when the duke was in trouble in 1756: "You are now being served as you and your brother served me." He could still be incisive when he wanted: in 1761, when Pitt spoke in cabinet of being "responsible to the people" he reminded him that at that board ministers were responsible to the king. His firmness over Pitt's intention of declaring war against Spain was the main cause of Pitt's resignation. His later years were not without their compensations. Political disappointment did not sour him. Before his death he had the satisfaction of seeing England glorious in a war conducted upon principles which were not dissimilar to his own, achieving "the most honorable peace, closing the most glorious war, that the nation had ever seen," and of hearing Pitt acknowledge his debt to the statesman whom he had once so arrogantly opposed.

D. B. Horn, *Great Britain and Europe in the Eighteenth Century*, 1967. B. Williams, *Carteret and Newcastle*, 1943.

WILLIAM STANHOPE, 1st EARL OF HARRINGTON (1690–1756) was Secretary of State in all for fourteen years and in office almost continuously for twenty-one years. Yet he has left but a small mark on the history of his time and one wonders if he has been underrated. It seems probable that his talents, like his training, were largely diplomatic, and that he was quiet, competent, and diligent, a man for the routines of office rather than for big initiatives and flights of policy.

Stanhope served in Spain as a colonel of Dragoons; after the Spanish Succession War he became a member of Parliament for Derby. He was much employed abroad in diplomatic missions, as a special envoy in Madrid (1717–18) and at Turin (1718–19). He was ambassador in Spain (1719–27) and in 1726 obtained from Ripperda the revelation of the articles of the secret Treaty of Vienna. He did not give, in return, Gibraltar, so ardently wanted by the Spanish, but successfully negotiated the Treaty of Seville whereby the English received trading privileges in return for acceptance of Parma and Piacenza being garrisoned by Spanish troops (1729). This was the climax of two years of negotiation at Aix-la-Chapelle and Soissons. In 1730 he was rewarded with the post of Secretary of State for the Northern Department, in succession to Townshend, whom Walpole had managed to oust. He was a suitable man to be under Walpole and in partnership with Newcastle, but he was not entirely happy about all aspects of Walpole's policy. He was George II's man and could take a discreetly independent line, for instance, in 1741 when he negotiated a treaty of neutrality for Hanover without Walpole's knowledge. He did not share Walpole's faith in France—and he took care not to share in his fall after two years of war against France. In 1741 he became Lord President of the Council; in 1742 he was created earl. In December 1744 he succeeded Carteret as Secretary of State, though by now he seems to have been regarded without enthusiasm by king or fellow ministers.

Queen Caroline once remarked of him that he needed "six hours to dress, six hours to eat, six hours with his mistress, and six for sleep." He was complaisant enough but not to be treated with such contempt as this might seem to imply. He may have seemed indolent when he failed to see ambassadors because he was laid up with gout. His written instructions were, however, invariably clear. He lost favor with George II, whose Hanoverian interests he had assiduously studied, by taking part with the Pelhams in the collective resignation of February 1746. In November of that year he resigned by himself, in protest against Newcastle's interference with the affairs of his department, and was replaced by Chesterfield, but he was promptly sent to Ireland as Lord-Lieutenant. It was the usual shelf in the eighteenth century for ministers thought to be too important for mere dismissal.

J. Black, *British Foreign Policy in the Age of Walpole*, 1985.

PHILIP DORMER STANHOPE, 4th EARL OF CHESTERFIELD
(1694–1773), a man who embodied many of the characteristic
virtues and failings of the time, is deservedly known for his *Letters
to His Son*, an epistolary code of conduct in polite society. He was
also a statesman of higher repute in his day than may be inferred
from the bare record of his achievement.

The grandson of Halifax the Trimmer, whom he resembled in
his "large and cautious mind" (Macaulay on Halifax), the son of
the morose Jacobite third Earl, he was brought up under the wing
of his grandmother, Lady Halifax, herself a woman of wit and
sense. His tutors and Cambridge produced a finished classical
scholar, although he looked back upon that "illiberal seminary"
with some scorn for his own pedantry: "when I talked my best, I
quoted Horace; when I aimed at being facetious, I quoted Martial;
and when I had a mind to be a fine gentleman, I talked Ovid." His
connections led him naturally into politics, and at the age of twenty
he represented the negligible electorate of St. Germans. Disqualified for sitting underage, he found a congenial retreat in Paris,
where he found the modes of the Regency much to his taste. Upon
the death of his father he took his place in the Upper House,
where his oratory shone all the brighter for having few rivals of his
scholarship or taste. His detached and fastidious spirit did not commend itself to Walpole, who would have liked to bind him to his interest. In 1720 he accepted the post of Captain of the Yeomen of
the Guard but made no use of its opportunities for gain. In 1723
he refused Walpole's offer for the garter, "one of the tags Bob gave
his boys," and his support of the Prince of Wales's interests earned
him the dislike of George II and Queen Caroline. His embassy at
the Hague enabled him to gratify his taste for gambling, the only
vice to which he was immoderately addicted; there he "courted the
good opinions of the Dutch by losing great sums at play." He also
conducted his more serious business with skill and played a large
part in the negotiations of the Second Treaty of Vienna, in 1731,
when the Emperor agreed to abolish the Ostend Company and England guaranteed the Pragmatic Sanction. Any credit he gained
with the administration was lost, however, when he opposed the Excise Bill in 1733. His greatest parliamentary performance was his attack upon Walpole's bill of 1737 to compel theatrical managers to
submit plays for license to the Lord Chamberlain. The measure
found its place in the statute book and stayed there, the despair of

producers and the butt of satirists, until 1968. But Chesterfield made his point in a speech "full of wit of the genteelist satire and in the most polished classical style."

Governors-General of Ireland were not always conscientious, and appointment to Dublin was regarded at Westminster as notice of dismissal. Chesterfield was appointed Governor-General in January 1745, after the fall of Carteret on the insistence of the Pelhams. George II may have been pleased to see him removed to Dublin, but Chesterfield also served his interests well. He earned respect by his tact, courtesy, and strength of purpose, and his efforts ensured that Ireland was quiet during the dangerous crisis of '45. His informal entertainments at the castle pleased Dublin society, but he showed sympathy too with the plight of the peasantry: "the poor people in Ireland are worse used than negroes by their lords and masters." He returned in April 1746, leaving his new plantations in Phoenix Park as his memorial, and became Secretary of State for the Northern Department in place of Harrington. Like his predecessor he found it hard to "tug at the oar with one who cannot row, and yet will be paddling so as to hinder you from rowing." He was not prepared, as he said, to act as a mere "commis" to forward Newcastle's instructions, and so resigned in February 1748. Newcastle found in Holderness a more complacent colleague and Chesterfield found compensations in what he termed "philosophical quiet," the pleasures of gaming at White's, building a fine house in what is now South Audley Street, cultivating pineapples, and collecting works for his library. He did not again take office but played the leading part in the Reform of the Calendar in 1751. Newcastle urged him "not to stir matters that had long been quiet" and may have thought himself justified in the ignorant clamor of the mob who thought they had been cheated of their "eleven days." But Chesterfield could afford to be more detached and his speech was luminous; even if he did not understand the astronomical arguments with which he was supplied by Bradley, Astronomer Royal, and Lord Macclesfield, he was proud of the harmonious periods of his speech. It was a minor triuph of the age of reason, and suitable that Chesterfield was the man to promote it.

His letters to his son convey the best and worst of the polite values of the time. *Suaviter in modo*, a phrase which he liked, might have been his motto. The general tone is not elevated: enthusiasm is to be abhorred and moral values take second place to graceful manners. It should be recalled, in his defense, that he was penning advice to his illegitimate son about the ways of the world, not a textbook of morals. His detached and witty appraisals may command our admiration: "In my mind, there is nothing so illiberal and so ill-bred as audible laughter"; his attitude to women is, however, displeasing: "They have in truth but two passions, vanity and love; these are their universal characteristics." He seems to have been consistent in this respect. In 1733 he married Petronilla von der Schulenberg, natural daughter of George I by the Duchess of Kendal: a political and financial arrangement which did not prevent his taking a new mistress to his house while his wife retired to occupy a house next door.

B. Dobrée, *Chesterfield's Letters*, 6 vols., 1932.
S. Shellabarger, *Lord Chesterfield*, 1935.
B. Willey, *The English Moralists*, 1964.

PHILIP YORKE, EARL OF HARDWICKE (1690–1764) was a great Lord Chancellor at a time when the law and its high officers enjoyed more esteem and power than at any other time. The Church and its affairs had retreated from their dominant position in politics; the bishops were appointed on political grounds and behaved, in their political capacity, as puppets; even the High Church. Dr. Johnson declared that he would rather be a judge than a bishop. The mystique of the law replaced that of the Church, a natural consequence of 1688 which had been, in spirit and terminology, a lawyers' revolution, the work largely of the great Somers. Its acts enshrined the notions to be found in the pages of Locke, for whom the chief end of civil society was the preservation of property and of the rights of the individual. Law was the guardian of the people, but "the people" narrowly conceived, as by Sidney Smith in 1830, as "the great mass of those who have opinions worth hearing, and property worth defending." In practice the law was the expression of a minority, disinterestedly firm in defense of the constitution but conservative in its view of society. There were 160 felonies punishable by death by the end of George II's reign and no significant movement for reform of the criminal law. At the same time, the subject enjoyed a measure of protection under the law which was unique in Europe. At the apex of this brutal but majestic system was the Lord Chancellor. For nineteen years this supreme office was occupied by Lord Hardwicke.

Like many great lawyers of the time, his origins were humble; he was the son of a country attorney, but a brilliant career at Westminster and the patronage of Lord Macclesfield provided him with an opening in Parliament: he sat for the Pelhams' borough of Seaford. When he was asked by his prospective father-in-law what property he possessed, he had, he replied, a perch of ground in Westminster Hall. He was loyal to his patrons and richly rewarded for it. In 1720, aged only thirty, he became Solicitor-General, three years later Attorney-General. In this capacity he prosecuted for the Crown, amongst others, the notorious criminals Jonathan Wild and Jack Sheppard. In 1734 he became Lord Chief Justice and Baron Hardwicke. In 1737 he succeeded Talbot on the Woolsack. From 1742 to 1756 he played an important political role, as the partner of the Pelhams. The best head among the ministers, he provided a conciliatory influence amid the intrigues of the various groups; he was efficient and cool, notably in the flutter of '45. His handsome presence and unfailing lucidity dominated the House of Lords. On occasions he could be devastating. When Henry Fox tried to ingratiate himself after opposing Hardwicke's Marriage Bill and describing its author as a giant spider, he replied: "I despise the scurrility and reject the adulation." In 1754 he was entrusted with the reconstruction of the cabinet and rewarded with an earldom. He had already acquired a fortune to hand on to his sons. He did not underrate his own abilities: his pomposity is understandable but not endearing. He was an influential if cautious politician, but it was as a lawyer that his work was of lasting significance.

He had the advantage of being as familiar with the common law as with equity, and he completed the work of previous chancellors in harmonizing the two systems. *Aequitas sequitur legem*, as he said in one of his judgments: equity existed to supplement and not to replace the common law. Over a hundred years were to pass before the equity and common law jurisdictions came to be administered in the same courts, but his work prepared the way for this partial fusion. As Holdsworth said of him: "Hardwicke laid the foundations and erected a large part of the edifice of modern equity." He saw in rules the safeguard of liberty, and Chancery's intricate rules were stabilized under him. There was danger in this as we are reminded by the later condition of Chancery that Dickens exposed. It was to Hardwicke's credit, however, that at a time when politics were venal, the law courts were respected for impartiality. The importance of this lay partly in the fact that England was changing rapidly in his time, while the union with Scotland created new problems because of the differences between the two legal systems. In 1708, the House of Lords held that its jurisdiction extended to appeals from the Scottish courts, though no comparable appellate jurisdiction had been known in Scotland before. In 1719 the same was extended by statute to Ireland. He had wide powers and he used them to establish a general code of precedents by which his successors might be guided. In Scotland he had specially to legislate for the clans after the rising of '45: aiming at a unified government in Scotland, he curbed the rights of the clans, abolished their private jurisdiction, and proscribed their peculiar dress.

At home he drew upon his large experience of runaway marriage cases to draw up the Marriage Act of 1753, which is still the basis of modern marriage law: provisions were made for the consent of guardians in the case of minors, and for the calling of banns, and licenses were required for any departure from the general rule. Hardwicke was attacked for promoting this measure by conservative or romantic-minded politicians, like Charles Townshend, on the ground that it was indelicate, or an infringement upon personal liberty. Normally he aimed at clarification rather than radical alteration of laws: "Certainty is the mother or repose, and therefore the law aims at certainty" was his favorite maxim. He believed that all important legislation should be initiated in the House of Lords, and it was on this ground, as much as on the poor drafting of the measure, that he opposed Pitt's urgently required Militia Act of 1756. He clashed with Pitt too over the interpretation of *habeas corpus*. Pitt framed a bill to provide for the gap in the Act of 1679 which had become evident when a man was seized by the press-gang, applied for a writ of *habeas corpus*, and had been refused on the grounds that it only applied to criminal cases. Hardwicke secured the rejection of the bill, on the grounds that it took away the judges' discretionary power. Pitt was precipitate and he should have consulted legal advisers before rushing into the technical field of writs, but Hardwicke was taking a narrow view: an act extending the operation of the writ was passed later, in 1816.

Hardwicke was convinced that the law must be adamant in an age of license; characteristically he disliked the freedom of the press, and it was on his advice that his son, then Attorney-General, advised Grenville's ministry in its proceedings against Wilkes. He was a conservative, who believed that England had "by far the best body of laws that human wisdom can claim," but he was no blind reactionary. In a century when the continental monarchies were all exploiting the principle that the will of the monarch is the supreme law of the state, England owed much to Hardwicke's conception of the supremacy of law.

Hardwicke was a handsome man, a good story-teller, impressive in society, but thought to be mean. The counterpane of his bed, people said, was made by sewing together the bags in which the Great Seal was delivered to him. He set out to create a great family: it was after his death that his son, thrust too precipitately into the office of Lord Chancellor, committed suicide.

P. C. Yorke, *The Life of Lord Chancellor Hardwicke*, 3 vols., 1913.

GEORGE BUBB DODINGTON, LORD MELCOMBE (1691–1762) had his memorial on a grassy knoll above West Wycombe, where stands a hexagonal mausoleum of flint raised by Sir Francis Dashwood. He had been one of Dashwood's Medmenham "Franciscans" and had sported with him in the damp caves under the hill. It is a suitable memorial to Dodington: pretentious, deplorable, a little absurd.

But Dodington was not the inconsequential figure that these frolics, and his thin record of political achievement—Junior Commissioner of the Treasury (1724–41) and Treasurer of the Navy (1744–49)—might suggest. He owed his start in politics to his wealth: from his uncle, a successful careerist, he inherited a fortune and a Vanbrugh palace, Eastbury Park in Dorset. His reputation was grounded upon some skillful work as an envoy in Spain from 1716 to 1719; his status was assured by his sensible speaking from the Treasury bench and methodical cultivation of his borough interests; he was a Newcastle in a minor key, for whom personal obligation was the stuff of politics. His diary is a shameless document in which all issues are reduced to the level of stock-jobbery, but invaluable to historians for its insight into the workings of Parliament and elections at the time. Pope saw him as

"Bu—with pay and scorn content," and he made an odd figure, very fat, with porcine features and the old-fashioned full wig that he affected to fit the part of country gentleman—Noll Bluff as he liked to be called. In fact no man knew more than he of the patronage which greased the wheels of eighteenth-century government. But he was capable of rising above the meaner interests of the sinecurist. No Clerk of the Pells showed such concern as he for the interests of Ireland; there was no political reward in his championship of the Irish linen industry. As befitted the friend of Voltaire, he defended Admiral Byng. Though his political usefulness had passed with him to the grave, he attended the funeral of the Prince of Wales in 1751. Nor was he notably dishonest in his capacity as Treasurer of the Navy.

Dodington's special talent was for organizing opposition, and he played a major part in the destruction of Walpole in 1742. This talent did not, however, commend him for office any more than the adherence to the Prince of Wales which made him *persona non grata* to the king. Even in his last years, after the accession of George III when he was gratified by the award of a peerage, he was being spoken of as a possible Secretary of State. It is appropriate that his features should have been preserved for posterity by Hogarth's cartoon, Chairing the Member, but ironic that this should have commemorated a by-election which he actually lost.

J. Carswell and L. A. Dralle, eds., *The Political Journal of Bubb Dodington*, 1965.
J. Carswell, *The Old Cause*, 1953.

THOMAS PELHAM-HOLLES, 1st DUKE OF NEWCASTLE (1693–1768) was fortunate to live in the eighteenth century when the political system was such as to afford his talents the widest scope. George II thought him unfit to be a chamberlain at a minor German court, but was forced to accept him in high office throughout his reign. The man who was derided by the wits and snubbed by his fellow ministers has left an imposing answer to his critics. He was Secretary of State from 1724 to 1754, with a break of only two days, in February 1746, and one shift, from south to north, in 1748. Then he was First Lord of the Treasury from March 1754 to November 1756 and again from June 1757 to May 1762. It is a unique record. Newcastle had the means to make himself indispensable even if he did not have the personality to make himself respected. Wealth, borough influence, understanding of the workings of patronage, a readiness to serve abler men, and to betray them when necessary: all these contributed to his position. But more important than anything was his passionate interest in the political game. To stay at the center of affairs he seems to have been ready to make any sacrifice of pride.

Newcastle canalized the various sources of influence that were available to governments of the time: boroughs, places in dockyards, excise and institutions under the Crown, grants from the civil list or secret service money, clerical and academic preferment. He directed them to the one end of securing a parliamentary majority. But he was no mere political jobber. Despite the flurry and effusion of his huge correspondence, the apparent lack of sense of proportion, the moments of timidity and the obsessive jealousies that made him such a tiresome colleague, Newcastle had a talent for management, patience, subtlety, a good memory, and insight into political behavior. He also delighted in electioneering. In every election from 1715 to 1761 he took a prominent part, in his own counties, Sussex, Nottinghamshire, Lincolnshire, and Yorkshire, but also as general agent for the government throughout the country. His guidance of the riotous elections of 1734 was perhaps his masterpiece; the opposition had a good cry in "No excise" while bad harvests and trade were damaging government prospects; the ministers yet secured a comfortable majority.

Newcastle had been Lord Chamberlain in 1717. In 1724 he became Secretary of State in place of Carteret and despite Pulteney, who must have hoped for the position. Townshend snubbed him as Carteret did later, but he played a leading part in the downfall of that minister in 1730. Besides his encyclopedic handling of the patronage he made himself useful to Walpole by his sensible debating. He was at his best when he could accept the dominance of a greater man. But when first Carteret, and then his brother Henry Pelham, led the administration, Newcastle's phobia about being left out of things became a menace. With Carteret (1742–44) he was especially uneasy, for he rode roughshod over even the formalities of cabinet consultation and committed the economical Pelhams to lavish expenditures. In August 1743 he complained "No man can bear long what I go through every day, in our joint audience in the Closet." The king might humiliate Newcastle in the closet, but he could not impair his hold upon the House; he was forced to accept Carteret's resignation in November 1744. Unless power in the House and favor in the closet could be combined, eighteenth-century government was impossible: this is the reason for the power of the Pelhams. They were at least prepared to compromise, to reconcile the opposites of Hanoverian king and anti-Hanoverian Parliament, to prosecute a war while looking for peace, to bring even Tories like Phillips and Cotton into minor ministerial posts. Because they were interested as much in power as in measures, they made government possible. In 1748, Newcastle overcame his phobia about sea travel to conduct negotiations at Aix-la-Chapelle. Louisburg, England's only conquest of the war, was handed back to the French; Don Philip got the Duchies of Parma and Piacenza. In India the *status quo* was restored. England kept Gibraltar and Minorca; Prussia kept Silesia. "Bête comme la paix" was the saying in Paris. But Newcastle was pleased with his efforts to end the war which, in Carlyle's phrase, was "an unntelligible, huge, English-and-Foreign Delirium." Frederick the Great knew what he wanted, a greater Prussia, for the present Silesia— and he got it. Charles Emmanuel of Savoy was bent, in Gibbon's phrase, upon "plucking more leaves of the Italian artichoke." France was "consulting her traditions rather than her interests." Unfortunately the loose ends left untied by the peace of Aix-la-Chapelle were to cause another war. Newcastle could not prevent it, since it was desired by both France and Austria. Culpably he did nothing to prepare England for the resumption of the war. He neglected the vital task of building up the navy. He was affected by George's anti-Prussian prejudices. While Kaunitz, disenchanted with the English alliance, set the diplomatic revolution in train, Newcastle busied himself with his "Great System, the great object of my life, in foreign affairs": this was to secure, by lavish bribery, the election of Maria Theresa's son as king of the Romans. Henry Pelham grumbled about this expensive "moonshine"; Frederick was self-righteous about interference in German affairs; the Austrians themselves contemptuously rejected the scheme as an impertinence and came to terms with France.

Hard hit by his brother's death in 1754, Newcastle pressed on with his system. Russia was brought in by a defensive treaty in September 1755, then Prussia, alarmed by the prospect of attack from Russia, by the Convention of Westminster. France and Austria then made their alliance, to be joined by Russia. Newcastle was gullible in supposing that his treaties with Prussia and Russia were not incompatible; a more serious objection voiced by Pitt was that the center of England's diplomatic interest appeared to be Hanover. When England floundered into war in 1756 it was to the accompaniment of disasters for which Newcastle was responsible; the defeat of Braddock, the wrong type of general, sent too late; the abortive naval action of Byng and the subsequent loss of Minorca. "Indeed he shall be hanged" said the agitated Newcastle, after the débâcle—he was shot. But the poor state of the navy and the confused orders given to England's naval commanders can be laid at the minister's door. Pitt had been dismissed from the paymastership in November 1755 and had since been jeering at Newcastle's alliances and followers, "Xerxes' troops." Now Newcastle was forced to come to terms with him. At first Pitt attempted to rule without him, from November 1756 to April 1757. Against the king, against the closet, against Newcastle, and denied the boon of early victory, he was ineffective. From April 6, when he was dismissed, until June 29, when he joined with Newcastle, the country was without a government. The country wanted Pitt, but he could not have a free hand in Parliament or enjoy the confidence of the king without Newcastle. From 1757 to 1761, the partnership subsisted on this uneven basis. The accession of George III, Pitt's determination to carry the war into a further phase by attacking Spain, and his haughty and uncooperative ways were among the causes of his fall in October 1761; Newcastle did not wish it, for all their differences of policy. George's determination to recover control of the patronage meant that Newcastle's own days were numbered. In the negotiations which led to the Peace of Paris he fought for recognition of the claims of Frederick without success; opposed in everything and edged out of power, he eventually resigned in May 1762.

Some of the best stories of the eighteenth century are told about Newcastle. Horace Walpole's account of his conduct at Westminster Abbey during the funeral of George II is typical: "He fell into a fit of crying at the moment he came into the chapel, and flung himself back into a stall, the Archbishop hovering over him with a smelling-bottle; but in two minutes his curiosity got the better of his hypocrisy, and he ran about the chapel, with his glass to spy who was or who was not there, spying with one hand and mopping his eyes with the other. Then returned the fear of catching cold; and the Duke of Cumberland, who was sinking with heat, felt himself weighed down, and turning round, found it was the Duke of Newcastle standing upon his train, to avoid the chill of the marble." The accounts of Hervey, Waldegrave, and Smollett show that it was fashionable to laugh at him. The solemn Lord Wilmington said possibly the truest thing about him: "The Duke of Newcastle always loses half an hour in the morning, which he is running after the rest of the day without being able to overtake it." His worse fault was meddling. During the peace negotiations of 1746–48, properly the province of his fellow Secretary of State, Harrington, he corresponded secretly with the envoy in Holland and sent instructions contrary to those of Harrington. He could not leave well alone and it was his mother, to whom he was devoted, who spoke of him "perpetually fretting your friends with unjust suspicions of them." He was easily agitated. Of a dinner party with Granville he wrote: "My Lord President had dined and talked very unguardedly . . . I was frightened the whole time."

Newcastle always showed, however, a high conception of public duty. If it was his fault that he thought himself indispensable, he had the talents to make himself so. He devoted himself to the handling of pension and place, but he made nothing from it for himself; considering the fortunes made by lesser men, like Henry Fox, we may respect his self-denial. His kindness and his patriotism deserve better from the historian than they received from contemporaries.

J. B. Owen, *The Rise of the Pelhams*, 1957.
R. Browning, *The Duke of Newcastle*, 1975.

THE HONORABLE HENRY PELHAM (1695–1754) had an unspectacular career and personality. In the words of his biographer, Coxe, "his understanding was more solid than brilliant." He himself disclaimed "Court ambition" and had "very little interested views" but made reduction of the nation's debt the main aim of his administration. Yet "Harry the Ninth" was a leading minister from 1743, when he was promoted from paymaster to First Lord of the Treasury and Chancellor of the Exchequer, until his death in 1754; from 1746 at least he was in effect prime minister, as his brother acknowledged. During this period he established such an ascendancy in the House that opposition virtually ceased. In November

1753 there were no amendments to the royal address. In his time, more than even in Walpole's, stability was achieved by a minister who enjoyed the confidence both of king and Parliament. This was the Whiggery, "the politics of stock-jobbers, and the religion of infidels" which the Tory Dr. Johnson denounced. The collapse of opposition had an unhealthy aspect. It was the triumph of a system which depended upon securing personal allegiance by individual bargains: "men before measures." At the same time the system provided a period of tranquillity during which useful reforms could be promoted. Such measures as there were bore the stamp of Pelham's sane and reasonable mind, even where he did not initiate them. He was not a great man, but a deservedly well-liked one. He had the tenacity of Walpole, his mentor, who had made him paymaster in 1730, but without his coarseness and greed; the patience of Newcastle, his brother, to whose grasp of the system he owed his position, but without his pettiness. There was also tragedy in his life: after the death of his two sons in 1734 work may have been anodyne.

On February 10, 1746, after George II had proved more than usually difficult, Newcastle and Harrington, Secretaries of State, were followed into resignation by Pelham, Bedford, Gower, Monson, and Pembroke, the larger part of the ministry. Two days sufficed to show that George could not have an alternative ministry. The Pelhams therefore returned on their own terms: the supporters of Bath and Granville were dismissed. Pitt was brought in as paymaster and appropriate honors were distributed among "the old gang." It was a decisive political victory for the old Whigs against the new, as well as a constitutional event of some note. By 1746, every important politician had been drawn into the Pelham circle. The Pelhams were effective because they operated as leaders of the group in which every man had his place. Henry Pelham confirmed the mastery of the group by his skillful conduct of business in the Commons; it was also a tribute to him that George II came not only to accept but apparently to trust his administration. There were tensions such as arose over the disagreements about foreign policy between Newcastle and Harrington and the fall of the latter after Newcastle's persistent interference in his business. In this Newcastle was acting, in his own intrusive and fussy manner, in the interests of George II. On the whole, however, the triumph of the Pelhams was owing to the fact that Henry Pelham had the trust both of the king and of Parliament. He had temporarily solved the dilemma of the century, the legacy of the Glorious Revolution.

Pelham regarded peace as worth almost any price and celebrated the Treaty of Aix in 1748 with drastic reductions in the size of the armed forces: the navy from 51,000 to 10,000 in two years, the army from 50,000 to 18,850. He balanced the budget within four years and was able to reduce the Land Tax. Unpreparedness for the next war was the price of these economies, but they found general favor. He simplified the management of the National Debt, swollen alarmingly to £77 million, and secured the reduction of the interest to a uniform three percent: the "consols" as the new consolidated stock came to be called. This involved him in a running battle with the vested interests in the city, the financial rings which had floated loans on the basis of a closed subscription. His success in the battle, gained by conciliation and firmness, provided an example of the good effects of continuity of administration of the sort that the Pelham system provided.

Pelham promoted measures to stimulate trade: he supported Oglethorpe's Bill of 1750 creating the Free British Fishery Company to develop the herring industry, and allowed the export of wool from Ireland, hitherto forbidden. Despite his brother's nervous warnings about the indignation of the populace, he supported Chesterfield's measure for Reform of the Calendar and he spoke warmly in favor of the Jew Naturalization Bill in 1753, aware perhaps of his obligation to Gideon, the city banker, for support of his policy; but he allowed his brother, and mob clamor, to cause its repeal in the same year. Whig oligarchs could not afford to be insensitive to public opinion in the year before an election. The growth of gin drinking had not been checked by Walpole's Act of 1736 and its degrading effects were brought home to public opinion, already conscious of the brutality and violence among the lower classes in the larger towns, by the satirical prints of Hogarth. "Gin Lane" and its illicit vendors were brought under control by Nugent's bill, the Tippling Act of 1751. In 1753 Hardwicke, Lord Chancellor and the faithful ally of the Pelhams, steered through his Marriage Act to control clandestine and irregular marriages. Henry Fox, though a member of the administration, defended the "Fleet marriages" and labeled Hardwicke "a giant spider." There was room for public as well as personal disagreements within the loosely bound administrations of the time. Much of the legislation of the years of the Pelham supremacy was humdrum, much directed toward private interests, enclosure, turnpike road building. Some was directed toward the perennial problem of the smuggler; there was a medley of measures to deal with specific problems: the width of wagon wheels, for instance. The record reveals a steady advance in the economic strength of the country and a slow-growing interest in the morality of society. Respectable, amiable but shrewd, Pelham was a loss to his friends and to his country. He was the only eighteenth-century "prime minister" to die in office. Now there ensued a prolonged period of political instability. His king recognized his worth and his comment is no bad memorial: "Now I shall have no more peace."

Coxe, *Memoirs . . . of Henry Pelham*, 2 vols., 1829.
J. B. Owen, *Rise of the Pelhams*, 1957.
J. Wilkes, *A Whig in Power, The Political Career of Henry Pelham*, 1964.

RICHARD BOYLE, 3rd EARL OF BURLINGTON (1695–1753) is the embodiment of eighteenth-century "taste." An engraving by Hogarth, "The Man of Taste," of about 1732, depicts the great gateway of Burlington House in Piccadilly. William Kent is standing on the pediment; Pope is on a scaffold whitewashing the front and bespattering passers-by below him. Ascending the ladder is a laborer, Lord Burlington himself. His house is now the Royal Academy, and *The Burlington Magazine* is the principal journal of art history. More than any other man this generous and devoted nobleman was responsible for the trend of architecture in the early eighteenth century, away from the native baroque of Vanbrugh and Hawksmoor, toward a stricter Italianate style.

Richard Boyle, who had succeeded to his father's estates at the age of nine and was educated by a private tutor, spent several years in Italy before he was twenty-one and there acquired his passion for Palladian architecture. There too he met the painter William Kent, who was to be his life-long associate, and encouraged him to undertake architecture. Burlington soon made his mark in London, to the admiration of Horace Walpole, who was entranced by the Palladian conversion of the house which Burlington inherited, the new facade and balustrade and its curving colonnade which linked the wings flanking the forecourt after the manner of St. Peter's. This house became a center of artists and writers. Kent lived there, Handel for a time; Pope, Swift, and Gay were constant visitors. The house has been transformed in the process of turning it into an art gallery, but the elegant Chiswick House, now faithfully restored, can be seen today as Burlington designed it, in Lord Hervey's words "too small to inhabit and too large to hang to one's watch." Burlington designed other houses, such as General Wade's in Old Burlington Street which again arouses the criticism that it was very fine on the outside but uncomfortable to live in. Houses which imitate the Italian tend to be drafty in the English climate. Burlington was essentially academic in his approach, and he carried out an extensive literary propaganda to convert the taste of wealthy patrons to the pure principles of Palladio and his followers. In this he was helped by the fashion that set in after 1713 for travel to Italy and especially to Venice.

To what extent was Burlington's a creative mind? How much did Kent and other architects, such as Campbell, do for him? The question is unlikely to be resolved, for it turns largely on technical questions about which authorities differ. Horace Walpole assumed that Burlington designed his buildings. The earl's own designs were, he thought, "more classic and chaste than Kent's," but "he was more studious to extend his friend's fame than his own." It seems probable, however, that Burlington sketched and determined the main features of the buildings he "designed," leaving his professional helpers to turn out the working drawings. Certainly he was influential and, unlike so many patrons, surprisingly modest. Indeed, little is known of his personality or private life. During his last years he lived quietly and took small part in artistic movements.

WILLIAM KENT (1684?–1748) was a painter and a landscape gardener, but is known chiefly as the leading architect of the Burlington school. The early eighteenth century in England witnessed a reaction against the baroque style of architecture whose principal monuments in England were St. Paul's Cathedral and Blenheim Palace. Young gentlemen traveling to France and Italy on the Grand Tour contemplated the relics of classical antiquity, and saw that they were good. The publication in 1715 of Colen Campbell's *Vitruvius Britannicus* and of a translation of Palladio's *I quattro libri dell'architettura* reminded connoisseurs of the fundamental canons of classical architecture, as formulated by Vitruvius in the time of the Emperor Augustus, and as resuscitated by Palladio in the sixteenth century. Judged by these canons, the later work of Wren, much of the work of Vanbrugh, Archer, and Hawksmoor, indeed all work denoting the baroque style, was seen to be impure, even barbaric. Of English architects, only Inigo Jones was admitted within the pale; and, under the talented patronage of Lord Burlington (1695–1753), a school of architecture developed in England to a pitch of dominance, which assumed that the architecture of antiquity was a comprehensive system, and regarded as an impertinent solecism any detail which could not be justified by the severe precepts of Vitruvius, Palladio, and Jones. In this movement, Burlington's most conspicuous colleagues were Colen Campbell (who rebuilt Burlington House for him) and William Kent.

Burlington had met the young Kent in 1714 in Rome, where Kent had gone to study, not architecture, but painting. In spite of the disparity of rank—for Kent had been promoted from a humble station by the generosity of Yorkshire squires who sent him to study in Rome "donec Raphael secundus ens"—a friendship grew up between them which, while it went deeper than a common interest in the arts, bore its most precious fruit in the artistic collaboration of the two right up to the death of Kent in 1748.

Burlington brought Kent home to England in 1719, set him to work on the decorative painting at Burlington House, and soon contrived to have him substituted for Sir James Thornhill, the sergeant painter himself, in the painting of the interior of Kensington Palace. But Kent was never more than an indifferent painter; and Burlington, poring over Palladio's drawings, and recognizing perhaps the true direction of Kent's genius, gave him (in 1724) the job of editing a book to be entitled *The Designs of Inigo Jones*. The book was published three years later, augmented with designs by Burlington and Kent, and the work on it seems to have decided Kent's career. Though he continued as a painter and was even appointed portrait painter to the king in 1739, he was now properly an architect, and an architect who, on being appointed to high positions in the Board of Works in the 1730s, exhaled in all his official tasks (and despite his fifty years of life) the fresh if austere breath of Palladianism. The outstanding products of his official work were the Horse Guards in Whitehall (completed to his designs after his death), the Royal Mews (demolished 1830), and the Treasury Buildings. He projected, but never realized, the new Royal Palace and Houses of Parliament.

Meanwhile he had been busy on private commissions also. As early as 1727, he was helping Burlington with the interior of his Chiswick villa, that epitome of English Palladianism, a worthy imitation of Palladio's own Villa Rotonda near Vicenza. He worked on the interior of Sir Robert Walpole's house of Houghton (newly built for him by Campbell) and was then engaged by the Earl of Leicester to design Holkham Hall. Kent's designs were later executed, and even modified, by his pupil Brettingham; but Holkham is Kent's (and, through Kent, Burlington's) memorial in domestic architecture. The exterior, which is like that of the Horse Guards without the clock-tower, is severe enough, massive, and overplain; but the interior, where Kent allowed himself some deviation from the strictest rules, is very fine, and shows how adroitly and carefully he could realize his idea (which the brothers Adam adopted); that an architect should be responsible equally for the internal details, down to the *trivialia* of furniture. The majestic hall, designed to display Lord Leicester's antiquities, is the *coup de maitre*—though it was shortly to be rivaled by Kent's hall at 44 Berkeley Square.

In short, Kent laid a finger of style on houses all over England, and even on cathedrals. But the country houses of England owe another debt to him. For, not content with his architecture and his painting, with designing furniture, with illustrating books, and with sculpture (he designed for Scheemakers and Rysbrack), he conceived a new plan for landscape gardening. The formal gardens of the seventeenth century irked him: the notion that the garden was something distinct, a portion of nature civilized and enclosed from the uncouth wild. Influenced by the landscapes of Claude, he "leaped the fence, and saw that all Nature was a garden." It was a pleasure to him to contrast the formality of the great house itself with studied informality in its surroundings; to dislocate the equipment of the formal garden—the ornamental water, the parterres, the temples—and scatter them about serpentine alleys far from the house; and to use sunken fences to prolong the view over the nearer lawns to the sweep of the park beyond. Rousham is Kent's masterpiece here.

The artist, versatile if not illustrious, died a painful death, and, as he had long made Burlington House his home, so he was buried in the vault of his patron, fellow-artist, and friend, at Chiswick.

M. Wilson, *William Kent: Architect, Designer, Painter, Gardener, 1685–1748*, 1985.

JOHN MICHAEL RYSBRACK (1693–1770), sculptor, a Fleming of an artistic family, came to England in 1720 as not the earliest, but (bar Roubiliac) the most distinguished, of that irruption of foreign sculptors which dominated English sculpture in the first half of the eighteenth century and breathed new life into the native school. He came with an introduction to James Gibbs, the architect, and was at once engaged in carving, from Gibbs' designs, a series of works which included a bust of the Earl of Nottingham. The bust is significantly a portrait in the Roman manner—not that veneration of the antique was anything very new, but that it was more closely observed in the days when victorious Englishmen were first making the Grand Tour, building houses in the Palladian style, and really thought themselves a Rome revived. By the time of Flaxman, the attitude had become regnant in English sculpture. But it is the blending of the antique with the late baroque which made, and makes, the particular attraction of Rysbrack's work.

To which it must be added that he was a supreme portrait sculptor in the years falling between the death of Kneller (1723) and the return of Reynolds from Rome in 1753, when much of the finest portraiture in England was done in terra-cotta and marble. Indeed portrait sculpture, which had too often been simply the perquisite of funeral monuments, came of age in the hands of Rysbrack and Roubiliac, as an autonomous class of English art, that of the portrait bust, greatly prized for its heroic associations. By 1732, Rysbrack had done sixty or more busts, often in two versions (terra-cotta, then marble). Among the contemporary portraits were Gibbs himself and Alexander Pope, both brilliantly figured; but there were also heroes of the past, the Black Prince and Oliver Cromwell, Spenser and Milton, emblems of England's glory, busts of a sort which went to honor the libraries and grottoes of the new palaces, and fill the Temple of British Worthies at Stowe. Rysbrack went on to do busts of the royal family (e.g., the tender "Queen Caroline," *c.* 1739, in the Wallace Collection), the prime minister (Walpole, 1738, N.P.G.), and a long list of aristocrats, writers, artists and professional men.

Not that, in giving currency to the bust, he neglected the funeral monument, the traditional forum of English sculpture: in 1731 his monument to Sir Isaac Newton was revealed, perhaps the finest postmedieval tomb in Westminster Abbey, and in about 1732 the monument to the 1st Duke of Marlborough at Blenheim. To say that in both of these he worked partly from designs by the architect

William Kent is not to depreciate the large contribution of the sculptor: the animated figures are carved in perfect equilibrium within the formal pyramid, the expression is restrained and very moving. Rysbrack had always more restraint than Roubiliac: he tended to prefer the ideal above the real, and what is taken from naturalism is given to nobility. After 1750—perhaps owing to the rise of Reynolds and Gainsborough—the number of his portrait commissions fell off, but he kept his freshness, even modified his style, and continued to create monuments which are the treasures of our churches.

LOUIS FRANÇOIS ROUBILIAC (1695–1762), one of the greatest English sculptors—if he can be called English—was born at Lyons and came to England only in his thirties. But he was the greatest of the immigrant artists who transfigured English sculpture in the first half of the eighteenth century—greater than Scheemakers and Delvaux, greater even than Rysbrack—and all his mature work was done in the country of his adoption.

Born therefore in the city which had bred Coysevox, trained by Permoser, the German sculptor who had learned the baroque from Bernini himself, working in a Paris indelibly marked by the artistic hegemony of Le Brun—a variety of influences went to the making of Roubiliac's style. What emerged was something relatively simple and composite and very much in tune with the France of Louis XV: Roubiliac was a rococo sculptor, by which we understand that he accelerated the broad emphatic *andante* of baroque into something more mercurial and more elegant—like a musical change into semiquaver time. Rococo sculpture is particular about details; it rejoices in density of rhythms, in a multiplicity of surface planes; it would rather record a transitory mood than an immortal longing; it finds the real physiognomy—"warts and everything"— more to the taste than the ideal. Rapid movement is of the essence of such sculpture; and drapery is no longer suffered to fall in patterns of its own, but is sought in aid to accentuate the movement of the figure below it. Take, for example, Roubiliac's statue of Forbes of Culloden in the Parliament Hall in Edinburgh: see here how multiplied detail can avoid confusion: the features are unflattering, the veins stand up in the hands and stockinged legs; the deep curls of the wig, the stiff creases in the satin robes, make a hundred little rhythms; beam light on the statue, and the light disintegrates on a thousand angled planes; yet all these particulars are drilled into informing the single, superb gesture of pacification. Or compare one of Roubiliac's busts of Pope with Rysbrack's: the one explores the lines of pain, in pity it portrays the magnificent cripple; the other forgoes the pathos in its eagerness to declare the nobility of the poet. Each is a masterpiece; only the point of view is different.

On his arrival in England in the early 1730s, chance gave Roubiliac a patron in Edward Walpole, the natural son of the prime minister. Through Walpole he met the sculptor Sir Henry Cheere, who obtained for him his first commission, a statue of Handel for the Vauxhall Gardens. Tyers, promoter of the Gardens, pleased with Roubiliac's skill, found him sitters for busts. His advancement, as it was made in the shadow of his predecessors, was a little slow; but by 1745 he was teaching sculpture at Hogarth's Academy in St. Martin's Lane, a popular and respected figure. Already he had done some distinguished work: the busts of Pope which have been mentioned, and a bust of Hogarth (N.P.G.) which is that pugnacious humorist to the letter; and he was to go from strength to strength in this vein, showing special aptitude for the portrayal of ugly men, but also (in 1751–57) creating, from painted portraits and from his own imaginative genius, the series of past celebrities of Trinity College, Cambridge.

In the 1740s he began on his great series of funerary monuments, of which it is to be noticed as an innovation that the central figure, the commemorated, no longer reclines in an attitude of postmortal calm, but regularly takes a part in the action of the group. And such action is often most vigorous and dramatic. The Duke of Argyll, cast as the dying hero, is certainly calm enough amid a scene of activity (1745, Westminster Abbey); but Bishop Hough (1746, Worcester Cathedral) starts up like a latter-day St. Paul, blinded by heavenly light; while Captain Hargrave in the abbey (1757) is trapped between the toppling pyramid of Time and the discomfiture of Time himself and Death. As for the abbey monument to Lady Elizabeth Nightingale (1761), where Death, again a skeleton, emerges from below the tomb and stabs at the unfortunate lady—well, that is a byword for the dramatic monument and is certainly a trifle grotesque. By way of contrast, to see what Roubiliac could achieve in a mood of serenity and grace, one should go to the monuments of the Duke and Duchess of Montagu in Warkton Church (Northamptonshire) or, better still, to the ante-chapel of Trinity College, to the perfectly noble statue, that of Sir Isaac Newton,

> with his prism and silent face,
> The marble index of a mind for ever
> Voyaging through strange seas of thought, alone.

JOHN HARRISON (1692–1776), chronometer maker, was one of the finest of the instrument makers who advanced the science of measurement during the eighteenth century. In 1726 he devised a self-compensating gridiron pendulum and a maintaining mechanism by means of which a clock continues to go during winding. Seamen had long been thwarted by the difficulty of calculating longitude. In 1714 the board of longitude at Greenwich was empowered to grant rewards of up to £20,000 to encourage research into the problem. Harrison made the breakthrough by his inventions, and his chronometer, modified by others and assuming its modern form about 1785, became the standard instrument. It was long before he received his reward, the whole sum coming only after he had completed the fifth chronometer of the series in 1773. He was opposed by the astronomer Maskelyne, who preferred the method of stellar observation, but there was no denying his accuracy. The chronometer, which is really a large watch, with a heliacal balance-spring, the whole being suspended in gimbals and poised to stay horizontal despite movements of the ship, kept time to within a minute in six months. Cook was one of many whose voyages would have been less successful if it had not been for the work of "chronometer Harrison."

JAMES EDWARD OGLETHORPE (1696–1785), Tory, philanthropist, colonial planter, is an interesting figure to meet in Hanoverian England. He saw service as an ensign in the last campaigns of the Peninsular War and later in the army of Prince Eugene that captured Belgrade in 1717. In 1722 he entered the House of Commons and soon acquired a Jacobite label by his defense of Bishop Atterbury. There was, anyway, little prospect of advancement for a member of his robust Tory views. He remained in Parliament and in 1750 promoted a useful bill to improve the herring fishery, but he found more congenial work in prison reform. He was roused by the fate of a friend, one Castell, who was imprisoned for debt in the Fleet and there died of smallpox. In 1729, he secured a parliamentary inquiry which unearthed conditions of squalor: malnutrition, barbarous use of manacles and the thumbscrew, and the lack of basic sanitary amenities which caused endemic jail-fever. The main assault on the state of the prisons had to await the efforts of John Howard and Elizabeth Fry; Oglethorpe's investigations, meanwhile, set him on to his great project, the settlement of Georgia, since he came to think that colonies provided the most practical means of relieving the misery of the poor.

In 1732 he obtained a charter for a new colony south of the river Savannah. He stated his aim in a pamphlet as: "The increase of our people, and the employment and support it (the colony) will afford to great numbers of our own poor, as well as foreign persecuted protestants." Walpole was indifferent, but the scheme was widely backed by philanthropists such as Lord Egmont and Thomas Coram, several bishops and the SPCK Private subscriptions amounted to £18,000, including £600 from the king. To ensure a spirit of self-help, he enacted that there should be no slave labor; he recruited poor men but tried to avoid wasters and tramps. In 1732 he sailed with 120 pioneers; they were followed by some Moravians who had been driven out of Austria because of their quietist views, and some Scottish highlanders. Townships were founded at Savannah and Frederic. For two years Oglethorpe ruled the colony by his masterful personality, but when he left in 1734 the settlers ignored his stern ordinances, squabbled, and drank the forbidden rum. The next year he came back with the Wesley brothers to provide for the spiritual needs of the colony. Great though the colony's impact was upon the Wesleys, their spiritual mission was a failure.

Upon the outbreak of war with Spain in 1739, Oglethorpe had to look to the colonists' defense against more tangible enemies; he raised a volunteer regiment of 600 in England and made bargains with Indian chiefs. By bluff and bravery the Spanish were foiled in their attacks. Whitefield, who had taken the place of the Wesleys, thought that the 500 colonists had been saved by divine providence; it was certainly not the work of the English government, who neglected to make any financial provision for their defense. To raise money, Oglethorpe returned home in 1743 but found himself called on for service in the Jacobite rebellion of 1745, under the Duke of Cumberland. Defeated in a small skirmish in Westmorland, he was then court-martialed: his alleged Jacobite past was recalled, but he was acquitted. He did not return to America but lived on at home to a great age, long enough to see, first, the trustees give up their charter to the Crown in 1754, later the secession of the colonies of America from the mother country.

His ambitious plantation brought him disappointment, but he was ever a man to be "animated rather than daunted" by his difficulties. Alert, dapper, a little Punch-like in profile, he was a trusted friend of Dr. Johnson and he makes some pleasant appearances in Boswell's *Life*, arguing against luxury, defending dueling, or expounding upon the adventures of his life.

A. A. Ettinger, *James Edward Oglethorpe*, 1936.

WILLIAM WARBURTON (1698–1779), theologian, a voluminous and controversial writer upon many topics, occupied a larger place in the view of his contemporaries than seems to be justified either by his scholarship or his personality. The son of George Warburton of Newark and of Elizabeth Holman, he was educated at Oakham School and articled to an attorney. He forsook law for Holy Orders, but never lost the lawyer's method and manner. He was presented in 1723, by the influence of a patron, with a Cambridge degree. Was there some element of inferiority complex in his assertive careerism? Whatever the cause, he was as earnest in his pursuit of influence as he was ruthless with men or ideas that he disagreed with. He passed from living to living; Greasely, Brant Broughton, Frisby all knew his name, but his energies were given to study and writing. He described his life as one of "warfare on earth; that is to say with bigots and libertines." He saw himself as animated by a desire for truth and regard for the Church of England, which might have been derived "solely from the contemplation of nature and the unvariable reason of things." His writing was intemperate, his arguments paradoxical to the point sometimes of absurdity, and his defense of the Church, on the grounds of convenience and discipline, unspiritual and unconvincing. Formidable in learning, he yet lacked common sense and restraint. He attacked with relish deists, atheists, Methodists; most of his intelligent contemporaries were fools, knaves, or "cox-combs"—a favorite word. Johnson, Smollett, Garrick, Young, Priestley, all were damned in turn. The Moravian hymn book was "a heap of blasphemous and beastly nonsense." With *The Divine Legation of Moses Demonstrated* (first part 1737, second part 1741) and *The Alliance between Church and State* he established a name, however, for solid advocacy. Though he may have been to Bentley a man of "monstrous appetite and bad digestion," Dr. Johnson, pleased by his assault on Bolingbroke, dubbed him "the last man who has written with a mind full of reading and reflection." In 1738 he became chaplain to the Prince of Wales and prebends followed. The highest rewards were nevertheless slow to come. Not until 1757 did he become Dean of Bristol, in 1760 Bishop of Gloucester. He married an exceedingly lively girl, the daughter of Ralph Allen of Bath. Perhaps his closest friend was Bishop Hurd, the scholarly divine who was eccentric enough to refuse the primacy. It should be added that some of his targets were worthy ones: a famous sermon in 1766 denounced the slave trade.

Warburton seems to have been lukewarm in his own religious life. Was he also insincere in his theology, which often seems to be an academic exercise, devoid of feeling? For instance, the main argument of *The Divine Legation* was the paradoxical one that Mosaic laws must be divine in origin, since they did not contain a doctrine that was socially essential. Isaac Disraeli believed that he was inspired by "the secret principle" of "invention," a love of novelty for its own sake. He was an admirer of Bayle whom he resembles in erudition and liking for logical exercise. His failing was most in sensitiveness. He could accept no limitations to his sphere. He complacently put out the theory that Gothic architecture developed from the habit of "this northern people having been accustomed to worship the Deity in groves" and he produced an unusually bad edition of Shakespeare (1747). When he became a friend of Pope and was left as his literary executor, he became involved in a savage quarrel with Bolingbroke. His gifts might have made him a splendid lawyer. As it was, he served a God whom by his reasoning he reduced to the status of "a mere heap of verbal formulae."

Leslie Stephen, *History of English Thought in the Eighteenth Century*, 3rd ed., Vol. I, Chap. VII, 1902.
A. W. Evans, *Warburton and the Warburtonians*, 1932.

JOHN WESLEY (1703–91), evangelist and founder of Methodism, by his fervent preaching and good organization, reawakened in thousands a sense of personal religion and created a movement of lasting social importance.

He was one of the youngest of nineteen children born to Susannah and Samuel Wesley at the rectory of Epworth. His father was a stern man who made it his life's work to minister to the primitive people of the North Lincolnshire marshlands. His own father and grandfather had been ejected from the Church in the purge of 1662, but Samuel was a High Churchman, a supporter of Sacheverell, and an irrepressible character; arrested once for debt, he had taken the opportunity to catechize his fellow prisoners in Lincoln jail. His wife came of good family and was proficient in Latin and Greek. She educated the children herself and inculcated in them her own intense faith in God. Concern for salvation and abhorrence of sin, a sense of living precariously between extremes, pervaded this household and affected the lives of all the children. The girls endured varying degrees of unhappiness in love and marriage, but two of the boys, John and his younger brother Charles, repaid their training by ardent evangelism. John was rescued at the age of six from a fire that destroyed the vicarage, "a brand plucked from the burning" in his mother's phrase, and it is not fanciful to see a compelling sense of destiny even in his early years. From this isolated and self-supporting background he was sent to the Charterhouse and thence to Christ Church with an exhibition. Ordained deacon in 1725, he was made a fellow of Lincoln College in 1726. Here the influences of George Whitefield, then at Pembroke College, and his brother Charles, his own careful reading of religious works and thoroughness in everything he undertook, with a habit of rigorous self-analysis, helped to turn him from the conventional course of scholar and tutor. From Jeremy Taylor's works he absorbed something of Christian life; from the mystic William Law he learned to think of a "world sunk in sin" and to see the remedy in a change of spirit and in the deliberate cultivation of holiness that was needful "if a man is to be in the favor of God." Accepting the Bible as "the one, the only standard of truth and the only model of pure religion," he tried at the same time to train himself by methodical devotion to the fasts and ceremonies of the Church. The founder of Methodism was by instinct and design a High Churchman.

For two years he acted as curate for his father at the neighboring hamlet of Wroot. In 1729 he returned to Lincoln and founded, with Charles and fourteen undergraduates, the "Holy Club," whose austerities startled Oxford and killed one of its frailer members. They lay on the grass on frosty nights, fasted and denied themselves sleep, but they also visited sick people and prisoners. Their "methodism" had the approval of the Bishop of Oxford, but it was inward-looking for all its melodrama and challenge; it brought Wesley no sense of personal salvation and few of his companions went on with him to the next stage of development.

In 1735 he went with Charles to Georgia, General Oglethorpe's new colony, to bring the Gospel to the settlers and Indians. It was a disastrous venture into a more complicated society than he could have envisaged. John may have fallen in love with a Miss Hopkey, whom he subsequently banned from Communion when she married someone else; in a claustrophobic and hysterical situation he seems to have behaved willfully, and without much tact or self-control. So he was driven out amid recriminations which dogged him for years. He had, however, met on the voyage out some Moravian brothers whose notions of personal salvation seemed to answer his need. To the question of their pastor Spangenburg, "Does the spirit of God bear witness with your spirit that you are a child of God?" he thought he saw a clue to his future course. He attended Moravian meetings in London and talked to the brethren in a mood of contrition. On May 24, 1738, at Aldersgate he experienced the mystical experience which brought him the sense and glow of certainty; "I felt my heart strangely warmed. I felt that I did trust in Christ alone for salvation; and an assurance was given me that he had taken my sins, even mine, and saved me from the law of sin and death." This revelation was a moment of release and commitment for a new work. From then, until his death, Wesley's efforts were directed toward his personal mission to the country. "I look upon the world as my parish," he said.

During the next fifty-three years he traveled over 200,000 miles, preached over forty thousand sermons, read, wrote, edited, organized, and prayed. No second of his day was left to chance—an uncomfortable regimen, as Dr. Johnson found: "John Wesley's conversation is good but he is never at leisure. He is always obliged to go at a certain hour. This is very disagreeable to a man who loves to fold his legs and have out his talk as I do." We should not picture a wild fanatic. In his appearance he was small and neat, in manner calm. His directness of appeal, with the suggestion of pent-up force behind it, gained in emphasis by his restrained demeanor. He kept a journal which overflows with the spirit of missionary zeal but is free of the unctuousness which some of his followers displayed. It is a record of physical endurance and high courage; of the inspired and necessary egoism of the prophet. He wished to speak in churches and was reluctant to follow Whitefield's example and take to the fields. He was opposed, however, at all levels; not only by the prejudiced country parson but by the fairminded Butler, then Bishop of Bristol, to whom the style and content of his sermons was uncongenial, too direct, too "enthusiastic," and too liable to misinterpretation.

There was little space in the rational churchmanship of the eighteenth century for the personal appeal: Are you saved? Moreover Wesley's gradual estrangement from the Church was due to faults on both sides. Wesley thought nothing of infringing the cherished freehold of the vicar; his mission took no account of local circumstances; he displayed a spiritual pride and autocratic temper which justified his enemies' label "Pope John." Above all, his style of preaching caused hysteria and the instability of undirected religious feeling. For all that, Wesley's appeal was strong, because it supplied a need. The formal devotions of the church did not cater for the simple needs of the semiliterate and illiterate; its appointments and even its teaching reflected the class structure of the time. Large areas in the big towns and the new manufacturing and mining districts were missed out, because few adjustments were made to the traditional parishes. The need of these dispossessed folk drove Wesley to begin open-air preaching, beginning with a mass meeting of miners outside Bristol, and to start a new ministry outside the church. Step by step he moved toward schism, though he continued to profess membership of the Church. In 1739 he opened his first chapel; in 1744 he set up a central organization at the Foundry in London. Lay preaching led to lay ordination, a decision forced upon him by the needs of the rapidly growing church in North America, in 1784. By then there were 356 chapels, served by preachers operating in circuits. The basic unit was the class, a group of about a dozen members from one district; above this was the band, subdivided according to sex and then again into unmarried and married. These groups reproduced the ideal of the Holy Club: communal confession of sins, prayer, and giving. Even the poorest were expected to give something to the funds of the movement; the sense of responsibility this instilled, together with the puritan emphasis upon self-discipline, had an incalculable effect upon society in these years of accelerating industrial change.

Methodism, zealous, dynamic, coordinated, could have been a revolutionary force in a period ripe for revolution. That it was not was owing partly to the character of the founder. He was autocratic: the annual conference was simply a forum for his views and exhortations. He was also a profound conservative who denounced the American colonists as rebels and the French revolutionaries as children of Satan. He believed that society could be transformed only by individual and spiritual conversions. Salvation was not for him the end, nor preordained as Calvinists taught: it must be proved by good works, by practicing the qualities of thrift and temperance. Wesley was intellectually curious (he was much impressed by a lecture of Benjamin Franklin's about electricity and embarked upon experiments of his own), but he was also absurdly credulous. He believed in witches, and to find guidance in any problem he would open the Bible at random. With his absorption in his mission, it was inevitable that he should become narrow in his interests. He liked to sing but he was blind to beauty; the theatre he regarded as "Satan's own ground." He may have been no more than naive and insensitive, but his conduct was exasperating enough to cause estrangement from his wife. His life was indeed too much swallowed up by his work for satisfactory personal relationships. He married Mrs. Vazeille, a merchant's widow of 41, in 1751. She was a scold, and he would not curtail his journeyings; they separated finally in 1776. His views about the upbringing of children would have been absurd if they had not been so influential. He believed that the rod was necessary to drive away the devil, that idle minutes were a danger to a child's soul, and that a knowledge of the Bible and of the catechism was sufficient education. The movement for primary education was positively discouraged by Methodist parents at a time when there was an ever increasing demand for child labor in mine and mill. Irrational in a rational age, enthusiastic among men who abhorred enthusiasm, conservative in its teaching to the miserably poor, puritan in the midst of slums, the paradoxes of Methodism reflect the paradoxes in the life of John Wesley.

N. Curnock, ed., *Journal of John Wesley*, 8 vols., 1909–16. (Everyman edition in 3 vols.)
C. E. Vulliamy, *John Wesley*, 1931.
R. E. Davies and E. G. Rupp, *A History of the Methodist Church in Great Britain*, Vol. 1, 1965.
B. Dobrée, *Three Eighteenth Century Figures*, 1962.
V. H. H. Green, *Young Mr. Wesley*, 1961.

CHARLES WESLEY (1707–88) was the younger brother of John and son of Samuel Wesley, the rector of Epworth. He became a sound scholar at Westminster and Christ Church and was ordained in 1735. In this year he went with John to Georgia as Oglethorpe's secretary. On his return he served for a spell as curate at Islington, but he soon became a regular itinerant preacher. From 1740 till he returned to London in 1771, he lived at Bristol. Less able than his famous brother and a less imposing personality, he was nonetheless an eloquent preacher. Though he mistrusted the raptures of the more fervent lay preachers, he expressed in his hymns the force and faith of a sensitive, poetic soul. In the Wesleys, ministry of conversion hymns played a large part, and Charles was prolific in the art of representing simple faith in essential terms. The lyrical force of the best of these hymns can still be felt. What is Advent without the impressive thunder of "Lo, he comes with clouds descending" or Christmas without "Hark, the herald angels sing"? "Love Divine, all loves excelling," and "Soldiers of Christ, arise," to name only two more, are among the best-loved hymns of English church people. He may have written as many as 7,000 hymns, for he had the inexhaustible vitality of his family. In the words of John's preface to the collection of 1780, which included also some from Watts and some translations from the German, the hymns formed "a little body of experimental and practicing Divinity." Imperative, urgent, vivacious, less astringent than those of Donne and Herbert, but surer in sentiment than those of most of the nineteenth-century writers, Charles Wesley's hymns have played a large part in both Anglican and Nonconformist worship.

He married in 1749 a Welshwoman, Sarah Gwynne, whose beautiful singing voice led the singing in his congregation. Their two sons, Charles and Samuel, make their mark in turn as organists and composers. The latter entered the Roman Catholic faith in 1784. His father was no more distressed by this than he was by

John's decision in the same year to ordain his own ministers; he was essentially a moderate, conservative man.

M. F. Brailsford, *A Tale of Two Brothers*, 1954.

SELINA, COUNTESS OF HUNTINGDON (1707–91), "Queen of the Methodists," as Horace Walpole called her, was a formidable patron of the evangelical revival of the eighteenth century. Her fame has been obscured by the achievements of the Wesleys; theirs became the central movement while her puritan connection was rejected alike by Church and Methodists. But the impact of her personality and the scale of her achievement were both immense. She may be seen as one of the greatest of female eccentrics, "Pope Joan," or as a noble "Mother in Israel" (Whitefield's description). Either way her sincerity and power are undeniable.

Second daughter and coheiress of the second Earl Ferrers, she was lucky in her husband, Theophilus, 9th Earl of Huntingdon, who accepted without fuss the enthusiasms of his wife, embarrassing though they must sometimes have been. His own sisters, who were notably pious, contributed to the evolution of a proud woman with a strong sense of duty into a single-minded missionary. "Since I have known and believed on the Lord Jesus Christ for life and salvation," she declared, "I have been as happy as an angel." She turned her house in Leicestershire, Donington Park, into a center of religious life where, said Whitefield, "We have the sacrament every morning, heavenly conversation all day, and preach at night." Maids and gardeners were examined about the state of their souls, and two schools were set up for the religious teaching of local children. But her main effort was directed toward the improvement of the upper classes where, as she saw, cynicism and loose morals stemmed from the decline of personal religion and the increase of wealth, without a corresponding sense of duty. In her drawing room the luminaries of society were exposed to the preaching and prayers of her evangelists. Polite acquiescence was the most she could get from men like Chesterfield or Bolingbroke. The Duchess of Suffolk, George II's mistress, thought that Whitefield's remarks were aimed at her. The Duchess of Buckingham thought it "monstrous to be told that you have a heart as sinful as the common wretches that crawl upon the earth" and could not "but wonder that your Ladyship should relish sentiments so much at variance with high rank and good breeding." Some, however, were converted: Lady Frances Gardner; two sisters of Lord Chesterfield and his ex-mistress who, as Horace Walpole said, bestowed "the dregs of her beauty on Jesus Christ"; Lord and Lady Dartmouth. Elegant chapels were built or restored in London and the fashionable spas. The chapel at Bath, with its comfortable red cushions and air of sober luxury—a balcony for elect ladies and a special pew, with its separate mahogany entrance, for visiting clergy who might want discreetly to hear the Word—expresses the flavor of Lady Huntingdon's work.

Lord Huntingdon died in 1746 leaving her in control of family and fortune. She assumed the leadership of the Calvinist element among the Methodists. She gave money to many causes, Whitefield's mission to Georgia and his tabernacle in England, to deserving preachers and not always deserving beggars. Besides her own personal following of enthusiastic men in and outside the Church, she controlled a connection that grew to include over seventy chapels. Despite uncertain health she worked intensely, corresponding, lobbying, organizing at every level. Preachers were saved from being pressed into the army, Garrick was persuaded to take off a play which contained a skit on Whitefield, her homicidal cousin, urged to repent (and prevented from seeing his mistress) in his last hours before being executed for murdering his steward. George III admired her and, on her prompting, delivered Archbishop Cornwallis a strong rebuke for holding unseemly routs at Lambeth on Sundays. "I wish there was a Lady Huntingdon in every diocese," he said to a bishop who complained of her interference. Her work was aided by a growing reaction against what she called the "system of heathen ethics, varnished over with the name of Christian morality," but she also helped to foster the new puritanism in a section of the ruling class.

In 1779 the Consistory Court of London disallowed her claim to appoint as chaplains as many Anglican priests as she wanted; she therefore registered her chapels as dissenting meeting houses. On the other flank she broke with Wesley when he and his followers rejected predestination; he also resented the intrusion of the countess and "my lady's preacher." After her death the connection did not grow. But the college which she founded at Trevecca, already the center of Howell Harris's crusading Methodism in Wales, produced trained, godly pastors eager to preach the Gospel of salvation to a selected few. Today there are only thirty odd chapels left, mostly in the south. The college is now at Cambridge. Abroad there is an active mission in Sierra Leone that was founded in the year after her death. Dogmatic, humorless, narrow—these traits can be discerned perhaps in the lines of her long face, wearing what Edith Sitwell called a "sunken look of piety," thin-lipped and severe. She was also very brave. She nursed a friend through an attack of smallpox and she bore stoically the loss of two sons from smallpox.

S. Tytler, *The Countess of Huntingdon and her Circle*, 1967.

GEORGE WHITEFIELD (1714–70), religious revivalist, was the son of an innkeeper, though of clerical family. Like Dr. Johnson, he was a servitor at Pembroke College, Oxford, where he made the acquaintance of Charles Wesley. After his ordination in 1736 he began his life's work of preaching. He adopted the tactics already pioneered by Harris and Rowlands, who were engaged upon evangelical tours of Wales. When he was excluded from the pulpit by clergy who did not preach "the true doctrine of Christ," he preached in the open air. An ugly man with a squint, not always dressed in his canonicals, unrestrained in his language by scholarly scruples, he used to gain an extraordinary command of his audience. His vivid style and his habitual themes of death, judgment, and salvation had their greatest impact upon simple people. It was at a mass meeting of miners near Bristol, in 1739, that John Wesley became convinced that Whitefield's methods were justified, as a means of touching the people outside the parish system. His sincerity and passion also won more sophisticated minds. The diary of Lord Egmont, a devout churchman, records impressions of Whitefield after two sermons and a subsequent discussion. The service had begun with the singing of a psalm and "a long pathetic prayer." Then Whitefield "preached by heart with much earnestness and spreading his arms very wide and was at no loss for words, and the people were very attentive." Whitefield defended his methods: reprobates and dissenters, who would not normally go to church, might come from curiosity and go away edified. Egmont believed that he was sincere: "He does indeed work a considerable reformation among the common people." Less pious and more skeptical was Lord Chesterfield, who went to hear him from curiosity but was so caught up with Whitefield's account of the condition of the sinner trembling on the brink of the abyss as to exclaim: "Good God! He's gone!"

Whitefield went with the Wesleys to Georgia in 1737 and made altogether seven visits to the New World; on the last, he died, in a small town in Massachusetts. At first he wished for a broad evangelical front, along with the other dissenting sects. Unlike the Wesleys, he was not institutionally minded, and the hold of the established church was never strong. Later his breach with them was widened by his adoption of Calvinist tenets, notably that salvation was preordained. In 1741 he opened his first tabernacle in London. In 1748 he became chaplain to Selina, Countess of Huntingdon, the pious founder of the old connection, who patronized with her money and interest a number of evangelical preachers and chapels. Whitefield was derided by those to whom any sort of enthusiasm was absurd. Horace Walpole wrote that "he made more money than disturbances: his largest crops of proselytes lay among servant-maids; and his warmest devotees went to Bedlam without going to war"—allowing at least that the sermons were not inflammatory. His extravagances of language might cause hysteria but they also brought some color, hope, perhaps, into drab and hopeless lives.

L. Tyerman, *Life of Rev. George Whitefield*, 2 vols., 1876.
J. Downey, *The Eighteenth Century Pulpit*, 1969.
J. D. Walsh, "Origins of the Evangelical Revival" in G. V. Bennett and J. D. Walsh, *Essays in Modern Church History*, 1966.

JOHN WILLIAM FLETCHER (1729–85) was a saintly parish priest who found his vocation in serving an obscure Shropshire parish; he refused all offers of preferment but became one of the most influential voices of his day. Born Jean Guillaume de la Flèchere, he was of Swiss origin. From the time of a seemingly miraculous delivery from drowning, he resolved to devote himself to God. He came to England to earn a living and found employment with Mr. Hill of Tern Hall in Shropshire. In 1757 he was ordained, and in 1760 Hill presented him to the living of Madeley, a rough district now that mines were being opened up in the vicinity; here he stayed until his death. He wrote books, but said one of his admirers, "I would rather hear one sermon from Fletcher than read a volume of his works." People flocked to hear his sermons and he would also journey as much as twenty miles to preach, returning to his vicarage in the small hours of the morning. He was fragile but fearless; sometimes he would go round Madeley with a handbell to summon his parishioners to church. They were notoriously unruly, profane, drunken, preferring cockfights and bull-baiting to the ministrations of the Church, but "Fletcher spoke to their condition and won their respect." Memories linger in the neighborhood about Fletcher: he had "a lovely voice, a gentle, grave way and an enchanting smile" and "to know John Fletcher was to know a saint." On his death, thousands filed through his chamber to see his face.

LORD GEORGE ANSON (1697–1762) is especially well known for his wonderful voyage round the world from 1740 to 1744. He was the most important admiral of his time; thereafter he made a second career of naval administration which bore fruit in the victories of the Seven Years War.

He came from Staffordshire. As a nephew of Lord Macclesfield he was Whig in sympathy; through his father-in-law, Lord Hardwick, he was to acquire useful political connections. He entered the navy at 15, was a captain at 27. In 1739 he received command of a Pacific squadron of six vessels which was intended to synchronize with Admiral Vernon, operating in the West Indies. He sailed from Spithead in the *Centurion* in September 1740. With this ship alone out of six, and only 200 men, emaciated and weak, he returned to Spithead in June 1744. In the meantime he had made naval history. The preparation for the voyage reveals the incompetence of the government of the time. Instead of regular troops for storming parties he was provided with 500 Chelsea invalids. Most of these vanished before they could be got on board. Of those who sailed not one returned. When he eventually left he was short of sailors and too late to enjoy favorable winds to round the Horn. Meanwhile the Spanish knew all about his plan and were preparing their defenses. He avoided the Spanish fleet which was dispersed by storms. His squadron suffered in the terrible passage round the Horn; only four met at the rendezvous at Juan Fernandez (Robinson Crusoe's island), and scurvy had halved their crews. Anson captured a treasure ship and despoiled a town on the coast of Peru. As the sketches of Lieutenant Brett of the *Centurion* convey it, the voyage had idyllic moments as well as grim ordeals. Anson himself suffered from scurvy at one stage, but we see him too in a happier state, at Juan Fernandez, with his tent standing on a lawn between clear streams, surrounded by groves of sandalwood. Eventually they reached Macao in China. The remaining ships had to be scuttled and the crews transferred to the *Centurion*. Anson was the first British officer to pay a visit to the mainland of China; his calm, dignified manner fitted him well for this diplomatic exercise. Another prize, the *Nuestra Senora de Cabadongo* galleon, with a crew of 550 and armed to the teeth, fell to him off the Philippines. The treasure, of value £600,000, was later paraded in triumph through the City of London. Anson and his men had risen to great heights of courage and endurance. The commander himself, a self-contained man and noted for his silences, put his hand to any task, helped to carry the sick to land, worked to repair spars, and did other necessary jobs. He added a great deal to knowledge of the Pacific shores and islands by his careful charts and notes. By his endurance, his technical skill, even by his humanity and courtesy, he provided a superb example to the young officers in his squadron. When it is realized that these included Saunders, Saumarez, Augustus Keppel, Hyde Parker, Byron, and Howe, it will be evident that this voyage was also an invaluable school for seamen.

Anson served subsequently as a member of the Admiralty Board but in 1747, when news was received of large French preparations in dockyards for relief expeditions to India and Canada, he was put in command of a large fleet to watch in the Bay of Biscay. On May 3 he contacted de la Jonquiere's fleet coming out of harbor. In the subsequent chase all the French men-of-war were captured and most of the merchant vessels. Six weeks later, a detachment under Captain Fox fell upon another convoy and captured no less than forty-eight merchantmen. This destruction of commerce forced France to come to terms and crippled her efforts to defeat England in the colonies. It is astonishing that, with such clear evidence of the value of the fleet, the ministers should have cut the navy down to a quarter of its wartime strength as soon as peace was made. Anson became First Lord of the Admiralty in 1751, and his work should be seen against this background of cheeseparing. He cannot evade responsibility for the disaster of Byng at Minorca in 1756; the admiral was scandalously ill-equipped for his task. But the main cause of weakness was that insufficient money was allocated to the navy by ministers preoccupied with the

National Debt. The victories that followed during this war owed much to Anson's planning though, as with Ligonier and the army, it is difficult to apportion the credit justly between military and political heads. Perhaps he did more in the field of administration than of strategy; he introduced a more scientific method of classification, with a more intelligent program of building the ships. Thus there were eighty-two frigates available at the start of the Seven Years War. He could not do much to correct the disparity of sailing quality between French and English. But in 1761 trials with copper sheathing led to an improvement which gave the English an advantage for some time. The quality of the men promoted at this time and entrusted with the important tasks—Saunders, Keppel, Howe—testifies surely to Anson's soundness of judgment as well as to the flair of Pitt. All in all it was fortunate that the patronage he enjoyed helped his promotion to the Admiralty Board and that he remained head of it, with only a short break in 1756–57, from 1751 to 1762. He died a rich man, with a fortune in prize money and property carefully tended. His great house at Moor Park testified to his success in the world. But it may be that he was never quite so much at home in the boardroom of the Admiralty or among the apricots and plantations of Moor Park, as he had been on the quarterdeck of the *Centurion*.

K. Walker, ed., *Voyage Round the World in Years 1740–4*, 15th ed., 1780 (based on Anson's own notes).
Sir J. Barrow, *Life of Anson*, 1839.
At Greenwich Maritime Museum: a model of the *Centurion*, made in 1748, on Anson's order.

THE HONORABLE JOHN BYNG (1704–57), admiral, did not, like his father, Viscount Torrington, win an important naval battle. The fourth son of the victor of Cap Passaro, advanced in his career to some extent by the influence of his father, Byng died ignominiously, by firing squad, upon his own quarterdeck. The incident and the events that preceded it are of sufficient importance to warrant a study of the unfortunate man.

Byng's early progress was sedate. He had a reputation as a hard disciplinarian. On shore he made some effort to be a man of fashion, and he was for a time in Parliament; aboard ship he was conscientious but unentertaining. He sat upon the court-martial that sentenced Mathews, convicting him of acting "contrary to discipline, in breach of his duty, the Fighting Instructions, and to the great danger of His Majesty's fleet." Mathews' conduct at the battle of Toulon is a matter of controversy. For better or for worse he had left the line—which, by the firm tradition of his time, was tantamount to inviting disaster. Upon many seamen, the fate of Mathews and the captains under him who were also cashiered lay as a weighty warning. "Preserve the line" became dogma.

At best Byng was somewhat phlegmatic. When, however, in 1756, he was sent to the Mediterranean with a small fleet, ill-found and inadequately manned, to meet the French threat to Minorca, he did not lack experience. He had been posted before to Port Mahon and commanded in the Mediterranean in the last year of the previous war. When he found himself in action, on May 20, 1756, with de la Galissonière, commander of a fleet equal in numbers but superior in equipment, he was not at a loss. He even showed initiative in his choice of strategy, bearing down upon the enemy at a slant to avoid the full impact of his first broadside. But the plan went awry through misunderstanding, inadequate signals, and Byng's reluctance to shift from his plan to a straight drive toward the enemy. It was at this crucial moment of the battle, when urged to turn, that Byng made his revealing comment: "Remember," he said, "the misfortune of Mr. Mathews." De la Galissonière slipped away, having inflicted some damage to the rigging of the English ships. Byng then made a mistake far more serious than anything in the battle. He sailed back to Gibraltar, leaving Minorca to the French. It was not for this error in strategy that Byng was tried by court-martial, however, but for cowardice and negligence in the face of the enemy. On the second of these charges he was unjustly found guilty and condemned to death. For political reasons, mainly because of the public indignation about the loss of Minorca the following year, and because the king, with whom subtle argument did not weigh, was adamant, Byng received no reprieve. He went stoically to his death at Portsmouth in April 1757. Voltaire made play with the notion that in England they shot admirals "pour encourager les autres"—and the effects did prove to be stimulating. It should be said, however, that if Byng's plan had been carried out as he had intended he might have won a notable victory; and that the attitude which gave the authority of gospel to the Permanent Instructions, and the negligence and cheeseparing of the politicians should have been arraigned in court, along with the admiral who had failed to beat the French. Horace Walpole, who was impressed by his dignity during the trial, was moved by his end: "While he felt like a victim, he acted like a hero."

Dudley Pope, *Mr. Byng was Shot at Dawn*, 1957.

SIR EDWARD HAWKE, LORD HAWKE (1705–81) was one of the foremost seamen of his time. "You have done your duty in showing me the danger, now you will obey orders and lay me aside the Soleil Royal." These words, spoken at the start of the battle of Quiberon Bay, characterize the man and explain the transformation that he and like-minded officers brought about in the Hanoverian army.

Hawke did not make a spectacular rise in his early career. He became a post captain at the age of twenty-nine and proceeded thereafter by merit, assisted by only the lightest breeze of patronage, his uncle being Commissioner of Trade and Plantations. He later succeeded him in his parliamentary seat at Portsmouth. He was present at the action of Mathews and Lestock at Toulon in 1744, his ship being one of the few to be handled with spirit in a feeble engagement, followed by a court-martial: an object lesson to an ambitious officer. In 1747, still the youngest of the rear-admirals, he made his mark when he attacked an escorted convoy off Cape Finisterre. He sank six of the warships and his message to Pocock, cruising off the West Indies, enabled the convoy to be intercepted and forty to be taken as prizes. In this action he changed a correctly formed line into a general chase, every ship pursuing its own objective. Upon the renewal of war, Hawke was employed mostly in the blockading role. In 1756 he was sent out to the Mediterranean to succeed Byng, after the débâcle at Minorca. In 1757–59 he commanded in the Channel. The latter year is known to us as "the year of victories," but when it began, French invasion was a serious threat. At Brest and Rochefort, fleets were held ready to escort transports to England. Hawke's plan was a new one, though it became one of the regular uses of English sea power: a coastal blockade, maintained in all weathers. In November the French fleet slipped out of Brest and made for Quiberon Bay, where the ships that Conflans was to guard were lying at anchorage.

On the morning of the twentieth Hawke's ships sighted the enemy. A squally northwesterly wind was blowing, and Hawke took a calculated risk when he decided to engage, on a lee shore, in high seas, among the shoals of an uncharted coast. He was justified because Conflans was caught in a trap. Seven of his ships were destroyed, others stranded; his fleet was broken up and the invasion put off. Hawke's dispatch closes on a memorable note: "When I consider the season of the year, the hard gales on the day of action, a flying enemy, the shortage of the day, and the coast they were on, I can boldly affirm that all that could possibly be done has been done . . ." Hawke had had somewhat strained relations with the Admiralty up to this point. He tended to be autocratic and was highhanded in matters such as provisioning. But he was always careful of the interests of his men, their diet as well as their discipline. It was not his fault that they were neglected afterward. As the sailors' sharp ditty put it:

> Ere Hawke did bang
> Monsieur Conflans
> You sent us beef and beer.
> Now Monsieur's beat
> We've nought to eat
> Since you have nought to fear.

Hawke was First Lord of the Admiralty from 1766 to 1771, but he was no more successful than his successor Sandwich in arresting the decay of the fleet upon a peacetime budget. When the fleet was called upon for action in the brief crisis which followed Spain's attack on the Falkland Isles, it was found to be sadly inadequate. Indeed Hawke's contribution to the navy was more in the sphere of tactics and in the inculcation of fighting spirit. Many of his captains, who witnessed the daring seamanship of Quiberon Bay— Keppel, Graves, Gambier, Alexander Hood, and Howe—were to be admirals in the War of American Independence. They had received a vital lesson in the value of sea power.

R. F. Mackay, *Admiral Hawke*, 1965.
G. Marcus, *Quiberon Bay*, 1960.

SIR EDWARD BOSCAWEN (1711–61), admiral, joined the navy from the aristocratic Whig background which flavored the politics and personalities of the navy in the middle of the eighteenth century when such men rose to be admirals. He was a talented officer of great spirit, whose victory at Lagos, together with Hawke's at Quiberon Bay, emphasized the importance of sea power at a time when England was threatened by invasion.

Boscawen, the third son of Viscount Falmouth, distinguished himself first at the taking of Porto Bello by Admiral Vernon in 1739 and at the siege of Cartagena in 1741. He had an important part in Hawke's victory off Cape Finisterre in 1747, where he was wounded in the shoulder. Perhaps it was because of this and for his habit of carrying his head on one side, that he was called "wry-necked Dick." He was also "old Dreadnought" to his men, after the name of the ship in which, in 1744, he fought a celebrated duel with the French battleship *Médée*. He captured it with 800 men, and enhanced his name as a fighting commander. In 1748 he commanded the East India expedition and conducted the retreat from Pondicherry with considerable skill. In 1755 he was ordered to intercept a fleet of French transports bound for Canada, but fog and unhelpful winds prevented his doing more than to take two stragglers. He presided over the court-martial set up to try the unfortunate Admiral Byng, and seems to have had little sympathy with his predicament, though sentence of death was mitigated by a strong plea for mercy. In 1758 Boscawen was in command of the successful expedition against Cape Breton which led to the fall of Louisburg. In August 1759, stationed in the Mediterranean to watch the invasion fleet of de la Clue, who was trying to join the other fleet at Brest, he met him as he emerged from Toulon harbor, chased him to Lagos, and captured or drove ashore most of his ships. He came home to receive the thanks of Parliament, a pension of £3,000 a year, a seat on the Privy Council, and the command of the marines.

The story is told of Boscawen that he was woken once by the officer of the watch to be told that there were two large vessels, apparently French, bearing down on them. "What shall I do?" the officer asked. "Do? Damn 'em, fight 'em!" was the admiral's reply as he scrambled out in his nightshirt. It was this spirit that endeared him to his men. Though he was a severe disciplinarian, he also cared for their welfare and efficiency. He was the first man, for instance, to take proper steps to ensure adequate ventilation be-

tween decks. Essentially a brave, fighting seaman, he had the sense
to realize that bravery was not enough.

SIR GEORGE POCOCK (1706–92), admiral, was a capable seaman who did valuable service without achieving any notable or decisive victory. He joined the navy in 1718 and received swift
promotion. He was in chief command in the Leeward Islands,
1747–48, where he captured a French convoy of forty ships. Upon
the outbreak of war again, he got his flag and was sent to command the fleet on the East India station in 1758. Off the Coroman-
del coast, in three successive actions, he battled with d'Aché, the
competent French commander, for the mastery of the sea which
was so vital to land operations. The third time, in September 1759,
after two indecisive encounters, Pocock fought a formal line engagement which shattered many of the French ships, though none
was sunk. The battle displayed the limitations of the old rule about
not breaking the line. Pocock could, one feels, have been more enterprising. But it was his duty to keep his fleet intact. Moreover
d'Aché subsequently withdrew his fleet and the English were able
to capture Pondicherry. Pocock became admiral and K.B. in 1761.
In the following year he commanded the fleet in the exemplary
amphibious operation that led to the capture of Havana and was
rewarded by prize money of £122,697. He retired in 1766 after a
career which had amply demonstrated the value of sea power
when put to intelligent use.

SIR CHARLES SAUNDERS (1713–75), admiral, may be a name
known to only one for every ten who can relate the story of Wolfe
and the capture of the Heights of Abraham. Yet the naval commander in the intricate operation which was completed by Wolfe's
brilliant assault must share the credit for the winning of Quebec
and consequently of Canada, not only for his competent navigation but also for his loyal cooperation, rare between sailor and soldier at any time. In Saunders the genius of Wolfe found its perfect
complement.

He was with Anson in his voyage round the world, an experience which, for the survivors, was uniquely valuable. Not only had
men like Saumarez, Hyde Parker, and Saunders shared in a sustained test of seamanship and endurance; they also enjoyed for the
future the patronage of the man who was First Lord of the Admi-

ralty for a vital decade. Anson was a good judge of men and Saunders was one of his special protégés. He served with distinction in the rest of the War of the Austrian Succession, being with Hawke in his victory of October 1747. He became a member of Parliament in 1750 and remained so for most of his life, and he became Controller of the Navy in 1755, but he was happiest at sea. In 1756 he went to the Mediterranean as rear admiral and did useful service, with Osborne, against the Toulon fleet. When Pitt and Anson worked out the ambitious plan to secure Canada by threefold attack, it was Saunders who was chosen to sail up the St. Lawrence, a long and notoriously hazardous passage. With him was Holmes, a man of cool nerve, and a young navigator, James Cook, whose survey of the St. Lawrence is a classic of its kind. Saunders and Holmes both thought that Wolfe was rash to attempt a landing below, and the ascent of the Heights of Abraham, but gave him whole-hearted cooperation. Saunders held the reach below Quebec and made feint attacks to distract the attention of the French, while Holmes looked after the landing. After the fall of the city, Saunders sailed home, making all sail to join Hawke when he heard of his engagement, but arriving too late to share in the victory of Quiberon Bay. He returned to the Mediterranean for a time, but had little more active service. Knighted in 1761, he became First Lord of the Admiralty for a short time in 1766.

C. P. Stacey, *Quebec*, 1959.

BENJAMIN HUNTSMAN (1704–66), ironmaster, was a pioneer, along with Cort and Wilkinson, in the development of the iron and steel industry which was to transform the economy and the face of the country. He was an ingenious man who found time, besides his regular work as a clock-maker in Doncaster, to be an oculist and to practice surgery. For some years he experimented in making fine steel for the springs of his clocks and blades for the knives that he used for his operations. In about 1740 he moved to Sheffield, and in 1750 he perfected his process and began to produce the superior steel with which the name of this town has been associated ever since.

Huntsman needed to keep the fluid iron intensely hot for many hours and for this purpose used sealed crucibles, small clay pots less than a foot high. To enable the crucibles to endure the heat he mixed several sorts of clay, and he also invented a flux to assist the particles to fuse. Though he tried to keep his process secret, even to the extent of working only at night, it was soon being copied by other Sheffield ironmasters. One of these, Samuel Walker, is supposed to have disguised himself as a tramp and to have got leave to warm himself by the furnace, where he was able to commit the process to memory. The conservative Yorkshiremen at first refused to buy his steel, which he therefore started to sell in France. Eventually some Birmingham manufacturers threatened to come and settle near Sheffield to use Huntsman's steel; only then did the cutters accept the fine metal which was to make the fortunes of their city. Huntsman was a modest and retiring man, a Quaker like the Darbys. He would not accept any honors and he even refused to become a member of the Royal Society. When he died, however, his works were already on a large scale, at Attercliffe outside Sheffield, and his son succeeded to a business which was to last into the twentieth century.

SAMPSON GIDEON (1699–1762), financier, of Portuguese origins, is the most prominent example of the improved status of Jews in the eighteenth century. They were only a small minority; in the whole country it has been estimated that there were about 8,000 at midcentury. Gideon was exceptional in the range of his affairs and the thrustful way in which he pushed aside barriers in government and society. At the age of twenty he founded his fortune by speculating in Change Alley and in coffee houses, lottery tickets, government bonds, and bank, East India Company, and South Sea Company shares. He then moved into the field of foreign funds and into marine insurance. He was consulted by Walpole and Henry Pelham. In the Austrian Succession War he strengthened his hand by raising loans among his fellow-Jews for the hard-pressed government, £350,000 alone in 1759. Although Newcastle's Jewish Naturalization Bill of 1753, allowing Jews to obtain naturalization by special acts, was repealed by the timid minister in the preelection panic of the following year, Gideon and the wealthier at least of his co-religionaires suffered little in practical ways from discrimination. Gideon himself became a Christian and married an English Protestant. He obtained a coat of arms, bought a mansion in Kent, and estates in several counties. He would have liked a peerage; the ministers refused this, but eventually conferred a baronetcy on his son, who was educated at Eton and Oriel, became a noted philanthropist, and founded the Evangelical Alliance. "Gideon Bibles" testify today to his Protestant zeal.

JAMES HARGREAVES (?–1778), by his invention of the spinning jenny, multiplied the output of individual spinners some sixteenfold and started the period of revolution in the textile industry. He was employed by Robert Peel (grandfather of the statesman) to construct an improved carding machine in about 1760. We may therefore treat with caution the traditional story of how, coming unexpectedly into the kitchen, Hargreaves so startled his wife that she knocked over her spinning wheel. As it lay on the floor the turning wheel is supposed to have set him thinking of a quicker and less toilsome method of spinning. Certainly he did contrive, about 1764, a machine that could spin eight threads at a time, and called it "jenny," in honor of his wife. Hargreaves operated the machine in the secrecy of their home for fear of reprisals by jealous neighbors. In 1768, however, his house and machinery were sacked by a mob. Hargreaves's machine, patented in 1770, would not by itself have destroyed the cottage weaving industry. The instinct of the mob may have been sound, however, for improved versions of the jenny were soon appearing which could spin over a hundred threads.

WILLIAM BECKFORD (1709–70) is best known as the keen supporter of the elder Pitt during the Seven Years War. His career illustrates the influence of the city, and of the plantations' interest in particular, upon political events. His father was Governor of Jamaica and he was born there. He made a fortune as a merchant in London and became a leading figure in city politics: he was twice Lord Mayor and at different times represented the city in Parliament. A stout Tory in name, he was really representative more of the tradition of civic independence than of any national policy. Pitt naturally enjoyed his support for his design of winning a colonial empire and, at first, before he became alarmed about the effect of a glut upon prices, for securing sugar islands from France. Later he backed Wilkes when he was charged with libel in the *North Briton*, in 1763, and again when a false return excluded him from sitting for Middlesex (1770). The impromptu speech that he made on this occasion, after receiving a tart message from the king, breathed defiance: the king, he declared, did not wish to hear the truth. Chatham was delighted and praised his independence, and "the spirit of old England" that he represented, and the city fathers had his speech inscribed on a monument erected in his honor in the Guildhall. Less sturdy in character, though, in his way, no less remarkable, was his son William, aesthete, eccentric, and recluse, who wrote *Vathek* and built the Gothic fantasy of Fonthill.

WILLIAM PITT, 1st EARL OF CHATHAM (1708–78), the elder, statesman, was born into a family already established by the efforts of his remarkable grandfather, Governor Pitt. Thomas Pitt had made his fortune in India, first in profitable operations outside the East India Company, later more respectably, poacher turned game-keeper, as Governor of Fort St. George. Fierce and eccentric in temper, he returned to see to the advance of his family. He had prepared the way by the acquisition of estates and a rotten bor-ough, Old Sarum. Wealth drew his children into aristocratic mar-riages: a daughter to Earl Stanhope, his short-lived eldest son Robert to Elizabeth Villiers. His family were, however, difficult; they were extravagant, while he was overbearing to the point, it seemed, of insanity. Only in Robert's younger son William did he find a kindred spirit. At ten, William was sent to Eton. Afterward he was to say that a sensitive boy was cowed there for life; but he made friendships, notably with the Grenville brothers and George Lyttelton, which served him well. "He is a hopeful lad," wrote his grandfather, "and doubt not but that he will answer yours and all his friends' expectations." In the year of his grandfather's death 1726, William went to Oxford. Already he suffered from the gout which had tortured his grandfather, though he did not yet show signs of the family temper. Governor Pitt never knew the meaning of repose; he described his own wife as mad, though she was no more than flighty. Elizabeth Villiers came from a family of genius and alarming instability. Most of Robert's fortune went to the elder son, Thomas, and William was forced to make shift with an income of about £200. Fortunately Thomas helped him to complete his ed-ucation.

From Oxford William went to Utrecht but made no serious preparation for any profession. In 1731, by the patronage of Lord Cobham, a connection by the marriage of his elder brother to Christina Lyttelton, he was made cornet in Cobham's Regiment of

Horse; his military duties did not prevent him from making a foreign tour in 1733. On his return he found politicians embroiled in the Excise Question. The great house which Lord Cobham had just restored was the center of a circle of his relations and dependents. Here Pitt met the leaders of the opposition whose views coincided with his own and whose plans fired his ambitions. In 1735 he became member for the family borough. He quickly revealed a talent for debate which raised him to the leadership of the "Cobham's cubs."

Historians have found it difficult to account for the power of Pitt. Using the language of psychology, one has called him "manic depressive," accounting for the intense force and passion of his rhetoric by saying that this derived from an uneven tempo of life: one phase of exaltation, insight, and energy being followed by another of dark, withdrawn depression. Others have stressed the gout which caused periods of agony and collapse. It seems that, for all his friendships, he was a lonely figure. He gained his effects in the House by studied and histrionic language, but its note of prophetic authority came from a sense of destiny which set him apart. The formal manner which kept ordinary men at their distance may have been his defense against his periodic awareness that he was not well.

The enmity between George II and his son Frederick gave Pitt his first chance to attract the attention of Parliament and the divided court. In 1736 Frederick married Augusta of Saxe-Gotha. The ministry avoided giving the matter space for debate, but Pitt used a congratulatory address to make the opposition's point in a speech of masterly sarcasm. For all his show of loyalty he cannot have been surprised when Walpole deprived him of his cornetcy. "Who will rid me of this terrible cornet of Horse?" George II is supposed to have said; but Pitt was to pay a higher price in exclusion from high office, for George had a keen memory for insults. Soon there was a greater occasion for oratory, and a real division of principle. The affair of Jenkins' Ear gave the opposition an excuse to hound the reluctant ministry into war with Spain (1739). Pitt believed that England's future lay in her pursuit of overseas trade: decadent Spain was in no position to resist the advance of England's merchants, if they were backed by the English navy. When he spoke of Walpole's Convention of Pardo as "a stipulation of national ignominy" and declared that "the complaints of your

despairing merchants—the voice of England—has condemned it,"
he was rousing a spirit as old as Elizabeth, lifting the greed of merchants and the opportunism of politicians to a level of patriotic
principle.

Walpole clung to power until January 1742. Carteret, his successor, secured the temporary neutrality of Frederick, built up the
"Pragmatic Army," and looked forward to the defeat of France in
the manner of Marlborough. In Pitt's view, however, England's war
was concerned primarily with Spain and with winning her trade: if
France had to be fought, it should be by sea. Since Carteret was
reckless in his use of subsidies and high-handed in his approach to
colleagues and to Parliament, Pitt found ready ears for his attacks.
"Neither justice nor policy required us to be engaged in the quarrels of the Continent . . . the confidence of the people is abused by
making unnecessary alliances; they are then pillaged to provide
the subsidies. It is now too apparent that this great, this formidable
kingdom is concerned only as a province of a despicable electorate." Philippics of this sort helped to destroy Carteret and made
the fortune of Pitt's group. Chesterfield, Cobham, Lyttelton came
to the Pelham administration after the fall of Carteret in November 1744; Pitt was kept out by the king. After the disasters and
shocks of the Jacobite rebellion in 1745, the Pelhams made a
strong case for his inclusion. George II was adamant against his
having the office of Secretary at War. But after the maneuvers of
February 1746, when the Pelhams resigned to prove that they were
indispensable, George was compelled to accept him: first as Vice-
Treasurer for Ireland, then, in May, as paymaster-general.

Eighteenth-century paymasters were able to speculate privately
with the money which passed through their hands between the re-
ceipt of army pay and the arrival of the bills; they received a lucrative cut from such transactions as the granting of foreign subsidies
or the raising of mercenary troops. Pitt, however, lodged his bal-
ances with the Bank of England. Though the step was taken with a
typical flourish and an eye on the public outside the House of
Commons, it was also a sincere sacrifice. Despite an eccentric
legacy from the Duchess of Marlborough, Pitt was a relatively poor
man, but he was interested more in power than in profit.

Paymaster for nine years, he made constructive use of the office, in the two years of war that ended with the peace of Aix-la-
Chapelle in 1748, and in the years of diplomatic activity that led

toward the next war which most people considered inevitable. He kept in touch with his agents abroad and studied the commercial statistics of England and France. Through such contacts as William Beckford, a London sugar magnate, Cumming, a Quaker with African interests, and William Vaughan, a fish merchant of New Hampshire, he gleaned information about the French colonies and planned a comprehensive strategy of empire. While he might not agree on all points with such advisers—Beckford, for instance, opposed the capture of French sugar islands on the ground that a glut of sugar would lead to a fall in price—and while the interests of colonists could not always be reconciled with those of merchants, there was a general agreement in Pitt's circle upon the main theme: trade must be made to flourish by war.

Attacks of gout and recurring depression could not always be countered by the distraction of work. After the removal of Henry Pelham's restraining hand, in 1754, he was disturbed by the trends of Newcastle's foreign policy. Newcastle's great system took no account of the determination of Austria to be revenged upon Prussia; when Newcastle eventually turned to Prussia as an ally, *faute de mieux*, he was only doing what Pitt had long urged. England drifted toward a war, crippled by the economies which had reduced her fleets and armies, without certain aim or emphatic leadership. Pitt was meanwhile made happier in his private life by his marriage in November 1754 to Lady Hester Grenville. With relish he turned to attack the government. He demanded a Secretaryship of State and a change of policy: tortuous negotiations occupied the summer of 1755. In November he denounced the government's German subsidy treaties, urging an alliance with Frederick even if this meant a break with Hanover, and a policy which gave priority to the defeat of France overseas in the interests of the colonists, "those long-injured, long-neglected, long-forgotten people." He was dismissed. The alignment was clear. He had the support of most in the city and of merchants everywhere. He had made himself once more obnoxious to the king and embarrassing to Newcastle. He could only be accepted if some national disaster forced the king to listen to the indignation of the public to whom Pitt, "the great commoner," spoke.

The Convention of Westminster (January 1756) secured the alliance of Prussia on terms which included a guarantee for Hanover's neutrality. But the Seven Years War started with setbacks.

In Canada, General Braddock was defeated and killed. In the Mediterranean, Admiral Byng failed to defeat the French squadron which was covering the expedition to Minorca, leaving the island's garrison to its fate. In December the king gave way to Pitt's conditions: he was to be Secretary of State with direct access to the king and responsibility for the formulation of policy—yet Cumberland, commander-in-chief of the allied land forces, refused to receive his orders. In April Pitt was dismissed, but the weeks that followed only proved that Newcastle could not form a ministry without him. While the country demonstrated its support with petitions and the freedom of cities, a coalition was devised. Newcastle, as First Lord, was to manage Parliament and find the money. Pitt, as Secretary of State, was free to run the war. Pitt had at last achieved real power, but on Newcastle's terms: only success could justify him and give him security of tenure. Fortunately he did not lack confidence: "I know that I can save this country and that I alone can."

In his first months of power, Pitt had remodeled the instructions to his commanders, but new plans and new men could not mature at once; the pace of war was slow in the eighteenth century. In India, luckily, the East India Company had a man who needed no order from England. Clive, victor of Arcot, as Pitt recognized, was "a heaven-born general." After Calcutta had been captured by the French, acting in concert with Admiral Watson, he counterattacked, recaptured Calcutta and Chandernagore, and in June 1757 defeated the huge army of Surajah Dowlah at Plassey. The victory enabled Pitt to concentrate his attention on what he considered the vital spheres: Canada and the West Indies.

Pitt's measures were inspired by two basic needs: to keep Frederick in the war and to secure the supremacy of the sea. To protect the country against French invasion and at the same time make available an army to protect Frederick's flank, he raised a militia from the counties and two regiments from the Highlands. Frederick was to receive subsidies and the French were to be distracted by a series of amphibious attacks upon their coastline. At sea, he set up a close blockade of the French bases, Brest, Rochefort, and Toulon. At first it was not apparent that much was being achieved by his "blue water" policy: the ships were in poor shape and French reinforcements slipped out of port to Canada and the West Indies. The operation against Rochefort was a fiasco and so was the first attack against Louisburg, in both cases because of incompetent commanders. Pitt ignored the rules of seniority and looked for commanders of initiative; his clear orders and confidence in victory encouraged them to be bold. He backed Grenville's Navy Bill (1758), which enhanced the attractions of naval service by speeding up the payment of seamen's wages. At home his determination to be honest, even about defeats, made for confidence: "I despise your little policy of concealments." Cumberland was defeated by the French at Hastenbeck and made his peace, but Pitt disowned his action as being authorized by the Elector of Hanover, and put his army under Ferdinand of Brunswick.

Success came first, in 1758, in Canada, where Pitt's scheme was grandiose, planned for total victory, risking disaster. Abercrombie was to move up the Hudson valley to Montreal. A combined force under Amherst and Boscawen was to reduce Louisburg, sail up the St. Lawrence, and attack Quebec. Forbes, a tough veteran, was to attack Fort Duquesne. Abercrombie was checked at Ticonderoga. Amherst captured Louisburg, after a careful siege. Forbes took Fort Duquesne, renamed it Pittsburgh, and died there. For the following year, Pitt shifted Amherst to the command vacated by Abercrombie. The army of the St. Lawrence he gave to the impetuous Wolfe. This officer, mortally sick with tuberculosis, shared Pitt's craving for victory and had also a keen concern for discipline, training, and commissariat. The naval force, under Admiral Saunders, cooperated closely and intelligently. After long delays, Wolfe decided to gamble on a night attack by way of the supposedly inaccessible face of the Heights of Abraham, and was justified by complete victory. In the following year Amherst and his fellow-commanders converged upon Montreal. The surrender of the city in September marked the end of French rule in North America.

Meanwhile Pitt's forces had been successful in West Africa. In 1758, Fort Louis, on the Senegal River, and Goree (Dakar) were captured, and with them the gum and slave trades. The price of slaves rose in the West Indies, where Pitt also had designs. General Hopson failed at Martinique, which was then left until 1782, but captured Guadeloupe, reckoned to be worth nearly ten million pounds. These victories overseas reflected the failure of the French navy to evade the stringent Mediterranean fleets—thus to protect invasion, which Choiseul planned in 1759, and leave a free hand to commanders across the Atlantic. Here Pitt was superbly served by his seamen. Maintaining the blockade of Brest and

Toulon in all weathers, Hawke and Boscawen had already played their parts; then Hawke won a famous victory at Quiberon Bay, in the face of a gale (November) among the shoals of a treacherous part of the Brittany coast. He destroyed the Brest fleet which had finally run the blockade. Boscawen sank a large part of the Toulon fleet whom he had chased to Lagos. News of Minden, where (August) Ferdinand of Brunswick won a great victory over the French, completed the "wonderful year." Pitt was idolized by the populace and respected even by the old king, not insensible to the glory of his nation.

Attention to detail, a strong nerve, an infectious craving for victory, and a sound grasp of the principles of strategy—all played their part in Pitt's success as a war minister. So, it should be added, did the work of Anson, First Lord, and Cleveland, Secretary, at the Admiralty. In his political management he was less happy. He treated Newcastle, Hardwicke, and, more justifiably, Bute, the chief advisor to the Prince of Wales, with sarcasm and condescension. Yet Newcastle served him well, finding the money for schemes in which he did not believe, under the most provocative circumstances, for Pitt did not hesitate to criticize his financial management. The accession, in 1760, of George III, prone to see political questions in personal terms and taught to believe that Pitt had "the blackest of hearts," created a raw situation. In March 1761, Bute became Secretary of State. Pitt could not work with a man whom he knew to be inexperienced and believed to be in office primarily to find means of ending what George III, in his first speech, had called a "bloody and expensive" war (Pitt substituted for "bloody" the words "just and necessary"). Pitt appreciated that Frederick the Great, even after his victory at Torgau in November 1760, was near the end of his tether, but when talks began in 1761 he was primarily concerned with winning more counters for peace. In June naval and military forces captured Belle Isle at the mouth of the Loire. In July came news of the occupation of the island of Dominica and Pondicherry on the coast of India. Pitt was thus strengthened in his haughty tone and unbending attitude. Over the question of the Newfoundland fisheries, which Choiseul was driven by French commercial opinion to demand, he would not budge. Cod was Britain's gold. Sure that Spain was planning to come into the war (and rightly), he wished to strike first. His fellow ministers demurred at his proposals. "Being responsible, I will direct, and will be responsible for nothing that I do not direct," said Pitt, and resigned hi seals and his war. The almost hysterical notes of humility with which he accepted from his ungrateful king £3,000 a year from the sugar duties and a barony for his wife suggest a man near to the end of his tether. His judgment may have been astray too in his attitude toward peace. Newcastle and Hardwicke knew the discontents of the squires who paid the Land Tax, and they appreciated the dangers of abusing a strong position: the classic mistake of victorious statesmen. Ultimately, however, Bute made a peace which only seemed to the Pittites a feeble one: the sugar islands were returned, with the trading stations in West Africa and fishing rights in Newfoundland. Pitt attacked these concessions in a speech of three hours: France, he urged, had been given the means to become once more formidable on sea, while England's ally Frederick had been betrayed.

He only commanded 65 votes in the House; but in the streets the crowd shouted for him. Political power, however, called for some readiness to meet colleagues halfway, to work inside the system and not merely to ignore it. Pitt's physical and mental condition combined to deprive him of that patience and tact which were required. At times now he was a caricature of himself, in his appearances in the House, gaunt, pale, legs wrapped in rolls of flannel, or in Dorset at the house at Burton Pynsent, left to him by a wealthy admirer, where he directed ambitious projects of landscape gardening without thought of the cost. A devoted wife, four children, and a beautiful house provided a background in which he sometimes relaxed. But his usual manner, strained, unnaturally histrionic, lay on the surface of a manic frenzy. The ostentation of his household, his postilions in blue and white, armies of servants around his children, were the outward signs of a restless ambition. Neither content to retire nor competent to play the exacting political game, he wished to be a force in politics, operating from the outside: "unattached to any party I am, and wish to be, entirely single." He was splendidly inconsistent: at first standing out for Newcastle, later refusing to work with him. He was determined, if he were to return to office, to do so on his own terms. That he could still rise to a great occasion he showed when he made a fine speech upon the Stamp Act, in January 1766, urging that there should be no taxation of free subjects without representation. The Stamp Act was repealed, but he was unable to dissuade Parliament from provoking the colonists by unnecessary assertion of the principle that it had the right to tax them; so the Declamatory Act was passed.

In July 1766 he got at last the sole and unconditional direction of affairs. The problems which faced the governments were those which he was specially fitted to tackle: the observance of the Treaty of Paris by France and Spain, the tension between the American colonists and the mother country, and the status of the East India Company. He made several striking appointments: Charles Townshend went to the Exchequer and Shelburne to order American affairs. He set about his duties with tempestuous energy. Yet in October 1768 he resigned after a catastrophic ministry. What had gone wrong? He had embarked upon an experiment in rule, not only without party but almost without cabinet: "sole minister" indeed. Then he became really ill and so remained, on the threshold of madness, for the rest of his ministry.

He selected his ministers upon their merits, so far as he knew them, without regard for their connections. That Charles Townshend was unreliable was unfortunate; with careful handling he might have made great use of his talents. But it was Townshend who complained that Pitt treated his ministers "like inferior animals." His brother-in-law Temple, proud himself, refused to serve, anticipating that he would, like the rest, be regarded as a subordinate official. If he had stayed in the Commons he might still have held together "an administration checkered and speckled," as Burke called it, "patriots and courtiers, King's friends and republicans; Whigs and Tories; treacherous friends and open enemies . . . indeed a very curious show"; but in the most surprising act of his life he took an earldom, removed himself from the sphere where he ruled with acknowledged mastery, and forfeited the sympathy of the people, for the doubtful advantages of the authority of a title and the pleasure of a king whom, with his veneration to royalty, he proposed to serve by "destroying all party distinctions." After a month Chatham collapsed. He made a show at first of ruling the country, from Bath where he wintered in 1766–67 and then from his house in Hampstead. But he was unable to impose his authority upon his ministers. When Townshend produced his unfortunate duties, in May 1767, light but offensive to the colonists whom Chatham understood so well, the prime minister was out of touch, so distracted that he would not even see his wife, sunk in agonized brooding, a prey to sudden whims such as pulling down some house which obscured his view. Grafton described his condition in shocked words: "his nerves and spirits were affected to a dreadful degree . . . his great mind bowed down." But the king clung to the hope that he would recover, while the ministry drifted rudderless; eventually Chatham himself, emerging from his shadows, forced his resignation upon the king.

It was a sad episode. The damage done was immense, ironically greatest in his special sphere of interest. As he realized the gravity of the American situation, partly restored to his former spirit Chatham once more played an active part in the opposition. He was delighted by the letters of "Junius," akin to his style in their fierce, polemical tone. He declared that "he would be in earnest for the public" and "a scarecrow of violence to the gentle warblers of the grove, the moderate Whigs and temperate statesman." But the latter had found a prophet in Edmund Burke who wrote of Chatham at this time, that he wanted "to keep hovering in air, over all parties, and to swoop down where the prey may prove best." Over the renewed case of Wilkes and the question of general warrants, he did indeed come near to destroying the ministry of Grafton. It was a cause after his own heart, with a smell of injustice, a threat to the liberties of the subject and a wider audience outside Parliament listening angrily to his words. He was eloquent and Grafton resigned, but in Lord North George III found a successor more pliable and more amenable to his wishes.

With North secure, and little scope for effective opposition, after this brief resurgence of effort, Chatham retired to a watchful isolation. He pushed no further his suggestions for a modest reform of Parliament. He pressed warmly the case for reform in India, where the less scrupulous servants of the East India Company were making fortunes for themselves at the expense of good government and the good name of the mother country. For a time he turned to active farming, and housed his cows in typically palatial stalls. Debts and mortgages piled up while the creditors were warded off by his indulgent and determined wife. His warnings about the condition of America went unregarded until the eve of war. Then brave efforts to present his case, passionate and deeply pondered, for the concession to America of the fundamental liberties—no taxation without consent, independent judges, and trial by jury, along with the recognition of Congress—foundered upon the ignorance and prejudice of Parliament. His intuition that France was waiting to exploit the crisis, his intimate knowledge of the American colonies, lent passion to his words. In his last years he found again a certain nobility and showed that he had not lost the stagecraft of his great days. But in January 1775 the House rejected his bill for securing a reconciliation. Then after war had broken out he warned the Lords that America could not be conquered. He still, however, clung to the view that reconciliation was possible. In April 1778, he went once more to the Lords where the Duke of Richmond was pressing a motion to grant American independence. His mind wandered, he was incoherent, sometimes inaudible; only phrases here and there recalled the passion and intellect of the statesman. It was a speech of hopeless resolution. His last words before he collapsed were: "My Lords, any state is better than despair; if we must fall, let us fall like men."

Carried from the House, he was driven to Hayes, his favorite home. His eldest son he sent back to his regiment at Gibraltar. William read Homer to him, the passage about the death of Hector; so heroically he died and was buried in Westminster Abbey with fitting pomp. In the Guildhall Burke's inscription summed up what he had meant to the city; he was the minister by whom "commerce was united with and made to flourish by war."

M. Peters, *The Elder Pitt*, 1998.
Lord Rosebery, *Chatham, Early Life and Connections*, 1910.
Basil Williams, *William Pitt, Earl of Chatham*, 2 vols., 1913.
J. Brooke, *The Chatham Administration, 1766–8*, 1956.
S. Ayling, *The Elder Pitt, Earl of Chatham*, 1976.
R. Middleton, *The Bells of Victory: The Pitt-Newcastle Ministry and the Conduct of the Seven Years War*, 1985.

HENRY FOX (1705–74), politician, was the son of Sir Stephen Fox, by a second marriage; when he was born, his father, formerly steward of Charles II, was over seventy. Fox was at Eton, a contemporary of William Pitt, and at Oxford. He gambled heavily, made the Grand Tour, and eventually entered Parliament in 1735. He began, as he continued, a supporter of the administration of the time and he was soon rewarded with a place as surveyor-general. In 1743 he became a Lord of the Treasury; in 1746, at the same time as Pitt was made paymaster, he was made Secretary at War in the Pelham administration. War was not his *métier;* if he was a specialist at all, it was in parliamentary affairs and patronage. He was assiduous, however; he had a rapid mind and he was effective in debate. In 1744 he had eloped with Lady Catherine Lennox. The marriage caused some stir; it brought Fox great happiness. He was ever ready to abandon public business for the delights of domestic life, sweetened by the wealth which he inherited, and increased by his political investments. His young son Charles James Fox was his special idol, and he indulged him absurdly, encouraged him in every whim, let him gamble or smash watches as the mood took him.

In the political disequilibrium that followed the death of Henry Pelham in 1754, Fox sided temporarily with William Pitt, his rival and opposite. Newcastle soon recognized that he needed his support and made him spokesman for the ministry in the Commons. In November 1755 he became Secretary of State, but in less than a year he had resigned. His parliamentary reputation stood high, but foreign policy was not to his taste, and the Minorca affair threatened to be troublesome. When Pitt emerged as chief minister in 1757, Fox was grateful to be paymaster, a lucrative office as his commissions increased with the subsidies and other costs of war, and suited also to his business talents. He had the pay office for eight years, consolidating his fortune at the expense of his fame. Whereas Pitt, in this office, had advertised the virtues of disinterested patriotism, Fox became detested for his cynical conduct. He even clung to the paymastership in the new reign. With promises and presents he managed and eased the passage of the Peace of Paris through Parliament in 1763 and was elevated to the peerage as Lord Holland. Out of office after 1765, he remained effective in the closet. He seems to have suggested to George III that he should govern by influence, without regard to party.

Henry Fox embodies a political type which recurs in every generation. If he stood for anything it was the effective use of power. Genial, kind in his self-centered way, deplorably weak with his family, especially with Charles, whom he removed prematurely from Oxford in order that he might enjoy his company abroad, he was neither base nor contemptible. He had an equable temper and a very marked ability. But we need feel no sympathy for the father when we learn that he had to pay Charles's gambling debts, amounting to £140,000, just before his death.

WILLIAM HOGARTH (1697–1764), painter and engraver, the first great artist of English birth, stepped into a field which was practically vacant of talent, and where Van Dyck and Samuel Cooper were only a silver memory. But his virtues were such as to have blazed in any company.

He was born of North Country yeoman stock fallen on bad days; he was brought up in the City of London, among alleyways the more noisome for having been spared by the Great Fire, leading on to a world which threw together the powdered beau and the verminous beggar, and set in motion from their reaction to each other, not a pageant, but a terrifying parade of vice, misery, prodigies, and excess. This was Hogarth's theatre for much of his life; and it is right to talk of a "theatre" because, taking the drama which he saw on his doorstep, he selected from it, epitomized certain features of it without (let it be noted) undue exaggeration, and then—using the accuracy of his scrupulous memory—transferred them to canvas or plate in pictures which have all the air of theatrical sets and which, like any good play, point a moral. He remained a townsman all his life; people intrigued him; and, while it is easy to overvalue his ethical intention, the eyes through which he looked at society were those of the evangelist as much as of the reporter. There is no mistaking, for example, his anger and shock at the cruelties perpetrated in Bedlam or the House of Correction at Bridewell. And if it be said that his characterization was unmerciful and violent, it must be admitted that it was largely accurate. Those who look for touches of compassion in his work can find them, in some of the female figures, in the children, perhaps most of all in the animals. What other artist of the day would have given to his dog (typically, an uncompromising pug) the foreground in his "Self-Portrait"? What other artist could have taken heart to paint his "Servants" with such ingenuous tenderness, or to distill the nobility from the vulgarity in the wonderfully spontaneous "Shrimp Girl"?

His first artistic work was the graving of heraldic designs on silver plate; from which he learned to engrave copper with designs to be transferred to paper as book illustrations or prints. In his twenties he became acquainted with Sir James Thornhill, the master of baroque decoration, and repaid Sir James's interest by eloping (1729) with his daughter, who made him a devoted wife and the loveliest of his models. Hogarth said it was Sir James's murals at Greenwich and in the Dome of St. Paul's that first awoke his interest in painting; but, when the early conversation pieces began to appear in 1728–29, they showed a mastery of pigment and a subtlety of color which long practice alone teaches. From the beginning he seems to have painted with the idea of multiplying copies of his pictures by engraving. Sometimes the engravings did not follow the painting; but as often, and particularly in his maturity, the engravings preceded the painting, which in turn was sometimes omitted. The process of engraving he often, and it seems wisely, entrusted to foreign masters.

In 1728 Gay's *The Beggar's Opera* was first played. Not surprisingly he found it congenial, and the scenes he painted from it may well have led him to his next step of painting scenes from everyday life *as if* they were on the stage. In 1732 his paintings of "The Harlot's Progress" were published as engravings; they made his first real success, and confirmed him in the idea (now vulgarized in the strip cartoon) of using a sequence of dramatic scenes to tell a story as a social document. Other series followed, notably "The Rake's Progress" in 1735, "Marriage à la Mode" ten years later, and "Gin Lane" in 1750–51. The last and richest series, "The Election," appeared in 1755–58. It is the merit of all these that, while they satirize vices with a candour which earned Hogarth the love of Swift and Fielding, they do not fall short as pictures: the draftsmanship is distinguished; though they are full to bursting with invention and incident, the composition of them never disintegrates, being built up along the serpentine "Line of Beauty" which was a pet thesis of the artist; and in all but a few, strokes of humor moderate the pathos.

But "Honest Bill Hoggart" (as he liked to call himself) was not content to be merely a satirist; he was resolved to beget a strain of art which should be purely English. His life was a long act of rebellion against the "connoisseurs" of the day, who neglected English talent in a veneration for paintings however second-rate, so be it they were aged and smoky (especially should the smoke have risen in a shrine of the Apennines or Lombardy)—all of what the brothers Redgrave described as "the goddess and shepherdess school, the Roman Emperor period of portrait-painters and their patrons, the collectors of fiddle-brown saints and ropy-tendoned martyrs, of pseudo-Titians and secondhand Raphaels." In the breadth of his indignation, Hogarth smote *every* foreign influence—the classical in painting, the Palladian in architecture—and treated of harlots and rakes, forgetting perhaps how much he owed in such pictures to the Dutch school of *genre* painters surrounding Jan Steen. The practical result of his "rebellion" was to alienate, not educate, the patrons; and but for the wide sale of his engravings, Hogarth would have been not only unregarded but penniless. As it was, he enjoyed a steady income from the time (1735) of the operation of "Hogarth's Act," which protected artists' designs from piracy.

Nevertheless this would-be rebel could not check a certain ambition to have his adversaries applaud him, to prove to them that he could (if he chose) paint in the fashionable modes as well as any. And so he covered the walls of St. Bartholomew's Hospital with scriptural subjects, and was disappointed when he could not sell "Boccaccio's Sigismonda Weeping over the Heart of Her Murdered Lover." For the Foundling Hospital (of which he was a governor and which offered the first substantial public exhibitions of pictures) Hogarth did the famous portrait of its founder "Captain Coram"; but his other portraits too often want the ingredient of character—and in any case he was not prepared to flatter to succeed. For his orthodoxy, he was made sergeant-painter; but those were not the ways of his genius.

He died in 1764, before the conclusion of a bitter and unseemly quarrel, waged over two years, with Wilkes and the poet Churchill. Garrick and Johnson wrote him an epitaph. The Life-School he resurrected in St. Martin's Lane was a forerunner of the Royal Academy, but as an artist he had no disciple of importance.

H. M. Atherton, *Political Prints in the Age of Hogarth: A Study of the Ideographic Representation of Politics*, 1974.

HENRY FIELDING (1707–54), novelist and magistrate, was born at Sharpham Park, the Somerset seat of his grandfather, Sir Henry Gould. His mother died when he was eleven. His father, Edmund Fielding, served under Marlborough and finished as a general. When he married again, to the Roman Catholic widow of an Italian, there ensued quarrels and a lawsuit. But Henry was soon reconciled to his father, who paid him, irregularly, an allowance of £200 a year. At Eton, Fielding was often flogged but "came away uncommonly versed in the Greek and Latin authors" and made at least one lifelong friend in George Lyttelton, to whom he dedicated *Tom Jones*. He wore his learning lightly, but the discipline of the classical writers permeated his writing and framed his philosophy of life. Of the Greek philosophers, he once wrote that "they elevate the mind and steel and harden it against the capricious invasions of fortune." In later life, under the stress of illness and poverty, he would retire to read Cicero's *De Consolatione*. Fielding was six foot, robust, and handsome, a long Grecian nose dominating the profile which Hogarth's sketch was later to immortalize. He was passionate, susceptible, impatient but good-natured, much like Tom Jones, into whose character he may have put some of what he knew to be his faults and hoped to be his merits. Murphy, whose introduction to the edition of his works published soon after his death was based upon firsthand experience of Fielding, wrote of his "vivacity of humor and high relish of social enjoyment." Deep learning, a strong intellect and an eye for incident and character which is similar to that of his friend Hogarth were the foundation of his literary work. He acquired, too, a technical knowledge of the workings of the criminal law, of those who operated it, and those whom it was supposed to deter; add the practical interest in social problems which he displayed as a London magistrate and his great and original achievement becomes intelligible. Fielding was the first great English novelist.

At the age of nineteen, Fielding attempted to run away with an heiress from Lyme. Between then and 1734, when he married Charlotte Cradock, his life was fashionable and rakish, alternating between poverty and splendor; he made a living by the writing of plays, until the Licensing Act of 1737, on the model of Congreve and Wycherley. Apart from their interest to the student of Fielding's life and novels, these have some merit. At his best, as for instance in *The Author's Farce* and *The Virgin Unmasked*, they have a sharpness of characterization and a raciness which anticipates the more extended work of his novels. In *Rape upon Rape*, he gives Mr. Justice Squeezum a portrait which combines high farce with indignation in the manner of Dickens. As Thackeray said of him, Fielding had an eye that "brightened up a rogue like a constable's lantern." One at least of the twenty plays survived to become famous: *The Life and Death of Tom Thumb the Great*, a burlesque of the grandiose tragedies being written at the time. Swift once said that this was one of the only two things that ever made him laugh. But Fielding owed much to the fact that he secured the patronage of Mary Wortley Montagu, a distant cousin, and got Mrs. Oldfield and Mrs. Clive to act for him, while the plays' interest today lies more in the light they throw upon the contemporary scene than in their intrinsic merit.

His marriage was happy, though strained by Charlotte's painful confinements, loss of children, and his own reckless generosity. Her beauty and sweetness he depicted in Sophia and, more directly, in Amelia; both are among the happiest portraits of women in the English novel. Three idyllic years they spent on a small country estate at East Stour, echoes of which may be found in "Mr. Wilsons' Story" in *Joseph Andrews*. In 1736, to make more money, Fielding became manager of the New Theatre in the Haymarket. After the Licensing Act of 1737, however, he sold his estate and started to read for the Bar. He had earlier spent some months at Leyden University, but this decision and his feat of accomplishing in three years what usually took six, witnesses to an inner resolve unsoftened by the "wild enjoyments of the town." At the same time he edited one of the ephemeral journals which sought to exploit current political excitement in the declining days of Walpole, the anti-Jacobite *Champion*. Called to the Bar in 1740 he started to travel the Western circuit which was to provide the setting for his novels. But about this time too his health broke; gout ravaged him, he was unable to practice much, and he experienced a poverty which was all the more distressing because of its effect upon his wife. Out of misfortune came a work of original genius, in the shape of *The Adventures of Joseph Andrews*.

To appreciate this work properly, it is necessary to remember that, before it, the only names in English fiction were those of Bunyan, Defoe, and Swift. Now Fielding produced his "comic romance," differing, as he said, from serious romance by introducing persons of inferior rank and manners. It began as a parody of Richardson's *Pamela*, an autobiographical romance, but went on, within a loose peregrinatory framework, clearly derived from Cervantes, to present a series of incidents and a gallery of characters of pleasing artistry. Notable among these is Parson Adams, whose unworldliness is comic, touching, ultimately even dignified, because Fielding, like all great comic writers, was deeply serious in his study of the situations which he embroiders in comic style. If Fielding had written nothing else, his reputation would be high. But in *Tom Jones*, published in 1749, he produced an extended masterpiece, one of the world's great novels. His character had been deepened by suffering. In 1743 Charlotte died, and Fielding, his friends

thought, nearly lost his reason. Fortunately, in their maid and intimate, Mary Daniel, he found a placid and faithful successor. He
married her in 1747. In the following year he was appointed Justice
of the Peace for Westminster, an office in which he could use effectively the encyclopedic knowledge of the London underworld already displayed in his *Life and Death of Jonathan Wild the Great*,
volume 3 of the *Miscellanies* which appeared in 1743. This was a
short, brutal account of the life of a celebrated criminal, set against
a Hogarthian background of highwaymen, card-sharpers, drabs,
and Newgate bullies. The work would be but a crudely effective tale
if not for what Austin Dobson called the "sustained and sleepless
irony" with which a rascal, who is "a great man in his underworld,"
is used to provide analogies with the career of the statesman, "a
great man" in rank and office. Fortunately Fielding turned from
the study of crime and the rule of wrong, to the intellecual challenge of a complicated plot and a panoramic field of characters.

Coleridge said that *Tom Jones* was one of the three perfect
plots. Within its elaborations, the heart of the story is the interplay
of the characters of three young people: Tom, exuberant, unsuspi-
cious, sensuous; Blifil, cold and heartless; and Sophia, whom, in
their different ways, both desire. Round their relationships are
bound adventures which provide superb entertainment. The characters of Squire Western, Miss Western, his sister, Mr. Allworthy,
Harriet Fitzpatrick, Jenny Jones, and Partridge are all in their way
successful. The reader of *Tom Jones* has the two greatest pleasures
that can arise from a novel: the characters whom he recognizes for
their life and actuality, and the handling of the story in a way
which provides the constant shock of surprise as well as the development of these characters. Dr. Johnson, in perverse mood, said
that Fielding was "a blockhead" and later "a barren rascal." Possibly his attitude was affected by Fielding's unblushing sexuality and
the coarseness of some of his descriptions. But the happily married
Fielding dealt with matters of sex without suggestiveness, plainly.
Set him against the society of the time and he will seem to be
truthful, even reticent. Gibbon spoke nearer to the mind of most
of Fielding's readers when he said that "that exquisite picture of
human manners would outlive the palace of the Escurial." Johnson, however, preferred *Amelia*, which Fielding wrote two years
later, and read it through at a sitting. It is a more serene work,
largely domestic in its scope, centering on the marriage of Amelia

and Captain Booth. The strength of the novel lies in its pictures of real life; notably in the contrast between the squalor of Newgate, the pawnshop of Monmouth Street, and the bailiff's lockup in Gray's Inn Lane and the domestic bliss which Booth enjoyed in the virtuous person of Amelia. But the book is only really animated when he is writing about Amelia; in her, his own love affair is resurrected. This may have been what made the book so popular. Fielding was paid a thousand guineas for the copyright and a second edition was called for on the first day of publication. Today *Amelia* is perhaps the least favored of Fielding's three major novels.

Fielding was a magistrate for only five years, but in that time he did much to better the lot of London citizens. From his house in Bow Street, assisted by his blind half-brother John, he waged war upon criminals and the turnkeys, attorneys, clerks, and constables, who battened upon the victims of the law. He made his own court a model of honest justice, sacrificing substantial revenue by his refusal to take the customary cut from fines imposed in his court. As Chairman on the Sessions, in 1749, he delivered a charge to the Westminster Grand Jury, who appreciated it so much that they insisted upon its publication. In it he showed his conception of the role of the citizen in the processes of the law. "Grand jurors . . . are in reality the only censors of the nation. As such the manners of the people are in your hands and in yours only." With characteristic energy he produced an analysis of the situation in the shape of *An Inquiry into the Cause of the Late Increase of Robbers*, 1751, which focused attention upon the evils of gin-drinking. A few weeks afterward his friend Hogarth produced his Gin Lane series; within months, Parliament had passed the Tippling Act, imposing restrictions upon the sale of spirits. He insisted that the roots of crime lay in the conditions of society: overcrowding and unemployment. His humanity and common sense are revealed by his pamphlet of 1753, *A Proposal for Making Effective Provision for the Poor*, though this scheme for a community of hostels, workshops, and infirmaries was never acted upon. The remedies he suggested for punishing crime were acted upon more speedily than his proposals for preventing it. In 1752 two acts for preventing thefts and robberies and "the Horrid Crime of Murder" joined the already crowded ranks of statutes for the punishment of the criminal. In 1753 Newcastle called on Fielding to devise a plan to break up the robber gangs which were terrorizing London. He was ill with gout, but sacrificed a projected cure at Bath to undertake this work: with entire success. In midsummer of the following year, having been advised that he should not endure another winter in England, he resolved to visit Portugal. There he died soon after landing, but in the *Journal of a Voyage to Lisbon* he left a document of great charm and interest. With courage and humor he retailed the incidents of the voyage so that they are immediate and fresh. In the character of Captain Veal, he found idiosyncrasies that would have graced one of his novels, and he kept to the end his interest in the ways of the world, the incompetence of bureaucracy, the insolence of Customs officers. One of his last entries records a meal in a kind of coffee house above Lisbon where they were charged as much "as if the bill had been made on the Bath road between Newbury and London." The last words of the journal were "Hic finis chartaeque viaeque."

Elizabeth Jenkins, *Henry Fielding*, 1947.
F. Homes Duddon, *Henry Fielding*, 2 vols., 1952.
Donald Thomas, *Henry Fielding*, 1990.

LAURENCE STERNE (1713–68), author, who achieved fame largely upon the basis of one novel, was born at Clonmel in Ireland where his father, an army officer, was then stationed. His mother was the daughter of a regimental sutler. He followed the regiment around but at the age of ten was sent to Halifax school where he stayed for eight years. Then his father died and his mother was left penniless, but he was helped by a cousin to go as a sizar to Jesus College, Cambridge, where he made the friendship of Hall-Stevenson, Eugenius in *Tristram Shandy*. In 1736 he took his degree and Holy Orders. In 1738 he acquired the Yorkshire living of Sutton, to which he soon added a second parish and a prebend of York, where his great-grandfather had been archbishop. In 1741 he married Eliza Lumley, though he did not for long remain satisfied by her companionship. They had one child, Lydia, to whom he was attached with a consistency of feeling which was rare in him.

Sterne's habit of shirking his responsibilities made him unpopular with his parishioners, although he was welcome in houses where a keen, none too fastidious wit was appreciated. In 1758 Mrs. Sterne went out of her mind and was removed to an asylum; Sterne started the composition of *Tristram Shandy*. In 1760, after the publication of two volumes of his masterpiece, he came to London to savor its success. He was adopted by such influential patrons as Lord Bathurst, but he did not lack critics. Goldsmith attacked him, Dr. Johnson predictably detested him, and he drew the wrath of Whitefield: "O Sterne, thou art scabby, and such is the leprosy of thy mind that it is not to be cured like the leprosy of thy body, by dipping nine times in the river Jordan." Sterne invited abuse by impersonating the character of his hero. On the success of *Tristram Shandy* he hoped that he would climb from provincial obscurity to preferment in the Church. He hoped that his book would advertise his talents; meanwhile he puffed it by his ostentatious behavior. "I wrote," he said, "not to be fed but to be famous."

Tristram Shandy may be enjoyed at different levels and critics disagree, inevitably, about its author's intentions and skill. But there is no dispute about the importance of the work in the development of the novel. The popularity of the work of Fielding and Smollett carried with it the danger that the novel might stay upon the level of everyday life. A film can be made of *Tom Jones* because it reproduces scenes of contemporary life round an organized narrative. It would be hard to make a film of *Tristram Shandy*, because Sterne deliberately departed from the "Life & Adventures" scheme and set out to make a channel for the opinions and whims of his characters. In asserting his own liberty, he cleared the field for those who followed him. Goethe found the characteristic quality of Sterne's genius to lie in his freedom of spirit and his readiness to withdraw into the citadel of his inner self; what was unsatisfactory in his character as priest and friend was part of his quality as a writer. "Sterne," he said, "is a free spirit, a model in nothing, in everything an awakener and suggester." E. M. Forster discovers a "charmed stagnation about the whole epic—a god is hidden in *Tristram Shandy* and his name is muddle, and some readers cannot accept him." But if there is an appearance of anarchy, it is not for want of scheme or of a rational approach in the writer. Even his sentimentalism, which some detest, is deliberately cultivated and highly wrought. His wit is learned, legalistic, logic-chopping, physical, the last child of the age of reason rather than the first effusion of the romantics. Thus he states his Shandean philosophy: "True Shandeism opens the lungs and forces the blood and other vital fluids of the body to run freely through its channels, makes the wheel of life run long and cheerfully round." Not all find Sterne's humor satisfying. "The man is not a great humorist," said Thackeray, "he is only a great jester." Many have found his prurience, his peep-hole suggestiveness offensive. Indeed no great novelist has to have so much forgiven him. If his reputation survives, despite all the obvious blemishes, it must be primarily because of a psychological subtlety which transcends mere oddity and foible. His caricatures have recognizable life. Walter Shandy, Uncle Toby, Corporal Trim, each have their own hobbyhorse. They pursue their delusions with a fervor that is lovable and just credible. All is rooted in Sterne's theory that when man becomes deeply attached to a favorite occupation, his character takes shape and coloring from the materials belonging to it.

Sterne's life, after his arrival in London, seems to have been dominated by his desire to cut a comic figure. But it should be recalled that in 1762 he suffered a breakdown in health; for some time he had suffered from a weakness of the lungs; ultimately he died of pleurisy. His flirtations were primarily affairs of sentiment which subsequently he could regard with ironic detachment. In 1760 he acquired the living of Coxwold, and his wife recovered, but he did not reside there long. He published his sermons and produced from time to time further installments of *Tristram*, finally completed in 1767. In 1762, with his wife and daughter, he went to France. He was received with rapture in France, where his way of thinking was in tune with the mood of the salons: there ensued two years in the south of France. In 1764 he divided his time between London, Bath, and York. In 1765 he embarked upon a tour of Italy from which was born the *Sentimental Journey*. Yorick's voyage of sensibility is a catalog of incidents, preposterous, touching, base. If Yorick is betrayed by a hopeless instability of purpose and feeling, then he is partly Sterne himself. Sterne, in London, in 1767, enjoyed the last of his sentimental treats in a prolonged affair with Mrs. Draper; when she was recalled to India by her husband, Sterne set down the record of his feelings in his *Journal to Eliza*. "It had ever," he made Yorick say, "been one of the singular blessings of my life, to be almost every hour of it miserably in love with some one."

W. Sichel, *Sterne*, 1910.
T. Yoseloff, *Laurence Sterne*, 1945.
Peter Quennell, *Four Portraits*, 1945.

TOBIAS SMOLLETT (1721–71), novelist, was born at Dalquhurn, Cardross, Dunbartonshire. His father died soon after and Tobias was brought up by his mother, aided by a small allowance from his grandfather, Sir James Smollett, a Scottish judge, member of Parliament, and commissioner for the drafting of the Union. He was educated at Dumbarton School and at Glasgow University. He was then apprenticed to a Glasgow surgeon but at the age of eighteen he took the road to London, with a play in his pocket and a fervent belief in his own talents. Failure to secure the production of *The Regicide* put his hackles up. Garrick and Lyttelton were among the early targets of his sarcasm; in the course of his life he quarreled with most of the literary figures in London. Touchy and opinionated, he could yet be affectionate and generous at times. He took a commission aboard the *Cumberland*, bound for the West Indies with Admiral Vernon, but after the failure of the attack upon Cartagena he went for a short time to Jamaica; he returned, in 1744, with Anne Lascelles, a planter's daughter whom he subsequently married, and a store of naval experience.

He combined a surgeon's practice in Downing Street with occasional writing, but without notice until the publication of *Roderick Random*, in 1748. Its deft loose framework, upon the plan of Le Sage's *Gil Blas*, gave him scope for characterization, and a brisk narrative, abounding in violence, earthy detail, and rough humor. Dickens liked *Roderick Random*, but he is a shameless fellow who seems to exist primarily for the purpose of describing his adventures. Smollett lacked any discernible view of life and conduct; furthermore he sees men and women from the outside. But within the limits of the picaresque tradition the novel has great verve and one special feature, the English sailor. In the Hanoverian navy, Smollett found a rich field for the study of human nature; in such men as Oakum and Jack Rattlin he started the literary tradition of the British tar, just at the time when the navy was about to acquire its special place in English hearts. In 1750 Smollett traveled to Paris to find material for a new novel; the fruit of this was *The Adventures of Peregrine Pickle* (1751). Pickle himself cannot be admired: he is a bully, amoral, witty mostly at the expense of others. But in Commodore Trunnion, for all his prolixity, Smollett created a character of the first order. The simple, salty sea-dog shows that for all his faults, clumsiness of construction, prurience, the "Smelfungus" side of him that Sterne so aptly hit off, there was more than knockabout in Smollett's art. He had a vein of comic genius. After failing to make his way as a physician at Bath, it is typical that he should write a pamphlet to show that Bath water was no more efficacious than any other—but equally typical that he should utilize his experiences for some of the best scenes in *Humphrey Clinker.*

After 1751 Smollet abandoned medicine and, settling in Chelsea, at Monmouth House, devoted himself to a literary career. Here he was visited by Johnson, Garrick, Sterne, and the hacks whom he installed in his "literary factory," an enterprise for the publication of large works, in which he was to do the lion's share of the writing. This produced over £600 a year, but he was a large spender and debt and ambition drove him on. The *History of England,* ultimately in nine volumes, for which he said that he had read more than 300 works, was written in haste, in order to anticipate Hume, who was also engaged upon a history. That he could be generous is shown by the praise that he gave in his volume to Fielding, with whom he had quarreled bitterly, and to Hume. As he became established, he mellowed somewhat. But he played little part in the social life of literary London. The preparation of Dodsley's *Compendium of English Voyages,* including Smollett's own account of the Cartagena expedition, the compiling of a universal history, a series of excursions into journalism, the editorship successively of the *Critical Review* (1756), the *British Magazine* (1760), and the *Briton* (1762) (the latter fated to become the chopping block for Wilkes's *North Briton)*—all taxed Smollett's nervous energy. Meanwhile he did not abandon fiction. *The Adventures of Ferdinand, Count Fathom* (1757) is among the less successful of his efforts, but *Lancelot Greaves* (1760) has its admirers. Sir Lancelot and Sir Timothy Crabshaw are pale imitations of their great originals in Cervantes, and the fun is largely horseplay, but there are several good minor characters. There is no better guide than Smollett to Georgian England, not only in the caricatures that enrich his novels but in the description of places—a country estate in *Lancelot Greaves* or Bath in the period of its hectic building in *Humphrey Clinker.*

Smollett's life was not unadventurous. In 1759 he was imprisoned in the King's Bench prison for three months for impugning the courage of Admiral Knowles in the *Critical Review.* His health was broken by overwork and fretting. He had some of Matthew Bramble's crossness with the world, and perhaps, too, his essential good nature. It was a great blow to him when in April 1763 his only child, Elizabeth, died at the age of 15. With his disconsolate wife he embarked upon a long tour of France and Italy. In 1765 he published the account, carping in tone, but for all that a mine of interesting and entertaining information. His spleen may be contrasted with the more serene temper of the journal of the last voyage of the dying Fielding. He saw everything—inns, Roman Catholicism, pictures—with jaundiced eye. On his return he made a visit to Edinburgh, where he was received with acclaim. Revisiting Scotland, and Bath again, now as a patient, he gathered material for his next novel. But before this he delivered himself of a Rabelaisian commentary upon the political scene, as seen by an atom while in the body of a Japanese. *The Adventures of an Atom* may reflect his disappointment at what he regarded as the neglect of his talents by successive ministries; it is Smollett at his most gross and unpleasing. In the same year, 1769, he left England to reside in a villa at Leghorn; here, in 1771, he died, but here, too, he wrote *Humphrey Clinker*. This work, conceived in a gentle mood of recollection, without the rancor and with less of the crudity of earlier works, is written in the form of letters; the story is straightforward and not overlong. The characters are more rounded than most of Smollett's. Matthew Bramble, his sister Tabitha, Winifred Jenkins, the Welsh maid, and Lismahago (original of Scott's Dugald Dalgetty?) are memorable. Smollett could, in few lines, create a type with a skill in which only Dickens, an admirer of his work, excelled him. The evidence of *Humphrey Clinker* is that Smollett died at the height of his powers. After his death there was published an *Ode to Independence*. The work is no greater than other poems that he wrote, but the subject is typical of his defiant temperament; its title makes a fitting epilogue to his truculent life.

Lewis M. Knapp, *Tobias Smollett, Doctor of Men and Manners*, 1949.

ROBERT DODSLEY (1703–64), bookseller and writer, was a more interesting character than an outline of his career suggests. The son of a schoolmaster in Sherwood Forest, he was for a time in service as a footman. His employer, Mrs. Lowther, took notice of his literary gifts and encouraged him, without apparently suggesting that he should leave her service. The eighteenth century is full of surprises and Dodsley's poems are among them: *Servitude* (1729) and *A Muse* *in Livery* (1732) are uncomplaining, uncomplicated thoughts on his domestic employment. In the seventeenth century, said his future friend and client Johnson, it was thought surprising if a man composed in his chariot, but "how much more the wonder would have been increased by a footman studying behind it." In 1735, when his little play, *The Toy Shop*, was successfully performed, Dodsley left service and set up as a bookseller: Pope lent him a hundred pounds for the purpose. He wrote assiduously, poems, burlesques, plays, including a moderately successful tragedy which, said Johnson, "had more blood than brains in it."

It was, however, as a publisher that Dodsley made his mark. Combining a publisher's enterprise and flair with an artist's taste, he projected a series of useful periodicals, magazines, and collections. *The Public Register* (1741), *The Museum* (1746), *The World* (1753), and *The Annual Register*, for which invaluable and surprisingly impartial record he secured Edmund Burke as his first editor, provided a forum for the most notable writers of his day. In 1757 he took the lead in producing a new evening paper, *The London Chronicle;* novel in form, with eight quarto pages, with few advertisements but plenty of news, it was seldom brilliant but interesting and safe: the first "family newspaper."

Dodsley and his brother James, whom he took into partnership with him, were universally liked and respected. Posterity owes him a large debt, too, as the man who backed the talent of the young Samuel Johnson before he became famous. He gave him ten guineas for *London* in 1738, suggested the *Dictionary* and was one of the syndicate of publishers who produced it; he also published *Irene, The Vanity of Human Wishes*, and with Strahan, *Rasselas*. Johnson, whose sensitive, independent spirit made him a difficult man to have business relations with, was happy to call him his patron. Very different from the arrogant, neglectful Earl of Chesterfield, who treated Dr. Johnson as he would not have treated a footman, was the ex-footman who acted as midwife to the work of Dr. Johnson, Goldsmith, Shenstone, and Gray. He indeed had the instincts of a gentleman.

R. Straus, *Robert Dodsley, Poet, Publisher and Playwright*, 1910.

JOHN NEWBERY (1713–67), publisher, was a quaint character, friend of many notable writers such as Goldsmith and Dr. Johnson.

He was for a time the assistant editor of the *Reading Mercury*. When he came to London he published some standard works such as the *Guide*, a gazetteer of buildings and monuments, and the *Medicinal Dictionary* in three volumes (1743–45). He made patent medicines and sold Doctor James's Powders, an infamous compound of antimony and phosphate of lime, in St. Paul's Churchyard. He found fame in writing, or at least presenting, books for children, using them sometimes to advertise his medicines. With Mrs. Margery (or Goody) Two-Shoes, Giles Gingerbread, and Tommy Trip and his Dog Jowler reaching an avid public, Newbery may claim to be the discoverer of the profitable market in books that were written specially for the young.

Austin Dobson, *Eighteenth Century Vignettes*, Vol. 1, 1892, p. 118.

DR. SAMUEL JOHNSON (1709–84), lexicographer, poet, biographer, essayist, was highly regarded in his time for his literary work. The impact of his personality upon his friends was such that he is known to us through an incomparable record of anecdotes and *obiter dicta*. He attracted a biographer worthy of his subject, whose method it was essentially to let the doctor speak for himself. Boswell knew him after the great creative period of his life; our image of Johnson is likely therefore to be of a shambling, gruff, opinionated, elder statesman of literature, a polymath, an independent Tory, a law unto himself, a man with time for his friends. This splendidly ripe autumnal figure has passed into legend. There were also years of struggle and doubt which were the making of the great man.

He was born at Lichfield in September 1709, the year in which his father, a bookseller, was sheriff of the city. As a child he was touched by Queen Anne for the King's Evil, his mother making a special journey with him to London for the purpose. He wore his touch-piece round his neck for the rest of his life and never renounced his sentimental attachment to the House of Stuart. His face was pitted by a severe attack of smallpox, he suffered from a pronounced nervous tic or convulsive start, and his eyes were weak. He suffered always from periods of depression of spirits and inability to concentrate, but he had a nearly photographic memory, a feeling for words, and ability to extract the meaning from the books which he read hungrily but seldom finished. He was educated at

Lichfield School, famous for the teaching of Dr. Hunter, and briefly at Stourbridge. Unpractical and moody, he made little effort to fit himself for his father's business, though he learned how to bind a book and acquired an extensive knowledge from his father's collection. With a small legacy and help from a friend, Andrew Corbet, he went to Pembroke College, Oxford, with the reputation of a prodigy in classical studies, but found the tutoring indifferent and may not have added greatly to his academic store during his thirteen months of residence. Already he seems to have acquired a habit of procrastination and already he was enduring bouts of introversion and self-examination; later it was said of him that he could not bear to be alone, and he was always at his happiest in company. Tall, raw-boned, shambling, shabby, twitching, embarrassingly clumsy at table, he was sometimes a butt, more usually an object of some awe. He was dogmatic in his talk, but impressive because he knew so much. His choice of friends was catholic and unpredictable. One was Henry Hervey, a good-natured, reckless young ensign of good family; another, Gilbert Walmisley, Register of the Ecclesiastical Court at Lichfield, urbane Whig and scholar. The fees not forthcoming, Jonson did not complete his course at Oxford and was afterward hampered in his search for employment by his want of a degree; fortunately, since his brief experience as a schoolmaster, at Husbands Bosworth and later at his own small school at Edial House, showed that he had little aptitude for teaching. In 1731 his father died, encumbered in debts. In the following year, after some unhappy months at Bosworth, he went to Birmingham, where he lived for about three years, writing sporadically some essays which have been lost, for the *Birmingham Journal*, and a translation from the French of a Portuguese Jesuit's travels in Abyssinia. The severe but orotund style, the antitheses and stately generalizations, show that Johnson's style was already setting in the mold of his later work.

At the age of twenty-five, without profession or income, he married Elizabeth Porter, a florid widow twenty years older than himself. His friends disparaged her, but she brought him a modest sum and the comfort of a ripe personality. Johnson's exuberant attentions to his wife aroused the ridicule of the pupils of his school, amongst whom was David Garrick, but he seems to have been devoted to his "Tetty"; later he neglected her at times and she grew difficult with age. Leaving his school, but taking with him the unfinished manuscript of *Mahomet*, a tragedy, he set off for London, in 1737, with Garrick, aged nineteen. Johnson said of London that "when a man is tired of London he is tired of life," but his early years were spent in "drudgery and garrets" and he tried to escape by applying for posts as a schoolmaster. In 1738 he began to contribute to the *Gentleman's Magazine*, for Edward Cave, and he soon asserted some literary control over this miscellany of reports, essays, and extracts from other works. He was for some time the reporter of debates in the House of Commons. Since, after April 1738, reports were held to constitute a breach of privilege, these were concocted by Johnson from scraps of notes under the guise of "debates in the Senate of Magna Liliputia." The speeches may have borne little resemblance to the originals; Johnson himself never attended the debates and he was Tory in bias ("the Whig dogs shall not have the best of it"): but they attain a consistent level of excellence which is remarkable considering the speed at which they were written, once ten pages between noon and early evening. He abandoned this work in 1743 when he decided that it was an unjustifiable fraud, but they were long afterward thought to be genuine; indeed two of his speeches appeared in the collected works of Chesterfield. In April 1739 Johnson produced a political pamphlet, *Marmor Norfolkiense*, and in May the *Compleat Vindication of the Licensers of the Stage*. They were unworthy of his intellectual powers, as were the short biographies he undertook. But toward the end of 1743 he wrote a lively life of his friend Savage, to whom he was attracted, despite his blatant faults, because of his talents and sufferings. The book, acute in its perception of the conflicts within Savage's personality, reveals as much of Johnson as of his subject. It brought some good reviews but little money. While his contributions to the *Gentleman's Magazine* tailed off, he began, at the end of 1742, a venture in bibliography, working upon the Harleian Library for the bookseller Thomas Osborne. He wrote the *Proposals* for printing the catalog of this vast collection by subscription and again for the *Miscellany*, a collection of the scarcer documents. But he left this work in dudgeon, actually coming to blows with his unappreciative employer, and turned to the production of a new edition of Shakespeare. His conception was grand, but he shelved it, after producing an essay on Macbeth, when he learned that Warburton was also working on an edition.

Still searching for an enterprise of a heroic sort, he decided upon a dictionary. The plan for this work, so suited to his magisterial, exact mind and his ability to select from a mass of material, was issued in 1747 and addressed to the Earl of Chesterfield. More practical help came from the printer Dodsley, head of the group who sponsored the dictionary. At the cost of grinding toil, Johnson was given a degree of security. He took a house in Gough Square, hired six amanuenses, settled to an immense program of reading, and committed himself to producing something which, in France, a team of forty academicians had taken nearly a century to compile. He still found time to write outside his self-imposed task. In January 1749 appeared *The Vanity of Human Wishes*, the first poem to bear his name, but his second imitation of the satire of Juvenal. Whereas *London*, written in 1738 and praised among others by Pope, stayed close to its original, *The Vanity of Human Wishes*, ostensibly derived from Juvenal's Tenth Satire, is distinctively modern in its examples of ambition disappointed, essentially Johnsonian in its stoical mood and morality. Johnson believed that much is to be endured, little to be enjoyed in life. After death he feared "being sent to Hell, and punished everlastingly." So he equipped himself to meet life's trials, composing prayers for his own use, a scheme of life which enabled him to live chastely among the temptations of the town and to overcome his self-confessed enemy, sloth. The sheer output of these years is astounding. In March 1750, he launched *The Rambler*, which appeared twice a week for the next two years: a periodical essay with a limited circulation of about five hundred which set a standard of quality to its more popular contemporaries, and eventually attained popularity itself on being reissued in volume form. *The Rambler* invites comparison with the spectator. The stories and allegories suffer from the same weakness that prevented his succeeding in drama: too much logic and too much of the moralist. His characters show a deep knowledge of human nature, but they are too abstract and generalized to make much impact. Addison's purpose had also been didactic but no one, reading about Sir Roger de Coverley, would guess that he was being taught philosophy or urged to reform. Johnson aimed at "the propagation of truth" and his serious purpose was obvious even in his lighter passages.

Concluding *The Rambler*, Johnson stated that he had labored "to refine our language to grammatical purity, and to clear it from colloquial barbarisms, licentious idioms, and irregular combinations." If this had been the only achievement of the *Dictionary*, which was completed in 1755, it would have been useful as pioneer work in the etymological jungle which had grown up around the rapidly expanding language. But Johnson's *Dictionary* is also a work of art. Aiming to fix the language and preserve its purity, he succeeded in establishing a standard of reputable use. He accepted no authorities earlier than Sidney or Spenser. But with typical lack of pedantry he included dialect words, Scottish in the main but also some from his native country. He used quotations to illustrate the use of words: often from memory, these do not belong to a scientific approach to lexicography but they are usually accurate, an instance of his prodigious knowledge. His great strength lay in definition, for which he had a genius, as readers of Boswell will recognize. He was the first to attempt a thorough distinction between the different meanings of words: *come*, for instance, is subdivided into fifty sections. Sometimes he was sportive, with words which gave him a chance to air his prejudices: *oats*, for instance, "which in England is given to horses, in Scotland to men," but his definition of the *patron* (with Lord Chesterfield in mind) strikes a harder note. It recalls the wonderful ending of his letter to the neglectful peer: "for I have long wakened from that dream of hope in which I once subscribed myself. My Lord, your Lordship's most humble, most obedient servant, Samuel Johnson." The flavor of his definitions remains where the vast *Dictionary* itself has long passed into limbo. But no one valued it more than those who followed in his tracks and produced more scientific compilations.

Johnson was acclaimed for his production of the *Dictionary* and began to enjoy a licensed lordship in literary circles. That did not prevent him, in 1756, from being arrested for a small debt and released only after the intervention of Samuel Richardson. He still hankered after grand projects, scheming to edit a journal of European studies, then issuing new *Proposals* for an edition of Shakespeare. But most of his work was such as required less sustained effort. He had exhausted himself in his work on the *Dictionary* and suffered acutely from bouts of depression, conscience-stricken during the intervals of leisure which he needed to recover from his intense bouts of work. It was in these years that he became the Dr. Johnson known to us through Boswell's pages: sage, philosopher, obdurate Tory, the presiding genius of the "Club." Fanny Burney saw a grotesque figure, "very ill-favored, tall and stout but stoops terribly" and noticed his body "in constant agitation, see-sawing up and down." Besides his talent for conversation, he had a compelling need of company, to ward off his black moods and prevent his mind from turning in on itself. He contributed to Kit Smart's *Universal Visitor*, undertook the control of the *Literary Magazine* (1756–57). The latter saw his celebrated defense of tea, which he preferred to any form of alcohol and drank copiously. He helped friends with their books, wrote a life of Sir Thomas Browne (1756) and of Roger Ascham (1761). He produced a second series of essays in the *Idler*, a section of another journal, *The Universal Chronicle*. Here may be seen a lighter touch than he displayed before and at least one of his characters, Dick Minim the critic, lives as something more than a type. But his single novel, *Rasselas, Prince of Abyssinia* (April 1759), written in haste to pay for his mother's funeral, is less a story or a study of characters than a series of discussions upon the human condition. It is pure Johnson, in style and philosophy, and levies a severe tax upon the reader's patience. He arrives at the end with a stock of aphorisms and a sense of a deeply serious but not unhappy man. Prefaces, dedications, reviews flowed from his pen, but not until 1762 and a sharp attack from the abrasive Churchill, did he resume work on Shakespeare; with a pension of £300, surely the most deserved of royal bounties, and financial independence, he was able to complete it by October 1765. His common sense, his perception of the genius of Shakespeare, and his knowledge of Elizabethan English contributed to the value of this edition. Some of his comments are still to be found in modern editions. Of all that had hitherto appeared, this was the most accurate and the nearest to the originals. Some clues to his quality as a man may be seen in his modesty. The "great Cham," who was so autocratic, even a bully, in his conversation, did not intrude conjectures or prejudices where the evidence did not support them.

   In 1763, Johnson met Boswell; in 1764, with his close friend, Reynolds, he founded the club; in 1765 he met the Thrales who provided a domestic setting for his middle age. In these years he wrote less but lived more richly than before; he was still generous with his time in causes that appealed to him, writing political tracts, dictating arguments for Boswell's law cases, and generous in his purse toward unfortunates, and with his time in conversation, which fortunately has been preserved for us. In the late summer and autumn of 1773 he traveled with Boswell to the Western Isles of Scotland; it was adventurous in a confirmed Londoner of advanced years. The reader finds interest in his comments about the clans, superstition, emigration, and other Highland themes, but the fascination of the book arises from the picture that it conveys—at once intrepid, inquisitive, and droll, the philosopher not afraid to get his feet wet, to sit in a small boat, or to vault over a fence to show his agility. At Easter, 1777, a deputation of booksellers waited on him to persuade him to write biographical prefaces to a collected edition of the English poets. Conceived in jealousy of a similar project in Edinburgh, the work proved congenial to Johnson and he gave of his best; the prefaces were published in 1781, without the texts, under the title of *The Lives of the Poets.* Earlier, George III, in a happy moment, had proposed that Johnson should write the literary biography of his country. He was specially interested in the man, and the poetry is seen in its relation to the personality and career of the poet. Thus they remain authoritative as biographies, although long superseded as criticism, partly because he did not know enough, partly because he is subjective, at his worst when he does not sympathize with the character of the poet, as with Milton, the puritan, or Swift, the bitter Tory. In the three years of infirm health that remained to him he endured the blows that usually accompany old age, the loss of friends, Thrale of Stretham, Levett, and blind Mrs. Williams, his pensioners at Bolt Court, with the courage and enterprise that made him such good company for a younger man like Boswell. In July 1785 he set out on a tour of old haunts, Lichfield, Birmingham, and Oxford. He came back to London to die, on December 13. He was buried in Westminster Abbey among some of the poets whom he had so nobly commemorated.

Dr. Johnson was a Tory and a churchman. His Toryism may have been based more upon family tradition and an antipathy toward the Whigs than upon serious Jacobite principles. It was baseness, arrogance, pretentiousness in politics, that he detested; above all anything that smelled of the hireling. His churchmanship stood upon a rock-like sense of the value of order, but it was nourished by regular and sensitive private devotions. He stood at the still center of the currents of the age: against "enthusiasm" on the one hand, also against the divagations, intellectual and moral, of the laxer figures of the established Church. Sometimes he was unfair:

one recalls a devastating judgment upon Fielding, a steely reluctance to see the merit of Gray. Even his lighter prejudices could lead him into heavy rudeness, to Scotsmen, to Whigs, and to nervous tyros. But we should remember that his reputation carries the heavy load of almost verbatim reporting by an uncritical devotee. Furthermore, beneath the orderliness of his definitions, the emphatic dogmatism, lay an inner turbulence. Even his friends complained of his habits; he admitted to having no love of clean linen. But could they fathom the stress of his life, the disorder of emotions, near at times to madness, that his *Journals* reveal? For years the genial house of the Thrales provided him with a secure refuge. But he could never be long with himself. To the end he had to be writing, talking, or traveling. Is it the secret of this man's greatness, the note of authority which we recognize even today, that we know that it came from struggle and heartbreak? Dr. Johnson lived at the full stretch of his emotional and mental capacity. Feeling vibrates through his most trenchant statements, and these are acceptable because they expose humbug and cant. In life he stood for reverence, for truth, and a high standard of decency. His death, wrote Murphy, "kept the public mind agitated beyond all former example. No literary character ever excited so much attention."

G. B. Hill, ed., and James Boswell, *Life of Dr. Samuel Johnson*, 6 vols., 1887.
R. W. Chapman, ed., *Letters*, 3 vols., 1952.
J. L. Clifford, *Young Sam Johnson*, 1955.
Richard Holmes, *Dr. Johnson and Mr. Savage*, 1993.
W. J. Bate, *Samuel Johnson*, 1977.

DAVID GARRICK (1717–79), actor, dominated the London stage for nearly forty years. What Handel was in music, Reynolds in painting, Garrick was in acting, the master whom many tried to imitate, none with complete success. His career was not, however, without vicissitudes, nor does he escape the critics quite unscarred.

He was born at Hereford, the grandson of a Huguenot refugee, son of an army officer. His mother, a clergyman's daughter, contributed some Irish blood. Rhetoric, imagination, sentimentality, above all a certain effusiveness we may trace to this source, all the more confidently when we recall that Burke, Goldsmith, and Sheridan were all Irishmen. Garrick was Dr. Johnson's first pupil at his little school at Edial near Lichfield. Dr. Johnson was not to be taken entirely seriously as pedagogue, but Garrick learned to value him as friend and patron when they went to London together. Garrick grew vain and garrulous; Dr. Johnson was outspoken and claimed almost proprietary rights in the man who "has made a player a higher character"; but their association was fruitful. Johnson introduced Garrick, who was trying to be a wine merchant, to Case, and he wrote for a time in his *Gentleman's Magazine*, but an essay in authorship, *Lethe*, performed at Drury Lane in 1740, was followed by an appearance on the stage as Richard III which brought such acclaim that his vocation was plain. There ensued a succession of roles too various to record in full. In 1747 he took a half-share in Drury Lane and kept the management for the rest of his career. His reign was magnificent but turbulent. Other actors like Quin and Macklin were jealous; actresses were temperamental. Mrs. Cibber resented his marriage; "Peg" Woffington, for some time his mistress, was quarrelsome; even the admirable Kitty Clive would let her attention wander to beaux in the audience when she should have been following Garrick's actions and eye. Audiences were fickle and rough. In order to curb the jeers and howls of critics and rowdies put up to it by rival managements, Garrick once had to post pugilists in the pit. A row of iron spikes ran along the front of the stage. He has been blamed for pandering to popular taste in dress and manner. He played Lear and captivated the town, beardless, with a white wig, a short robe of velvet, trimmed with ermine, white silk stockings, and high-heeled shoes; but when he ventured upon an Othello in Moorish attire, he was received with ridicule. He accepted that "The Drama's laws, the Drama's patrons give," for he was a businessman and knew too that "Actors live to please and please to live." What he stood to lose, if rioting became serious, can be seen from his experience in 1755 when the appearance of some French dancers in a ballet caused six nights of disorder culminating in a free fight, bloodshed, and damage costing £4,000. He then closed the theatre for a time and was compelled to again in 1763, when higher prices produced an almost hysterical reaction from the mob.

To maintain his position, Garrick had to be ready to adapt, to rewrite and play to the gallery. It was a battle of wits in a profession which had more than its share of feuds, intrigues, and heart-burnings. Garrick often had to rewrite plays that he was offered by amateurs with little sense of the demands of the theatre. Less justifiably he mutilated Shakespeare to suit the conventions, but in a way which underestimated the intelligence of playgoers. In 1772 he presented a *Hamlet* without Osric or the grave-diggers; Laertes became a sentimentalist, Gertrude went mad, and Hamlet fought a duel with the king. A new dying speech was written for Laertes and, when it was much applauded, Garrick, a somewhat elderly Prince of Denmark, took it for his own part. Dr. Johnson said that to praise Garrick for his Shakespearean revivals "would be to lampoon the age." Yet Garrick, in one of the prologues which he wrote so felicitously, declared his wish and plan "to lose no drop of that immortal man." The sophistications of Garrick may be regretted, because he seems to have been an incomparably great actor who could adorn any part in tragedy or comedy, turn an ordinary into a memorable part, and act a great role, a Richard III or a Lear, with a force like a Mediterranean storm, overwhelming in orchestration of color and sound. It may be that his impact was enhanced by the relative incompetence of the minor parts. For all the mannered elegance of the age, audiences were susceptible to a full-blooded assault on their feelings. Garrick was not a great declaimer, nor did he let himself go utterly, but kept an absolute command of his emotions. Because he was more restrained, his fellow-actors had more chance and he could bring the best out of the female lead. So much was he master of the whole range of feeling and characterization that he could appear natural, vary his pace, and achieve a degree of realism that was lost again under his successors, Kemble and Mrs. Siddons.

Garrick was vain in small things but always willing to learn. He returned from a tour of the Continental theatre in 1763–65 with new ideas about lighting, scenery, and even acting method; well received by connoisseurs abroad, he returned to a glow of admiration which lasted until his retirement in 1776. A great procession of the famous and fashionable followed him to his grave in Westminster Abbey. Johnson, who thought him "the first man in the world for sprightly conversation," had nothing but contempt for most actors, but recognized that Garrick had left the stage more respected than he had found it. He was extremely generous, but made a larger fortune than any actor except Alleyn. Not least, in an actor, he was faithful and tender to his wife, who seems to have been charming and survived him by forty-three years.

F. W. Hiller, ed., and Joshua Reynolds, *Portraits*, 1952.
D. Little and G. Kahrl, eds., *Letters of David Garrick*, 3 vols., 1963.

OLIVER GOLDSMITH (1728–74), author, was born at Pallas, a small village near Ballymahon, near Longford. His father was then a curate of his uncle's living at Kilkenny West, to which he succeeded in 1730. Thereafter he lived at the hamlet of Lissoy in Westmeath which students of Goldsmith have identified as the original of *The Deserted Village*. Here his imagination was fired by the fanciful tales of an unusual schoolmaster, Thomas Byrne, ex-quartermaster, local rhymer, and dealer in legends. But it appears to have been Patrick Hughes, the master of his last school at Edgeworthstown, who brought on his aptitude for the classics and came to terms with his sensitive temperament.

A likely cause of the self-consciousness which affected him all his life was a severe attack of smallpox, when he was about eight, which left his face terribly pitted. He was a clumsy little figure but proficient at games and could score by repartee against those who teased him. He was sent to Trinity College, Dublin, as a sizar, because his father, with a generous improvidence which was characteristic of the family, had spent most of his money on providing a dowry for his daughter. He was miserably poor there, despite the generosity of his Uncle Contarine, and he suffered from an unsympathetic tutor, Theaker Wilder, specialist in the mathematics that Goldsmith loathed. He led a lounging existence within the limits of his purse, wrote some ballads which have not survived, and left the university in 1749 without regret. Armed with a degree he could now prepare for ordination, but instead led an aimless existence at the house of relations, fishing, otter-hunting, playing his flute, and it is not surprising that he was considered unfit for Orders at his examination by Dr. Synge, Bishop of Elphin. His uncle financed one or two ventures which came to nothing. He never reached England when he set out to read law, because he allowed himself to be tricked out of the £50 with which he had been provided. Eventually, however, in 1752, he went to Edinburgh to study physics; he never saw Ireland again. After two years he proceeded to Leyden. He subsequently entitled himself M.B., but it is uncertain where he took this degree. He peregrinated through Europe, making an unconventional Grand Tour on foot, disputing, writing part of *The Traveller*; he arrived home in February 1756 with a few halfpence in his pocket.

In London he found his way into Grub Street, after vicissitudes which included a time as apothecary's assistant and another as poor physician in Southwark. He was taken on by the bookseller Griffiths as reviewer and copywriter for his magazine *The Monthly Review*. To his literary work he brought unusual qualifications. Academically he had smatterings from different studies upon the firm basis of a sound knowledge of the classics. He was well read in the English poets and was a close student of several French writers, notably Voltaire. His unorthodox Irish background and his subsequent travels had given him a useful experience of humanity. He did not stay long with Griffiths, but he persisted in his new calling. In February 1758 appeared under pseudonym his translation, free, racy, and exciting, of the *Memoirs of Jean Marteille of Bergerac*, a victim of the Revocation of the Edict of Nantes. *An Enquiry into the Present State of Learning in Europe* was planned to raise funds for a medical appointment in a foreign station. It did not materialize, but the *Enquiry*, superficial as it was, received some attention. He produced for a while a new periodical, *The Bee*, which contained several rhymed contributions of which only *The Death of Wolfe* is wholly original. But he displayed a talent for the occasional essay and secured the notice, not only of Dr. Johnson but also of Smollett, who recruited him to serve his *British Magazine*, and the bookseller Newbery, who was starting a new paper, *The Public Ledger*. For Smollett he wrote two of his best essays, for Newbery the "Chinese Letters," afterwards published as the *Citizen of the World*. He was emerging as a student of manners, but not in the hard, satirical vein. His style of living always keeping one move ahead of his income, he moved first to a house in Fleet Street, later to Islington, with expensive rooms in Brick Court. Friends were amused by his extravagance of dress. Unfortunately his constant need of money drove him to undertake hack work: in 1762, a life of Richard Nash of Bath, a task that he may have found congenial, in 1764 a history of England, in a series of letters from a nobleman to a son. He translated; he even wrote an English grammar. Yet he displayed literary qualities beyond what might have been expected of a literary drudge—lucidity, elegance, and the plainness which came naturally to an unspeculative mind: "Let us, instead of writing finely, try to write naturally."

Fortunately Goldsmith did not allow himself to be swamped by his self-imposed tasks. He was engaged upon *The Vicar of Wakefield* as early as June 1761; it was purchased by Collins in October 1762. Before it appeared, he had completed *The Traveller*, a didactic poem in rhyming stanzas, dedicated to his brother Henry, now curate of Kilkenny West, which sought to show "that every state has a particular principle of happiness." The poetry has outlived the poet's purpose. Dr. Johnson declared it was the best poem since the death of Pope and contributed several lines toward it. It sold nine editions before the author's death, though he had sold it for only £21. What most pleased contemporaries was the simple beauty of the descriptive passages: sweet without sickliness, because of the restraint of the poet's language. It has the same quality of charm that enables also *The Vicar of Wakefield*, for all its faults, to survive. This novel was brought out in March 1766 in two volumes by reluctant publishers and it sold slowly at first. It has appealed perhaps more to later generations than to his own: safe to put into the hands of Victorian children for whom Fielding and Smollett were too strong. It is an untidy book, artless in its wanderings, the plot inconsistent and often broken up by intrusions into the narrative of sermons, poems, and irrelevant tales. The character of the vicar is a little smug, while none of the other characters is so developed that we know his inner life. It lacks the virility of Fielding or the insight of Jane Austen. What we may specially like is the feeling, surely autobiographical, that the author conveys in his study of the family group of the Primroses: "All equally generous, credulous, simple, and inoffensive." The generalizations which clothe the vicar in a vague but kindly light are more effective in the more disciplined form of verse.

The Deserted Village, which was published in May 1770 and ran through five editions in the year of issue, is Goldsmith's masterpiece. It is Augustan in its measure, gravity, and poise; the contrasts of rich and poor, city and village, are familiar ones. But the poem again has the charm of a sympathetic personality, restrained from the vulgarities of mere sentiment by his control of the verse.

One advantage of play-writing to the indigent author was the prospect of immediate payment, but Goldsmith also held strong views about the nature of comedy which, he maintained, should involve comic situations rather than the "delicate distresses" which were fashionable in the theatre of his time. He wrote two plays. *The Good-Natured Man* was given to Garrick who, however, avenged himself for earlier criticisms by Goldsmith of the "histrionic demon" by prevaricating about its performance, then eventually passing it on to Coleman, who produced it at Covent Garden in

January 1763. It ran for nine days and brought in £500. Despite this success, Coleman demurred before putting on *She Stoops to Conquer.* An ingenious plot and broad fooling brought immortality to at least one of the characters, Tony Lumpkin, but he was at first deemed to be "low." Dr. Johnson, who was always ready to espouse Goldsmith's cause, pressed for its performance. He would sometimes snub his friend, who was always trying to cut a figure and often succeeding in cutting an absurd one, stuttering, thrusting himself forward: "Goldsmith should not be for ever attempting to shine in conversation: he has not temper for it, he is so much mortified when he fails." But for all his consequential and self-important manner, Boswell admired what he called the "frankness and simplicity of his natural conduct."

In April 1774, Goldsmith died, deep in debt and weakened by immoderate use of Dr. James's patent medicine. It was not the least of the merits of this delightful man that he could never resist the claims of charity upon his purse, and he was mourned by many poor people as well as by the literary world. Even if his abilities were flattered by Dr. Johnson's famous epitaph in Westminster Abbey, his character deserved the tribute: "he touched nothing that he did not adorn." He could write charmingly about anything. He frittered away money on fine clothes and Madeira; he tried the patience of his friends, by his vanity and fecklessness; yet "Let not his frailties be remembered, he was a very great man."

R. M. Wardle, *Life of Goldsmith,* 1957.
K. C. Balderston, ed., *Collected Letters,* 1928.
J. H. Plumb, essay in *Men and Places,* 1963.

JAMES THOMSON (1700–48), poet, was born at Ednam, where his father was minister, and spent his early life in the border country of Tweed and Jed. He went to the abbey school at Jedburgh and thence in 1715 to Edinburgh University. He was intended for the Presbyterian ministry, but was encouraged by friends to make a living as a tutor while he pursued his bent toward poetry. He came to London in 1725 and had his first important poem, *Winter,* ready for publication by March 1726. It was popular and was soon followed by *Summer* (1727) and *Spring* (1728). Completed by *Autumn,* the quartet was published under the title of *The Seasons* in 1730. The form of this poem was suggested by the *Georgics* of Virgil to whose themes and manner Thomson is clearly indebted. Johnson praised his originality: "His numbers, his pauses, his diction are of his own growth, without transcription, without imitation." But he owed much, for instance in his ornamental use of proper names, to Milton, and something also to another imitator of Milton, John Philips, author of *Cyder*.

Thomson's distinctive contribution was his choice of subject. At a time when most poets followed the pronouncement of Pope, that "the proper study of mankind is man," he described the phenomena of nature. He is not properly to be called a forerunner of the Romantic movement, for his skill was essentially descriptive and his language is as much restrained by the conventions of the time as by the limitations of his own outlook. He painted nature in fine and sometimes appropriate language; he did not write about himself under the form of writing about nature. His merits include, however, a patent delight in what he records, a felicity of phrase which evokes the image even in the most generalized of descriptions, and where he is more particular, an accurate and subtle sense of touch, smell, and sound. His popularity with contemporaries owed much to the sentimental stories with which he pointed a moral and adorned the tale in a fashion suited to the season. A description of a thunderstorm, for instance, evokes the story of Celadon and Amelia, lovers parted by a thunderbolt. Nothing else that the poet touched had the same success as *The Seasons*. For the rest of his life the poet revised, improved, added to it.

Thomson enjoyed the support of patrons whom he rewarded with fulsome dedications and mention in his poems. Among the warmest of these was Lyttelton, himself a poet and better fitted for this than he was for politics; when he was Chancellor of the Exchequer, in 1744, he provided Thomson with the surveyor-generalship of the Leeward Islands, though it is unlikely that he knew where they were. Thomson thus became naturally the poet of the anti-Walpole faction, although he had dedicated one of his earlier poems to the minister. With his sinecures (he was also for a time Secretary of the Briefs of Chancery) and the profits of his poems, he was not obliged to toil for a living. Earlier in life he was tutor to the two boys of Lord Binning and later to the son of Lord Talbot, with whom he traveled to France and met Voltaire. Later he turned to tragedies such as *Sophonisba, Edward and Eleanore*, and *Coriolanus*, of no special merit. Not all his poems deserve to be read; he was at his worst when engaged upon the lengthy discussion of an abstract theme. *Liberty*, in five books, tried the patience of a diminishing number of readers as it proceeded upon its prolix course. His last poem, the *Castle of Indolence*, which appeared in the year of his death, was, however, a success. In the course of this sustained allegory, the Knight of Art and Industry finds his home in Britain, guarded by Britannia and aided by Liberty. Thomson was, in his amiable and undemanding way, a "patriot," as the Prince of Wales and his faction understood the term, and he wrote the words of *Rule Britannia* which appeared in a masque written for the Prince of Wales. It was upon the water, being rowed from Hammersmith to Richmond, where he lived for the last twelve years of his life, that he caught the chill from which he subsequently died.

G. C. Macauley, *James Thomson*, 1908.

THOMAS WARTON (1728–90) was the son of Thomas Warton, vicar of Basingstoke, and professor of poetry at Oxford; an unconventional but much-loved Oxford figure, he became a better poet than his father, and also a historian of poetry, a biographer, and an antiquarian.

He entered Trinity College, Oxford, in 1744, and was elected Fellow in 1751. The college, whose great gates ever stood shut until a Stuart should come to the throne again, was his home until his death. But he was no cloistered don. He attracted notice as a poet by a poem in praise of Oxford, *The Triumph of Isis;* he contributed to a series of Oxford collections of verse and edited two of them: *The Union* and *The Oxford Sausage*. From 1758 to 1768 he was professor of poetry. In 1785 he became Poet-Laureate. His official odes were justly ridiculed. Some of his earlier verse is interesting, however, because, like his brother Joseph, the Headmaster of Winchester, Warton revolted against the limitations of good sense and expressed himself with unfashionable feeling. His criticism, too, expresses a romantic sensibility. His *Observations* on Spenser's *Faery Queen* appeared in 1754. The later years of his life were taken up mainly with the vast *History of English Poetry*. Only three volumes were finished by his death, taking the story up to the end of the Elizabethan age, but he also published a useful edition of Milton's poems. This is a Gothic work, rich and various like his personality, reflecting his extensive reading of the classics as well as of early English texts.

Warton was a church-fancier and a lover of the picturesque. Tireless in his travels with pen and notebook, he liked to dwell upon old ruins and the "flaunting ivy, that with mantle green invests some wasted tow'r." His short essay of 1762 upon Gothic architecture was a scholarly, if inaccurate, prelude to the Gothic Revival. He was a friend of Dr. Johnson, who relished his conversation and tapped his knowledge of the poets. "I love the fellow dearly, for all I laugh at him," he said, and a pleasant passage in Boswell describes their walks in the Oxfordshire countryside. Warton was too fond of academic life to pay much attention to his duties as vicar of Kiddington but, characteristically, he wrote a history of the village. He cared little for social convention and liked to drink and smoke with the Oxford bargees. "A little, squat, red-faced man" is a contemporary description of this engaging polymath who became Camden professor of ancient history in 1785, but might prefer to be known for the seven manuscript volumes of his archaeological tours which repose in Winchester College Library, for his skit on Oxford guide books *A Companion to the Guide,* or even for the lines he wrote on a blank leaf of Dugdale's *Monasticon:*

> Nor rough, nor barren are the winding ways
> Of hoar antiquity, but strown with flowers.

C. Rinaker, *Thomas Warton,* 1916.
W. P. Ker, *Collected Essays,* Vol. I, 1925.

THOMAS PERCY (1729–1811) published the *Reliques of Ancient Poetry,* which were a mine of riches for the romantic imagination to work upon, a work of scholarship, and the start of a literary movement. Percy was a grocer's son of Bridgnorth in Shropshire, who went from the local grammar school to Christ Church, where he showed an interest in early literature. He had already made a collection of Chinese poems and proverbs when he made the discovery which led to his great work. Staying with his friend Humphrey Pitt at Shifnal, he found on the floor a dusty manuscript volume which a maid had been tearing up to light fires. There remained, in a Jacobean hand, nearly two hundred sonnets, ballads, historical songs, and metrical romances from the time of Chaucer to the seventeenth century. With this for a beginning, Percy collected and edited assiduously. The *Reliques* (1765) were followed by *Northern Antiquities* in 1770. As more and more readers turned from the artificiality of contemporary verse to the Gothic and Romantic of a less settled age, and antiquarian pursuits became fashionable, taste was prepared for Sir Walter Scott, and Percy was rewarded with preferment in the Church. He became Dean of Carlisle and, in 1782, Bishop of Dromore, where he added a new transept to the cathedral. His last years were bleak, since he lost his sight in 1805 and his wife in 1806. But a Percy Society was founded to keep his name alive and his portrait was painted by Reynolds. Few men who have not themselves been original artists have had such an effect upon the culture of the time. Though he expended some time upon a fruitless attempt to show that he was descended from the Northumberland Percys, he was a modest man and a true scholar.

PRINCE CHARLES EDWARD STUART (1720–88) was born at the Palazzo Muti, in Rome, in December 1720. At this time his father, the Old Pretender, or James III, as he might be called, according to allegiance, was a disappointed man of thirty-one, melancholy and resigned to a life of exile. His mother, Maria-Clementina Sobieska, was devout, intense, and somewhat delicate; she gave birth to a second son, Henry, and then retired temporarily to a nunnery. The cause of her estrangement from her husband was religious: she objected to the appointment of a Protestant tutor, James Murray, for her elder son. James III, who was not prepared to alter his own religion for the sake of a throne, was tolerant nonetheless, and allowed Charles to grow up without settled religious convictions. He was fairly clever and learned Italian, French, and English without difficulty, but his education was as haphazard as his family background was unsettled. He grew up a restless boy, agile, active, a good rider, and a good shot; tall but slight, with the coloring of his ancestress, Mary Queen of Scots: light brown hair and chestnut eyes (though the iconography of this prince is controversial, some paintings give him fair hair and blue eyes; when he grew a beard it was red).

Charles Edward came to be regarded by Jacobites at home as the hopeful prospect, while he himself became absorbed by the cause. He made plans for fortifications and hardened himself by long walks and other feats of endurance. In January 1744, in secret and in disguise, he left Rome for France, where an expedition was being prepared. Unfortunately the Brest fleet which was to have escorted the transports to England was scattered by a storm and Marshal Saxe turned to other plans. For over a year Charles dallied incognito, impatient and frustrated by the half-hearted attitude of the French government. Then he decided to cross alone. For this single act of courage and initiative Charles deserves his place in legend. He raised a small loan from Waters, the Jacobite banker in Paris, bought some arms, ammunition, and brandy, hired a brig and a man-of-war, and set sail for the Western Isles.

After a running fight with an English ship, leaving the brig to put back to France, the *du Teillay* landed the prince with six companions at Eriska at the end of July. On August 4, Charles dismissed the ship where he had held his first hopeful audiences. On the nineteenth he raised his standard at Glenfinnan: by his side was Murray of Broughton, a Lowlander, appointed to be his secretary and suspect to the Highlanders from the start. After an agonizing wait, the pipes of the Camerons announced the arrival of his most substantial aid. With 700 of this wild clan were some Macdonalds, Stewarts of Appin, MacDonnells, Clanranalds and MacLeods. Like some other August crises, this venture found the English government unprepared. In Duncan Forbes of Culloden they had a shrewd Lord President whose influence helped to damp down support for the Pretender. But Sir John Cope had neither troops nor talent enough to hold the Highlanders. On September 17 they entered Edinburgh unopposed, now under the command of Lord George Murray, a veteran of the '15. There Charles accepted the huzzas of the people in the courtyard below Holyrood, while his father was proclaimed James VIII of Scotland at the Mercat Cross. Four days later he met Cope, who had shipped his troops south from Aberdeen, at Prestonpans. The two forces, at about 2,500, were equal but Cope's troops were panicky and handicapped further by a morning mist. "They escaped like rabets," the prince wrote to his father, after an action that lasted for a bare ten minutes. Cope himself brought to Berwick the news of a defeat which had exposed England to the rebel army. Charles wanted to march direct upon England. Still a somewhat detached figure in all the excitement and the intrigues of his counselors, he was overruled, stayed in Edinburgh for five weeks, and did little more than to declare the Union with England at an end. Edinburgh Castle held out, and the bankers whose money was so important took shelter within its walls.

On November 1 the army marched southward, not toward Newcastle where Wade lay, as Charles wanted, but toward Carlisle and the west, where Murray hoped that they would find recruits. On the fifteenth, Carlisle Castle surrendered. At Lancaster, Preston, and Manchester, there was enthusiasm but a scarcity of recruits. They reached Derby, 130 miles from London, on December 6. There were about 5,000 men, but the attitude of the local gentry did not encourage them to expect much response farther south. Wade at Wetherby, Cumberland at Lichfield, another army assembling at Finchley Common—some 30,000 in all were waiting to resist them. Not knowing the full extent of the panic in London, it is not surprising that Charles "could not prevail upon a single person" to carry on with the march. So the Highlanders turned back, losing the advantage of surprise and morale. The decision must have been wrong: if the cause had slight hope before, it had no hope thereafter. Indeed, it is hard to resist the view that it was forlorn from the start. But all that Charles achieved had been by bluff and audacity; now he was reduced to campaigning under the conventional conditions in which he was bound to be at a disadvantage. On January 17 his men won a small victory at Falkirk. But at Culloden on April 13 only a miracle, such as the success of his projected night attack, could have saved his starving, ragged men from defeat at the hands of Cumberland's drilled professionals, supported by artillery and by faith in their cool commander. Charles, who had grown steadily more moody amid the quarrels of his followers and who had been seriously ill with pneumonia in February, had to watch the battle develop in ground wholly unsuited to the Highlanders' tactics and he did not stay to see their final rout.

When Lord Lovat discussed plans of further resistance, he showed no enthusiasm. He was worn out, broken *au fond* by disappointment as much as by the hardships of the campaign, and bitter with his commanders, notably Murray, who had crossed him upon several vital occasions, though with valid military arguments. The cheerfulness and toughness which had so impressed the Highlanders did not wholly desert him. He may even have enjoyed some of his adventures during the months of danger, April to September, when he was being sought by the troops with a price of £30,000 upon his head. With his gallant companions—among them, for a time, Flora Macdonald—in the bothies and hills of Stornoway and Scalpay, Corrodale and Skye, the legend of Prince Charlie received its final touches. After he had eventually departed, with Cameron of Lochiel, Lochgarry, and about a hundred others, he left behind some brave and affecting memories. But with hundreds of wretched prisoners rotting in the prison hulks of the Thames, crofts burned, the clans broken up, the Jacobite chieftains dead, proscribed or in exile, the cause was dead. Its ghosts lingered on. Charles Edward did not at once give up hope. For years he wandered, so successfully disguised that historians today cannot trace his movements. In 1748, with peace, came orders to leave France. In January 1755 his father wrote that he had not known of his whereabouts for six years—though the English government might have been able to tell him. But "James Douglas" occasionally wrote to Waters, in Paris: once he scribbled, "What can a bird do that has not found a right nest? He must flit from bough to bough." There is evidence that he lived in Lorraine, in Paris, that he visited Spain, Russia, Sweden, Scotland again. A typical rumor was that he had been complaining of being badly shaved in an Oxfordshire village. Certainly he visited London, in the spring of 1750, met Jacobite sympathizers, inspected the Tower and St. James, and was received, at St. Mary's le Strand, into the Anglican Church. In 1753, the Elibank plot was unearthed: its object was the capture of the entire reigning house, its principal casualty Dr. Cameron, Lochiel's brother. About this time he took a mistress, Clementina Walkenshaw, whom he had briefly met in England in '45, and by her had a daughter. It is possible that she was a spy; she left him in 1760. He had never been much in the company of women; he had long been a heavy drinker and by now was consuming a bottle of brandy a day.

Early in 1766 his father died and Charles awaited his recognition as Charles III. Neither the Pope nor any European power would do this. It was convenient, however, for France to have another "Young Pretender," and in 1772, for marrying the eighteen-year-old Princess Louisa of Stolberg, he received the promise of a small pension from Louis XV. There was no child, and before his death the "Compte d'Albanie" recognized his daughter by Clementina as his heir. In his last years, in Florence and in Rome where he died on January 30, 1788, she was a sympathetic companion. His wife had left him for a convent in 1780, after a scene when he actually hit her, and then became the mistress of an Italian poet. Charles was probably not such a degraded figure as hostile rumor depicted him, but it would have been better for his fame if he had been killed in 1746. What the few Jacobites, faithful or curious visitors, saw was a dreary and somewhat incoherent old man; the contrast between this shambling figure and the young adventurer of '45 must have been poignant indeed.

C. H. Hartmann, *The Quest Forlorn,* 1952.
F. McLynn, *Charles Edward Stuart,* 1988.

HENRY BENEDICT YORK (1725–1807), cardinal, last of the Stuarts, "Henry IX, King of Great Britain" as the few remaining devotees of the family preferred to call him, was the younger son of James Edward Stuart and of Maria-Clementina Sobieski. Since his mother retired to a convent and his father was of a melancholy disposition, his boyhood lacked excitement. He was devoted to his more active elder brother Charles Edward, but was not let in to the secret of '45 and took no part in that adventure. Devout and gentle as his father, he became ordained and was provided with three Italian bishoprics and made cardinal: nothing could be imagined better calculated to kill any hope of a legitimist restoration to the British throne. By the time "James III" died, the Papacy had concluded that the Stuarts had no political future and refused to recognize Charles Edward as king. When Charles Edward died, however, in 1788, Henry styled himself king, in the words of his medal, "Not by the will of men, but by the Grace of God": last sad formula of the Stuarts. When the French invaded Italy his palace at Frascati was sacked. George III, hearing of his plight, sent him, as one gentleman to another, a pension to ensure his comfort. Jacobitism was dead, laid into the earth with fitting gesture of chivalry and generosity. Henry bequeathed his remaining Crown jewels to the Prince of Wales.

LORD GEORGE MURRAY (1694–1760), Jacobite general, was a son of the Duke of Atholl. He spent an unruly youth, failed to settle at Glasgow University, and went into the army. He gladly exchanged a cornetcy in George I's army for a colonelcy in "James

III's," but his participation in the revolt of 1715 led to exile, and he did not improve his position by acting with his brother William, Marquis of Tullibardine, as leader of the abortive rising of 1719. A dominant motive in his life was service to the exiled king, whom he came to see as personification of Christian hero and knight. In 1725, however, he secured a pardon and came to live at Tullibardine Castle. In 1739, in the interests of his family, he at last took the oath of submission to the Hanoverian king. He believed that the Jacobite cause was moribund and wanted to serve his country. He even suggested the employment of Highland troops in the government service.

The events of 1745 seem to have taken Murray by surprise, and the landing of the prince may well have appeared a forlorn adventure. He was drawn to engage himself in the cause by his brother William, who had remained chivalrously loyal to the Prince, by his own military ambitions, and by a strong sense of honor. At Perth, in September, he was appointed joint lieutenant-general of the army, with Lord Perth, under the prince. From the start his position was difficult. The only experienced soldier, he had to bear the garrulous advice of Mr. O'Sullivan, self-appointed military adviser, quartermaster-general, and adjutant-general, but ignorant of war and the country, as well as the uncertain whims of the prince. The Highland army of about 3,000 was as undisciplined as it was brave; that it did not behave worse was owing largely to his sensible discipline. Because Murray was forthright with the prince, who liked the flattery of the Irish group, he was subsequently held to have been disloyal. But this came with the bitterness of defeat and exile, and during the early campaign disagreements were stilled by victory at Prestonpans and the exhilaration of the march to Derby. In December the lack of recruits compelled him to counsel retreat, with the approval of the rest of the council; thereafter the prince blamed him for all that went amiss.

The splendid victory at Falkirk showed that, in Lord Mahon's words, the prince had a general with whom none could vie "in planning a campaign, providing against disasters, or improving a victory." Perhaps ultimate disaster was inevitable in the face of the larger, well-found force of Cumberland; but there is little doubt that the overwhelming defeat of Culloden was caused by the constant interference of the prince, too sanguine to the last, and especially by his insistence upon battle at Culloden on April 16, 1746, when his troops were exhausted and starving. The conduct of the battle is still surrounded by controversy. Lord George Murray emerges, however, as a commander of foresight and bravery, "first and last upon the field." After the battle he remained in hiding for eight months in the hills near Tullibardine. Then he took ship and landed in Holland on Christmas Day. Charles Edward refused even to receive him, but he settled down to live contentedly enough in exile near Cleves.

Katherine Tomasson, *The Jacobite General*, 1958.
J. Black, *Culloden and the 45*, 1990.

DUNCAN FORBES (1685–1747), Lord President of the Court of Session, was the man above all on whom the Whig government depended for the security and order of Scotland in the years leading up to 1745. It is ironic that the great seventies which followed the suppression of the Jacobite rising should be associated with the name of his family house and estate of Culloden, for he was an amiable man who sought peace in Scotland, the bettering of its inhabitants, and friendship amongst the clans. His family was strong Whig, and Duncan was trained as a lawyer in Edinburgh and Leyden. In 1715 he helped to rescue Inverness from the Jacobites with a force which he raised himself, and was rewarded with the office of depute-advocate. He protested against the trial of the Scottish rebels in England, but this did not hinder his professional progress. In 1725 he became Lord Advocate; in 1735 he succeeded his elder brother in the family estate; in 1737 he was made Lord President in succession to Sir Hew Dalrymple, a pleasant man who left huge arrears of business. The Lord President presided over civil cases in which, since the jury system was obsolete, the judge was arbiter both of law and fact. He carried out swift reforms. No case was to be left undecided for more than four years, and a proper rota of judges was instituted. Forbes appointed a registrar whose task it was to rescue the Scottish records from damp, and rats and he ended most of the chicanery of agents in the courts. His own judgments were clear and decisive enough to earn the praise of Lord Hardwicke.

The career of this able lawyer, who combined whole-hearted support of the Union with warm defense of Scottish interests, was marred at the close by the rising of 1745. Lord George Murray, the

Jacobite general, was his personal friend. Forbes, however, played no passive role but strove with the Earl of Loudon to hold the north of Scotland while the prince occupied Edinburgh. After the battle on bleak Culloden Moor above the park and policies of his stately house, he spoke out for justice and clemency but without avail. He who had spent and suffered so much for the government was slighted by the Duke of Cumberland and unrewarded by the king. Forbes indeed seems to have been an admirable character: a conservative who was much alarmed by the insidious growth of tea drinking, a lawyer who was notable for his humanity, and a patriot who tried to hold the middle course between extremes.

G. Menary, *Life and Letters of Duncan Forbes of Culloden*, 1936.

GEORGE KEITH, 11th EARL MARISCHAL (1693–1778), was a gallant Jacobite, later in life the servant and friend of Frederick the Great; a splendid example of the adaptable Scotsman whose life is mostly spent abroad, but who yet retains the independence and toughness of his native country.

He was the eldest son of the 9th Earl. His mother was a Drummond. The feudal office had become a hereditary title, but the tradition of the Aberdeenshire family was one of loyalty to the Crown. His father had protested against the Union; George, an officer in Anne's army, joined Mar's rising in Scotland, with his brother James. They fought strenuously at Sheriffmuir, urged the army to make another stand, and refused to leave with Mar. Eventually they escaped to France and then went to Spain, where Alberoni was planning to use the Jacobites as an instrument in his ambitious schemes. The Earl Marischal, attainted, led the small Spanish company which landed in Lewis. He established a base at Eilean Donan on Loch Duich, opposite Skye, but was given little support. With Tullibardine and Lord George Murray, he was defeated in Glen Shiel; he returned, wounded, to Spain, only to be coolly treated by James, who thought him an honorable fool; he, in turn, distrusted the prince's councillors. "Nothing but ill management on this side of the water has kept or can keep the Elector on the Throne of Britain."

Keith opposed the 1745 rising and after its failure went to Vienna. His brother James, meanwhile, had thrived as a mercenary, first in Russian service, then as Field Marshal of Prussia. Keith went to Frederick the Great who employed him as ambassador in France and Spain during the Seven Years War. Since Frederick was then an ally of England, he was able to secure the reversal of his attainder and the succession to the earldom of Kintore, his by heredity. It was he, in 1760, who gave Pitt news of the signing of the Family Compact between Charles III and Louis XV. After the Peace of Paris he returned to Scotland but was persuaded by Frederick, who seems to have been truly fond of the robust old man, to return to Prussia. He lived on affectionate terms with this lonely and unloved king for the rest of his life, in his villa at Potsdam enjoying a way of life "half-Aberdeenshire, half-Spanish." He was by no means the simple person that his manner suggested. He corresponded with Voltaire, and he invented the game out of which Kriegspiel grew.

DONALD CAMERON OF LOCHIEL (1695–1748) is a fine example of the Highland chieftain, a leading figure in the '45 revolt who risked danger and suffered exile for a prince whom he had advised not to come till the times were more propitious. "The gentle Lochiel" was a civilized man among barbarians, well educated and acquainted with the world, handsome in an almost delicate way. He could be fierce, however, with his clansmen. He threatened to burn down the house of any Cameron who did not turn out for the '45; before the capture of Edinburgh he declared that he would shoot any clansman who looted or drank—and none touched a drop. It was the sound of the Cameron pipes coming over the mountain at Glenfinnan that first told the prince that he had an army, while on the last field of Culloden, none fought more bravely than the clan Cameron. Their chief was wounded in both legs. The remaining people of the clan were harried in their glens, while Lochiel himself is supposed to have watched from a hillside as his house, Achnacarry, burned to the ground. His estates were forfeited to the Crown and his younger brother Archibald was subsequently executed, on a flimsy charge of conspiracy.

F. McLynn, *The Jacobites*, 1985.

FLORA MACDONALD (1722–90) was the daughter of Ronald Macdonald of South Uist; he died when she was a child and her mother married again—Sir Alexander Macdonald. She was brought up in turn by Clanranald, chief of the clan, and Macdonald, and sent to finish her education in Edinburgh. In June 1746 she happened to be staying on Benbecula. Her stepfather was at the time in command of the militia out looking for Prince Charles Edward, fugitive since Culloden. On June 21 Captain O'Neil, an old acquaintance, asked her to help to convey the prince to Skye. She arranged for a pass from her stepfather for herself, manservant, "Betty Burke" (an Irish spinning-maid, needed, she said, to help her mother), and six boatmen. They crossed the Minch and, after being first driven off by some militia-men, safely reached the house of Lady Macdonald. Sir Alexander was serving with Cumberland's army, but she agreed to shelter the prince. He stayed at the house of her factor, Macdonald of Kingsburgh. On June 30 Flora accompanied the prince to Portree and saw him off to Raasay. He had weeks of anxiety and concealment to endure before he returned to France. But she had done more than anyone to save his life.

Flora Macdonald was arrested on her return to Benbecula and sent to the Tower. On her release she was adulated in society but was in no way affected by this. She had acted, she said, not from any high-flown loyalty but as she would "for any person in distress." In 1750 she married Allan Macdonald of Kingsburgh; it was then that she received the celebrated visit of Dr. Johnson and Boswell, who recorded that she was "a little woman of a genteel appearance and uncommonly mild and well-bred." In the following year, impoverished like so many Highlanders at this time, she and her husband emigrated to North Carolina. He was a loyalist in the Rebellion and was captured; she returned to Scotland and was wounded on the way in a fight with a French frigate. Reunited with her husband after the war, she lived for the rest of her life in Skye. In either army or navy, all her five sons served King George III.

Eric Linklater, *The Prince in the Heather*, 1965.
F. McLynn, *Charles Edward Stuart*, 1988.

WILLIAM AUGUSTUS, DUKE OF CUMBERLAND (1721–65) was included by Horace Walpole in his list of the great men whom he had known in his life. Since today he is remembered primarily as "the butcher" of Culloden, and by the Scots as "stinking Billy," it is right to recall that he was once admired for his courage and leadership.

The second surviving son of George II and Queen Caroline, he was born at Leicester House. At the age of four he was made first knight of the revived Order of the Garter. According to Lord King, then Chancellor, the Prince of Wales, before his accession, planned to disinherit his detested elder son and make Cumberland heir to the throne. This came to nothing but, perhaps because he never stood first in line of succession, George II always enjoyed easy relations with his son. Originally intended for the navy, he chose the army and displayed courage and devotion to his service. He was first in action under his father at Dettingen, and was there wounded in the leg; the wound healed, but imperfectly, and gave him further trouble. In 1745, at the age of twenty-four, he was made captain-general of the British forces attached to the allied army at Flanders, in place of the septuagenarian Wade. This appointment reflected the dearth of military talent in England after years of peace, but he distinguished himself nonetheless at Fontenoy, in April, where the English forces took the brunt of the French attacks before retreating in good order. One of his colonels, Joseph Yorke, wrote afterwards: "I never saw or heard of such behavior as the Duke's: he rode everywhere, he encouraged the wavering, he complimented the bold, he threatened the cowards . . . Had the nation seen him they would have adored him."

The nation soon had need of him, after Prince Charles Edward's landing in Scotland and his southward march. He was brought home in October to command the principal army at Lichfield, where he covered London during the prince's march to Derby. He then marched by slow stages toward the Highlands, on the tail of the retreating Jacobites; then Stirling, on February 2, Aberdeen on February 27, Nairn on April 1. As he proceeded he took characteristic measures to ensure that his men would not run before the Highlanders, as had happened at Prestonpans and Falkirk. They were trained to fire with concentrated effect and to stand their ground. Cumberland's reputation, energy, and thoroughness restored the morale of his men, and the battle of Culloden Moor was won before it started. The Highlanders who faced Cumberland's fresh troops and efficient artillery on April 16, with the cold rain driving in their faces, were tired and starving, and the frenzied courage of their attacks was useless in the face of accurate fire. Cumberland's victory was complete when he sent in his cavalry on the flanks, and with 2,000 dead or captured, the remnants of the Highlanders dispersed. Cumberland, who had but 300 casualties, was satisfied but, out of temper with the rebels whose rising had threatened his father's throne. He ordered their systematic extermination, the burning of their houses, and the confiscation of their cattle. Cumberland stayed three months to see the operation launched, then returned to London to find that his heroic image was becoming tarnished by the stories of savagery assiduously circulated by his political opponents and by Jacobites. Dr. Johnson once visited Bedlam and was struck by the sight of an inmate beating at his straw under the impression that he was punishing Cumberland for his cruelties in Scotland. The poor lunatic only expressed the popular view.

The story of the pacification of the Highlands is a distressing one; but Cumberland's conduct should be seen in perspective. The manners of the Highlanders were savage, their methods ferocious. Treason was an ugly word, and the cruelties of Cumberland's troops are paralleled by the grim reprisals of the law, which knew no distinction of birth or rank. Some of the worst atrocities were committed by Scottish Whigs, eager to pay off old scores. Cumberland's personal appearance told against him in the growth of the legend. He weighed eighteen stone and had porcine features and manners to match. Yet the responsibility for the policy remains his: he did nothing to mitigate the cruelties of Hawley's dragoons and showed no sign of regret. He was not a sensitive man.

He returned to Flanders in 1747 but did not add to his military reputation. At the battle of Laffeldt the allied army was again defeated. His dispositions were faulty and only the handling of the cavalry by Ligonier saved the army from disintegration. He was no more successful when he commanded again, at the start of the Seven Years War. Defeated by the French at Hastenbeck in July 1757, he retreated northward, was encircled by superior forces under Richelieu, and signed the Convention of Klosterseven securing the neutrality of Hanover, in September. His orders had been inhibiting: George II was primarily anxious for the safety of Hanover and gave him full powers, as Pitt pointed out to him, to secure it. Cumberland was recalled and made to resign, while Pitt whom he had opposed and driven from office in April, promptly disavowed his convention. He consoled himself with his racehorses and with the pleasures of the table, for which he had a true

Hanoverian appetite. He died, exhausted, at the early age of forty-four.

Cumberland's most important military contribution was in the unspectacular work of reform of discipline and training, and the inculcation of professional standards. It may be recalled that, when the garrison of Minorca was attacked in 1756, almost all the officers were absent in London. Amateurism and slackness were Cumberland's targets; he attacked them with Germanic thoroughness. He was not able to end the purchase of commissions, but he insisted upon evidence of soldierly fitness. He attempted to limit the amount of leave that officers might take and the number of carriages they could take with them on campaigns. He might have attached less importance to the cut and color of uniforms and spent more time on thinking about strategy, but he had an eye for merit in his subordinates and promoted forward and humane young officers such as Howe, Coote, and Wolfe. It was the latter, the least conventional of soldiers, who said of Cumberland's dismissal that it was "a public calamity."

Evan Charteris, *William Augustus, Duke of Cumberland, 1721–48*, 1913.

J. A. Houlding, *Fit for Service: The Training of the British Army, 1715–1795*, 1982.

ROBERT MACQUEEN, LORD BRAXFIELD (1722–99), the most arresting figure among the legal portraits in Cockburn's *Memorials of His Time*, achieved a notoriety outside his native Scotland by his conduct of the treason trials of 1793–94. "But the giant of the Bench was Braxfield. His very name makes people start yet." Political temper was charged with furious anti-Jacobinism in these years. Reformers and radicals whose activities were in some way suspect to the government might expect to encounter biased juries. In Scotland, however, the judges themselves failed to maintain impartiality. Foremost among these was Braxfield, who presided at the infamous trials of Muir, lawyer and founder of the Scottish Friends of the People, and Palmer, a leading Scottish Unitarian, sentenced to fourteen and seven years' transportation, respectively. In Braxfield's view the constitution was perfect, and it was seditious, therefore, even to propose change. He was exceptionally well-versed in the details of the law; at the same time he was a boor and a bully.

"Strong built and dark, with rough eye-brows, powerful eyes, threatening lips, and a low growling voice, he was like a formidable blacksmith. His accent and his dialect were exaggerated Scotch; his language, like his thoughts, short, strong and conclusive." His gross repartee provides the Scottish bar with some of its best stories. Even if he was not, as has been said, the judge who told a former chess crony whom he had sentenced to be hanged, "That's checkmate to you, Matthew," he did make a habit of adorning his judgments with a mordant humor all his own. To a clever culprit he once said: "Ye're a vera clever chiel, man, but ye wad be nane the waur o' a hanging." With reference to his aged and trusty clerk, he used to boast: "Hoot! just gie me Josie Norrie and a gude jury and I'll do for the fellow." Others too in that robust age doled out brutal punishments without regard for their victims' feelings. The particular blot upon the record of this masterly lawyer is that he gloried in the prejudices that could make a travesty of justice. His eminent career reveals the rough underside of the civilization of the eighteenth century—and in Edinburgh at that.

Ed. and abridged W. F. Gray, *Henry, Lord Cockburn: Memorials of His Time*, 1946.

DAVID HUME (1711–76), historian and philosopher, was born in Edinburgh, the younger son of a Berwickshire laird of good family but small means. He went at twelve to Edinburgh University but after a regular course of three years he plunged into deep, somewhat random reading. His passion for literature proved stronger than his father's wish that he should read for the Bar. His mind was wonderfully stored but his health suffered; eventually, to cure himself of morbid depression, he tried to make a career in commerce. After a few months in a merchant's office in Bristol, he traveled to France, drawn, it may be instinctively, to the land of the *philosophes* which was to become his second home.

After three years, spent mostly at the Jesuit college of la Flèche, where Descartes had been educated, Hume came home to arrange for the publication of his work, *A Treatise of Human Nature*, the first two volumes of which appeared in 1739. In Hume's disappointed words, the books fell "dead-born from the press," though there was at least one long review. Indeed the force and lucidity of his philosophical arguments went largely unrecognized until he achieved fame as moralist and historian. Hume began, it seemed, in the rationalist tradition whose weaknesses he sought to expose: his subtitle was *An Attempt to Introduce the Experimental Method of Reasoning into Moral Subjects.* But he sought (as Newton had for the physical world by his principle of attraction) for some principle which should unify the moral world. He found it in Association, which introduces an order into the world of ideas by means of the relations of Resemblance, Contiguity in Time or Place, and Cause and Effect, and hence derived his complex ideas: Relations, Modes and Substances. Dealing with the problem of External Existence—the relation between things and ourselves—he declares that man is contained within the compass of his own ideas. He asks: How can real things be distinguished from illusory? He answers: By an appeal to common sense. Accepting the existence of an external order, he denies that it is based upon reason: "belief is more properly an act of the sensitive than of the cognitive part of our natures." Belief in the "order of nature" is determined by certain principles which associate together the ideas of these objects and unite them in the imagination. "Causation" is a "vivacious" feeling, arising from the customary connection of certain ideas in a pattern, shared with other sensible people. This he calls Nature which, in this sense, he defends as against deism which does not contain all the keys to existence. So he demolishes the claims of religion, whether based on revelation or on deduction, but at the same time admits, with sprightly detachment, the limitations of philosophical speculation: it could be thought, but it could hardly be lived. Hume himself admitted that when he left his study all his doubts vanished: "I dine, I play a game of backgammon, I converse and am merry with my friends." Returning from these amusements he found his speculations "cold and strained and ridiculous." One warms to him.

The third volume of the *Treatise* and, in 1741, *Essays, Moral and Political,* attracted greater notice and Hume was encouraged to work more at popularizing his reflections than at extending his inquiries. They had not been nugatory, as may be seen from the judgment of Bertrand Russell: "These skeptical conclusions are equally difficult to refute and to accept. The result was a challenge to philosophers which, in my opinion, has still not been adequately met." The philosopher had, however, also to live and so, having failed twice to secure a university professorship against the influence of the orthodox, he spent a year as tutor to Lord Annadale whom he found to be mad, and then in 1746 accompanied General St. Clair as secretary upon a farcically inefficient expedition to France. In 1748 he went on mission to Vienna and Turin and in the same year published a third volume of *Essays, Moral and Political* and another collection of essays, later to be known as the *Enquiry Concerning Human Understanding*, which presented the reasoning of the *Treatise* in revised form. In 1751 came his *Enquiry Concerning the Principles of Morals* in which his conformity to accepted social standards is made plain: he rejects all supernatural and physical sanctions for morality and finds all the sanctions he needs in human nature: so his ethical and philosophical positions come into line. Good is what is approved of, an "object of esteem"; to say something is bad is to say that it is disapproved of, which "arouses aversion."

Hume regarded the *Enquiry* as the best of his writing, maybe because it corresponds with his own complacent instincts. He believed that questions of ethics, as well as those of taste, could be referred to the corporate good sense of respectable society. Could such a claim have been made at any other time in the history of Europe? He made a virtue of conforming to the precepts and behavior of a society that was as narrowly conceived as it was solid in self-confidence. His skepticism, no less bland for appearing to be modest, enraged Dr. Johnson, to whom he seemed to be destroying all things firm and certain. Hume was also, however, invalidating the weaker sort of skepticism and pointing the way to a new authority, in instinct; for after he has accepted that nature is a habit of mind, morality a sentiment of the heart, and belief a product of the imagination, he comes near to advising men to allow faith in its place as well: "Our most Holy religion is founded upon Faith, not on reason; and it is a sure method of exposing it to put it to such a trial as it is by no means fitted to endure." Outside reason? There lay another field where reason's laws did not apply. There he might experiment but he could not conclude. So he remained a skeptic, but never became the atheist depicted by hostile propaganda.

In 1752 Hume published a volume of *Political Discourses* which, translated into French, introduced him with *éclat* to the literary world of Europe. He was also made keeper of the Advocates' Library in Edinburgh, against the clamor of the "unco' guid," louder still when he was found to have introduced some French novels. Now he had some income to support him in his design of writing history. Voltaire showed what could be done in his *Charles XII* by the application of literary skill and a philosophical mind. Discouraged by the early failure of his philosophical works and believing anyway that the mind was only capable of sensible experience, Hume came to look for such experience in the empirical study of past events and men. The first volume of his history, upon the Early Stuarts, appeared in 1754; it was not approved, partly because his Scottish ignorance of common law led him to misunderstand the motives of the parliamentary leaders whose opposition was part of the sacred Whig tradition. The second volume, ending in 1688, was, however, successful; then he worked backward, later, somewhat superficial volumes on the Tudor and Middle Ages, completing the study. Its sales, by 1761, had made him "not merely independent, but opulent." Rational, impartial as might be expected from a Tory who could no more accept Divine Right than he could the extreme Whig view of the constitutional struggle, the history suffers from the characteristic and distorting eighteenth-century passion for uniformity. Hume has all Gibbon's urbane confidence in the superiority of his own age, without the latter's meticulous research; the style is lucid but does not mount to the sustained grandeur of Gibbon. So Hume is now valued more as philosopher than historian, but his achievement was nonetheless remarkable; in the last years of his life he was able to savor it. For above two years, 1763–65, he was Secretary to the English Embassy at Paris, possibly through the influence of the Comtesse de Boufflers, a passionate admirer, maybe even for a time his lover. He was received with acclaim in the salons and academies, and even Louis XV found something to say to him. He befriended among others Rousseau, but the neurotic genius repaid his kindly attentions by provoking an absurd quarrel, then bombarding him with insults which were the talk of Europe. Few who met him, however, failed to be pleased by his unassuming manner and radiant good humor. "Verbum caro factum est," exclaimed d'Alembert profanely when he first saw the plump philosopher.

From 1767 to 1769 he was in London as an Undersecretary of State. Then he settled finally in Edinburgh, where he attracted to himself a society which may have been less scintillating than that of Paris, but did not lack a sober distinction of its own. The Edinburgh of Robertson, Adam Smith, Lord Kames, was coming into its golden age, and of the Edinburgh literati Hume was acknowledged leader. At the same time his name was mud to the zealots of the kirk. "Le bon David" he might be in Paris; in Edinburgh "the Atheist Hume." His enemies chuckled over the story that he had gotten stuck in a bog under the Castle Rock and only been assisted to dry ground by a pious old woman on condition that he recited the Lord's Prayer and the Creed—which he did with alacrity. In truth he was as amiable as he was mild. He was capable too of stoicism. When a wasting form of dysentery had made him, in the eyes of Boswell who came to probe him on the question of the immortality of the soul, "lean, ghastly, and quite of an earthy appearance," he showed that he could jest in the face of death, and maintain a cheerful pose of infidelity to the end. "He was an Atheist!" someone shouted as his coffin was carried out, but at once a voice retorted: "He was an honest man!"

M. Mossner, *David Hume*, 1954.
J. Y. T. Greig, ed., *Letters*, 2 vols., 1932.
B. Willey, *The Eighteenth-Century Background*, 1940.

ALLAN RAMSAY (1713–84), portrait painter, was born in Edinburgh, where his father's poetry was almost the first fruit of that grand literary harvest of the eighteenth century. Young Allan studied art in London (attending Hogarth's St. Martin's Lane Academy for some of his time) and in Italy; and from 1738, though he had and used a studio in Edinburgh, he worked chiefly in London. The foreign *timbre* of his work, the lack of which kept Hogarth unfashionable, and the patronage of Dr. Mead (who had cared for the consumptive Watteau in 1719) helped him to early popularity. By 1751 the critic Vertue thought his pictures "much superior in merit than any other portrait painter's." In the same year Ramsay, who had lost by death his first wife and their three children, eloped with Margaret Lindsay, later to be the subject of "The Painter's Wife," the flower of his work. He took her to Rome from 1754 to 1757, and it must have been her example which formed in his head that marvellous vision of womankind which he realized during the following years, and which prompted Horace Walpole to say that Ramsay was "formed" to paint women. He had painted George III as Prince of Wales and had reached an intimacy with him which was continued on the prince's accession: Ramsay was created Painter-in-Ordinary, and had to employ a throng of assistants to meet the overwhelming orders for royal portrait-copies to be sent, as imperial symbols and as marks of favor, to the furthest parts of the world. At about the same time his star became eclipsed by those of Reynolds and Gainsborough; and when an accident to his arm (c. 1773) made painting difficult, he moved gracefully from the world of artists to the world of philosophers and *litterateurs*. Now he traveled for health and diversion, and his struggle to return from Italy (to die at Dover) in 1784 is reminiscent of Scott's last return to Abbotsford.

Ramsay was a man of great charm, an accomplished scholar, who spoke several languages, exerted himself as an essayist, and was welcome to men of learning everywhere. He knew Rousseau and Voltaire; corresponded with Diderot; was specially appreciated—"loved"—by Dr. Johnson; entered the group which surrounded Mrs. Montagu; and in Edinburgh formed the Select Society, members of which were Hume, Adam Smith, James Adam the architect, William Robertson the historian, Lords Kames and Monboddo, and Boswell.

His portraiture is uneven in quality. It is also undramatic. He was a "still-life" artist: his subject-figures, though full of potential vitality, do not "move'; they are caught in moments of repose, not in action, but they are caught with loving care. Ramsay later made a habit—which was uncommon at the time—of doing chalk studies before setting to work in paint. Thus his painting is peculiarly disciplined and delicate. He made some memorable male portraits: "Dr. Mead" (for the Foundling Hospital), "David Hume," "Rousseau." But in his portraits of women—where from billowed costumes of lace and coruscating satin there looks out all that is most lovely, most frail, and most tender—he touches the heights.

STRINGER LAWRENCE (1697–1775) has been aptly called "the father of the Indian army" for he started a tradition of strenuous soldiering which lasted as long as the British Raj. Under him and his fellow officers, Indians who could be inept and cowardly under their own countrymen fought superbly. He served at Gibraltar, in Flanders, and on the field of Culloden before being sent to India as "major in the East Indies only" to command all the company's troops, in 1747. He was captured by the French at Madras but released at the peace of Aix-la-Chapelle. In 1749 he was made civil governor and military commandant of Fort St. David. Although Clive's seizure and defense of Arcot steals the fame, Lawrence taught Clive much about commanding small bodies of troops. He was responsible too for the forward policy of cooperation with such Indian princes as would be friendly. In 1752 with Clive he defeated the French-backed Chanda Sahib and restored Muhammed Ali as Nawáb of the Carnatic. When war was renewed in 1757 he was made brigadier-general and in the following winter he commanded Fort St. George in its successful resistance to siege. He left India in 1759. Eyre Coote succeeded him and completed the discomfiture of the French by the victory at Wandewash.

ROBERT CLIVE, BARON CLIVE (1725–74) created a territorial empire out of war between the East India Company and its French rivals. "A heaven-born general," in Pitt's phrase, Clive was one of the conquistadores of British imperialism. In the face of the perils and opportunities that faced the handful of Britons in India, conventional moral judgments can be set aside. Clive was not a scrupulous administrator, but an adventurer of genius at a time when he and his fellow-servants of the company had to choose between fighting and grasping—or abandoning India to the French and their puppet rulers.

Clive was born at Styche Hall, Moreton Say, the Shropshire village where his family had been for 300 years. He was sent to school at Market Drayton, where his initials are still to be seen, carved on a desk. Could the bored schoolboy have dreamed of anything so dramatic and glorious as the defense of Arcot or the victory of Plassey? His boyhood shows him strong-willed, daring, perhaps a bully. He climbed the church tower to mount a gargoyle and led gangs in window breaking and petty blackmail. His family and local shopkeepers may have been relieved when he was shipped out to India at the age of sixteen. The climate was enervating and the writers in the company were poor; inactivity made Clive irascible and suicidally depressed. He fought a duel with a man who had accused him of cheating at cards and attempted to kill himself. By his own account he would have done so had not his pistol twice misfired, whereupon he was convinced that he was "reserved for something." To survive he needed a great challenge; this took the shape of Dupleix's campaign to drive the English from their trading stations. In 1747, after the French had seized Madras and he had helped in the defense of Fort St. David, he was given a commission. He learned about soldiering in Indian conditions under Stringer Lawrence. Reluctant to return to his counting house after the peace, he grabbed the chance to serve in an auxiliary force that was sent to help Muhammed Ali, a claimant to the Mahratta principality of Tanjore.

Clive realized that it was vital to aid an Indian Prince who was prepared to be friendly, even if for his own purposes; Dupleix seemed, however, to have a stronger ally in Chanda Sahib. In 1751 he planned to place him on the throne of the Carnatic and he besieged Muhammed Ali together with a handful of British in Trichinopoly. If Trichinopoly fell, the British would be left without ally or credit. At this point Clive, now a captain, asked leave to take a force to capture Arcot. With 200 Englishmen and 300 sepoys he marched to the town and prepared to be besieged. It was a diversionary move which, for boldness and imagination, though on a tiny scale, may be compared with Marlborough's march to the Danube in 1704. On September 24 he was besieged by a force which outnumbered him by more than ten to one. Under a torrid sun, short of water and food, the sweltering redcoats and sepoys enacted an epic of valor and endurance. "Our people sickly, not above eighty fit for military duty," wrote a sergeant after forty days. In mid-November they were relieved; then they turned on their besiegers and defeated them. Dupleix was never to have the chance again, so Arcot was the turning point. The good judgment and staunchness of Thomas Saunders, President of Fort St. David, who backed Clive throughout, the fortitude of his officers and men, "the character of Britons in a clime so remote from their own," share the glory with Clive; but his was the plan, his the command.

In 1752 Lawrence was able to relieve Trichinopoly. Clive was furiously active in a series of small engagements, Conjeveram, Coveripauk, Covelong, and Chingleput. When he sailed home for his first leave in 1753 he was a sick man. He spent some of his prize money in redeeming his old home and paying his father's debts, more in contesting a seat in Parliament, only to be unseated on petition. He returned to India a lieutenant-colonel and governor of Fort St. David. Again events in India did not wait upon declaration of war in Europe. Bussy, Dupleix's successor, had made the French paramount in Hyderabad; confident in his alliances and revenues, he seized English factories in the Deccan.

In the same year (1756) Siraj-ud-doulah succeeded to the rule of Bengal and promptly captured Calcutta. News of this calamity and the deplorable incident of the Black Hole reached Madras just as an expedition was being prepared against the French in Hyderabad. Clive was conveyed to the scene by Admiral Watson, with 900 British and 1,500 Indian troops. In January 1757 he recovered Calcutta. The Nawáb, indecisive and incompetent, made peace and Clive went on to take the French post of Chandernagar. He was no less resourceful as diplomat than as soldier. Mir Jafar offered himself as an alternative to Siraj-ud-doulah in return for the confirmation of the company's privileges, a million and a half compensation for the loss of Calcutta and its inhabitants, and substantial offerings to individual company servants. Pathetically, the Nawáb clung to Mir Jafar though he learned of his plan by June. He was only an onlooker of the battle among the mango groves of Plassey in which Clive destroyed the motley horde that faced him, 50,000 against his 3,000, of whom only 800 were European. On the eve of this battle Clive was irresolute: but the odds proved meaningless and the action little more than a cannonade. Mir Jafar was set on his throne and Siraj was executed.

Clive's position was jeopardized, however, by financial miscalculation. The treasure of Murshidabad turned out to be a mere million and a half and Mir Jafar was hopelessly indebted; he looked to recoup himself from his outlying provinces. So Clive had to defend Mir Jafar against revolts, to uphold subordinate Hindu officers against Mir Jafar's rapacity, and to protect Bengal against external attack. He rebuilt Fort William, suppressed internal risings, and collared the Dutch East India fleet and their factory at Chinsurah, regardless of the fact that Great Britain was not at war with Holland. He also drove off Ali Gauhar, heir to the Moghul throne, who was trying to strengthen his claim upon Delhi by acquiring Bengal. "Sabaj Jang" (the tried in battle), as Clive was entitled by the Emperor, had shown himself to be an executive of genius. In three years he had established a tradition of British suzerainty and laid a strong base for it to grow. It was precarious still, because it depended so much on his own effort. When, however, he came home to enjoy his fortune, to receive an Irish peerage and the thanks of king and Parliament, and to take a seat in Parliament, he did not lose his interest in India, where the greed and lack of restraint of the Bengal civilians had created "a scene of anarchy, confusion, bribery, corruption and extortion." The words are Clive's, but he had set a bad example himself: he had received altogether £234,000 and a *jagir* of £30,000 a year on his own suggestion that a revenue grant was required to maintain the dignity of an imperial noble. Enjoying unlimited credit, involved in government at all levels, free to trade, to work contracts, to receive "presents," the company's servants enriched themselves regardless of Hindu law and susceptibilities and of the interests of the company. They were in the position of gamblers; for the likelihood that they would die young or return diseased they compensated themselves by quick returns on their investment.

The company was alarmed for its profits and the security of its position and sent Clive back to India to restore fair and firm rule to Bengal. When he arrived in May 1765 he found that the battle of Baksar, in the previous October, at which Hector Munro had defeated Mir Kasim and Shuja-ud-doulah, had made the British masters of Bengal once more, no longer trying to rule through existing authorities but recognized now by the Shah. Clive must have been strongly tempted to march on Delhi, to turn by one stroke of war a commercial concern into an Indian empire. Fortunately the instinct of the adventurer was tempered by the calculations of the soldier. He realized that the company was not yet strong enough to take on the warlike Rohillas, the Sikhs of the Punjab, the Jats of Bharatpur, or the Marathas of the Deccan in possible combination. He resolved to limit the area of the company to Bengar and Bihar, with Oudh as a buffer between the company and invaders from the North. An agreement was made with the Shah: he was given certain districts of Oudh; in return he conferred upon the company the *Diwan*—power of collecting revenue—of Bengal. Oudh was returned to Shuja-ud-doulah, who was more afraid of the Marathas than of the company, and well content to be a puppet ruler.

In Bengal the company governed in effect through its own deputies, though in theory the authority was divided between company and Nawáb. In this situation of indirect administration the quality of the government depended upon the integrity of the Calcutta Council. Whatever his motives, Clive undoubtedly brought a stiff broom into the stables—and he knew where to look for the muck. He appointed a select committee, Carnac, Verelst, with two newcomers from England, Sumner and Sykes. Officials had either to submit or to return to England; presents above the value of 4,000 rupees had to be handed over to the company. Clive tried to regulate private trading so as to limit its abuses while allowing the company's servants to make some extra money to supplement meager salaries. At first a Society of Trade was set up to administer the salt monopoly, and the company's servants received shares: the directors protested and the system was replaced by one of commissions on the revenues of the province. Inevitably revenues were subject therefore to extortionate increase. Clive also limited military allowances and dealt firmly with the resultant "White Mutiny." With foresight he set on foot a pension scheme for officers forced to retire early.

Clive retired from his second governorship in February 1767. He left the company with territories clearly defined and, for the present, secure. Company servants were working under recognized rules; corruption was at last reduced. The old days of a "free-for-all" were gone, never to return. He did not understress his own achievement. At home many were convinced that Bengal would now bring riches to the company, and so to the state. Chatham proposed to declare sovereignty over the whole of India before leasing the subject parts to the company, but after his collapse Grafton compromised by exacting a payment of £400,000 a year. Bengal, however, brought problems as well as profit, for the famine of 1769–70, in which up to a third of the people are said to have died, caused a steady decrease in the company's profits. The directors failed to insist upon necessary reforms: too many of them stood to gain directly, or through relatives, by private trading. While "nabobs" returned with fortunes to invest in property or politics, shareholders grew restive. In 1767 the company was involved in an alarming though short-lived war with Hyder Ali. Company stock, much inflated, suddenly fell, and the political group led by Sullivan and Vansittart, who had bought stock to have a say in company affairs, burnt their fingers. There was a crisis of confidence in the affairs of the company, and angry men sought a scapegoat. Clive, by now the recognized leader of a Shropshire group in the House, was also the outstanding example of a "nabob." A propaganda campaign mounted by shareholders and humanitarians alike led to the setting up of Burgoyne's committee to study the problems of India. It persuaded the House to vote that all territorial acquisitions belong rightly to the Crown but had been wrongfully appropriated by private persons, but the motion which focused the issue upon the greatest personality failed. The House did not accept that Lord Clive had been guilty of promoting his private fortune "to the dishonor and detriment of the state"; rather they declared that, while he had obtained £234,000, he had at the same time rendered "great and meritorious services to this country." History confirms the verdict.

Clive had fought for his name and fame with the direct and passionate energy that marked his whole life. He had indeed received presents. Had he not also created an empire? When he considered what he might have taken he "stood astonished at his own moderation." He did not live long, however, to enjoy his triumph or his riches. The strain of the trial told on his health, and to cure sleeplessness he had recourse to opium. The pent-up violence which had never been far from the surface welled up again. On November 2, 1774, he took his own life. It was the last egotistical stroke of a man who needed always the prospect of action to keep him from the demon of despair.

P. E. Roberts, *British India*, 1952.

H. H. Dodwell, *Dupleix and Clive*, 1920.

P. J. Marshall, *East India Fortunes: The British in Bengal in the Eighteenth Century*, 1976.

Lord Macaulay, *Essays*, 1911 edition.

SIR EYRE COOTE (1726–83), general, was born at Ash Hill in County Limerick, entered the army early, and was one of the keen young officers who rose under the eye of Pitt and the Duke of Cumberland. He served against the Pretender in 1745. In India during the Seven Years War, he played an important part at the battle of Plassey, but Clive came to dislike him. In this there may have been jealousy, but Coote was greedy, even by Indian standards, and had an ungovernable temper. He was also, however, heroic and persistent in conditions which soon took their toll of weaker men. In 1759 he was sent back to India with a reinforcement of royal troops. In 1760 he defeated the French at Wandewash. His capture of Pondicherry in the following year completed the discomfiture of Lally de Tollendal and the ruin of the French cause in India. What this meant to the French can be guessed from the fact that Lally was afterwards tried for cowardice and executed.

In 1770 he became a K.B. and returned for a short time to India, only to quarrel violently with the Madras Council over the precise area of his authority and to return after six months. Hastings then wrote: "God forbid that he should ever return." But when he came back, in January 1779, once more commander-in-chief with a seat on the Council of Bengal, he was given wide powers. Hastings faced a grave crisis when he was confronted by the Maratha Confederacy. The fight against the Maratha princes prospered, but when the Madras government incited Hyder Ali to war again, in 1780, Hastings sent Coote himself to take command in the Carnatic to save Madras in the hour of peril. Hastings was both magnanimous and energetic. Coote was given a field allowance of £18,000 a year and discretion to campaign as he wanted. Gold, rice, and bullocks were got by all possible means to maintain Coote's army in the hot, barren plains around Madras. Coote was short of cavalry and tents; supplies reached him by sea from Bengal, and the French were active off the coast. He himself was suffering acutely from the climate. He showed no great strategical insight, but his toughness inspired the sepoys and kept his army in the field. He was rewarded by two victories against Hyder Ali and the Frenchman Bussy, at Porto Novo in 1781 and at Arni in 1782. In the latter year he had a stroke. In April 1783 he was struck down with paralysis and died at Madras. Peace was made with Mysore in the following year. The victories in India were small and unspectacular in the public eye, but they helped to counterbalance the loss of America. Coote was not an agreeable man. He had old-fashioned views about his native troops—"the blacks"—and he quarreled with everybody. He was generally agreed to be avaricious. But he was also ready to die in his saddle and his spirit did much to save British India.

Ramsay Muir, *The Making of British India, 1756–1858*, 1915.

JEFFREY AMHERST, BARON AMHERST (1717–97), whom Fortescue judged to have been "the greatest military administrator between Marlborough and Wellington," was the son of a squire in Kent. Like his younger brother Billy, subsequently a lieutenant-general, he went early into the army and gained rapid promotion in the war years when the army was being rapidly expanded. He was a cornet in Ligonier's regiment and his aide-de-camp at the battles of Dettingen, Fontenoy, and Roucoux. In 1747 he served on the staff of Cumberland and was subsequently gazetted lieutenant colonel in the First Foot Guards. After the duke's surrender at Klosterseven, in 1757, he became responsible under Prince Ferdinand of Brunswick for the administration of the Hessian troops in British pay; then he was appointed, despite George II's misgivings, to command the force which was being prepared to attack Louisburg, the French stronghold in Canada.

The initial attack on Louisburg, "the Gibraltar of the West," was executed with skill and daring. The landing on an open beach at Fort Breton, under fire from the garrison and from French ships, was followed in July by the final assault upon Louisberg. Amherst then led the center thrust of the triple advance, advancing toward Montreal by the chain of the Little Lakes. The problems of transport amongst the woods and lakes of mostly untracked country, the opposition of the French, the prickly attitudes of the loyalists, and the uncertain position of the native Indians, combined to make this a hazardous operation. The unsatisfactory record of previous and subsequent campaigns, the fate of Braddock and Burgoyne, make this clear. Amherst's capture of Montreal, in 1760, with a task force composed equally of regulars and loyalists, was the product of excellent staff work, resolution, promptitude, and care for detail. Amherst introduced a new tactical conception in his use of irregular riflemen as skirmishers. His good humor enabled him to preserve good relations with awkward colleagues, Admiral Boscawen and General Wolfe. He was happy, too, in his dealings with the colonists. In August 1761 he reported to the King: "There is a *bonne volonté* for anything that the king is pleased to order." If all English soldiers had been as cooperative there might have been no colonial revolt; at least Washington might have served the king, not the rebels. Unfortunately Wolfe's open contempt was more typical of the regular soldier's view of the irregular loyalist. To the Indians Amherst was benevolent, in the best tradition of the British imperialist, but he was efficient and prompt in suppressing the Pontiac revolt in 1763.

When he returned from Canada Amherst was played out. His sister remarked how thin he was and how tired, "with fatigues and being weatherbeaten he has strong lines from his eyes down his cheeks which make him look ten years older than he is." In 1753 he had married a Miss Jenny Dalyson—"the duchess of Louisburg"—who had a name for being proud and unsociable. They had no children and she may have become possessive. Certainly Amherst seemed hereafter to have no further ambition or inclination to serve, and the rest of his career is somewhat of an anticlimax. In July 1768 he refused the invitation of George III to become Governor of Virginia. After he had resigned all his military offices in a mood of exasperation, he was restored to favor and to his colonelcies; a grant of 20,000 acres of land in New York State indicates the king's desire to recover the services of Amherst as the man who might be able to deal with the troublesome colonists. In 1775, he was urged to go to America in place of Gage, again after Saratoga in 1778. Twice he refused, and yet in his capacity as lieutenant-general of Ordnance he advised the government and supervised the administration of the war. He seems to have had no scruples about the conduct of the war, but he may have been reluctant to fight against his old comrades. Commander-in-chief in 1780, he showed some energy in putting down the Gordon riots by the use of troops, but less severity might have been necessary if he had acted earlier. In 1793, upon the outbreak of another war, now with revolutionary France, he was recalled to the office of commander-in-chief. The discipline, status, and training of the army left much to be desired, and as the man responsible for its administration for many years he must share the blame with economizing politicians and the all-enveloping system of patronage. His torpor may be accounted for by tiredness or indifferent health, but the sharp contrast between the two parts of his career remains a puzzle.

J. A. Houlding, *Fit for Service: The Training of the British Army, 1715–1795*, 1982.

JAMES WOLFE (1727–59), general, was the son of major-general Wolfe, an Irishman, and Henriette Thompson. He entered the army at fourteen; two years later he was adjutant of his regiment, the Twelfth, at Dettingen. He died at the head of his troops on the Heights of Abraham. The ensuing capture of Quebec was the beginning of the end of French rule in Canada; Wolfe was only thirty-two years old. His daring exploit ensured his fame, but there is more to remember him by than this. Intelligent, ambitious, as scrupulous in training as bold in action, Wolfe had already established himself as an exceptional commander.

He was born at Westerham in Kent, and it is there that we meet him, "the youngest lieutenant-colonel in the army," in Thackeray's novel *The Virginians:* "Very lean and very pale; his hair was red, his nose and cheek-bones were high, but he had a fine courtesy toward his elders, a cordial greeting toward his friends and an animation in conversation which caused those who heard him to forget, even to admire, those homely looks." The shock of hair, long upturned nose, and receding chin lent themselves to caricature and Wolfe was physically fragile too. He was, however, both ardent and thorough; he sought active service and he learned from his experiences. After serving under Wade in Flanders, he missed Fontenoy, but was at Falkirk with Hawley and on the staff at Culloden. He was certainly no sentimentalist: of the British troops in Scotland he wrote: "I knew their discipline to be bad and their valor precarious. They are easily put into disorder and hard to recover out of it." He was proud, however, of the bayonet-work of his regiment at Culloden. He was not party to the brutalities that followed the battle. "Pistol the rebel dog," said Hawley of a young wounded Jacobite lying on the ground; but Wolfe refused, and offered his commission instead. Later, however, on garrison work at Inversnaid, he combed the area for fugitives. The Highlanders, he believed, were "better governed by fear than favor." Six years later he proposed a plan which, had it been carried out, would have involved a deliberate massacre of the Clan Macpherson. "Would you believe I am so bloody?" he wrote. "'Twas my real intention." Yet it was to be the Highlanders who, kilted in the government's black tartan, scrambled up the Heights of Abraham.

The British army has always had a few officers who have not been content with the routines of regimental soldiering in peacetime. Like Wolfe, they have usually been derided by their fellow officers. He was sharply critical of ignorance and inertia. He studied Latin and mathematics. In the winter of 1752 he got leave to go to Paris to perfect his French, but he was not allowed to study the French or other Continental armies. In the invasion of 1755 he practiced his men in tactics specially devised to repel landings. He saw this problem from the other side when he took part in the abortive expedition to Rochefort in 1757. His conspicuous gallantry there was recognized by Pitt, who appointed him to serve under Amherst in Canada. In the attack upon Louisburg in May 1758 he led his part of the landing party to success through angry surf and fierce fire. He went home to recover his health for he was "in very bad condition both with the gravel and rheumatism." In the same letter he said: "I have signified to Mr. Pitt that he may dispose of my slight carcass as he pleases." Pitt chose him to command the expedition being fitted out against Quebec. Newcastle demurred to George II, on the ground that Wolfe was mad. "Mad, is he?" replied the old King; "Then I hope he will bite some of my other generals."

Wolfe meanwhile became engaged to Miss Katherine Lowther, of the great northern family. He was in love, but he did not hesitate before the call to glory. He found Quebec well prepared, apparently impregnable. Montcalm had ample warning and 16,000 men in a natural fortress. Wolfe was attacked by fireships: spectacular affray but harmless. In an attack upon Montcalm's lines in July he suffered a costly repulse. He was fertile in expedients, his troops learned to adapt themselves, and the fleet under Saunders was effective. But the operations of Amherst on the lakes did not cause any significant diversion and Wolfe was faced by failure. Under strain he ordered the wholesale burning of outlying settlements. In August he grew ill, but recovered enough to project an audacious attack. The plan to land at the Anse du Foulon and climb the Heights of Abraham seems to have emanated from his brigadiers, Monckton, Townshend, and Murray; but Wolfe made it his responsibility. His soldiers had come to love their narrow-shouldered commander, feverishly bright-eyed but pale and worn. He was too much a professional soldier to underestimate the risks, but he faced them with stoicism. He used the fleet, drifting up and down the river, to keep the French guessing. On September 12 Wolfe issued his last orders, and ended: "The officers and men will remember what their country expects from them, and what a determined body of soldiers inured to war is capable of doing against five weak French battalions mingled with a disorderly peasantry." What they had to do was to climb the Heights of Abraham, 4,800 strong, in the teeth of twice that number.

Admiral Saunders made a noisy diversion ten miles away while preparations were made aboard Holmes's squadron anchored off Cap Rouge. On the night of the twelfth, Wolfe told Jervis, commander of the *Porcupine* and his school-fellow, that he expected to die the next day, and gave him his miniature of Miss Lowther to return to her. At about 2 A.M. the small boats cast off with the current and bore their infantrymen silently down the St. Lawrence. In later life, John Robison, professor of natural history at Edinburgh, but then a young midshipman, would tell how Wolfe recited Gray's *Elegy* to the other officers in his boat. "Gentlemen," he said, "I would rather have written those lines than take Quebec." They came up to a cliff wall of rock and forest. Sentries were answered by a French-speaking officer. From the landing-place volunteers scaled the Heights and secured an outpost, then somehow the troops scrambled up and formed squares on the plateau above. There at dawn the choice was victory or ruin: there was no retreat. Montcalm attacked him before his best regiments were ready, and the French, white-coated regulars, colonial militia, and war-painted Indians, assaulted Wolfe's scarlet lines in vain. Wolfe was three times wounded as he led the countercharge on the English right, but he lived long enough to know that the day was won. His last words were an order to cut off the French retreat at the bridge over Charles River; then: "Now, God be praised, I will die in peace." Montcalm, too, was taken into the city to die. "Never was rout more complete than that of our army," said a French official. Quebec itself need not have fallen, but it was abandoned almost at once. In England the news was received with acclaim. Walpole wrote: "They triumphed and they wept; for Wolfe had fallen in the hour of victory." Wolfe's "path of glory" had seized the imagination of people who yet could scarcely have measured the significance of the capture of Quebec.

W. T. Waugh, *James Wolfe, Man and Soldier*, 1928.
F. Parkman, *Wolfe and Montcalm*, 1884.
C. P. Stacey, *Quebec*, 1959.

GEORGE AUGUSTUS ELIOTT, 1st BARON HEATHFIELD (1717–90), general, crowned a tough career by his splendid defense of Gibraltar against the Spanish and French. Gibraltar was of the utmost strategic importance, key to British power in the Mediterranean; when the siege was begun, in the summer of 1779, the British were losing their grip on the American colonies and looked likely to lose the European war as well. When the siege ended after three years and seven months, some credit had been restored. Gibraltar's Rock was confirmed to the British by the Treaty of Versailles in 1783 and has remained so ever since, though the Spanish resent and periodically challenge the British presence.

Eliott was the son of Sir Gilbert Eliott, of Stobs, Roxburghshire; he was educated at Leyden and at the French military college of La Fere. In the War of the Polish Succession Eliott served as a volunteer in the army of King Frederick William of Prussia: apprenticeship in the most stringent discipline to be found. He specialized at first in field engineering and artillery, subsequently served in the Guards through the War of the Austrian Succession, and saw action at both Dettingen and Fontenoy. In 1759 he raised a regiment of cavalry upon the Austrian model and commanded it under Prince Ferdinand, 1759–60. In 1761 he played a leading part in Pocock's capture of Havana; he returned a lieutenant-general.

In 1777 he was sent to command the Gibraltar garrison which was never larger than 7,000 men, with about 100 guns. Asked to send a battalion to Minorca, which was also in straits, he refused: a typical piece of obstinacy and, as it turned out, a wise decision. When the siege began, his force proved barely sufficient; its efficiency and morale were, however, sustained by his rugged and distinctive personality. In January 1780 Rodney brought some supplies and mauled the Spanish fleet; in April 1781 Admiral Darby brought in a fresh convoy. From that point, however, the siege became more intense; after their capture of Minorca, in February 1782, the French joined in and with summer came the crisis: in May, ten floating batteries were sent in, screened by damp sandbags, but Eliott's red-hot shot pulverized them. By September the British were faced with 47 battleships and 40,000 men, with 200 guns on land. The attack of September 13 and 14 came nearest to success but by the end of the 14th, the British had destroyed every floating battery. As a *tour de force* of engineering and gunnery Eliott's defense is measurable enough: the embrasures hewn out of the solid rock for the guns can still be seen. No less vital was the battle of morale, fought against scurvy, hunger, fear, and drunkenness. Eliott dominated by personal example. He was a vegetarian and a teetotaller; he could eat anything but he was especially fond of suet puddings. Reynold's celebrated portrait in the National Gallery captures his heroic, indomitable side; we may guess that his sense of humor was almost as important. When a soldier was charged with having said he wished to join the enemy, Eliott would not have him shot but said he must be mad: he was therefore to be bled, put into a strait-jacket, prayed for in church, and fed on bread and water. He was not always so humane but he seldom failed to be original.

JOHN MANNERS, MARQUIS OF GRANBY (1721–70), was commander of the British contingent under Ferdinand of Brunswick from 1759 to the end of the Seven Years War. His force, larger than the British contingent which had served in Marlborough's army, won a series of remarkable victories, small in scale but important in the overall strategy of the war. Today only the expert has heard of Warburg and Kloster Kampfen, Vellinghausen, Emsdorff, and Wilhelmstal, but swinging inn signs recall the name of a brave and spectacular general.

Granby was the elder son of the Duke of Rutland and went to Eton and Trinity College, Cambridge. He had a seat in Parliament from 1741 to his death. Wealth and influence smoothed his way, but a blockage occurred when Ligonier was preferred for the coloncly of the Blues: George II disliked his father. He raised a regiment in 1745 to fight against the Jacobites; later he served in Flanders. A lieutenant-general in Germany under Ferdinand, he had the mortification of sharing in the failure of the cavalry to complete the splendid victory of Minden. Sackville, commanding the cavalry, would not move; Granby, in command of the second line, was about to charge on his own initiative when Sackville rode up and ordered him not to. What the troops thought may be considered unprintable; what Ferdinand said was that had Granby been in command, the French would have been annihilated. Sackville was dismissed and Granby succeeded him. In the next four years, with the intelligent backing of Ligonier at the War Office, he won a series of battles, usually against odds.

If it is true that "Canada was won on the banks of the Elbe," then not only Frederick the Great but Ferdinand and Granby should share the credit. The cavalry were brought to a high pitch of efficiency, and Granby led them with tactical skill and reckless daring. "One could see nothing finer and more fit," said Ferdinand in 1760 of the cavalry. Waldegrave's infantry battalions were also impressive. The battle of Warburg in 1760 affords a good example of this army in action. When it was obvious that the infantry could not catch the French, Ferdinand ordered Granby to move against their flank. Two hours' riding with cavalry and horse artillery brought them to the French corps of 20,000. Then a massive attack shocked the French into rout. Granby led his men in bareheaded. They drove the French back to the river Diemel, where they were decimated by Phillips's artillery; in all they lost about 8,000 men. Of his performance at a later battle, Wilhelmstal, in 1762, Ligonier wrote: "No man ever acted with more courage or more like a commanding officer. The Blues did almost beyond what was ever done by a cavalry regiment." His only criticism of Granby was that he was too bold, "exposing himself like a hussar."

In 1763 he was recalled to be Master of the Ordnance; in 1767 he was made commander-in-chief. He was a poor administrator, however, and his later years were inglorious. He had spent a fortune on his own regiment, largely recruited from Belvoir tenantry of Leicester and Rutland, he drank too much, and he died heavily in debt. He was also a victim of Junius's acid pen. It was an unequal encounter: he was happier with the sword.

R. Whitworth, *Field Marshal Lord Ligonier and the British Army, 1702–70*, 1958.

JONAS HANWAY (1712–86), philanthropist, had an adventurous life abroad before he devoted himself to benevolent works at home. He was apprenticed to a merchant's office in Lisbon. He then became a partner in the business of Robert Dingley in St. Petersburg. When the firm looked for an agent to replace Elton, the enterprising seaman who had opened up Russian trade in Persia but had then deserted his employers, Hanway volunteered. For two years he traveled, with a caravan laden with English cloth; he survived fever, pirates in the Caspian, a revolution in Astrabad. In 1750 he left Russia and came to live in London. As he wrote of travelers at the end of the journal in which he described his adventures in the Middle East, "their own country must necessarily become the dearer to them, according as they discover the superiority it enjoys in laws and governments above other nations." But he determined to do good where he saw need. He was especially concerned with the well-being of poor children. With Fielding, among others, he founded the Marine Society for training boys for the sea. Seventy years before Shaftesbury he exposed the sufferings of the child sweeps. He visited poorhouses and foundling hospitals in France and Holland as well as England. Like Howard, the prison reformer, he based his demands for reform upon massive statistics, culled from assiduous visits. An Act of 1761, inspired by him, obliged all parishes to keep registers of their "infant poor." A House of Commons committee which examined the registers in 1767 showed that only seven in a hundred of the children under twelve years old survived more than two years. Hanway's Act in that year obliged parishes to send their children under six into the country to be boarded for not less than 2s. 6d. a week. Indentures had to be signed by two justices but the boys were thereafter, till twenty-four (subsequently twenty-one), at the mercy of their guardians: too often they were cheap, exploited, expendable hands. Hanway himself said that "the apprenticeship of some parish children is as great a scene of inhumanity as the suffering others to die in infancy."

Although he earned the censure of Dr. Johnson for attacking "the pernicious custom of tea-drinking," Hanway was prominent among those who urged the government to check the consumption of gin. Endlessly fertile in expedient, he was the first man to walk the streets of London under an umbrella, derided but dry. He contributed to the improvement of the townsman's health by his campaign for adequate street paving. For prostitutes he showed a sympathy far in advance of his time, and he founded a hospital for venereal diseases. As a reward for his public services he was made, in 1762, a Commissioner of the Victualling Office. After his death a monument was erected to him in Westminster Abbey, but the lives that he rescued from death and depravity were the best memorial of this busy, kind, and practical man.

Austin Dobson, *Eighteenth Century Vignettes*, 1892.
J. S. Taylor, *Jonas Hanway, Founder of the Marine Society: Charity and Policy in Eighteenth Century Britain*, 1985.

THOMAS GILBERT (1720–98) was an energetic and public-spirited man who interested himself especially in improvements to the Poor Law. The laws of Elizabeth's reign for poor relief were designed for a virtually static society and it was apparent by Gilbert's time that they were inadequate. At first trends of change were toward preventive measures. The Act of 1722, while authorizing parishes to group themselves together to build workhouses, channeled all applications for relief through the overseer, and authorized churchwardens and overseers to farm out the poor. With the need for cheap labor and the unsatisfactory nature of many overseers, this led to exploitation. Enlightened observers like Fielding and Crabbe denounced the waste and dishonesty endemic in the system. Their concern was reflected in more compassionate legislation.

The general opinion of reformers, notably the clergymen Alcock and Tucker, was that able-bodied should be separated from infirm, that larger workhouses should be created and managed under the aegis of magistrates and parsons. These became common in Norfolk and Suffolk, but were unpopular; the running of large institutions called for experience, honesty, even a sense of vocation. To Gilbert, who became a member of Parliament in 1763, belongs the credit for putting on to the statute book an act which, though inadequate in the face of an expanding population and the enclosures which were altering many English villages, made life tolerable for some of the poor. The preamble to his Act of 1782 spoke of "the incapacity, negligence, or misconduct of overseers." It allowed parishes to join in unions: by 1834, when the next significant act was passed, 67 of these had been formed, covering nearly a thousand parishes. The rates for these were to be collected by overseers, the money allotted by paid guardians, one for each parish, appointed by the justices from lists presented by the parishioners. A visitor overlooked the work of the guardian, whose business it was to find work and to keep it going for those who could not find it for themselves: if the money earned was inadequate he was to pay the deficiency. The workhouse was to be preserved for the aged, infirm, orphans, and babies with their mothers. The variations in the system were great and it is hard to discover how well it worked. There were two great weaknesses. The position of the parish apprentice was still unprotected. Later, the well-meaning action of the Speenhamland magistrates in supplementing the wages of the able-bodied without discrimination developed into a demoralizing system of outdoor relief: the farmer was subsidized sometimes by more than a third of the wage.

Gilbert had been active in other ways. He was the author of an act for enabling the clergy to reside by loans from Queen Anne's bounty (Gilbert's Act), and his proposals for helping Friendly Societies by parochial grants were embodied in an Act of 1793. He carried measures for the improvement of roads. He had been trained as a young man under Matthew Boulton, the engineer, and his first important appointment was that of estate agent to the Duke of Bridgewater. In this office he was responsible, with the engineer Brindley, for the planning of 365 miles of canals.

D. Owen, *English Philanthropy, 1600–1960*, 1965.

JOHN HOWARD (1726–90), by his courage and energy, exposed the squalor of English prisons. At his death he was described in the *Annual Register* as an "eccentric but truly worthy man." In an age when the public conscience was insensitive or ill-informed, only such initiative as his could stir Parliament or magistrates into action.

He was originally apprenticed as a grocer but, after his father's death, he enjoyed independent means. He married a middle-aged woman who had cared for him during a nervous illness. After her death he married again, settled at Cardington in Bedfordshire, and built model cottages and a school for the village people. His interest in prisons may have dated from his experiences in the Seven Years War when, traveling to Portugal, he was captured by a privateer and detained in a foul French prison. Sent to England on parole, he secured exchange for himself and release for his fellow-victims. In 1773 he became High Sheriff for the county; then he discovered that many prisoners could not be released after acquittal because they were unable to pay the jailers' fees. From this time he spent his life looking into the state of jails. Though delicate in health, he traveled 50,000 miles, spent £30,000 on his work, and visited every country in Europe. The record of his experiences at home is to be found in *The State of Prisons in England and Wales*, first published in 1777, but frequently revised.

He found that the prison population was small—4,084 in 1776—but utterly wretched. More than half were debtors, "the most pitiable objects in our jails." At Durham he found them living on "boiled bread and water," complaining of "that great nuisance of bugs." There were few convicts, for these were executed, transported, or branded. The county jails were insufficient for the simplest needs of the other prisoners, committed for minor misdemeanors or simply awaiting trial. They were in the charge of turnkeys whose living depended on bribes and perquisites. Many were kept in chains. At Lincoln, the jailer was authorized to relieve the prisoner of his irons for 2s. 6d. a week. Many prisons were ill-ventilated because the window tax encouraged the authorities to brick them in. Women and men were not always segregated. They were usually filthy, verminous, and diseased. At the Black Assize, held at the Old Bailey in 1770, four out of six judges and forty other officials and jurymen died from jail fever caught from New-gate prisoners undergoing trial. Howard endangered his life by his visits. He was compelled, though not fastidious, to ride on horse-back because the prison atmosphere made his clothes smell so offensive inside a post-chaise; he even had to disinfect his memorandum book in front of a fire before he could use it.

One fruit of Howard's labors was the Gaol Distemper Act of 1774, promoted by Mr. Popham, M.P. for Taunton. Prisons were supposed to be cleaned, whitewashed, ventilated; baths were to be provided, with proper medical attendance and separate rooms for the sick. By another act the county rates were to bear the expense of fees owed by acquitted prisoners. In Bedfordshire Howard could see the act put into force; in many places it was ignored. The prisons remained inadequate, as we know from the experiences of Elizabeth Fry. Howard was unable to initiate anything like a general reform, but he soldiered on. After outbreaks of jail fever in the hulks and the examination of a parliamentary committee, new hulks were started in 1786. In 1779 the Penitentiary Act provided for two new prisons, one of 600 for men, one of 300 for women. But they were not built, for the "supervisors," of whom Howard was one, could not agree upon a site. He was too restless to be a good committee man. He died, at work as always, of camp fever, at Ker-shan, on the shore of the Black Sea where he was investigating the condition of a sick Russian army. Today his name is commemorated by the Howard League for Prison Reform.

John Howard, *The State of the Prisons in England and Wales*, 1777.
D. L. Howard, *John Howard: Prison Reformer*, 1958.
R. Morgan, "Divine Philanthropy: John Howard Reconsidered," *History* 62, 1977.

THOMAS GRAY (1716–71), poet, was born in Cornhill. His father was a scrivener and broker, a person of surly temperament; his mother, a stoical woman who doted on Thomas and provided from the proceeds of her millinery shop for his education. At the age of nine he was sent to Eton, where an uncle was a master. There he became fast friends with Horace Walpole and Richard West: they called themselves "the Triple Alliance." Delicate, fastidious, disinclined to games, Gray, like his friends, preferred the private language and pastoral dreams of a clique to the gregarious life of the school. Though not so clever as West nor so self-possessed as Walpole, his exercises in Latin verse were thought to be good. The poet looked back on his schooldays with delight:

> Ah, happy hills, ah pleasing shade,
> Ah, fields belov'd in vain,
> Where once my careless childhood stray'd,
> A stranger yet to pain.

These years of intense feeling and intellectual adventure were probably the happiest of his life. After nine years at Eton he went to Peterhouse, one of about a dozen undergraduates in a glum atmosphere. He spoke of the Fellows of the college as "sleepy, drunken, dull, illiterate things" and found little to inspire him. Even in his younger days, however, he was prone to the despondent mood which tinges much of his poetry, and in the closing lines of the *Elegy* he remarked that "Melancholy marked him for her own" and wrote in the *Hymn to Adversity* the sad line: "My lonely anguish melts no heart but mine." But he studied deeply and he was a keen traveler. In 1739 he accompanied Horace Walpole on a Grand Tour; inevitably the hypersensitive friends fell out, but Gray's trip was not wasted. To someone as steeped in the classics as he, Italy could not fail to be stimulating. It is curious, however, to find that the poet spent weeks in Florence writing a didactic poem in Latin on the philosophy of Locke. West's death of consumption evoked a noble lament in stately Latin hexameters. This was followed in the same year, 1742, by an outpouring of English poetry. By the end of the year he had achieved a large proportion of his life's poetry; it included the *Ode on the Spring*, the *Ode on a Distant Prospect of Eton College*, the *Hymn to Adversity*, perhaps the beginnings of the *Elegy*. At the end of the same year, without enthusiasm, he returned to Cambridge as a Fellow and settled down to a life of study. He shrank from action that would involve him in public affairs. Thus he took his degree of Bachelor of Civil Law but never practiced. He resumed his friendship with Walpole and sent him, in 1750, the manuscript of the *Elegy Written in a Country Churchyard*. Walpole was thrilled by it and insisted upon publishing it; unlike some poems which have pleased contemporaries, it has lived in anthologies and in the hearts of all who have read it. It is a profoundly classical poem. The classical education which in the insensitive may produce mere pedantry, may so permeate a man of poetic sensibility that discipline is achieved without the drying up of inspiration. Gray's experience of life and his sympathy for the predicament of man are compressed in these beautiful stanzas. He knew the tranquil village of Stoke Poges, where for years he spent his summers, staying with his mother, and the imagery gains in simple impact by being based upon his everyday experience. Dr. Johnson, who was not an admirer of Gray, said that it "abounds with images which find a mirror in every mind and with sentiments to which every bosom returns an echo." Tennyson wrote of those "divine truisms that make us weep," but there is no banality, no mawkishness; rather an exquisite restraint which is a feature of the best eighteenth-century poetry.

Gray seems to have been ragged by some undergraduates of Peterhouse who raised an alarm of fire. Resentful of this, and of the cold treatment of the master and Fellows, he migrated in 1756 to Pembroke, then presided over by an eccentric and Tory master, Roger Long; there too was his close friend, James Brown, Senior Fellow. It was a more lively society: the average age of the Fellows was about thirty since they moved regularly off to country parsonages or other preferment. Among them was the volatile Delaval, a considerable scientist and a gifted musician. William Mason, whom Gray was to choose as his biographer and literary executor, had just moved to Yorkshire. Gray was lowered in spirits by the indifferent reception of his *Pindaric Odes*, published by Walpole in 1757. Allusive, printed without titles or explanatory notes, they were addressed to the serious world where they met mixed response. "They are Greek, they are Pindaric, they are sublime: consequently I fear, a little obscure," wrote Walpole. Other readers complained about their rhapsodical style, like Johnson in the *Lives of the Poets*. Stillingfleet wrote: "They require as much thought to understand them as a mathematical problem. The author can write for me and has done, but not in this gallimawfry style." The literary taste of the age was plain; readers required poetry to be intelligible. Gray may have exaggerated when he said, "Nobody understands me and I am perfectly satisfied"; sales were good and some enthused. But there was a sense of anticlimax after the rapturous reception of the *Elegy*.

Gray varied the even tenor of his Cambridge life with expeditions to the country and further afield. In 1765 he went to the Highlands, still a rare experience for most Englishmen. The castles, mountains, and passes of Scotland appealed to the romantic element in his nature: "The mountains," he wrote, "are ecstatic, and ought to be visited on pilgrimage once a year. None but those monstrous creatures of God know how to join so much beauty with so much horror." Unfortunately all this did not inspire his muse, which remained silent. Instead, typically, he spent his time upon such pursuits as natural history—he was one of a number of intelligent Englishmen of the day who were amateur naturalists—in annotating Linnaeus, usually in Latin, and in composing Latin verses upon the orders and genera of insects. He said that "to be employed was to be happy," and the Duke of Grafton appointed him, in 1768, regius professor of modern history. He had some conscientious scruples about his duty. The post was a sinecure and he was not expected to lecture or even to reside more than was convenient, but reform was in the air, at Oxford at least, and Gray tried to respond. He projected lectures, but shrank from the ordeal; in the end not even his inaugural lecture, which he started to compose in Latin, was delivered. But the Installation Ode in which he repaid his debt to Grafton, for all its insincerity, showed that his poetic fire was not wholly damped. As always he was most effective when he was writing about some place where he had struck roots—in this case Cambridge. He had the intense love of place and institution that sometimes goes with a temperament too reserved to find much *rapport* with the opposite sex. Even in his friendships with other men he was reticent and withdrawing. For a short time he allowed himself to be fascinated by the young Swiss patrician, Bonstetten, who returned his affection with a lasting devotion; briefly the old man knew again what he once described as "the sunshine of the breast," the sereniy of his Eton days. But he shrank from enthusiasm and from any break in the regulated existence; and he was as strict with himself as gentle with others.

Arnold said, in a phrase that has stuck to Gray's memory, that he lived in an age of prose, when "a sort of spiritual east wind was blowing"; that he would have been a different man if he had lived in the age of Milton or of Burns. Arnold was taking out of context the remark of his friend Brown: "He never spoke out." But Brown's remark was right in a different way; Gray's reticence was the product of the intellectual discipline in which he had been nurtured and the artistic principles prevailing in his age; but it was also the consequence of his temperament and his physical condition. "There would have been no remedy for Gray's particular sufferings," writes his biographer, Ketton-Cremer, "in the spiritual climate of any other age." "Delicate Mr. Gray" wrote the finest poem of the Augustan age; it was sufficient achievement.

R. W. Ketton-Cremer, *Thomas Gray*, 1955.
Lord David Cecil, "Poetry of Thomas Gray," essay from *Eighteenth Century English Literature*, 1959.
Lord David Cecil, *Two Quiet Lives*, 1947.

HORACE WALPOLE, 4th EARL OF ORFORD (1717–91), diarist, was the third son of Robert Walpole by his first wife, Catherine Shorter; he was devoted to his mother and hurt by his father's indifference in the later years of the marriage. At Eton he exhibited precociously the wit and the somewhat rarefied literary tastes of his subsequent life; one of the set of aesthetes of which he was acknowledged leader was the poet Gray. He was at King's for four years, though he resided but irregularly. While still an undergraduate he was presented with the first of the sinecures which helped to make his life agreeable: at different times he was Usher of the Exchequer and Controller of the Pipe and Clerk of the Estreats. While out of England on a Grand Tour with Gray he was elected member of Parliament. He enjoyed the advantages of being the son of a powerful minister and he was loyal to his father, but he was out of sympathy with his hearty way of life and did not attempt to emulate his career.

In 1742 Walpole made his maiden speech in the House which his father was just leaving: it was suitably filial and neatly phrased. He never entirely eschewed active politics. From 1757 until his retirement in 1768 he sat for King's Lynn, which occupied him more than the decayed boroughs of Callington and Castle Rising which he had represented before. He showed mettlesome spirit in his attempt, in 1757, to secure a stay of execution for Admiral Byng; but he preferred to exert influence through more indirect channels. For many years he championed the interests of his able relative, General Conway, whose comparative failure was a sharp disappointment to him. Meanwhile he recorded the political scenes of the age of the Pelhams and Pitt in letters, and in the memoirs (published after his death) which have provided rich material for historians, even where their inventive wit and biased views have disqualified them as serious evidence. His descriptions, among others, of the Duke of Newcastle at the funeral of George II, the trial of Lord Ferrers, and the "champagne" speech of Charles Townshend are rightly held to be classics of their kind. His letters, written to one hundred and fifty different correspondents, a large number of them to his friends, Horace Mann, minister in Italy, the Misses Berry and Mme du Deffant, friends of his old age, are self-conscious literary pieces intended for publication. The letters to Mann and Montagu, for instance, were returned by their recipients, edited, and left to his executors in the shape of a historical chronicle. But Walpole wanted more than to be the Mme. de Sévigné of his time: if he was a dilettante he was an active one. In 1747 he acquired Strawberry Hill, Twickenham, and set about creating there a Gothic house, modest in scale but unique in its fanciful antiquarianism. Sir Kenneth Clark has called it Gothic rococo; indeed it is far removed from the academic work of the professional architects of the nineteenth century, Butterfield, Street, and Scott. Essentially it was a fancy, for, as he wrote of his "small, capricious house," it was built "to please my own taste and in some degree to realize my own visions." His Gothic was that of an antiquarian and he always went to original Gothic work, nor did he invent new "orders," like some later enthusiasts. There was of course something ridiculous about carefully imitated perpendicular framing the gold and crimson of eighteenth-century furnishing at its most sumptuous, and the tomb of Archbishop Bourchier reproduced in the gallery in gold network over looking-glass. Gothic was hardly evolved to make a frame for pictures, but the walls of Strawberry Hill were crowded with paintings in a medley of periods and styles, for Walpole was an avid collector.

His *Anecdotes of Painting* were based on the notebooks of George Vertue, a comprehensive collection of information about artists and architects. Walpole worked hard on these and performed valuable service in presenting information which might otherwise have been lost. His literary skill dressed up the material pleasantly, while his judgments, often sound, sometimes introduced the spice of the unexpected. Walpole has been pilloried for saying that Reynolds could not paint women and that Hardwicke Hall was ugly, and for such passages of nonsense as that in which he praised Lady Lucan's watercolors. But many of his judgments stand the test of time, and if it is his weakness as a critic to slip into light-hearted discursions about inconsequential things, it is a large part of his attraction as a writer. He established his own printing press at Strawberry Hill; its output is now justly valued by bibliophiles. In 1757 Gray's *Odes* appeared, the first production, and never have author and publisher been more happily matched. Among other productions came his own essay in tragedy, *The Mysterious Mother*. The more interesting *Castle of Otranto* was published elsewhere; claimed by some critics as the first romantic novel, it is yet steeped in the atmosphere of Strawberry Hill.

Walpole was unfortunate in incurring odium for his part in the tragedy of Chatterton, when the most he could be accused of was failing to see straightaway through this elaborate deception. Although undoubtedly self-centered, he was not usually unkind; but he was prone to lapses of judgment that border upon absurdity. He lived usefully, in his own way, busily, elegantly. He appeared, however, for all his *finesse*, a trifle absurd to some of his contemporaries as to us, in his physical presence—he used, we are told, to enter a room as if he were stepping on a wet floor with his hat crushed between his knees—in his taste for melodrama in literature and architecture, in his febrile love of gossip, and in his last years, in an intense, exacting love for Mary Berry and her sister, less than half his age, but his "twin wives," "*mes très cheres Fraises.*"

R. W. Ketton-Cremer, *Horace Walpole*, 1940.
M. Hodgart, ed., *Memoirs and Portraits*, 1963.
W. S. Lewis, *Selected Letters of Horace Walpole*, 1973.

GILBERT WHITE (1720–93), author of *The Natural History & Antiquities of Selborne*, father of English naturalists, and one of the best-loved of writers, was born at Selborne. He was educated at Basingstoke under Thomas Warton and at Oriel College, Oxford, where he became a Fellow. He returned after brief tenure of a curacy at Durley and the incumbency of Moreton Pinkney to the chalky hills and beech woods of his native Hampshire. We may be grateful that he did not become Provost of Oriel, as he hoped he might, but consoled himself with the curacy of Faringdon near Selborne (1758). His life was a quiet one; scarcely any details have survived even of his appearance, no portrait was painted of him and we know only that he was very short, upright in figure with stumpy legs. He was a model village parson, devoted to his people and interested in their ways, but fortunately his work left him ample time for observation, inquiry, and writing. He started his natural history diary in 1751; in 1767 and 1769 respectively he began the irregular correspondence with Thomas Pennant and Daines Barrington, which forms the staple of the *Natural History,* eventually printed in 1788. The *Letters,* the *Naturalist's Calendars, Observations on Various Branches of Natural History and Antiquities,* together make only some 10,000 words, but they have been reprinted in over 150 editions.

Naturalists in the eighteenth century fell into distinct types, though the work of each was complementary. Most were preoccupied with classification, work that was made necessary by the opening up of new lands and observation of new species: among these were Buffon, Ray, and Linnaeus, who invented the binomial system of naming animals. Equally important, however, were the observers, concerned with their arrangement into species: of these Gilbert White was both typical and preeminent. Eventually, by the theory of organic evolution, in the middle of the nineteenth century the work of the classifiers and the observers was fused into a single science.

Gilbert White made some signal discoveries: the distinction between the English leaf warblers, chiff-chaff, willow-warbler, and wood-warbler; the species of noctule bat, the harvest bat, the harvest mouse, the lesser whitethroat. He anticipated modern theories of bird territory and also Darwin's conclusions about the origin of the domestic pigeon. His studies of the life history of the nightjar, swallow, martin, and swift are as accurate as they are pleasing. Sometimes he would shoot a bird to discover what would otherwise be out of reach, the anatomy of the cuckoo, for instance, to test the theory of an ingenious German about this bird's inability to hatch her own eggs. His work is redolent, however, of interest and sympathy for the creatures he observes; he was a gentle soul. Great naturalist as he was, he was no specialist. Everything comes under his eye—trees, fossils, local superstitions—and the result is a unique portrait of the countryside. A tiny corner of eastern Hampshire in the eighteenth century is preserved forever in his pages.

An intellectual without sophistication, a scholar without pedantry, a humorous man and modest, his world is a pleasant one, with some of the calm that one sees about an eighteenth-century landscape. Politics, material cares, are remote; the phenomena of nature alone have power to disturb the serenity of woods and fields.

Johnson, ed., *Journals of Gilbert White*, 1931.
W. S. Scott, ed., *The Antiquities of Selborne*, 1950 (there have been numerous editions).
C. S. Emden, *Gilbert White in his Village*, 1956.

GEORGE LYTTELTON, 1st BARON (1709–73) was the son of Sir Thomas Lyttelton of Hagley in Worcestershire, a gentleman of some standing and electoral influence in the county, and of Christian, daughter of the Earl of Cobham. He was, besides this connection with the Temple family, also related to the proud Grenvilles, since Christian's sister was the wife of Richard Grenville. An ancestor had been the legal expert and author of Lyttelton's *Tenures*.

After Eton, Christ Church, and the Grand Tour he entered Parliament in 1735, sitting for Okehampton, in the same year as William Pitt, who was also linked to the "Cobham cousinhood" by his brother Thomas's marriage to Lyttelton's sister. With this militant group he attached himself to the interest of the Prince of Wales, becoming his secretary, less because he admired Frederick than because he could attack Walpole. The destruction of this minister was the prime object of the "Cobham Cubs" for seven years, but after his fall Pitt continued to inveigh against the war policy of Carteret. Lyttelton was overshadowed by the ability of Pitt, but he found office before him, in December 1744, as a Lord of the Treasury. When Pitt continued to attack this ministry, he suffered from some embarrassment. One of Henry Fox's letters describes him sitting "silent and uneasy" on an occasion when he had voted against the government. But Pitt, too, joined the ministry in 1746 and Lyttelton himself retained his office until 1755, when he was made Chancellor of the Exchequer by Newcastle. This involved him in a more lasting breach with Pitt which was not healed until 1763. Since he had a notorious incapacity for arithmetic, he was unhappy in his post and resigned it the following year, with a peerage. Lord Hervey said of him that he had a flow of words, uttered in a lulling monotony, commonplace in the moralisms and maxims which were his stock-in-trade. Horace Walpole, who did not love him, declared that "absurdity was predominant" in his constitution. "With the figure of a spectre and the gesticulations of a puppet, he talked heroics through his nose, made declamations at a visit, and played at cards with scraps of history." Yet he allowed that "he was far from wanting parts; spoke well when he had studied his speeches; and loved to reward and promote merit in others."

Lyttelton approached literature with the same solemnity that amused Walpole. His verse contains many of the mannerisms of the Augustans and little that is specially pleasing or interesting. But some of the stanzas in the *Monody*, written in 1747 in memory of his wife, Lucy Fortescue (a selection of which may be found in the *Oxford Book of Eighteenth Century Verse*), invite comparison for feeling and elegance with the best of his time. In his prose works he shows the influence of the French master: Montesquieu, for instance, in his *Persian Letters*, sprightly and deist in turn; Fénelon, in *Dialogues from the Dead*, in which the tone is more serious, as benefited an ardent convert to Christianity. He was a zealous amateur historian and wrote a *Life of Henry II* which is, by all accounts, a heavy and uninspiring compilation. His letters, to his father and others, show, however, historical imagination and an excellent topographical sense. The man who helped James Thomson with *The Seasons*, to whom Fielding, his fellow-Etonian, dedicated Tom Jones, was worth something more, perhaps, than Lord Chesterfield's observation that he looked as if his head had already had one chop on the block, for it hung always on one shoulder or the other, or the devastating remark of Dr. Johnson about the *Dialogues:* "He sat down to write a book to tell the world what the world all his life had been telling him."

S. C. Roberts, *An Eighteenth Century Gentleman*, 1936.

LORD GEORGE SACKVILLE GERMAIN, 1st VISCOUNT SACKVILLE (1716–85), soldier and politician, has left a notorious name because of the events of a few hours on the battlefield of Minden in 1759. Moreover, he had a second career in politics less well-known than the first, more meritorious but equally unfortunate; for the military failures of the American War he must be held in some measure responsible.

Sackville, whose father was the first Duke of Dorset, was educated at Westminster and Trinity College, Dublin; he entered the army and Parliament. He served with credit at Fontenoy, where he was wounded, and in Scotland, during the "pacification" of the Highlands. From 1750 to 1758 he was Chief Secretary to his father, when Dorset was for the second time Lord-Lieutenant of Ireland. His reputation was good, though he was held to be arrogant. By 1757 he was lieutenant-general of the Ordnance and colonel of the Second Dragoon Guards. In 1757 his friend Pitt offered him command of the Rochefort expedition which, believing the plan to be misconceived, he refused. After its failure he sat on the commission which examined Mordaunt, the unsuccessful commander. He was second in command, in 1758, in Marlborough's abortive attack upon St. Malo. This failure may have affected his nerve or judgment. No adequate reason can, however, be offered for his lapse at the battle of Minden, where he was in command, under Prince Ferdinand of Brunswick, of all the allied cavalry. The infantry had broken the French line, six British regiments bearing the brunt of fierce fighting. Ferdinand ordered Sackville to advance and, when he took no action, repeated the order several times. Sackville would not give the order and the French were allowed to escape from what could have been a complete disaster. Furthermore he specifically ordered Granby, his fiery second in command, to stand still. He was "disobliged" with both Granby and Ferdinand. Was he a coward, as Fortescue thought? Did he, as seems more likely, make a sulky stand upon what he may have realized was an initial error of judgment? He suffered for it, for he was shunned in camp and drawing room, court-martialed, and disgraced. The sentence that he was "unfit to serve the King in any capacity" was read out, by express order of Pitt, at the head of every regiment "so that officers might be convinced that neither high birth nor great employment can shelter offenses of such a nature."

Yet Sackville was brought forward again by George III (who saw him as an injured man) because of his dislike of his father's ministers. In 1765 he became Vice-Treasurer of Ireland in Rockingham's administration—an appointment which caused Pitt to refuse to join the ministry. In 1770 he took the name of Germain, with the property of the widowed Lady Betty Germain, and fought a duel with one of his traducers. He adhered to Lord North's ministry in 1770 and was rewarded by appointment to be Secretary for the American colonies in 1775 (and Board of Trade). He now became imaginatively bellicose, urging decisive military action upon cautious colleagues. For 1777 he produced a Pitt-like plan to end the war. That it failed was no more Germain's fault than Burgoyne's or Howe's. Had it succeeded, as with closer cooperation between Howe and Burgoyne it might have done, Germain's reputation would have been recovered. As it was, in increasingly difficult circumstances after Burgoyne's surrender and the development of a full-scale European war, he showed at least more energy and resource than his prime minister, Lord North.

G. Saxon Brown, *The American Secretary: The Colonial Policy of Lord George Germain*, 1963.

JOHN MONTAGU, 4th EARL OF SANDWICH (1718–92), First Lord of the Admiralty, "Jemmy Twitcher," because of the fads and failures which characterized the last years of his long control of the Admiralty, has not received the credit that he deserves for devoted administration at a time when the government was more interested in reducing taxation than in maintaining the armed forces. Indeed, he is dismissed thus by a biographical dictionary: "The scandalous fourth earl, invented sandwiches to eat at the gaming table." Some rehabilitation may be required.

After early service in the army, Sandwich received political preferment in 1748 when he became First Lord. His prime political interest was henceforward naval administration and he was First Lord, in all, for fifteen years. Newcastle actually wanted to make him Secretary of State in this year, having a high opinion of the young landowner who had three boroughs at his disposal and was a close adherent of the Duke of Bedford. But he dismissed him in 1751 in order to force Bedford to resign from the secretaryship. On the accession of George III Sandwich moved toward the court, to enjoy a share of the patronage which the king was bent on controlling and to mend his fortune, ravaged by gambling losses. His affairs being, he said, "in the most confused condition," he accepted the post of ambassador to Spain. In 1763 he became First Lord again and then, in Grenville's ministry, Secretary of State. As such he belonged to the comparatively small group which decided major issues under Grenville's severe direction. The House of Lords witnessed an incongruous scene when Sandwich, acting for the government, read out passages from an obscene poem, the *Essay on Woman*, which Wilkes had printed. The government's intention was to discredit Wilkes's radicalism by tainting him with pornography, but some recalled that Sandwich—"Jemmy Twitcher" as he was called—had been an intimate of Wilkes and the Hell Fire Club. Sandwich was mainly concerned, however, with foreign policy: alarmed by the isolation of England after the Peace of Paris he wished to make some alliance with Austria. Austria, however, saw little advantage in this and Grenville refused to provide subsidies. Friction between Sandwich and Grenville increased and was one of the causes of the ministry's downfall in 1765.

In 1770, when North was seeking to broaden the basis of his government, he brought Sandwich back to the office of Secretary of State. In the following year he became again First Lord of the Admiralty; once more he was handicapped by the economizing spirit of his superiors. North tried to cut expenditure on the navy, but Sandwich made the most of limited resources. Copper bottoms were given to existing ships. But the penalty for North's retrenchments was paid in the American War, when the navy proved too small for the demands of a war against the American colonists, France, and Spain together. A fleet cannot be expanded in a few months. Problems of manning and of raw materials took years to solve. Meanwhile Sandwich believed that the threat of France was of the first importance. Graves had to meet the activities of scattered American privateers with a small fleet while a larger force patrolled the Channel. In any event the French controlled American waters for long enough to have a decisive influence on the colonial war, and the home fleet failed to inflict a proper defeat upon the French. Admiral Rodney's victory of the Saints (April 1782), which restored naval control of the Atlantic and ended the French threat to the West Indies, came too late to help Sandwich's reputation, for North's government had resigned a month before.

Sandwich had already been the target of a pamphlet war and the central figure in a crisis of confidence. As never before rivalries among senior naval commanders reflected political differences. The quarrel of Keppel and Palliser and the courts-martial which followed their indecisive battle of Ushant in July 1778 were embittered by the fact that Keppel was closely bound to the Whig opposition; his sister was married to the Duke of Bedford's heir. He became a public hero, many of the captains took his part and some refused to serve; aged admirals were sent out to sea, men such as Hardy and Geary, unfitted for active service. Fortunately, however, these political strains hastened the emergence of a new type of naval officer of the middle class, professional in outlook, often sons of the vicarage, like the Hood brothers or Nelson. Meanwhile distrust was engendered by the suspected corruption and known inefficiency of the Navy Board. Horace Walpole wrote of Sandwich's "passion for maritime affairs, his activity, industry and flowing complaisance," but he went too far when he said that this "endeared him to the profession." Sandwich's sophistication, the courtly air of effortless authority which is expressed by Gainsborough's celebrated portrait in Greenwich Hospital, was a further irritant to those who loathed the politics of North and the patronage of the court. Furthermore Sandwich was himself too much a product of the system to be able to carry out the radical reforms which were needed to transform the navy of 1780 into the navy of Nelson and Collingwood. He seemed to be more preoccupied with patronage than with policy. In his correspondence with Rodney occur constant requests to forward the career of some protégé or other. "There is," wrote the First Lord, after a reference to Lord Charles Fitzgerald, "another young officer of fashion now in your squadron. You will infinitely oblige me. I mean Lord Robert Manners." Lord Sandwich was an amiable man, obliging, zealous for the navy. But he never quite emancipated himelf from the image of the dilettante. Indeed, with his adored mistress, Martha Ray, whom he surrounded with pet dogs and parrots, with his taste for fine clothes, he lived in a very different world from the seamen whose operations he controlled.

N. A. M. Rodger, *The Insatiable Earl*, 1993.
G. R. Barnes and J. H. Owen, eds., *The Private Papers of the Earl of Sandwich*, 4 vols., 1932–38.

CHARLES TOWNSHEND (1725–67), son of the 3rd Viscount Townshend and grandson of Walpole's able colleague, is as puzzling to historians as he was to his contemporaries. His career was throughout inconsistent, his character impetuous and unstable; his talents were formidable, his achievements meager.

From his boyhood he suffered from some physical disability, hard to diagnose from his correspondence but very probably epilepsy. After adolescence he suffered bouts of malaise; under the sparkling guise of a buoyant personality there seems to have been much suffering from what he called his "crazy constitution." He

lived uncertainly poised between sanity and disaster, between brilliance and breakdown. His parents were separated after he was fifteen, and he stayed thereafter with his father, an intelligent man
but oppressive and demanding. Charles did not go to Eton, but
later went to Clare College, Cambridge, and subsequently to Leyden. He studied thereafter for the Bar at Lincoln's Inn, but in 1747
he was returned to Parliament as member for Great Yarmouth,
where his family had influence. In 1755 he married Lady Dalkeith,
eight years older than he, a lady of ample fortune. He was already,
by then, a junior minister with a place on the Admiralty Board and
soon became known as an expert in the affairs of the navy, the
colonies, and especially America. The effects of this mastery of
affairs were, however, diminished by his performances in Parliament though, as Horace Walpole tells us, his speeches appealed to
an assembly which relished fine phrases: "Charles Townshend as-
tonishes: but was far too severe to persuade, and too bold to convince . . . He only spoke to show how well he could adorn a bad
cause, or demolish a good one," he said of one characteristic effort.
Nobody knew on what side of the House he would be at the end of
the debate. He could speak with "infinite rapidity, vehemence, and
parts" but his very brilliance aroused mistrust.

In October 1759 Newcastle, reshuffling his ministry, was
tempted to make him Chancellor of the Exchequer, "but there is
no depending on him, and his character will not go down in the
City or anywhere else." Yet his abilities were such that they compelled attention and in 1761 he was made Secretary at War. He resigned in December 1762, but was made President of the Board of
Trade two months later. From now on his gyrations became more
erratic, his disloyalty a byword. He accepted a post under
Grenville, attacked his measures, resigned, and then, in the last
year of Grenville's administration, accepted the post of paymaster-
general: he retained this office under Rockingham but it did not
inhibit him from attacking him likewise. Meanwhile he was gravi-
tating toward Chatham and was rewarded by the post of Chancellor of the Exchequer in his administration of 1766.

He may have commended himself to Chatham by his interest
in American affairs—fatal irony as it was to turn out—but he was
surely the most ill-fitting piece in the "tesselated pavement" of
Burke's famous description. Chatham soon fell ill and left the ministers virtually without guidance. Townshend, in 1767, produced a

scheme to tax the colonies and mend the mother country's finances, which was reasonable in theory but calamitous in practice. It is fair to him to emphasize that there was a problem. When critics of the government forced through a reduction in the Land Tax from 4s. to 3s., alternative revenue had to be found. A few weeks before, Townshend had boasted that he knew of a way to raise money from America; it seems that when pressed to disclose his plan he hastily worked out the idea of Customs duties on American imports. The colonists had said, during their resistance to the Stamp Act, that they would only accept taxes regulating trade; under this guise taxes that were obviously designed to raise revenue were concealed as duties on lead, glass, paper, painters' colors, and tea imported from Britain. They could hardly have done more harm, for as taxes on British exports they raised protests at home, while across the Atlantic they symbolized Britain's determination to turn the Declaratory Act into hard cash. By asserting that the yield might help to pay executive officials in America Townshend implied that he sought to make Americans more dependent upon the British government. "Champagne Charlie," the handsome, reckless, bombastic minister, came to epitomize the arrogance of British government to Americans, who were already in a mood to question the whole relationship between their states and the mother-country. The Massachusetts circular drafted by Samuel Adams called upon all colonists to resist the duties. Having bequeathed this fruitful source of discord to the two great English-speaking peoples, Charles Townshend died suddenly on September 4, 1767, leaving his affairs in great disorder.

He was a lonely man; several of his closest intimates were disreputable men—like Theobald Taffe, professional gambler and swindler. He never gave himself a chance. Posturing and mimicry contributed to an impression of a man who was not to be relied on. The purpose of the statesman was lost in the turns of the clown. Paradoxically he was consistent in his most unfortunate act: the scheme of 1767 was that which he had first mooted as a junior minister in 1753. His last months were tragic in course and consequence; yet the comic image persists. Since he ridiculed his colleagues he was distrusted by them all. He could not have lasted much longer in office. To the end he joked about death, as naturally as he used to do about living. He was capable of tenderness as well as bravery, showed concern for the well-being of his children, and he worked, without success, for legislation to improve the condition of the insane, whose fate, we may feel, his might so easily have been.

Sir Lewis Namier and John Brooke, *Charles Townshend*, 1964.

JAMES LIND (1716–94), physician, has an honored place in the history of the navy as the man who did most to combat the scurvy and other deficiency diseases which lowered the efficiency of ships on long voyages. He served with Vernon in the West Indies in 1739–41 and later off the coast of Guinea. For the sufferings of men with scurvy, the reader should turn to Smollett, also for a time a naval surgeon, and the adventures of Roderick Random. Lind was subsequently physician to the Naval Hospital at Haslar and able to deepen his study of illness on board ship. We may wonder how men survived at all in the cramped, reeking quarters of these ships, on a diet that was too often reduced to weevily bread and biscuit, maggoty salt pork, and brackish water. Lind was not alone in realizing the importance of balancing the diet. But he brought scientific observation to bear, wrote treatises on the subject, and influenced thoughtful seamen like Anson and Cook. In 1754 he published his *Treatise of Scurvy*, suggesting green vegetables, fresh fruit, and lime juice as preventives. In 1768 he presented a fuller survey in his *Essay . . . for Preserving the Life of Seamen*. If it were no longer true at the end of the century that, as Lind said, "the number of seamen in time of war who died by shipwreck, capture, famine, fire or sword, are but inconsiderable in respect of such as are destroyed by the ship diseases and by the usual maladies of an intemperate climate," this was a fine memorial to him. His work was carried further by Gilbert Blane (1749–1834), who obtained free issues of soap and medicines for seamen.

N. A. M. Rodger, *The Wooden World: An Anatomy of the Georgian Navy*, 1986.

JOHN METCALF (1717–1810), "Blind Jack of Knaresborough" as he is better known, provides a rare example of spirit and achievement in the face of physical handicaps. As a constructor of roads along the boggy moors and uplands of the Pennine country which lay athwart the busy industrial areas of Lancashire, Yorkshire, and Derbyshire, he was a pioneer of real importance.

Metcalf was completely blinded at the age of six after an attack of smallpox, but people tended to forget his disability when they encountered him. He was at various times a horse dealer and carrier, and thus well acquainted with the mud, ruts, stones, and dust of eighteenth-century roads. He was prodigiously active and once for a bet raced a friend from London to Harrogate: on foot, he took six days; his friend, in a carriage, took eight. He was a notable horseman and an accomplished fiddler, much in demand at fashionable spas such as Harrogate. He married a beautiful girl, Dolly Benson, after a characteristic elopement. In 1745 he joined his county volunteers and served in the subsequent Scottish campaign under the Duke of Cumberland. At one time he seems to have thought of setting up as a spinner, but his great work was to be as road-maker.

A contemporary, Hew, described how he had seen Metcalf, "with the assistance only of a long staff," working on his roads, "ascending precipices, exploring valleys, and investigating their several extents, forms and situations so as to answer his designs in the best manner." When Hew inquired about the new road "it was really astonishing to hear with what accuracy he described the courses and the nature of the different soils through which it was conducted." Between 1760 and 1790 he constructed roads from Wakefield to Doncaster, Bury to Blackburn, Ashton to Stockport, Skipton to Burnley, Macclesfield to Chapel-en-le-Frith, and Whaley Bridge to Buxton, 180 miles of turnpike in all. His method was to dig out the soft soil, to spread out bunches of heather and broom on the earth-bed, and to cover them with stone and gravel on the surface, with a gentle convex slope so that rainwater ran off into the ditches on either side. He was taciturn about his ways and means, however, and preferred to make his surveys alone, so there is some doubt about his methods. There is none about his success or its importance in the evolution of the industrial north of England.

E. Pawson, *Transport and Economy: The Turnpike Roads of Eighteenth Century Britain*, 1977.

JAMES BRINDLEY (1716–72), the great canal builder, was born in a hamlet three miles from Buxton in Derbyshire. In his boyhood he was poor but slightly educated. He was taken off farm work at the age of seventeen to be apprenticed to a wheelwright, and he showed remarkable aptitude for making and repairing things. Ingenuity and persistence brought him along, and in 1742 he emerged as a millwright; soon he was employed by Josiah Wedgwood and was acquiring a local fame as a constructor of machinery for flour mills and water-driven silk mills. He also experimented in improvements to stationary steam engines. In 1755 he undertook the draining of a colliery near Manchester by means of a water wheel and a tunnel six hundred yards long. In 1758 he surveyed "a navigation" between Trent and Mersey. In the following year he came into contact with the young Duke of Bridgewater who had inherited a scheme, still on paper, for making the Worsley brook navigable, from his collieries to the river Irwell. Called in by his friend, the duke's agent, paid 3s. 6d. a day for his work and lodged at the Duke's house, Worsley Old Hall, Brindley planned and executed a new project that was both daring and expensive. After an "ochilor servey or ricconitoring," he designed a canal which had no locks but high embankments to maintain the level of water. Over the river Irwell he carried his canal at a height of forty feet, within a channel whose banks and base, inside masonry, were made of puddled clay. Across the spongy ground of a local "moss" his canal went, and by tunnels into coal mines at Worsley itself. There were many critics. Bridgewater, a recluse and dreamer, caring little for the conventional life of an aristocrat, spent his fortune in the work; he then had difficulty in raising mortgages and loans because he was thought to be insane. But the canal was finished within two years. The price of coals to Manchester was reduced by a half and Brindley, the almost illiterate engineer who made up in his flair for the work what he lacked in technical training, became famous.

He was required next to make an extension of the canal to the Mersey itself. Called on to give evidence before a committee of Parliament, Brindley explained his plans for a certain bridge that was part of the scheme by bringing in a large cheese and cutting it in half. Canals were an essential condition of industrial progress at a time when other factors were favorable, but the means of transportation were inadequate. Adam Smith later asserted that every sort of goods except live cattle could be transported more cheaply by sea than by roads. Coal was especially in demand; no less than ninety of the 165 acts passed between 1758 and 1802 were for concerns whose main object was to carry coal. There was also a growing demand among landowners to extend their markets for corn and root crops and also among manufacturers and builders for the cheaper conveyance of their materials and products, cotton, iron, brick, and slate. The confidence and money of men like Bridgewater and Wedgwood, not afraid to be thought eccentric and ready to wait for a proper return on their capital, played a vital part in the canal revolution in the period before the advantages of the new waterways were clear to the business community. Before Brindley's death, men were investing in canal shares with an enthusiasm similar to that which accompanied the development of the railways sixty years later. Brindley himself, with a typical single-mindedness, invested all his savings from his somewhat meager income in canal undertakings, and he died a fairly rich man.

The Mersey extension was opened in 1773, a year after Brindley's death. He had also been at work upon the Grand Trunk, which eventually linked the Mersey, Trent, and Severn. Wedgwood was keenly interested in the building of a canal which could carry his fragile products across the country, and Brindley cut the first turf in July 1766. He surveyed several canals in the Midlands and was consulted upon several others. At the age of fifty he married a surveyor's daughter of nineteen and had two daughters. When he died he was generally respected as the leader of his profession. Yet he can hardly be called an engineer in the commonly understood sense. He succeeded by common sense, intuitive skill in the face of physical problems, and a sturdy confidence in his own judgment. When he had to come to a decision involving intensive thought, so we are told by Samuel Smiles in his *Lives of the Engineers*, he would retire to bed for a day or two, then rise with the plan complete in his mind. He rarely drew anything, but he kept a journal, crudely spelled and expressed, which, with his surviving works, tell us his secrets and methods. Brindley avoided locks where it was possible, choosing a circuitous route rather than one where hills were encountered. He kept the "pound," or space between locks, at the summit level as long as possible; where the canal had to rise or descend, he placed locks close together, if necessary with successive gates as the steps went down. He provided weirs for overflows and floodgates which could be quickly closed in the event of a breach;

thus a length of the pound could be emptied and repairs carried out without the whole pound being emptied. At the summit levels he would have tunnels rather than deep cuttings. One such, the famous Harecastle tunnel, was 2,800 yards, took eleven years to dig, and was not finished until five years after his death. He always preferred an artificial to a natural waterway; once he even suggested that a canal should be built alongside the Thames, instead of keeping open the river's navigation.

It may be, for all his skill of contrivance, that Brindley's greatest talent was for organization. His laboring force of some 500 might be spread out over miles, engaged upon several different projects or under subcontractors. Rough men, these "navigators," hillmen from the Pennines, Irishmen, or Scots mostly, they had to be disciplined, encouraged, paid. Their picks and shovels dug a revolution in sixty years which changed the face of the country, the sites and the productive capacity of its industries, the size and nature of its markets. Of the canals they dug, some 360 miles were under the direction of Brindley. He was indeed one of the pioneers of the industrial revolution.

Samuel Smiles, *Lives of the Engineers*, 1861.
H. Malet, *The Canal Duke: A Biography of Francis, 3rd Duke of Bridgewater*, 1961.
Robert Harris, *Canals and Their Architecture*, 1964.

FRANCIS EGERTON, 3rd DUKE OF BRIDGEWATER (1736–1803), canal builder, is one of the more surprising figures of his century. He was the only survivor of a large family; he was scantily educated, despised by his mother, and left to amuse himself with servants and stable-lads. At twelve, he became the heir to the dukedom and was sent to Eton to be birched and bullied into an acute awareness of his awkward manners. At twenty-one he succeeded to title and estates. He had by then traveled in Italy; for a time he led a fashionable life in London. Soon, however, he retreated to his estate at Worsley, six miles northwest of Manchester, nursing the grief of a broken engagement, determined to eschew society. Here, with Gilbert, his agent, and Brindley, unlettered genius of canal building, he projected the first of the waterways which were to transform the industrial face of England. He found the money, saw to it that the necessary bills were passed in Parliament, negotiated with the owners of land through which the canals passed, and infected with his cheerful, robust spirit the "navigators" who dug the canals. With them the Duke was happy to spend time in amiable talk, and when they were working on specially hard cuts he would order them extra beer. A supper of beef and pudding rewarded them at the end of every stretch, a larger spread with music and dancing when the canal was complete.

The duke made a fortune from his coal-laden barges. The Manchester canal was famous for its aqueduct over the river Irwell and parties from Europe came to see the spectacle of ships passing over ships. The Duke was at his ease entertaining guests to cold feasts in hall or barge. He rebuilt his house at Worsley and filled it with pictures and porcelain. He was an early patron of Turner before he became famous. When England declared war on France he at once subscribed £100,000 to the funds. Of even greater value to the nation was the cheap transport provided by his canals.

H. Malet, *The Canal Duke: A Biography of Francis, 3rd Duke of Bridgewater,* 1961.

J. R. Ward, *The Finance of Canal Building in Eighteenth Century England,* 1974.

JOHN LOMBE (1693–1722) and his half-brother Thomas Lombe (1685–1739) are among the less well-known figures of the industrial revolution, but they deserve notice for they erected, on an island in the river Derwent, the first factory in England and gave an enormous impetus to the development of industrial capitalism.

English manufacturers of silk were confronted by great difficulties: they had to buy their raw silk abroad and when they tried to make their own thrown silk (the thread made by twisting together the filaments from the cocoons), smugglers put such cheap thread on to the market that they were badly undercut. It was rumored that there were, in Italy, machines for throwing silk, but they went unseen until, in 1716, John Lombe penetrated into a building in Leghorn where they were used. With the help of an Italian priest he secretly made some drawings and sent them to England hidden in pieces of silk. When he was reembarking, a brig was sent after him and he only narrowly escaped. Soon after his return home, however, he died, a victim to Italian poison, so rumor had it. Meanwhile he had set up, in 1717, silk-throwing machines upon the Italian model. His brother supplied the necessary capital and in 1718 obtained a patent for fourteen years. Soon afterward the famous factory was built, a huge barracks, five hundred feet long, five or six stories high, with four hundred and sixty windows. The machines were very tall, cylindrical in shape, and they rotated on vertical axes; several rows of bobbins received the threads and gave them the required twist by a swift rotary movement. At the top the thrown silk was automatically wound on a winder, ready to be made up into hanks for sale. The machine was a complex one. Defoe, who visited the factory on one of his tours, said that there were "22,586 wheels and 97,746 movements, which work 73,726 yards of silk thread every time the wheel goes round, which is three times in one minute, and 318,504,960 yards in twenty-four hours." The whole mechanism was worked by one water wheel. The workman's main task was to retie the threads whenever they broke; each man had charge of sixty threads.

This factory employed three hundred workmen. In a short time Thomas Lombe made a fortune, became an alderman and a sheriff, and was knighted. When Parliament refused to renew his patent in 1732, he was given £14,000 indemnity. He did not live long to enjoy his success, but he had the satisfaction of knowing that he, with his brother, had pioneered an entirely new form of industrial organization.

A. E. Musson and E. Robinson, *Science and Technology in the Industrial Revolution*, 1969.

JOHN WILKINSON (1728–1808), ironmaster, was one of the inventive and forceful personalities who helped to mold the industrial revolution. He grew up in the iron tradition, for his father, Isaac Wilkinson, was a resourceful ironmaster who took out patents for a number of inventions, the last being an iron blowing engine for coke-smelting iron ore. Other men grew rich on improvements on his ideas, but he died insolvent. His son, meanwhile, was sent to a dissenting academy at Kendal, typical of those schools which were such a valuable nursery of thoughtful and inventive minds.

Wilkinson married twice, in 1755 and 1763; both wives brought him the money which was a vital condition of success. Another was demand for his product: this was provided by the Seven Years War

and the expansion of armaments that went with it. In 1757 he set
up the first furnace in the Black Country to produce coke-smelted
iron, at Bradley. At the same time he became technical adviser to a
consortium of Bristol merchants and Shropshire landowners who
were building a foundry at Willey, on the opposite side of the river
from the Darby works at Coalbrookdale. The pattern of the iron industry was changing fast, from small forges, charcoal-burning and
scattered in forest areas, to the coal and iron-stone areas. East
Shropshire, round the Severn, where now all is green or preserved
in an admirable open-air museum, then provided the raw materials, and river transport as well. Wilkinson soon acquired complete
control of Willey's new furnace and directed the operations of his
growing industrial empire from Broseley until, in 1779, he went to
live in lonely state at Castlehead, Grange-over-Sands.

In 1762 he went into partnership with his father at Bersham,
near Wrexham, producing naval cannon, piping of every sort, and
parts for the new steam engines. He perfected his father's blowing
machine, and ousted him from active concern in the works. In
1774 he took out his patent for boring cannon from solid castings,
by rotating the piece while keeping the boring bar steady. He also
developed a cylinder-boring lathe on the opposite principle. These
improvements gave England a vital lead in the production of arms.
The French were concerned about the relative ineffectiveness of
their cannon and secured the services of Wilkinson's brother
William to build and equip a new ironworks. Technology then
knew no frontiers. But there grew up later a damaging myth that
John Wilkinson supplied the French with arms. In fact all he had
done was to supply the Paris Waterworks Company with forty miles
of iron piping—for which English travelers may have had cause to
be grateful.

In the 1770s Bradley and Birmingham were linked by canal; by
then Wilkinson was already supplying Boulton with castings. Now
the success of the partnership of Boulton and Watt in the manufacture of steam engines owed much to the accurate castings and bor-
ings of Wilkinson's works. The American War brought great
prosperity to the "Iron Parliament," as it was called. Wilkinson
spread out in other directions too, with interests in the copper industry of Cornwall, where he came to own six mines outright, and
in the lead mines of North Wales. But as his concerns grew more
extensive, troubles of every sort overtook him. He had no male

heir and he could find no satisfactory lieutenant. Eventually he took a nephew, Thomas Jones, into his service. He quarreled with his brother when he returned from France, and years were spent on wasteful disputes and an expensive suit in Chancery. He broke with Boulton and Watt when they found that he had been pirating their steam engine designs. They extracted large sums from him in compensation and then erected their own foundry. In the 1790s Cort's new process of iron-making set an example of cheaper production which he was reluctant to follow. Technical difficulties were accompanied by a decline in his private life. He had always been a difficult man, willful and imperious. When his only child married a Shropshire clergyman without his consent he "vowed never to speak to her again." While his second wife was still living at Castlehead, in about 1800, he took himself a mistress, Ann Lewis, who bore him three children. He later declared them legitimate, which led on his death to a further Chancery dispute instigated by Thomas Jones, who had hoped to succeed to his uncle.

When the old ironmaster died, he was already something of a legend. His iron bridge, iron barges, the iron pulpit, window sills, and tombstones of Coalbrookdale Church, were daily reminders of the iron revolution which he had fostered. For all his coarseness he was a man of literate tastes. His interests were wide; he reclaimed land, founded banks, invested in canals. He minted his own copper coinage, for the convenient payment of workmen in his various concerns, and the profile of his strong features was familiar to many who never saw him in the flesh. He was painted by Gainsborough; his brother-in-law was Joseph Priestley. He touched the life of his time at many points. But at the end all was narrowed down to his ruling passion. At his own request he was buried in an iron coffin under an iron obelisk. It was said that, on the seventh anniversary of his death, he would revisit his blast furnaces on his gray horse—and on July 14, 1815, several thousand people assembled at Bradley to see the event. This was a substantial man indeed whose anticipated ghost could arouse such excitement.

T. S. Ashton, *Iron and Steel in the Industrial Revolution*, 1924.
W. H. Chaloner, *People and Industries*, 1963.

JAMES HUTTON (1726–97), geologist, was the originator of the modern theory of the origin of the earth's crust. A Scotsman, like

so many big men in the intellectual life of the century, he was educated at Edinburgh, Paris, and Leyden. After widespread travels
abroad he became a partner with James Davie in the production of
salammoniac from coal soot. He settled in Edinburgh in 1768,
from where he traveled around Scotland, examining rock forma-
tions and collecting evidence for his theories from those wild and
beautiful places which, happily for the geologist, provide the best
hunting grounds for specimens and sections. In 1795 he was joint
editor of Adam Smith's *Essays on Philosophical Subjects.* In the same
year he published his *Theory of the Earth.* From his researches in
Glen Tilt, Galloway, Arran, and the Isle of Man he had satisfied
himself that it is mostly in stratification that fossils occur; that the
imposition of successive layers could not have occurred as a result
of a single great flood, but suggested rather a gentle and orderly
deposit over a long period. He therefore concluded that the strata
had once been the beds of seas, later of swamps. Scientific geology
takes its start from him.

JOHN HUNTER (1728–93), the son of a small laird of Lanarkshire, followed his brother William to London and to fame as surgeon and anatomist. Advances in medicine are rarely made by the
unaided efforts of a single person. He was only one among a number whose research and practice relieved us from some of the pain
of the sickbed, but he was in many ways the most remarkable.

At the start of the century there was no systematic teaching of
anatomy in Britain and men went abroad for the best instruction.
Guy's was yet to be founded and there were only two hospitals in
London: St. Bartholomew's and St. Thomas's; outside London only
one, at York. Surgeons were regarded as inferior to physicians, who
might be both rich and fashionable. In 1745, however, the Company of Barber-Surgeons was dissolved and the surgeons given a
company of their own. Yet as late as 1757 a majority of judges in
Common Pleas decided that a surgeon was "an inferior tradesman"
within the meaning of an Act of William and Mary. When medicine
was still contained within the classical tradition and learning valued
more than clinical experience, quacks flourished, but improvements had to wait for men of genius and persistence.

Among these, Scotsmen were to be found prominent as in so
much else. In 1720 Alexander Munro, the first of a family which
was to dominate the Edinburgh School of Anatomy for a century,

was appointed professor; he and his son had, by 1790, trained 12,800 students. From the Medical School of Glasgow, founded in 1718, William Hunter came in 1741 to learn dissection in London. He came to specialize in the practice of midwifery, which he learned from Smollett's friend, Smellie. His brother John took over his lecturing and carved a great career of his own, learning from Cheseldon, expert in operations for the stone, and from Percival Pott. As a surgeon at Belle Isle and in Portugal he studied the effect of gunshot wounds. He returned in 1762 and began the study of comparative anatomy with the aid of a collection of specimens at Earl's Court. His practical surgery was important; he started in 1786, for instance, the life-saving practice of tying the artery above an aneurism. His teaching of anatomy was, however, the more significant part of his work; among his pupils were Edward Jenner, pioneer of vaccination, and Abernethy. His lectures, which established the methods and principles of surgery until the advent of Lister, began in 1773. He was known to his pupils as "the dear man," but his minute studies in comparative anatomy reflect the method of an empirical scientist. "Don't think; try" was one of his favorite phrases. He never took shortcuts, but accumulated evidence until he was sure that he had verified every possible link in the chain of evidence. He was astonishingly wide in his field, working at different times on the problems of differentiation of sex, the fetus and embryonic studies, blood and the arteries, but also on geological time and the fossils. When so little was established, the experimental scientist was bound to be drawn into a number of related fields. One tangible product of his researches and collecting was his museum, begun in 1783 for the housing of his specimens and subsequently taken over by the College of Surgeons. Then there were such books as *Human Teeth, Venereal Disease, Animal Economy*, and *Gunshot Wounds*. Excitable, dedicated, graceless in social life but unwearying in his work, he helped to bring surgery and medicine into contact with science; in this respect he anticipated the age of Darwin.

G. C. Peachey, *A Memoir of William and John Hunter*, 1924.

JOSEPH BLACK (1728–99) made a lasting impression on science by his experiments on chemical combinations and on heat. He trained at Glasgow under William Cullen, head of the medical school and much in advance of his time in his emphasis upon chemistry, and then at Edinburgh where he graduated M.D. in 1754, with a thesis of seminal value: *De humore acido a cibis orto, et Magnesia alba.* The brief essay established with complete success, by cautious investigation and precise measurement, the composition of chalk, the relationship between quick-lime and the mild alkalis, and the reason for the milky appearance of lime-water when exposed to the atmosphere. He proved that chalk gave off a gas, when strongly heated, which he called "fixed air," but which is known to us as carbon dioxide, and that small quantities of this gas were present in the air. Add to these findings that he also showed that fixed air was liberated from chalk by the action of a dilute acid, and that a certain weight of chalk yielded the same weight of fixed air when treated in this way as when it was strongly heated, and it will be apparent that the methodical young Scotsman had revolutionized chemical knowledge. He was the first person to detect upon the balance the chemical changes at every stage in this series of reactions without isolating the "fixed air." He had thus found a gas which could be transferred from combination with one substance to another and had its own peculiar properties. So he pointed the way to a new line of research which was to occupy chemists for the rest of the century: the isolation and study of gases and their combinations.

In 1756 Black succeeded Cullen as professor of medicine and while there he practiced as a physician. He also investigated the nature of heat. About 1760 he introduced a method of measuring quantities of heat by the degrees of temperature imparted to a definite quantity of matter; at the same time he clarified the distinction between *quantity* and *intensity* of heat. He showed that every substance had its own "capacity for heat" (*specific heat* is the modern term) which appeared, in contra-distinction to the older theory, to have no relation to the quantity of matter in the body investigated. He showed too in subsequent experiments that definite quantities of heat vanish and reappear in changes of physical state, melting and evaporation, freezing and condensation. James Watt, then working on his steam engine, was able to use this latter discovery, *latent heat* as Black called it, in his contrivance of a separate condenser. The friendship of Watt and Black, who first came into contact with Watt when he made the barrel organ for him, provides a happy example of advance achieved by the partnership of scientist and inventor. Black was always a practical man. He gave valuable advice to the Linen Board, to discontinue the use of lime in bleaching, he took an active interest in Roebuck's sulfuric acid factory at Prestonpans, and he made an early demonstration of the possibility of aeronautics, twelve years before the first balloon was launched in Paris, with a membrane filled with hydrogen.

Like most Scots of this golden age of intellectual life, he took the chance offered by appointment to the professorship of medicine and chemistry (1766) to move to Edinburgh, and there he stayed for the rest of his life. In old age he provides material for one of the most memorable of Cockburn's portraits. "He was a striking and beautiful person; tall and thin and very cadaverously pale; his hair carefully powdered though there was very little of it except what was collected into a long, thin queue; his eyes dark, clear, and large, like pools of pure water. He wore black, speckless clothes, silk stockings, silver buckles, and either a slim green silk umbrella or a genteel brown cane. The general frame and air were tall and slender. The wildest boy respected Black."

E. J. Holmyard, *Makers of Chemistry*, 1931.
A. and L. N. Clow, *The Chemical Revolution*, 1952.

HENRY CAVENDISH (1731–1810) was a chemist, philosopher, and mathematician whose investigations unlocked several of the closed doors of scientific knowledge. With Boyle, Priestley, and Darwin he is a reminder of how much of the most important pioneer work in science was done outside the great universities. In this century it may seem to be appropriate that a leading scientist was the grandson of a Duke of Devonshire and a millionaire. He was, however, no dilettante; on the contrary, he was meticulous and patient, utterly absorbed in his self-appointed tasks of measurement and analysis. Because he would leave out no stage in argument and present no conclusions before they had been minutely tested, his work had an immediate and powerful influence.

In his first paper, sent to the Royal Society in 1766, he described his discovery of "inflammable air" (or hydrogen), a distinct, inflammable gas which was produced by the action of acids on certain metals. In his "Experiments on Air" (1784) he demonstrated that the only product of the combustion of "inflammable air" and "dephlogisticated air" (oxygen) was water, and gave an approximately correct estimate of the proportion of the two in water. In a superb series of experiments, confining ordinary air over a solution of caustic potash and sparking it repeatedly with additions of "dephlogisticated air," he demonstrated that niter (potassium nitrate) was produced. Thus he showed the way to the fixation of atmospheric nitrogen and the manufacture from the air of nitric acid. In 1783, using Priestley's method of testing the goodness of air by mixing it with nitric oxide, he found a contraction of 20.833 percent; this is almost identical with the modern value for the percentage of oxygen in the air. Only a few years before, Priestley had confidently announced that "atmospherical air" was "a simple elementary substance, indestructible and unalterable, at least as much so as water is supposed to be." It was after reading Priestley's account of Cavendish's experiments that Montgolfier set to work on his hot-air balloon; it flew for the first time in 1783.

Cavendish was anything but narrow in his scientific interests. He inquired into the density of the earth and experimented with electricity. He offered an experimental proof (not published until a century later) of the theory that the law of electrical attraction was the same as that of gravitational attraction, that of the inverse square of the distance. His work was, however, his life. If the legend of the remote, inhuman scientist can be traced to any one person it is Cavendish. He was so careless of his appearance that he is supposed to have worn the same shovel hat for forty years, and so shy that only one portrait could be made of him, and that surreptitiously. He disliked all meat except mutton, and quarreled with the bankers who handled his fortune. Conversation and women seemed to him to be alike superfluous. He might not, however, have been displeased to know that one of the world's most famous laboratories perpetuates his name.

A. and L. N. Clow, *The Chemical Revolution*, 1952.

MATTHEW BOULTON (1728–1809) was an enterprising manufacturer and merchant whose work and capital did much to establish Birmingham as the workshop of England. His father, a Northamptonshire man in origin, was a silver stamper; Matthew extended his business by the purchase of some wasteland at Soho, "a barren heath, on the black summit of which stood a naked hut, the habitation of a weaver." On this unpromising spot he built a large factory at a cost of £9,000: five buildings held 600 workmen, and a reservoir at the top of the hill provided water for a large wheel which "communicated motion to an immense number of different tools." Here Boulton produced iron, copper, silver, and tortoise-shell wares, metal buttons, snuff-boxes, and watch-chains; his tools were up-to-date, his sales enormous. He valued quality, however, before mass production. When in about 1765 he began to manufacture ornamental bronzes, he had the finest antique work sent him from abroad and he inspected the treasures of great houses.

Boulton fought a strenuous battle against the industrial frauds which besmirched the name of Birmingham. "I will do anything," he said, "short of being common informer against particular persons, to stop the malpractices of the Birmingham comers." He lavished care upon the invention and use of a process for coining which greatly improved the quality of the coins. This alone, in the opinion of James Watt, should have ensured him immortality: "If it be considered that this was done in the midst of various other important avocations, and at enormous expense . . . we shall be at a loss whether most to admire his ingenuities, his perseverance, or his munificence." Watt was associated with Boulton from 1774, when they set up their manufactory of steam engines at Soho with a patent lasting twenty-five years. At first the new engine was unprofitable and Boulton had to inject all his capital into its production. At the end of 1781 the partners were unable to pay their workmen in wages; not till 1786 were they able to meet their debts and think of profits. Till then Boulton's other manufacturers had subsidized the steam engine. Watt, the inventor, needed Boulton's skill in business, for several other firms were involved in the making, and of course in the use of these machines: the cylinders, for instance, were supplied by Wilkinson. Also his "active and sanguine disposition" served to counterbalance Watt's "despondency and diffidence," as the latter admitted.

Boulton was a cultivated man, whose friends included some of the most interesting people: Erasmus Darwin and the astronomer William Herschel, Joseph Priestley, like him a radical in religion and politics, and Josiah Wedgwood, another industrialist of comparable enlightenment and enterprise. At "the inn of friendship" on Handsworth Heath, as Boulton liked to call it, his "Lunar Society" friends would meet every month when the moon was full enough to light up their journey back along country lanes. Every meeting would have its agenda: scientific questions were usually discussed. Boulton was himself the most practical of men; his factory, in Mantoux's words, was "one huge laboratory of applied mechanics": he was the first to conceive the idea of the tubular boiler, chemistry was a favorite "hobby-horse," and he was interested in the new science of political economy.

He was a stalwart for fair prices and a scrupulous employer, who utterly rejected the idea that labor was only a commodity, marketable and disposable. His work-people admired him for his fair dealing and generosity and he knew them all personally. In the factory his men were trained to such regularity that any break in the steady noise and rhythm of steam hammers was enough to bring him from his office. He started a sick club to which every man subscribed according to his wage. There was also, however, something of the great magnate about Boulton. When his eldest son came of age, bells rang to summon work-people, 700 of them, to a banquet; led by music, trooping in squadrons according to their trades, they marched in procession. These men were craftsmen who could take pride in their work and their firm. Their tall, curly-headed, strikingly handsome employer, "princely Boulton," was an approachable figure with whom they could identify themselves. By precept and example Boulton taught a lofty code of business ethics: "A hard bargain is a bad bargain," he would say, and "Honesty is the best policy." He was unfailingly generous. When the Birmingham dispensary was started in 1792 and he became treasurer, he announced: "If the funds of the institution are not sufficient for its support, I will make up the deficiency." This "iron captain in the midst of his troops," as Boswell once called him, knew that the workman, upon whose shoulders rested the technological revolution that he did so much to promote, was also a human being.

W. H. Dickinson, *Matthew Boulton*, 1937.
J. E. Cole, "Finance and Industry in the Eighteenth Century: The Firm of Boulton and Watt," *Ec. Hist.*, IV, 1940.
R. E. Schofield, *The Lunar Society of Birmingham*, 1963.

RICHARD ARKWRIGHT (1732–92), inventor and factory master, was the son of a laborer of Preston. He started work as a lather-boy with a barber and rapidly became proficient with scissors and razor. Quick-witted and resourceful, he experimented with dyes and traveled about searching for country-girls' hair for wig-making. Marrying at twenty, he set up in business for himself in Bolton. By watching a clock-maker friend he was inspired to construct spinning machinery: after many attempts he succeeded in making a water-frame. He built a factory at Hockley in Lancashire in 1769 and installed a number of frames, using a stream for power. Early manufacturers were handicapped by the shortage of available labor: an advantage of the water-frame was that it could be minded by children. Women and some men were employed for the difficult tasks. Arkwright's example was followed by others in the same district; like them he was plagued by the opposition of the domestic spinners: one of his mills was destroyed, others damaged. He therefore moved to Derbyshire, built a large factory in a remote valley near Cromford, by the river Derwent, imported workhouse children from London, and housed his labor force on the spot. This mill, which might have provided an illustration for Blake's *Jerusalem*, still stands: it is built like a castle round a courtyard, with no windows facing outward.

Arkwright became very rich; he took out several patents on improvements on his first machine. He was knighted and became High Sheriff of Derbyshire. In his later years he built an imposing house overlooking his factory. His contribution to the country's economic progress was considerable; the water-frame produced a cotton yarn which was, for the first time, strong enough to serve as warp as well as weft. The new material produced in quantity by factory labor could be sold at a cheap price for a mass market. Figures here are eloquent: between 1780 and 1800 the amount of raw cotton imported increased eightfold. Even if some of his inventions were challenged as being copies, which involved him in lawsuits, the combination in him of inventor, capitalist, and manager was significant. He was entirely ruthless, a notably hard employer even for his time. Indeed, with his broad, coarse, somewhat porcine features, he is not an appealing character, but we may wonder if, without the brass and boldness of men like Arkwright, England would have become a great industrial nation.

S. D. Chapman, *The Cotton Industry in the Industrial Revolution*, 1972.
G. Unwin, A. Hulme, and G. Taylor, *Samuel Oldknow and the Ark-wrights*, 1924.

THOMAS CHIPPENDALE (1718–79) is perhaps the most famous name among the furniture-makers of the eighteenth century, when subtle craftsmanship and aesthetic sense combined to produce work which will surely never be excelled. He owes his special fame largely to his trade catalog, *The Gentleman and Cabinet-Maker's Director*, 1754, the first comprehensive pattern book for furniture, and the designs in this book were mostly executed by Lock and Copland. His reputation among contemporaries does not seem to have been especially high. William Vile, William Hallett, and William Ince were just as highly regarded, and there were many others who have left little record beyond the exquisite pieces which are the pride of great English houses and the object of foreign dealers. Chippendale may, however, deserve special mention, if only because, with Hepplewhite and Sheraton after him, his is the first name that comes to mind: rightly or wrongly, "Chippendale" represents for millions the elegance and ingenuity of the age.

He was born at Otley, in Yorkshire, where his father was a joiner; as a boy he made plain oak country furniture. Before the middle of the century he set up in London, first at Long Acre, then in St. Martin's Lane, the heart of the artistic quarter at that time. His workshop was not large at first and his reputation grew but slowly. In the sixties and seventies, however, he received large commissions and supplied furniture to, among others, Nostell Priory and Harewood House, in his native Yorkshire, Badminton, Renishaw, and Alnwick. *The Director* revealed Chippendale's organizing ability and commercial sense; he always had an eye for fashion too—Chinese, "Gothic," French, neo-classical—whatever it might be. Technically, Chippendale's work probably was best in his Adam period, after 1770, when he was making inlaid furniture in the neo-classical style. Good craftsmanship in many styles was characteristic of him: with solidity he combined lightness and delicacy. His name is usually, however, associated with chairs in the rococo style: a cabriole leg, carved with leaf foliage, hooped back and a central open-work splat, with delicate carved ornament, surmounted by a top rail, serpentine, or cupid's bow.

Chippendale was an unpretentious man, content to remain a joiner. He placed his son in his firm; he was a good craftsman but less successful and in 1804 was made bankrupt.

O. Brackett, *Chippendale*, 1925.

JOHN ROEBUCK (1718–94) was an inventor and entrepreneur who made an important contribution to the spectacular industrial advance of his time. He studied chemistry and medicine at Edinburgh and Leyden but soon abandoned medicine for technology. He established a chemical laboratory in Birmingham and invented some improved methods of refining precious metals and processes for the production of chemicals. Learning from the seventeenth-century chemist Glauber that lead was not attacked by sulfuric acid, he substituted lead for glass; this freed manufacturers from the use of fragile laboratory-scale apparatus and made possible cheap and relatively large-scale production. With Samuel Garbett he founded a vitriol manufactory, but he decided that better opportunities existed in Scotland, where the bleaching trade was expanding fast. In 1749 he established a sulfuric acid plant near an old salt works at Prestonpans to provide cheap chemicals for bleaching, but despite secrecy about his methods and material (he imported sulfur from Leghorn and saltpeter through the East India Company), his patent rights were dubious and widely infringed upon. His works remained the largest, but many others sprang up to supply a growing demand in the textile industry. His pioneer work was a big factor in the low cost and massive production of bleached and printed goods.

Roebuck was, however, unfortunate in other fields. In 1760 he founded the Carron iron foundry and in 1762 invented a process of iron manufacture involving the use of pit coal. The Carron works were to become famous, but Roebuck did not benefit from their success, for he lost money heavily in coal mines and salt works in Linlithgowshire, and in 1773 he became bankrupt. He was the friend and patron of James Watt, and it was he who suggested that Watt apply for a patent for steam engines, for he anticipated that they would be useful for pumping out his coal mines. His share in the patent was valued by his creditors at a farthing, but Boulton took it over in exchange for the cancellation of Roebuck's debts to him. Roebuck's enterprising career shows that great progress could be achieved by a man who was both scientist and technologist, but also what risks such men had to take to find a profitable way in which to make use of their technical discoveries.

A. and L. N. Clow, *The Chemical Revolution*, 1952.

ANDREW MEIKLE (1719–1811), millwright, invented the first effective threshing machine. Improving upon earlier designs, it could be driven by steam, by water, by horses, or by hand. The long process of threshing with flails and winnowing by draft created by a hand-turned wheel was shortened by this machine. Its widespread adoption in the corn lands of southern England led to much hardship among the laborers who had grown to depend on threshing employment in winter, and it was one of the causes of the revolt of 1830. Meikle, a Scotsman, had already invented a machine for dressing grain and made unsuccessful efforts to produce threshing machines before arriving at the drum type, which made its first appearance in 1786. It contributed greatly to the improvement of agriculture, if not to the well-being of the laborer.

JOHN SMEATON (1724–92), engineer, was born in June 1724 at Austhorpe, near Leeds. His father, a successful attorney, sent him to the grammar school at Leeds; at sixteen he started work in his office, copying legal documents. Smeaton, who had shown interest at school in mathematical problems and worked at ambitious projects in his workshop at home, even forging his own iron and steel, soon abandoned the law. He was apprenticed to an instrument-maker and set himself up in the trade. In 1750 he read a paper on the mariner's compass to the Royal Society. Three years later he was elected a Fellow. In 1755 a visit to the Low Countries introduced him to advanced problems of canal, harbor, and drainage works; he already had a large theoretical knowledge of hydraulic engineering.

Later in the same year he was commissioned, on Lord Macclesfield's recommendation, to build a new lighthouse on the Eddystone Rock in place of the wooden one destroyed by fire. Built in large blocks of dovetailed stone, rooted in the rock, Smeaton's lighthouse became famous and the engineer with it. It was a fine piece of engineering, only to be replaced in the late nineteenth century after dislodgment of rock.

In Smeaton's time, the specialized engineer was unknown. Like James Watt, his contemporary, Smeaton's field was necessarily wide. He was a practical man who tended to fight shy of theory. Thus, although he played some part in the development of the steam engine, modifying the valves of Newcomen's engine and providing it with a larger cylinder to give greater power to the atmospheric steam pump, he was skeptical about the idea of reliable circular motion from steam power. In November 1781 he told the Commissioners of His Majesty's Victually Office that "no motion communicated from the reciprocating beam of a fire engine can ever act perfectly equal and steady in producing a circular motion, like the regular efflux of water in turning a mill-wheel." His waterwheels were, however, ingenious and provided a useful service to Roebuck's Carron Ironworks in Scotland.

He might have been better known as a canal builder had he enjoyed the patronage of a rich man—such as the Duke of Bridgewater. He built the Calder and Hebble Navigation, from Wakefield to Sowerby Bridge (1758–65): a river improvement in difficult country. His greatest work was, however, the Forth-Clyde canal. Despite the patronage of Lord Dundas, his comprehensive scheme (December 1764), involving an expenditure of £79,000, met with procrastination and criticism and involved him in quarrels with other engineers whose views were consulted—notably Brindley, who wanted a narrower canal. In the end Smeaton's plan was adopted, but work on the canal was suspended owing to financial difficulties and completed later by Whitworth. He also built several fine bridges, comparable with those of Telford in England, notable examples being at Perth and Coldstream. But his bridge over the Tyne at Hexham collapsed during a flood in 1782, his only certain failure.

Smeaton was the first man to style himself "civil engineer," not merely as opposed to a military engineer, but also as a member of a distinct profession. He insisted upon high standards of ethical behavior, was cautious, for instance, about accepting commissions, and took an active interest in the development of his pupils. In 1771 he formed a society, with a group of followers, to discuss engineering problems—the forerunner of the Institute of Civil Engineers.

Smeaton died at Austhorpe in 1792. He had spent much of his last years there, in the study and workshops in the tower which he had added to his father's house. Straight and plain in his manner, a Yorkshireman who spoke his mind, in some ways he seems to anticipate the virtues of the Victorians in his public spirit and strong integrity. Though an engineer rather than an inventor, it was well said of him that he could touch nothing without improving it.

L. T. C. Rolt, *Great Engineers*, 1962.

ROBERT BAKEWELL (1725–95), farmer, was a central figure in the agricultural revolution of the century. Before his day, a start had been made by pioneers such as Gresley of Drakelow, breeder of longhorn cattle, and Webster of Canley, in the selective breeding of livestock. The survival of much open-field cultivation, the insufficiency, before the introduction of four-course rotation, of the breeding stock's winter diet, besides the conservatism of farmers who had not realized the potential value of controlled breeding, combined to hold back development.

Bakewell was born at Dishley Grange, near Loughborough in the pastoral heart of Leicestershire. Although he traveled widely to study other people's methods and stock, he never moved from Dishley, nor married; but he became nationally famous as what we should call a scientific farmer. Tall, heavy, and broad, methodical in his routines, unpretentious and patient, he may have appeared to perfection the yeoman farmer; he was, however, radical in his methods. By careful study and record of the factors and figures of production, by in-breeding and careful matching of two animals of the required type, he secured astonishing advances in the quality of his breeds. Starting with some Canley heifers he improved strikingly upon the longhorn breed in weight and milk production. The subsequent improvement of this breed, from the Shakespeare of Little Rollright, the greatest bull of his day, can be traced back to Bakewell's Twopenny, since his sire was twice the grandson of Twopenny and his dam a daughter of the same. But this breed was not destined to survive and Bakewell's work with sheep was of more lasting value. From a basis of the Lincolnshire long-wool sheep he produced in his lifetime a breed of Leicestershire sheep, barrel-shaped and fine of wool. His ram-lettings became an institution; the most famous of his rams, Two-pounder, was actually let for 800 guineas for the season.

Yet Bakewell, a tenant farmer to the end, died a poor man. He was interested in improvements for their own sake as much as for the money they brought. His critics indeed said he was concerned too much with the appearance of his animals. His black stallion, named K, was famous for his splendor and was for some time on display in London. But he was in most respects a practical man and his inventiveness turned always to useful ends. In irrigation, in wintering of stock, in control of sheep-rot, his object was always the same: to obtain more value from his 440 acres of land. To improve his water supply he even diverted a brook; down it he floated turnips from field to cattleshed, where, the water draining away by a grate, they were ready-washed and dried! He was as hospitable as Chaucer's frankeleyn: "It snewed in his hous of mete and drinke." People of every class, dukes and yeomen, sat down to meals in his kitchen. Round the walls and in the hall of his farmhouse they could see the skeletons of his more celebrated beasts and there were joints of pickled flesh, too, to display the breeding points. He was ever willing to help and to provide the means of improvement, but he guarded closely the secrets of his breeding methods so that little is known of them. "Like will produce like" was as far as he could venture, though visitors could see for themselves the results as they inspected sheep, horses, and cattle, all distinctive, all marshaled for them as if the whole farm were planned for public exhibition. It is pleasant to record that he pressed strongly for more humane treatment of animals and opposed the barbarities of butchers and drovers.

Bakewell was only the most prominent of several farmers who were using their capital to improve breeds. Others were Ellmann of Glynde with Southdown sheep, Collins with shorthorns. In the same county, Thomas Paget of Ibstock, another breeder, was carrying out valuable experiments in drainage and the treatment of permanent pasture. Bakewell stands out among such men, even though his longhorns are rare and the Leicester sheep have vanished from Leicestershire. Not only the farm, but the man epitomized the richness of the land upon which a country of expanding population must depend for meat, milk, and bread. That England has always since been a reservoir for the farmers of other countries in Europe, and virgin lands overseas, to draw upon, is witness to the value of his work. In the words of an obituary, he was justly celebrated because he was "a truly useful member of society."

H. C. Pawson, *Robert Bakewell,* 1957.

RICHARD KEMPENFELT (1718–82), admiral, is more famous for the manner of his death than for what he did when he was alive. He was in his cabin aboard the *Royal George* at Spithead when, some guns being moved, timbers of unseasoned wood gave way, and the ship heeled over and sank "with twice four hundred men." He deserves, however, to be known for his original work as strategist and reformer, for he was one of the most thoughtful seamen of his time.

His outlook was shaped by the fact that he rose without influence, slowly, by professional merit. Born in London, the son of a Swedish father and an English mother, he served under Vernon at Porto Bello, but did not reach post-rank until he was nearly forty. In the Seven Years War he saw service in the West Indies and Manila. In the American War he was captain of the fleet under three successive commanders of the Channel fleet. It may be that under the first two of these, Admirals Hardy and Geary, old men, indecisive and out of touch with tactical developments, he saved the fleet from worse mischance than the somewhat inglorious but undefeated cruisings which kept the French at bay. In these years he wrote letters, mostly to Middleton at the Admiralty, from which much can be learned about his views and methods. He believed that young landsmen "may in three months, if half that time at sea, be made to know every rope in the ship, to knot and splice, hand and reef, and be perfect at the management of cannon and small arms." He constantly preached the gospel of sailing quality. "We don't seem," he wrote from the *Victory*, "to have considered sufficiently a certain fact, that the comparative force of two fleets depends much upon their sailing. The fleet that sails fastest can engage or not as they please, and so have it always in their power to choose the favorable opportunity to attack. I think I may safely hazard an opinion that twenty-five sail of the line, coppered, would be sufficient to hazard and tease this great unwieldy combined Armada." We are reminded here that the English ships were inferior to the French, in sailing performance at least, for the most part of the century.

Promoted rear-admiral, Kempenfelt continued to serve in the Channel fleet, and he was on his flagship when the sudden fatal disaster occurred. It has been suggested that the loss was due to serious neglect on the part of some official on the Navy Board, and it may be significant that all attempts to raise the ship were frustrated and that evidence given at the court-martial was suppressed. The story makes an ironic epilogue to the life of a man devoted to efficiency and to honest service.

David Mathew, *The Naval Heritage*, Chapter 6, 1944.

GEORGE RODNEY, 1st BARON RODNEY (1719–92) was one of the most enterprising admirals of his time. Although not always popular with the government or men under his command, he rendered great service by his victory of the Saints after a war in which the navy had scant success.

Born in London, of an old Somerset family, and sent to Harrow by his guardian, the Duke of Chandos, he entered the navy in 1732. He was a captain at twenty-four and a rear-admiral at forty after brave and notable service. In 1762 he commanded the expedition which captured Martinique, but the next phase of his career was prejudiced by his extravagance and by the Admiralty's suspicion that he was liable to be truculent in delicate situations and that he wanted war to provide a chance to redeem his debts. In 1774 he was forced to evacuate to Paris in order to escape his creditors. He was recalled in 1780 to command in the West Indies, with Samuel Hood, a keen young officer, as second in command. After the failures of Byron and the resignation of Keppel and Barrington, the government was anxious for some success. "For God's sake go to sea without delay," wrote Sandwich; "You cannot conceive of what importance it is to yourself, to me, and to the public." Rodney was released from his creditors by the generosity of a French nobleman—a pleasantly civilized touch—but he was kept to his cabin by the gout, another enemy, when his fleet chased the Spanish in a night action off Cape St. Vincent and took six ships. In April and May he fought three drawn engagements with the French fleet. In February 1781 he seized St. Eustatius, with stores valued at £3,000,000. Rodney and the general shared the spoils and dallied on the island, behaving in a way that caused scandal in the fleet and questions in Parliament. Hood, complaining of his chief's dilatoriness, added, "The Lares of St. Austatius were so bewitching as not to be withstood by flesh and blood."

Rodney had already fallen foul of some of his captains. He was evolving, during these campaigns, a new tactical plan based upon breaking the enemy's line. He is said to have outlined the idea with cherry stones at the dinner table of Lord George Germain. But it is typical of him that he never took the trouble to explain the plan properly to his captains. He was very polite and equable, but an intolerant commander. While his private letters are redolent of his love for his family, his dispatches are often sharply critical of the men who served under him. Nor was he popular with them. Aloof, very much a man of the world, with a keen eye for property and prize money, a politician who had fought an expensive election for Northampton and could say that "a man in our country is nothing without being in Parliament," Rodney was the opposite of Hood, professional middle-class, a puritan about prize money.

Rodney had returned to England in August 1781 to face his critics and the planters' lawyers. He went back to the West Indies full of confidence that he could "restore the empire of the Ocean to Great Britain." In the heavy rollers of the Saints passage, between Guadeloupe and Dominica, the British squadrons waited to intercept the enemy under de Grasse. Here hurricane was as great a danger as the enemy's guns. When the two fleets were passing in line on opposite courses, suddenly, by the nineteenth of the thirty French battleships, Rodney ordered his captain to put over the helm and break through the French line; two others turned, each followed by a column of ships which in turn, with their broadsides, raked the French vessels at the point of rupture. Thus the French were thrown into confusion and five ships were disabled and taken. As night fell upon the victory, Hood urged that the fleet go in chase of the enemy, but Rodney made no attempt to pursue, saying to his indignant subordinate, "Come, we have done very handsomely." Hood exaggerated when he said that they could have taken the whole French fleet. Rodney's was the responsibility of keeping his fleet in being, and the French were fast sailors. Perhaps a few more damaged vessels might have come in as prizes. Ever since there has been controversy about the battle of the Saints: whether Rodney's tactics were deliberate or just improvised; how much he owed to the initiative of Commodore Afflick who led the second squadron to break the French line. Whatever the answers, Rodney had achieved something considerable in breaking away from the grip of the Fighting Instructions. He bequeathed to the admirals who followed him a good example of tactical initiative. He returned home to a peerage and a pension of £2,000 a year. He sailed no more, but there were still battles to fight, in the law courts, in matters arising from the damage to planters' property in the West Indies. He died, in 1792, a relatively poor man.

D. Hanney, *Rodney*, 1903.
A. H. Mahon, *Types of Naval Officers*, 1901.

SIR EDWARD HUGHES (1720–94), admiral, was one of the finest seamen of the century, lacking perhaps only in the originality which was needed to break through the cramping effects of rule book and tradition. It was his misfortune that in Admiral Bailli de Suffren he was opposed by a commander who was perhaps the best produced by France since Tourville. Before the crucial campaigns upon which the fate of British India depended he had already had extensive experience. Present at the capture of Porto Bello in 1739, he won post-rank in 1748. At the operations before Louisburg and Quebec, 1758–59, he had the battleship *Somerset*. In 1773–77 he commanded in the East Indies. In 1778 he became rear-admiral and K.B. He was sent out again to the East Indies in that year with a fleet which was at first inferior to the French, and with the knowledge that a defeat would jeopardize the British position in India at a time when their hold upon North America was already giving way. In 1782 he fought against Suffren a series of five battles which show him skillful alike in defensive line tactics against his aggressive enemy in the first two battles, and in the more flexible tactics required in the last two, when Suffren attacked in an enterprising way that made the keeping of formation most difficult. The third battle might have led to a more decisive outcome, if the wind had not died away: the English for once were able to attack with the wind and Suffren, game as always, stood his ground. In the course of these five battles, with a dozen or so engaged on each side, no ships were sunk or changed hands, though they were often battered and casualties were high. Hughes lost none of the battles: only in the last were his ships more damaged than the French. By the standards of Nelson he was unsuccessful. It should be recalled, however, that there had been, by Nelson's day, great improvements in guns and signals, and the French navy had been weakened by the Revolution. This doughty fighter was hampered by his scrupulous attention to the prevailing doctrine of "keeping the line," but his skill and courage did much to preserve the young British Empire at a time of crisis. He was admiral of the Blue in 1793, but did not live to see the great victories of annihilation which were to justify bolder tactics that he had felt able to use.

P. Mackesy, *The War for America, 1775–1783*, 1964.

SIR SAMUEL HOOD, 1st VISCOUNT HOOD (1724–1816), like his brother Alexander, became an admiral and peer. One evening in the autumn of 1730, when England was at war with Spain, a post chaise bound for London broke down in the village of Butleigh in Somerset. So Captain Thomas Smith, whose ship had been paid off after her return from the Mediterranean, was entertained by the rector of the parish, Mr. Hood. When he went to sea again in the following year, he took the rector's sons with him.

Samuel Hood became post-captain in 1756. His patron was related to the Lyttelton family and he was an intimate not only of the Lytteltons and Grenvilles but also of William Pitt, who subsequently entrusted his youngest son, James, to his care. But he owed his advancement also to a keen professionalism, an objective view which made him sometimes sharply impatient with his more politically minded fellow-officers, and an eager desire to serve. Kempenfelt was perhaps his nearest equivalent among contemporaries. In 1778 he was Commissioner of Portsmouth dockyard. In 1780, at the most critical time of the American War, when the navy was stretched too far for its strength and political feuds divided its senior officers, Hood was promoted out of turn to flag rank and appointed to serve as second in command to Rodney in the West Indies. In 1781 and 1782 he fought a number of actions against the French. The most famous of these was the battle of the Saints, in April 1782, when Rodney defeated de Grasse in a way which anticipated the tactics of Nelson. But Hood was severely critical of the easy going approach of his superior, in particular of his failing to follow up the victory: "Sooner than undergo a continuance of what I have so very painfully done for several weeks past, I would be content to be placed on a Welsh mountain to gather buttons as they drop from a goat's tail." He had grounds for confidence in his own abilities, having prepared for this victory by a brilliant series of engagements, while Rodney had been on leave in England. Indecisive in that Hood was unable to effect his main purpose, the relief of St. Lucia, they showed the French that they were confronted by a keen tactical brain and taught the captains of the fleet the advantage of working together in a team. One of these, Lord Robert Manners, described the crucial point of the first day of a battle off the Basseterre as "the most masterly maneuver I ever saw."

On his return, now Baron Hood in the Irish peerage, he was elected to Parliament as member for Westminster, standing against Fox, of all people, in a contest that was to become celebrated for the activities of the Whig ladies. In 1788 he was made a Lord of the Admiralty. He returned to active service upon the outbreak of the Revolutionary War. Originally his force was intended to support the attack launched from the east by Austria and Prussia. The contribution of the English was to be the seizure of Toulon, with its fleet and royalist inhabitants. But the failure of the first coalition's land campaign and the astonishing resurgence of the French republic spoiled the plan. Toulon was evacuated in December 1793. Thereafter, as the French marched into the Netherlands and Italy, Spain and Holland made their peace with France, the fleet was deprived of its Mediterranean ports, and Hood's operations were discouraging. The capture of Bastia and Calvi brought small satisfaction to the aging admiral. Under him, however, served Nelson, ardent to win glory. Nelson found in Hood a man whom he could admire unreservedly and with the warm feeling that characterized all his relationships. "Lord Hood," he wrote, comparing him favorably with Lord Howe, "is equally great in all situations in which an admiral can be placed," and later, when Hood returned to England in the *Victory* and struck his flag: "Oh, miserable Board of Admiralty. They have forced the first officer in our service away from his command." Lord Hood was ever a king's man who put country before party. He spoke up for Hastings when it was unfashionable to do so, in 1787, urging the House not to weaken the hand of servants of the state who had to act in an emergency.

THE HONORABLE JOHN BYRON (1723–86), admiral, was the precursor of Cook in circumnavigating the world, though with less spectacular results, and he was commander of the English fleet in the West Indies at what could have been a serious disaster. He was notorious throughout the navy for the bad luck which attended him. He set out with Anson but he was wrecked on the Chilean coast in 1741. His experience on this voyage qualified him, however, for command of the expedition sent out by the Admiralty the year after the end of the Seven Years War. He was by then a commodore. He took possession of the Falkland Islands early in 1765, discovering and naming the fine harbor of Port Egmont. Having an appalling experience with the Cape Horn route in 1741 he went through the Straits of Magellan (where he saw his rival Bougainville). His Pacific route was not original and he failed to explore the southern ocean where it was believed that Terra Australis might lie. But his voyage stimulated interest in the area and encouraged the Admiralty to plan the voyages of Wallis, Carteret, and Cook, and drew attention to the Falkland Islands, soon to become the center of an international crisis when the French encouraged the Spanish to seize the islands. That he failed to do more may be ascribed to the tempestuous climate of the south temperate zone and the ill condition of ships and men by the time he reached it.

In 1778 Byron was in command of the West Indies fleet. For the first time in the century, England's command of the sea was seriously threatened: a victory was badly needed; defeat might well prove to be disastrous. Byron sighted the French fleet under d'Estaing on July 6 as the French were leaving the anchorage of Georgetown. It was not plain, because of their pell-mell order, that they were in fact more numerous than his twenty-one ships. With alacrity he ordered the General Chase, but his own fleet was strung out and his ships found themselves in some cases overmatched in combat with the French line. Four ships were reduced to wrecks and might have been sunk if d'Estaing had been more experienced. The battle was indecisive. But it provided a sharp lesson, that boldness only succeeded when allied to good judgment.

R. F. Gallagher, ed., *Byron: Journal of His Circumnavigation, 1764–66*, 1964.

AUGUSTUS, VISCOUNT KEPPEL (1725–86), admiral, was the son of the 2nd Earl Albemarle. He served as a midshipman on Anson's voyage round the world from 1740 to 1744. After this incomparable schooling he rose steadily. He served under Hawke in 1757, captured Goree with a small expeditionary force in 1758 in one of the raids, perfectly planned and executed, that led to the capture of all the French factories on the West African coast. He was at Quiberon Bay in 1759 and at the capture of Belle Isle in 1761. To cap all this vigorous service he led the expedition which took Manila in 1762.

If Keppel's subsequent career was a disappointing anticlimax, this is more because of his political entanglements than any falling off in his professional skill. He was closely associated with the Whig group which opposed the American War, and was critical of the conduct of Lord Sandwich at the Admiralty, so it was thought surprising that he was appointed commander of the Channel fleet in 1778. Some Whigs, in a spirit more partisan than patriotic, thought that he was to be made a scapegoat, but in fact he was the ablest available man of his seniority. Under him, third in command, was Admiral Palliser who, nonetheless, kept his seat on the Navy Board. On July 27, 1778, the British fleet encountered the slightly superior French fleet under d'Orvilliers and fought a desultory action in which no ships were won or lost. The French had the weather-gage and could break off the action when they wanted. But the English fleet's fire was the more ineffective because of Palliser's failure to obey Keppel's signal to close. Palliser claimed that the foremast of his division's flagship was severely damaged. Enraged by news sheets which alleged that he was responsible for the failure to bring the French to action, he used his position on the Admiralty Board to secure a court-martial on Keppel.

Charged by Palliser himself with not marshaling his fleet, careless approach to the battle, scandalous haste in withdrawing from the action, Keppel became the central figure in a drama of personalities, with strong political overtones. It became the talk of fashionable drawing rooms and naval wardrooms alike—that at the height of a war in which England was fighting not only for her colonies but for her life, a Franco-Spanish fleet cruised about the Channel. Thus the nation paid for the political affiliations and interests of her leading seamen. Did not Rodney say that a man was "nothing without being in Parliament"? Palliser's charges were rejected as malicious and ill-founded. The verdict was regarded as a snub to Sandwich. Palliser was then court-martialed and acquitted—with the rider that he should have informed the commander-in-chief of the damage to his ship. He was given the governorship of Greenwich Hospital, but inn signs everywhere swung in honor of "Keppel's Head." He resigned, however, and was supported by his friends, Lord Bristol and Barrington, who refused to accept appointments from Lord Sandwich. Admirers such as Jervis and Duncan took his part and perpetuated the feud in the navy.

The genial and courteous Keppel may have been misled; somehow, too, he aroused violent animosity in Palliser, a blunt Yorkshireman, without influence. But he seems, too, to have been badly treated. Recompense came when he was made First Lord of the Admiralty in Rockingham's government of 1782 and luck with it, since the first news received was that of Rodney's victory of the Saints. His subsequent recall of Rodney was ungenerous; once again we see how politics affected the navy. In the circumstances it is remarkable that England emerged from this war with any credit. In December 1783 Keppel was replaced by Howe in Pitt's government; relatively free of political connections, he commanded general confidence and proved a more successful First Lord than Keppel could have been.

A. T. Mahon, *Major Operations of the Navies in the American War of Independence*, 1913.

ALEXANDER COZENS (?–1786) and **JOHN ROBERT COZENS** (1752–99) were painters, father and son. Alexander was born in Russia, and was for long thought to have been a natural son of Peter the Great. He studied in Italy; came to England in the 1740s; was thereafter drawing master at Eton (when the future George III was a pupil) and instructor to the fashionable set at Bath; and published a curious work on the use of chance markings on paper (e.g., ink-blots) as an aid to artistic invention. He painted chiefly in monochrome: his sepia drawings, reminiscent of the Chinese, sought out the bare structure of nature and asserted her sublimity in a way which was novel and daring at the time.

His son, John Robert, traveled a good deal abroad and once in the company of the younger William Beckford (to whom also Mozart was appointed tutor in music). John Cozens was one of the first English artists to come to terms with mountains, which were still to many of his contemporaries objects of horror and duress. His work deals mostly with the scenery of the Alps and Italy, being tinted in watercolor over an inked outline with few adventures in color beyond the barest requirements of light and shade, but clothed overall with such sensitivity, so impressioned, as to proclaim him the first of the romantic watercolorists. In point of time, Sandby was the founder of the English school of watercolor. In point of influence, John Cozens was the exemplar of those who sought to express the grandeur of nature; and especially of Turner, who copied Cozens's work at Dr. Monro's house. Constable, in a moment of enthusiasm, called Cozens "the greatest genius that ever touched landscape." The same Dr. Monro, with Sir George Beaumont, the patron and connoisseur, cared for Cozens during the imbecile close to his short life.

PAUL SANDBY (1725–1809), watercolor artist, is called "the father of English watercolor"—which needs explaining. Watercolor painting, whether done opaquely after the manner of tempera or transparently over a light ground, had been known for several centuries. The medieval missalists had used it; the portrait miniaturists of the seventeenth century had used it; and the Dutch, as usual, had perfected it. But the fashion for tinted topographical drawings (intended to be multiplied by engravings) grew apace among the estate-proud English squirearchy of the eighteenth century; and Sandby was the first to add to these the ingredient of *art*, to make (in other words) pictures out of pictorial records. Thus he was the founder of the English school of watercolorists, for there succeeded him all those artists who have made of English watercolor a unique contribution to the sum of pictorial art.

He drew employment chiefly from the army: first in the department of military drawing at the Tower of London; then as draftsman to the Survey of the Highlands which was carried through after '45; and later as chief drawing-master to the R.M.A., Woolwich. He was a public figure, being Director of the Society of Arts, a founder-member of the Royal Academy (1768), and an exhibitor at the Foundling Hospital. He demeaned himself by burlesquing Hogarth, but bought paintings secretly from Wilson to save him from starving. A collection of his work may be seen at Windsor Castle.

SIR JOSHUA REYNOLDS (1723–92), portrait painter, though not the greatest English painter, did more than any other to make English painting great. He gave it stature. Before him, we speak of English painters; but after him, of English painting, an indigenous gamut of art fit to be compared with the great European schools. For nearly forty years he worked in London at the hub of society, a bachelor, stable and industrious, highly influential, widely respected. In his old age he was described by Boswell as "he who used to be looked upon as perhaps the most happy man in the world."

He was born in Devonshire, the son of a clergyman who was also headmaster of the local school. His father rewarded the boy's talent by sending him to London as apprentice to Thomas Hudson, then a luminary in the world of painting. After four years, Reynolds returned to the West, and it was not until he was twenty-five that he had the good fortune to be taken to Italy by Captain Keppel (whom he later painted with distinction). He spent three years in the study of the Italian masters and must have used his time well, for on his return to London he made an immediate success. In 1755 he had 120 sitters for portraits; by 1764 he was earning £6,000 a year by his brush. From 1760 he kept a large house, including studios and a gallery, in Leicester Square, where he entertained liberally and played host to a galaxy of acquaintances. His friendships with the great Whigs deprived him of the favor of the court; but when the Royal Academy was instituted in 1768 and Reynolds's stature was such that he was seen as the only possible president, the king was obliged to acquiesce in the election, and indeed knighted Reynolds in the following year. Thereafter he was zealous in the work of regulating the academy and organizing its schools, and was a constant contributor to its exhibitions. To the academy he delivered his *Discourses*, which were probably polished by Burke and Johnson so that they can still be read with pleasure as well as profit, and which yet bear wonderfully little relation to Reynolds's own practice.

The number of his portraits declined a little with his absorption in the academy, and with the reasonable preference of would-be sitters to entrust their immortality to artists technically more "safe." But he remained the doyen of English painters until in 1790 his eyesight failed and he was compelled to cease working. After a melancholy period he died in 1792 and was borne to St. Paul's by a party which included three dukes and two marquesses.

His spectacles and ear-trumpet (deafness began with a cold caught while he was copying the Raphaels in the Vatican) make him conspicuous in the group portraits of the day. Some critics have found it difficult to believe that his character was as delightful as it seems to have been. Thus, because he was a rich man, he is said to have been avaricious; because he preferred good society, he is said to have been a snob. The truth is that he liked to live in style; that he was generous, though not to a fault; and that he frequented high places because he was welcome there. The man who was at the same time intimate with the Whig Lords and with Wilkes, with Mrs. Siddons and Horace Walpole, had reason to be proud of his social versatility. He was no mere lion-hunter: he cared for Goldsmith when Goldsmith was a nobody; and Johnson, who knew nothing of pictorial art, must have loved the man and not the artist ("There goes a man not be spoiled by prosperity," he said of Reynolds). It is clear, however, that he was somewhat jealous of his position; and the coolness toward Gainsborough (dramatically dissolved on Gainsborough's deathbed) was largely the result of the latter's antagonism to Reynolds's beloved academy.

In the reports of the immortal conversations of the Literary Club (later simply the Club), which he joined in founding in order, he said, to give Johnson unlimited opportunities for talking, and of which Burke, Goldsmith, Garrick, and Boswell were also members, Reynolds appears now as pacemaker, now as peacemaker, and always his presence was grateful. In Boswell's *Life* his name appears less frequently than Johnson's alone.

As artist, he was portrait painter first and foremost. His excursions into religious painting, into allegory, landscape, and history painting, are not to be considered beside his portraiture, but he painted portraits, not as portraits alone, but in terms of those other branches of painting. Thus his great portraits are highly allusive, and if we miss the spiritual in them—well, it was an unspiritual age. He excelled in painting men of authority and action ("Lord Rodney," "Lord Heathfield") and young children ("The Strawberry Girl," "Miss Bowles," "Lady Betty Hamilton"). In composition, as in all his art, he was often faultless, but often a borrower. So individually, however, did he treat his borrowings from earlier masters as to suggest that he seriously undervalued his own power of originality. "Damn him, how various he is!" said Gainsborough. The modest ambition of his youth was to be the successor of Kneller; but his true exemplar was Titian. Unfortunately he carried his devotion to the Venetians into the realm of chemistry, and in searching for the "Venetian secret," which to him was a kind of philosopher's stone, he made such rash experiments with his materials, using vehicles and pigments not only improper and unstable in themselves but mutually antagonistic, that much of his best work was the early victim of time. He himself jokingly admitted that he came off with "flying colors." But what colors! Ruskin called him one of the seven supreme colorists. And yet there was no one living to teach him such colors. Had he not experimented, he might have remained too truly the successor of Kneller and robbed our eyes forever of the brilliant flesh colors, and the triumphant golds and reds, which illuminate the work of his maturity.

F. W. Hilles, *The Literary Career of Sir Joshua Reynolds*, 1936.
N. Penny, ed., *Reynolds*, 1986.

GEORGE STUBBS (1724–1806), painter, was as considerable a figure in his own field of animal painting as Gainsborough or Reynolds in theirs. He was born in Liverpool in 1724, the son of a currier; painted portraits in his youth; studied and lectured on anatomy at York; and at the age of thirty traveled to Rome "to convince himself" (he said) "that nature was and is always superior to art, whether Greek or Roman." Such a viewpoint was scarcely intelligible to the partisans of the neo-classical, who were the patrons of England, and Stubbs's originality might have brought him no fortune had he not exerted it in a field of art comparatively untilled but very fertile. For this was the age of the apotheosis of the horse; and Stubbs was high priest.

Not that he courted popularity; he was too solitary and strong. But it happened that he was a scientist, and he loved horses; so he painted horses which are not only real horses—more real in particulars than any painted before or since—but are endowed with a character almost heroic.

> The horses show him nobler powers:—
> O patient eyes, courageous hearts!

By carefully declining, however, to ascribe to his horses *rational* powers, Stubbs both emphasized the dignity of their animal nature and avoided that sentimentality which has been the bane of so many animal-painters. The life-size portrait of "The Hambletonian Rubbing Down" (*c.* 1790) is that of the essential thoroughbred, equine from teeth to tail; there are no spurious attributes, no suggestion that the creature is more than the best of its kind. Nor did Stubbs excel at painting horses only: his scientific bent led him to share in that contemporary curiosity about rare animals which has raised a rash of menageries over Europe. Thus he painted for Lord Pigot a cheetah sent by his lordship to George III; for John Hunter (who kept a private menagerie at Earl's Court and formed the Hunterian Collection of anatomical specimens) a yak, an orang-utan, and an Indian rhinoceros; and for his brother William Hunter's collection at Glasgow University a nilgai and a moose. Stubbs seemed equipped to distinguish every prodigy of the animal kingdom.

Much of his anatomical experience he owed to having in his youth, in a lonely farmhouse in Lincolnshire, labored to compile over eighteen months the wonderful work of science and art called *The Anatomy of the Horse*. Stubbs's models were the very carcasses of horses, which he suspended, flayed, and dissected, injecting tallow into the veins, ignoring the offense of the decaying meat in his ardour to record what he saw. Then, as if that had not been enough, he engraved his own drawings because no one would do it for him. The book, deservedly, won European praise; and Stubbs was henceforth the prey of every gentleman with a thoroughbred to immortalize.

The patient discipline which had furnished *The Anatomy* revealed itself also, not only in the botanical accuracy of Stubbs's trees and plants, but in his faultless composition and use of perspective. "Phaeton and Pair," for example, is an essay in balance; and the splendid series of "Brood Mares and Foals," set both in landscapes and against plain backgrounds, have (for all Stubbs's disregard for the classical) the rhythm of a frieze. There are those who hold it against Stubbs that he does not give us enough of wind and weather (as Munnings has done) for his superb creatures to move in; but it is this very understatement which marks Stubbs's pictures with one of the signs of great art, the sign of mystery.

Stubbs was over six feet tall, of great physical strength; yet he who could manhandle a horse's carcass could also conduct minute dissections, make the finest anatomical drawings, and paint with an exquisite sense of texture the scales of a rhinoceros, the pelt of a foxhound, the whiskers of a tigress. And when he turns to give a picture of *human* life in the country, as in "Reaping," he can make even Gainsborough's pastorals smell a little of the studio. The high gloss of his paintings may be due to his having at one time made some enamel paintings on stoneware plaques for Josiah Wedgwood. He died in 1806, aged eighty-two.

Basil Taylor, *Stubbs*, 1960.

THOMAS GAINSBOROUGH (1727–88), portrait and landscape artist, was born at Sudbury, Suffolk, but his artistic promise took him while still a boy to study in London, where, despite the efforts of Hogarth and others, the prevailing attitude was still "Shakespeare in poetry, and Kneller in painting, damme!" Hubert Gravelot, the French engraver, taught him the ways of art; Francis Hayman taught him also, it seems, the ways of the world; and in 1746 Gainsborough returned to Suffolk as something of a celebrity. His marriage to Margaret Burr, the natural daughter of the Duke of Beaufort, brought him some financial independence by way of her annuity. During thirteen years, he painted fresh, charming landscapes, and set the provincial gentry in them (e.g., "Mr. and Mrs. Andrews"), until finally, one of his patrons giving him introductions to the fashionable world of Bath, he set up there as portrait painter at the end of 1759.

From then his success was immediate. He was widely employed. His work was shown in London and approved. He was a founder-member of the Royal Academy, and, although he took no part or interest in its management, he exhibited there periodically until 1784, when a dispute about the hanging of his work estranged him finally. From 1774 he worked in London, living first in Pall Mall, and later at Richmond. He became the favorite artist of the court, for which he painted the series of royal children now at Windsor. He died, probably of cancer, in 1788.

Gainsborough was a complicated man: on the one hand nervous, impulsive, sensitive, and moody, a man whose daughters both died insane; on the other he was handsome, humorous, and sociable, an ingenuous being who detested pretension and snobbery the more he had to serve them, who loved the simple life, to ride the countryside on an old gray horse, drink wine, with his friends and play any musical instrument he could come by. In one of his delightful letters, he writes: "I'm sick of Portraits and wish very much to take my viol-da-gamba and walk off to some sweet village where I can paint landskips in quietness and ease. . . ." Self-indulgent? Yes. Reynolds, who was Gainsborough's contemporary but opposite, could never have written that; and certainly Gainsborough never attempted to shoulder the public responsibilities which Reynolds thought were inseparable from his own position as an artist—the academy schools, the provision for young talent, and so forth. Nor does it appear that discipline played much part in

Gainsborough's work. When his fundamental love of painting was aroused (which generally happened halfway through a portrait), he painted well and could forget his earlier truculence at having to paint fashionable persons in order to provide a carriage for his wife. But the awkward and repetitive postures so often taken up by his subject-figures reveal an artist who was averse from the preliminary discipline of thinking a picture through to the end, an artist deficient (even) in the power of invention.

"Landskips," however, seem always to have been a labor of love with him: here his composition is so sure as to err toward a studio artificiality; and the mannered and accelerated foliage of his later landscapes was the product not of laziness, but of a search for a more rhythmic mode of expression than he had used in his youth, when (as in "Wood Scene, Cornard") he painted every oak leaf as an item. Indeed this progress from the static to the rhythmic, from the merely poetic to the lyrical, can be traced through most of his work and may be closely associated with his musical interests.

Artists of the day were accustomed (for better or for worse) to make a pilgrimage to the Continent at the start of their careers. But Gainsborough seems never to have gone abroad. He never labored at copying the Raphaels in the Stanze or noted the sun sinking below the Campagna (what might he not have wrought, if he had?). For his experience of the masters he had to rely on what he could see at home, and that, in the days before the National Gallery, was not a great deal. Van Dyck, however, powerfully influenced him, lending to him that silvery lightness which Gainsborough used so distinctively; and it was just in Gainsborough to acknowledge the debt on his deathbed when, being finally reconciled to Reynolds, he whispered to him, "We are all going to Heaven, and Van Dyck is of the party."

But, for the larger part, Gainsborough's style was his own. What Reynolds called "all those odd scratches and marks" are a method of hatching developed by Gainsborough to record spontaneously the most gentle changes of texture and (in his figures) the subtlest modulation of character. He painted thinner than Reynolds, and used safer techniques; and while there are those who prefer to think that English men and women have more beef and blood than Gainsborough gives them, there is no doubt that his method was particularly suited to fixing on canvas what there was of spirituality, let alone refinement, in his sitters. The division in his own heart

helped him to interpret the division in theirs, between the impedi-
ment and the aspiration. Thus his "Mrs. Graham" and "Mrs. Siddons," his "Benjamin Truman" and "Karl Abel," and his ventures
into the *demi-monde* like "Mrs. Elliott," are practically spiritual histo-
ries; and his portraits of youth—"Miss Juliet Mott," "The Blue Boy,"
"The Artist's Daughters"—express to perfection the joy of the
young which is not far from tears.

Basil Taylor, *Gainsborough*, 1953.

RICHARD WILSON (1714–82), landscape painter, was born on
the Welsh border where his father held a living. In those days
provincial artists of talent were practically obliged to go to London
to complete their training and find a market; Wilson was no excep-
tion. For years he painted portraits of no particular excellence,
and latterly was even engaged to paint the future George III and
his brother, the Duke of York. Then, at the age of thirty-six, he traveled to Italy, where the artist Zuccarelli persuaded him to turn
once and for all to landscape painting. Six years Wilson spent in
Rome, and when he finally returned to England his head was full
to bursting with the physical features—the noble ruins lit by the
level southern light and the grander illumination of antiquity, the
orderly sequence of plain, lake, grove and hill—which belonged to
the Campagna; full too with the work of those European artists
(particularly Claude and Poussin) who had made the scenery of
the Campagna their meal and drink. Those features Wilson proceeded to impress on the face of English landscape, so that even a
"View on the Wye" breathes the air of the Appennines. But he
painted some lovely pictures, the best of which ("Penn Ponds" and
"The Thames at Twickenham," for example) contain none of the
Italian furniture and are pure England. Yet from the time of his return, few bought his pictures. Although he was a founder-member
of the Royal Academy (1768) and exhibited there until 1780, only
his appointment as librarian to the academy saved him from the
extremes of poverty. A small property at Llanberis fell to him by
succession in time to allow him to die (1782) in his native country.

Wilson's landscapes were painted in the mold of Claude
Poussin and Salvator Rosa at a time when those masters' works
were the prey of the English lords and the quarry of their landscape gardeners. But it was also the time when an English "con-

noisseur" could say in public, "You surely would not have me hang a modern English picture in my house, unless it were a portrait?" Wilson was not a foreigner, and that was a portion of his ill-success. He was also a gruff and unaccommodating man, ill-disposed to flattery, who could describe Gainsborough's foliage as "fried parsley." Most important, he was not the pure classicist which the patrons would have had him. In his love for the paintings of Cuyp and van Ruisdael and the other seventeenth-century Dutch landscape masters still then unappreciated in England, in his neglect of detailed representation in favor of a unified effect, in his imparting to nature in some of his landscapes—especially the Welsh ones, "Cader Idris" and "Snowdon from Llyn Ogwen"—qualities of solitude and grandeur and the true antiquity of geological time, he shows that he was mature enough to have intimations of the Romantic. Thus he was a prophet, and like most prophets, unpopular in his day and a little overvalued by posterity. To call him, for example, "the father of English landscape" would be just, if George Lambert had not preceded him.

LANCELOT BROWN (1716–83), whose landscape gardening transformed the appearance of many fine estates, was born in a Northumbrian cottage, the child of humble parents, carefully taught by the parish clerk, and then at the little grammar school at Cambo; he was afterwards employed as a gardener on the estate of Sir William Loraine. Observant, shrewd, and ambitious, he grasped the possibilities of estate improvement, which was becoming fashionable even in the remote northeast. In 1739 he put his fortune in his knapsack, came south, and took service at Wotton, near Vanbrugh's new palace at Blenheim; thence he went to Stowe, where Lord Cobham had removed a village to improve the view. Here he rose swiftly to be head gardener, working in grounds which Kent's taste and Cobham's money made into a school of landscape gardening. He was soon being asked to advise upon, even to execute, the plans of neighboring grandees. In 1751 he set up as an independent landscapist; henceforward he was in continuous demand, for his sure grasp of the taste of the age, together with his extraordinarily brisk and competent method and manner, made an immense appeal. Low taxation, cheap labor, and landowners whose love of the countryside was often tinged with the classical painter's ideal of a landscape that was calm, ordered, and serene; a society which looked tolerantly on the whims of the rich, and rich men who had no qualms about pulling down old manor houses or grubbing up formal gardens—all combined to favor the landscape gardener.

Brown was himself no mean architect, as buildings like Croome, for Lord Coventry, and Belhus, for Lord Dacre, indicated; alterations to the house were sometimes a part of his overall design for the estate. Most of his work was, however, concerned with the fields, trees, and water which composed the view from the house: his vocation was to create agreeable scenes, to provide arcadian views to fill tall Georgian windows. To contemporaries his touch meant often a shaven sward, thin saplings, neat enclosures within railings, and new waterworks. Supremely fortunate the subsequent generations who have looked at the mature plantations and rushy lakes: artificiality became natural with age! Neither ideas nor personality escaped criticism. There were complaints about the desolating effects of his clearances, his ruthlessness: he thought nothing of clearing woods or damming streams, though he would usually leave good trees standing. "So many artificial mole-hills," said Horace Walpole about Lord Anson's Moor Park, where Brown sheered away a hillside to provide tree-capped undulations. Later he was to be attacked by the critics of the picturesque school for a lack of visual excitement and his preference for plain and open views. With more personal and cantankerous comments he was assailed by Sir William Chambers; but Humphrey Repton who, as an expert landscapist himself, had better reason to feel professional jealousy, acknowledged him as master.

Brown's analysis of "the capabilities" of the grounds was forthright and remarkably prosaic: in a role which suggests amateur enthusiasms he was stolidly professional. His confidence occasionally verged on the brutal: "My lord, there is nothing to be done here, unless you will plant one half of your estate and lay the other half under water," he is supposed to have informed one unfortunate gentleman. Another tried to seduce him to Ireland with a commission of a thousand pounds but Brown told him that he must wait till he had "finished England." "Thames, you will never forgive me," he is supposed to have said, after he had finished damming the river Glyme at Blenheim. The remark is not characteristic, for Brown was essentially a modest man. That he worked on the grand scale affected him no more than the fact that most of his patrons were aristocrats, many were pleased to make his acquaintance, some became fast friends. Chatham recommended him to Lady Stanhope as a man "of sentiments much above his birth." "Please to consider," he wrote, "he shares the private hours of the king, dines familiarly with his neighbour of Sion (the Duke of Northumberland), and sits down at the tables of all the House of Lords." He lived, however, when he was not traveling, in a modest manor house at Fenstanton. He was happily married, had several sons who made their mark, one an M.P., another a captain in the navy; a daughter, Bridget, married Henry Holland, the builder, with whom Brown worked in harmonious partnership. Despite tiresome asthma he was incessantly busy. Even a small selection of his commissions gives an idea of the scale of his achievement and the mark he left on the countryside. Burghley, Bowood, Castle Ashby, Ashridge, Harewood, Wardour, Longleat, Compton Verney, Claremont, Knowsley, Oakley, Wilton, Alnwick, Sion, not least his native Wallington: the very names evoke that elegant harmony of stately house and mellow park which is still one of the distinctive glories of England.

A typical Brown landscape resolves itself into several recognizable elements. The park is bounded by an encircling fringe of woodland, barring off the workaday fields but broken here and there to reveal striking objects or distant views. The inner line of the belt is irregular, following the contours and softened by outlying clumps or individual trees; elms and oak, chestnut, beech, and fir were most employed. If possible the middle distance was enlivened by water. The serpentine curve replaced the straight line of earlier plantings or the haphazard forms of nature. He aimed to create the same placid, uncluttered scenes, the serenity and delicacy that the poets and painters of the time pursued as the ideal of beauty. Within the limits of his somewhat dogmatic temperament and the aesthetic conventions of the time he was, however, both original and resourceful. At Blenheim he matched the grandeur of the palace by his waterworks, at Chatsworth he widened the Derwent; at Fisherwick he planted a hundred thousand trees; at Burton Pynsent he built for Pitt a memorial obelisk. He was ready to prepare designs for anything: a menagerie at Castle Ashby, a temple of Diana at Weston. He loved to work with enthusiastic patrons like the arboriculturist Lord Weymouth at Longleat. He never exploited his unique position to make excessive sums out of his com-

missions; indeed, if the expenses turned out to be less than his estimate he would scrupulously subtract the difference. He had one
official position, that of Royal Gardener, to which he was appointed
in 1765. He had only one big chance to carry out a corporate project of landscaping, but countless strollers in the Backs at Cambridge have appreciated the results. His memorials are to be found
in nearly every English county. Sometimes, as at Tong or Tixall, the
house has vanished; sometimes the axe and plough have altered
the scene beyond recognition. But enough has survived to impress
us with a sense of the debt that we owe to Capability Brown.

Dorothy Stroud, *Capability Brown*, 1947.
R. Turner, *Capability Brown and the Eighteenth Century Landscape*,
1985.

JAMES GIBBS (1682–1754), architect, was the last of the great English baroque artists, the last of that school which Vanbrugh and
Hawkesmoor had distinguished; but, in that he was influenced (in
middle age) by the succeeding movement, called English Palladianism, he can easily be seen as the bridge between Wren (*d.* 1723)
and the Burlington school (see WILLIAM KENT).

He was born in Aberdeenshire of a good family, and, on reaching majority, traveled to Rome, apparently to study for the Catholic
priesthood at the Scots College; but the material fabric of Rome al-
lured him more powerfully than the spiritual, and he turned to
study architecture under the famous Carlo Fontana. To work on
baroque building at its source, in the shade of Bernini, under the
direction of one of Bernini's most conspicuous successors, was a
training no other English architect of the time had enjoyed: it
made Gibbs something unique, a professional among amateurs.

He returned to England in 1709. Being a Catholic, a Scot, and
a gentleman, he had found his patrons among the Tory nobility;
and one of these, Edward Harley, son of the statesman, used his influence to have Gibbs appointed (1713) one of the "surveyors" to
the Commission for Building Fifty New Churches in London. This
ambitious concern was one of the crops of the harvest for which
the Great Fire had prepared the ground; and, although the fruit of
the commission was only twelve churches, these included Gibbs's
St. Mary-le-Strand, a lovely blend of the baroque of Wren with the
baroque of Italy. The baroque strain, however, was no longer popu-

lar: the atmosphere of the time was prevailingly Whig; and that meant, for architecture, a movement toward classical purity. Colen Campbell, the Whig architect and rival of Gibbs, was also the first of the English Palladians, the school which promoted this new movement; alluding implicitly to St. Mary, he censured the super-imposing of one order of columns on another, and other "absurd Novelties." In the Jacobite Rising of 1715, the Earl of Mar, an early patron of Gibbs, was defeated at Sheriffmuir by Campbell's patron, the Earl of Argyll; and for Gibbs the military defeat must have sym-bolized the rout of one trend in taste by another. When in the same year he was dismissed from his surveyorship by the new Whig government, it became clear to him that he must come to terms with the times. From then onward he reserved his baroque exuber-ance for the interiors of his buildings (where he was amply served by the genius in plasterwork of the Italians Artari and Bagutti), while his exteriors are increasingly restrained by the influence of Palladianism (though he was never a convert). Indeed, his country houses (Ditchley, for example) are, from the outside, sober almost to a fault.

In 1720 he persuaded a Whig committee to accept his designs for the rebuilding of St. Martin-in-the-Fields. The little St. Peter, Vere Street, was put up in the nature of an experiment for the larger project. St. Martin itself, one of the best-known churches in the world, is a brilliant compromise between the manner of Wren and that of the Palladians. Purists have always found fault with the notion of a Wren steeple (the steeple being essentially of Gothic extraction, as Gibbs admitted) rising above a classical pediment; the same combination had been used in St. Mary-le-Strand; but the success of the "barbarity" cannot be denied, and the idea of St. Mary has been repeated in a hundred distant colonies.

Otherwise the best work of Gibbs is to be seen at Cambridge, in the Senate House and the Fellows' Building of King's College; and at Oxford, in the Radcliffe Camera. The circular plan of the Camera was borrowed from Hawksmoor, who in turn had bor-rowed it from Wren; and this succession is symptomatic of Gibbs's achievement, the achievement of an artist who was not strikingly original, but was gifted, far above the average, to choose and amal-gamate the best of what he knew.

According to the custom of the day, the monuments in West-minster Abbey to Ben Jonson, Matthew Prior, and Dryden were designed by Gibbs to be worked in stone by Rysbrack. But of greater moment were Gibbs's published works, the first of which, *A Book of Architecture* (1728), was tremendously popular, was read in America, and was perhaps the most thumbed architectural textbook of the century.

SIR WILLIAM CHAMBERS (1726–96), architect, with Robert Adam, dominated the architecture of Britain in the second half of the eighteenth century. The affinity with Adam goes further: they were practically coevals; they both came of well-to-do families, and spent long years in travel and study before entering on careers in which success seemed to hold out her hand to them; they were both ambitious to a degree, and so self-confident that they could hardly choose but be rivals. Chambers was principally a public architect, who stood at the apex of the English classical tradition; Adam was a private architect, powerful but unorthodox in his originality.

Chambers's Scottish father was a merchant in Sweden, where William was born; the family came to Yorkshire when he was two, and he was brought up to join his father's business. Traveling, however, in pursuit of that aim to China, as supercargo on a Swedish ship at the age of seventeen, he fell under the fascination of Oriental architecture, began to make drawings, and was converted to the idea of an architectural career. But he did not take the plunge until 1749, when he went to study architecture, first in Paris and then in Italy. In Paris he met the great Soufflot, one of the fathers of the classical revival in France; and both in Paris and in Italy he was friendly with two other French classical architects: Le Roy, whose survey of the antiquities of Greece was to forestall Stuart and Revett's by a year or two; and Clérisseau, with whom both Robert and James Adam were later to be closely associated. Robert Adam was told in Rome in 1755 that Chambers "owed all his hints and notions" to Clérisseau. Certainly Chambers early became a confirmed classicist—always in the Roman strain, never in the Greek. But Adam was also told that Chambers had been considered, by Englishmen in Rome at the time, as "a prodigy for genius, for sense, and for good taste."

This aura of regard accompanied Chambers home in 1755. He soon encountered royal favor. Lord Bute introduced him to the Prince of Wales, to whom he became tutor in architecture; and on

the prince's accession, he and Adam were appointed "Joint Architects of His Majesty's Works." But meanwhile Chambers had been
taken up by the princess dowager also; and in 1757 he began work
on her estate at Kew, laying out the gardens and ornamenting
them with a Roman arch, an Orangery, and other "temples" mostly
in the classical taste, but adding, as a memento of his travels, the
well-known Pagoda. The Pagoda was not a freak in his *œuvre*, for in
1757 he published *Designs of Chinese Buildings*, and in 1772 was to
appear a remarkable *Dissertation on Oriental Gardening*, which was
pilloried by William Mason and Horace Walpole (the trouble was
that Chambers had a Scottish dearth of humor).

In 1759 appeared his major work, the *Treatise on Civil Architecture*, which is a distillation of all that the author had found best in
the decoration of classical architecture. Drawing especially on
those Italian architects who had kept alight the flame of purity in
the days of the baroque, when heretics were rife, he teaches the
purpose of the classical Orders, their use in schemes of decoration, their adornment, and how the details of a building should be
designed to harmonize with them. It is a personal statement; it
shows him to be a conservative in art; but it also shows how prof-
itably he had bent his wide experience to rationalizing the classical
ideal.

Meanwhile he had been engaged for tasks more demanding
than the garnishing of Kew. He was given commissions for country
houses: Castle Hill in Dorset, Peper Harow in Surrey (with its
splendidly simple front), Duddingstone in Edinburgh. Town
houses he designed too: Sir Lawrence Dundas's house in Edinburgh (now the Royal Bank and neighboring houses by Robert
Adam), and a London house for Lord Melbourne which has been
incorporated in the Albany. And where he built in a lighter vein,
he was no less thorough: the Lodge or Casino at Clontarf cost
Lord Charlemont £60,000, and is one of Chambers's most perfect
works. Indeed, his talents were especially suited to the smaller
building, as his work at Somerset House was to show.

By his appointment to the comptrollership in 1769 he became—since the senior post, the surveyorship, was still a place for
a politician—the chief royal (*sc.* public) architect. Unfortunately it
was a period when, for one reason and another, there was little
public building undertaken. It would have been expected, however, that when a scheme was finally mooted for housing several

government departments in the largest public building to be begun since Greenwich, the job would have gone at once to the Comptroller. Chambers was in fact commissioned to build Somerset House, but only after some difficulty and too late to save the remains of the old palace on the site (to which Inigo Jones had nobly contributed); so that his plan had to be made *de novo*. There were formidable difficulties in building down to the tidal Thames in the days before the Embankment, and in building on a site which measured several times on the river side what it measured on the Strand. Chambers confronted the Thames with an arcaded basement storey punctuated by watergates, above which he stretched the long riverfront in three main groups, with bridges above the watergates, and joined that to the Strand front by a system of inner courts. The effect of the whole is magnificent, but not unitary. It is a building to be looked at piecemeal; only so can one enjoy the fruits of Chambers's fastidious eclecticism, drawing (as he had done in the *Treatise*) on the best of Italian and French authorities. The work was not completed till after his death in 1706; and the riverfront was extended in the nineteenth century.

Chambers was the last and most distinguished of the Palladian school in England. In the search for sources, he spread his net wider than his predecessors in the school, but he professed to use only what was unmistakably in the Roman tradition. He insisted on the "correct" proportions in the Orders, on decorations which he conceived to be authentic—a conception which happily embraced much of the work of Louis XV's decorators, from whom Chambers borrowed liberally for interior ornament. It is hardly necessary to add that he was purer and more reserved in style than the Adams; their exuberance seemed to him not only "toy-work" (his own phrase) but something improper; and people turned from the Adams to Chambers as from an exciting novelty to a known article which is the best of its kind.

Burke's reforms were felt even in the Office of Works, and in 1782 Chambers became the first architect to be surveyor-general since Wren. If his official status was unquestioned, his position in society was equally high. He moved in the Johnson circle. He was the first Treasurer of the Royal Academy when Reynolds was the first president. He was knighted by George III. But he remained a professional to the fingertips; and the profession took new honor from him.

ROBERT ADAM (1728–92), architect and interior designer, with Sir William Chambers divides the honors in architecture of the period 1760–90. He was the second son of William Adam, a gentleman of means who, up to the time of his death in 1748, was also the foremost architect in Scotland. Four sons became architects, but it was the third son, James, who was most closely joined with Robert, who shared in most of his undertakings, and administered the firm which they set up together in London. And it is the work of Robert and James—in which it is accepted that Robert took the leading part—that has given the name "Adam" to the language.

Robert's career in the University of Edinburgh was cut short in the summer of 1745 by the southward progress of the Young Pretender—not that he espoused the cause, but, falling ill shortly after, he went straight into his father's firm on recovery. In 1754 he set out on the Grand Tour, which was rapidly becoming a *sine qua non* for a cultivated gentleman. Although the social *réclame* of traveling with the Earl of Hopetoun's brother was highly acceptable to Robert's ambition, he did not allow the *beau-monde* to absorb him. Being honored by the Italian academies, he took pains to deserve it. He submitted himself with unexpected modesty to the earthbound instruction of one friend, the Frenchman Clérisseau (a classicist in architecture with some *avant-garde* ideas). At the same time his sketches and designs began to take wings in harmony with the soaring fancy of another friend, the Italian Piranesi (whose elaborate reconstructions of the glories of ancient Rome resuscitated the classical revival in Britain). Among Robert's drawings for 1757 is one for a royal palace which is practically a city in itself, a very Leviathan of a building. And where others before him had worked hard enough on the great public monuments of Rome, Robert was more interested in the remains of the "private" dwellings, the baths, and the palaces. Then, learning that the Palace of Diocletian at Spalato (the modern Split) was largely intact, he crossed the Adriatic, and in five weeks, with the help of Clérisseau and others, executed the sort of scientific survey of the antiquities which Piranesi was executing for Rome, and Stuart and Revett for Athens. The final drawings, engraved by Bartolozzi and sumptuously published in London in 1764, served to seal a reputation already widely proclaimed.

For, on his return to England in 1758, this fashionable young man took the patrons by storm. It helped, of course, that he was *de bon ton;* it helped too that the Earl of Bute extended to him, however tardily, the umbrella beneath which so many young Scots advanced to prominence; but chiefly it was his own tenacity in courting clients, and the evident promise of the work he showed them, which made his reputation. Already we notice his superb confidence in his own ideas; already he recognizes that Chambers is the only rival worth his salt. On the same day in 1761, he and Chambers were appointed "Joint Architects of His Majesty's Works." For Robert it was practically a sinecure: he had built the Admiralty screen in Whitehall—it was his first big commission; but it was also the last public work he was to execute for some time. Chambers was always the *public* architect of the two, and important private clients were making approaches to Robert. Edwin Lascelles wanted him to advise on the improvements to Harewood; Sir Nathaniel Curzon desired him to complete Kedleston. The interesting thing is that in these commissions as in others, Robert was to supplant architects who were well known and still practicing—that is a measure of the impression he was creating. During the 1760s he and James (they were now working together) were more frequently employed to extend and improve existing buildings than to design from the beginning; the great houses they built new were Mersham-le-Hatch and the old Lansdowne House in Berkeley Square; but in the same years they operated on and transformed, not only Kedleston and Harewood, but Syon and Osterley, Luton Hoo, Croome Court, Kenwood, and a roll of others.

Warmed by prosperity, they embarked upon a huge private speculation, the building of the Adelphi (Greek for "the Brothers"); it nearly ruined them; they had to resort to a public lottery to save themselves; but the work was finished and, being made of materials as modest as brick and terra-cotta, served as a pattern for future terrace planning.

It is commonly said that after 1775 there was a decline in the quality of their practice. Certainly they felt the economic draft of the American War; and it is possible that patrons were tiring of the exuberance of what Chambers sneered at as their "filigrane toywork." But it was in 1775 that they began work on the town houses—demi-palaces—at 20 St. James's Square and 20 Portman Square. And, although their greatest achievements thereafter were in Scotland, those were of a high quality. It may be objected that in the Register House and the University of Edinburgh, they proved that their talent, being essentially for decoration and detail, was not virile enough for public buildings on the grand scale; but their designs for the north and northeast sides of Charlotte Square can hardly be faulted. Really, Robert's fecundity was marvellous. As if his work was not enough, he dabbled in landscape painting, and even sat as member for Kinross—one wonders how much the electors saw of him. In the last years of his life, he is said to have designed eight public and twenty-five private buildings. He died in 1792, in the same year as Reynolds, and, like Reynolds, was attended by pallbearers of the nobility. James Wyatt was the first of his disciples, but countless minor artists, at home and abroad, adopted his canons of taste—at least until Nash gave them something fresh to think about.

The "Adam style" was not an entirely new thing. William Kent and others of the Burlington School had already seen, as the brothers Adam saw, that the early Palladians had confined themselves too rigidly to the ABC of the classical Orders of architecture; they had dimly realized, as Piranesi was to demonstrate, that Vitruvius was not Holy Writ, that the Romans had used, and used successfully, more freedom in their private architecture than attention to their public buildings would ever suggest, that (in short) the "rules" of classical architecture were more a matter of feeling than of measurement. What distinguished the Adams was the apparently inexhaustible fund of invention which they applied to reinterpreting the classical rules. "We flatter ourselves," they wrote in the Preface to the published edition of their *Works*, "we have been able to seize, with some degree of success, the beautiful spirit of antiquity, and to transfuse it, with novelty and variety, through all our numerous works . . . Nothing can be more sterile and disgustful than to see for ever the dull repetition of Dorick, Ionick, and Corinthian entablatures, in their usual proportions, reigning round every apartment where no order can come, or ought to come . . . " Given this charter of originality, how did they behave? In the exterior of buildings, they were governed by the principle of "movement," which they partly defined in the same Preface as "the rise and fall, the advance and recess, with the diversity of form in the different parts of a building," comparing it with the spatial variety offered by a landscape set with hills. In the interior, they sought first to design rooms which lead, one to another, in an airy progress of contrast and convenience. And when it came to the decoration, they

reached for their cornucopia: it is all more felicitous, more fanciful, more buoyant than before—rococo, really; the only "rule" is
that of infallible good taste. They conceived (as Kent too had
begun to conceive) that the decoration, not only of each internal
surface, but of every item of furniture, should harmonize with that
of the others and with the stone itself in an overall expression of
the architectural idea. Thus the care which they lavished on a
Corinthian pilaster (yes, it is Corinthian at heart, though genius
has straitened it to the point of weakness, and then fed it strength
in the form of gilded arabesques), they lavished equally on a can-
dlestick or a clock, a fender or a soup tureen. Many of the decorative schemes, many of the furniture styles, are French in origin.
The "Etruscan" myth—the supposition that vases, figures, and
medallions had been the household decoration of the Etruscans—
came to the aid of their invention, as it came to Wedgwood's aid in
the factory which he named "Etruria," and was used by them to enrich and supplement the strictly classical embellishments. As for
their stucco, it seemed that, whether they drew on Etruscan, Imperial, or Renaissance Italy, there was nothing they could not execute
in the way of arabesque or serpentine rhythm, with the subtlest effects of chiaroscuro—though it would be unjust to ignore the contribution of the craftsmen who interpreted the designs. All these
strands can be seen comprehensively drawn together at Syon
House and Osterley Park, which are among their masterpieces;
and, if that is not enough, there are 8,000 drawings by the brothers
in the Soane Museum.

J. Lees-Milne, *The Age of Adam*, 1947.
G. Beard, *The Work of Robert Adam*, 1978.

EDWARD GIBBON (1737–94), historian, was born at Putney, eldest of seven children but the only one to survive beyond infancy.
When he was ten his mother died, but he was already being cared
for by his aunt, Mrs. Catherine Porter. He was an ailing child, but
she tended him devotedly and encouraged him to read: Pope's
translations from Homer and the *Arabian Night's Entertainments*
were "the first two books of which I retain a distinct and pleasing
idea." It was as well that he devoured books, for his regular education was scant. He was for two terms at Westminster, later for a time
at Winchester, Bath, and Putney. But the real center of his life was

Buriton Manor in Hampshire, the family house to which his father repaired when he tired of Parliament and society. The elder Edward Gibbon was an erratic parent. After placing his diminutive son at the house of Philip Francis, clergyman father of Warren Hastings's future enemy and a casual tutor, he suddenly sent him up to Magdalen as a gentleman commoner. Gibbon later censured the college, which he entered just before his fifteenth birthday, in words which have lost none of their sting with time. The dons were "decent, easy men," whose "conversation stagnated in a round of college business, Tory politics, personal anecdotes, and private scandal," "whose dull and deep potations excuse the brisk intemperance of youth." The empty days of this awkward schoolboy may not have been typical of the Oxford where Johnson was undergraduate and John Wesley a Fellow, but it is likely that he learned little and that his tutors were inactive.

In a mood of disenchantment with the Established Church Gibbon sought out a Catholic priest, the chaplain of the Sardinian embassy in London, and was solemnly received by him into the Roman Church. He was sent down, and his indignant father arranged for him to live with a Monsieur Pavilliard, Calvinist pastor at Lausanne. Gibbon, still only sixteen, remained polite under provocation and stood up for his new creed until intellectual doubts got the better of him. He was kept on short allowance by his father but made good use of his solitude by systematic reading of the classics. Gibbon the historian who steeped himself in the records until he breathed the air of Rome, and Gibbon the skeptic who learned to trust in his own powers of reasoning, were born in these years. He was not, however, exclusively engaged with his texts. He made a lifelong friend in Deyverdun, and he had a warm affair with Suzanne Curchod, a radiant girl, two years younger than Gibbon; they met in the summer of 1757. He was the smaller, little more than five feet tall, not handsome but a character, in her opinion "spirituelle et singulière." It seems likely that when he departed for England, disguised for his journey across French soil as a Swiss officer, in April 1758, he intended to fulfill his promise to return and claim her. But his father, now married again, would not hear of it and Gibbon acquiesced: "I sighed as a lover, I obeyed as a son." Instead he settled contentedly to the life of a gentleman scholar, dividing his time between lodgings in Bond Street and Buriton. The library of his father's house attracted him more than farming and shooting, but his ordered life was enhanced by friendship with his intelligent stepmother.

In 1759 he obtained a commission in one of the militia battalions formed at that time to meet the threat of invasion. For more than two years he served in different parts of England with the South Hampshire Grenadiers. A "bumperizing" commanding officer and "companions who had neither the knowledge of scholars nor the manners of gentlemen" made this service a somewhat distasteful one, but he had an encounter with Colonel John Wilkes of the Buckinghamshire militia, learned something of military exercises and more of the social life of the southern towns where they made their quarters. He learned to hold his drink when "hospitality was often debauch" and believed that the militia made him "an Englishman and a soldier." Major Gibbon, as he was when his regiment was disbanded in December 1762, was ready to play a larger part than man of letters. But when he traveled abroad again in 1763 he had entry to several salons in Paris. In Switzerland again he firmly rebuffed Mlle. Curchod. He went to Rome after nearly a year by the Lake of Leman, and he began to write occasional pieces. He was overcome by the excitement of an experience for which all his reading had hardly prepared him. It was in the ruins of the Forum, on October 15, 1764, that he felt inspired to write a historical epic: "As I sat musing amidst the ruins of the Capitol, while the bare-footed friars were singing vespers in the Temple of Jupiter, . . . the idea of writing the decline and fall of the city first started to my mind." Thorough and single-minded as in everything, he spent the next four months on a complete examination of the classical ruins. Then he continued his tour, but from Venice he hurried home, alarmed by news that his father was in financial trouble. He stayed long enough in Paris, however, to meet Suzanne Curchod in her new role, wife to the banker Jacques Necker. His father died in 1770. In the intervening years he continued to write, classical studies mainly, but also with Deyverdun an annual review of British arts and manners.

After 1770 Gibbon flowered. By judicious sales and by letting Buriton his finances were secured. He took a house in Bentinck Street and there, in his elegant library with walls of pale blue and silver, he began the great project. An unfailing grace of style conceals intensive effort. The first chapter was rewritten three times, but gradually he became more fluent. He was already a well-known figure. He belonged to several clubs, White's, Brooks's, Boodle's; in 1774 he became a member of the Club, though not much liked by Johnson. "An ugly, disgusting little fellow," wrote Boswell. In the same year he became a member of Parliament for one of the boroughs in the patronage of his cousin, Edward Eliot. He enjoyed the oratory and voted steadily for Lord North, but he never spoke. He was conspicuous in his appearance, his plump body, large head with pendulous cheeks above a tiny round mouth, set off by the vivid clothes that he liked to wear. Then in February 1775 the first volumes of *The History of the Decline and Fall of the Roman Empire* appeared in the bookshops—and sold out immediately. As edition followed edition, Gibbon basked in fame. He accepted contentedly the sinecure of Lord Commissioner of Trade and Plantations (1779). He received the assaults of academic and clerical critics of his history with complacency, though he was sufficiently roused to compose a vindication in answer to a Mr. Davies of Oxford, who questioned his scholarship. He expected deference and became very vain. An occasion is recorded when, worsted in argument by Pitt, he retired from the company in a huff. He was chiefly immersed in his great task and the story steadily unrolled. In 1781 the second and third volumes appeared. He lost his seat in Parliament after some differences with Eliot, but soon reappeared as member for Lymington. Time was running out for placemen, however, with the fall of North, and in May 1782 his sinecure was abolished. The axe sharpened his instinct to escape altogether from public life and give himself to literature. He settled with Deyverdun at Lausanne and there, in a pleasant house with grounds running down to the lake, with cultivated society around him (the Neckers were back, since M. Necker had been dismissed from his controller-generalship), he proceeded to the sack of Constantinople and the end of the Byzantine Empire.

In his autobiography Gibbon describes the sense of elation, shaded with melancholy, as he laid down his pen between 11 and 12 of the evening of June 27, 1787, in a summer house in his garden, "took several turns in a berceau, or covered walk of acacias, which commands a prospect of the country, the lake and the mountains" and felt "joy on recovery of my freedom . . . perhaps, the establishment of my fame." He came to England to act as midwife to the concluding volumes. On April 27, the author's fifty-first birthday, they were presented to the public. Before he returned he had the gratification of hearing Sheridan deliver a stately tribute before the fashionable gallery at the trial of Hastings, whose misdeeds were without parallel "in ancient or modern history, in the correct periods of Tacitus or the luminous page of Gibbon."

There is a satisfying completeness about Gibbon's life. As if he knew that Rome had been his life, he attempted to write nothing more beyond some autobiographical essays which his friend Lord Sheffield subsequently made into a continuous memoir. The death of Deyverdun in 1789 brought a rare moment of sadness. The French Revolution filled him with disgust; its excesses and its assaults upon established forms were alien to his orderly mind. Then in April 1793, learning that Lady Sheffield had died, he traveled home past the battlefields of Europe to console his friend. Soon it became obvious that he must have an operation for he was monstrously fat. Under the spell of the beauty of Lady Elizabeth Foster, a visitor at Lausanne, he dropped to his knees with a proposal of marriage; but he was unable to rise and had to be rescued by servants from his predicament. Though he endured three operations with stoicism, his case was beyond repair. After the third operation, on January 16, 1794, he died peacefully.

The reputation of *The Decline and Fall* is secure. Inevitably, later research has invalidated many of his conclusions and some of his facts. The work suffers in balance from his unsympathetic view of the Byzantine Empire. His treatment of personality tends to reflect his own experience: heroes are cool, urbane, and responsive to reason; the opposition is provided by wild men who offend against the laws of good taste and common sense. He is notoriously prejudiced against the Church: that was the cause of vehement but sometimes unwise attacks in his day. It is not so much that he was inaccurate but that he reveals the limitations of a mind that was insensitive for all its subtlety, leather-bound with the complacency of the sheltered bookman. He cannot measure the moods and actions of human beings in mass except in terms of mockery, but he approaches scenes of indecency and violence with a distinct relish. "Nor does his humanity ever slumber unless when women are ravished or the Christians persecuted" (Porson). Such criticisms only serve, however, to enhance the real qualities of his work. He rose sufficiently to the level of the greatest of subjects. Subsequent historians have revised and supplemented; they have not replaced the whole. In an age of specialization we must be impressed by Gibbon's grasp of a long period, a variety of subjects. He is sure upon the growth of Mohammedanism, the institutions of the republic, the details of Roman Law. "If," wrote Bury, "we take into account the vast range of his work, his accuracy is amazing and with all his disadvantages, his slips are singularly few." Accurate, lucid, Gibbon is, above all, a master of harmony. Hume could not believe that the book was written by an Englishman. Formed by his reading of the Romans, Livy, Tacitus, and Cicero, besides French and English contemporaries, Voltaire, Robertson, and Hume, Gibbon's style is yet distinctive: stately, but delicate in the use of words to convey precise meaning and nuance. He can unfold a story, sustain an argumen in sentence, paragraph, even pages long, without becoming either pompous or obscure. A fine mind, a sensitive ear, control the flowing pen. We are left awed, with a sense of finality, of the constant victory, under the direction of the historian, of reason and light over the material: the material being, in his own words, "little more than the crimes, follies, and misfortunes of mankind." The work, like the man, represents the height of eighteenth-century civilization. The man, in bag wig, ruffles, and flowered velvet, forever tapping the lid of his snuffbox, never quite achieved the effect of dignity that he sought. But he was content, for he had lived his life by a consistent plan. He had practiced "the profane virtues of sincerity and moderation," and he had accomplished a masterpiece.

J. B. Bury, ed., *The Autobiographies of Edward Gibbon*, 1896.
J. E. Norton, ed., *Letters*, 3 vols., 1956.
G. M. Young, *Gibbon*, 1932.
R. Porter, *Gibbon*, 1988.

GEORGE III (1738–1820) came to the throne at the age of twenty-two at the height of the Seven Years War. During his reign the country was transformed by an accelerating industrial revolution. The American colonies were lost but an Indian empire was won. A protracted war against France brought in the end glorious and decisive victory. Five years after Waterloo he died. Only Victoria's reign of sixty-five years exceeds that of George III in length or compares with it in the scale and variety of events. This is the age of Pitt, Burke, and Castlereagh, Reynolds and Gainsborough, Nelson and Wellington, Adam Smith and James Watt, Jane Austen, Wordsworth, and Shelley. At no other time, perhaps, is one aware of such a range of genius, such a creative, dynamic, purposive spirit in society.

It was a great reign. But George III was in no sense a great man. As was perhaps predictable, royal power decreased. During the last twenty years of his life he was virtually *hors de combat*, for the last ten years irremediably mad; the constitutional rights of the Crown were atrophied. His heir and regent after 1812 was so un-popular that it was uncertain whether monarchy would survive at all. It did, but in a limited form. After 1820 the initiatives which George III had striven to keep and use passed from the Crown. If he had been an abler man, if he had been mentally stable, would the constitutional balance have been in any way different? It seems unlikely. The combination in him of high aims, petty methods, and an awkward manner has, however, provided ammunition for the debate of Whig and Tory partisans. George III was not "behav-ing like Charles I when he should have behaved like Queen Victo-ria." Nor was he, however, the blameless prince, firm in exercise of undoubted rights, of some of his extreme apologists. He was a staunch, intense, narrow-minded man, admirable in private life but prejudiced and often perverse in public matters; he may win our sympathy but not yet merit the gallons of ink that have been spent upon his personality and rule.

George was eleven when he learned to read; when the death of his father, Frederick, left him heir to the throne, he was twelve. He was lethargic and found it hard to concentrate, but what he learned he clung to. He was very literal in his understanding, un-sure in judgment, naive in hopes and intentions. At the age of twenty he still wrote like a child; whenever he was thwarted he lapsed into a sort of childish despair. Beneath the dull exterior there were, however, strong feelings. He dearly loved his brother Edward. At eighteen he became devoted to his mother's friend, the Earl of Bute, and made him Groom of the Stole in his own estab-lishment. George craved for support and sympathy in the heavy tasks which would fall to him, for beneath his apparent composure there were misgivings about his ability to rule. An inferiority com-plex is indeed the first clue to understanding the callow acts and pronouncements of his early years. Another is his own reading of the immediate past: in his view his grandfather had been weak— "Newcastle's lackey"—his mother shamefully treated by king and ministers. Pitt, the superb war minister, had "the blackest of hearts," while Lord Sackville, disgraced at Minden for disobedience and cowardice, was set up as "an injured man" and marked for future promotion. He took seriously the resounding phrases of his father's opposition group: they talked of corruption because they were out of office, and he conceived a mission to purify politics and eliminate faction. Only gradually did he learn to temper his missionary zeal with political cunning, and to use those weapons of influence and patronage which he denounced in other hands.

George lost his heart to the fifteen-year-old daughter of the Duke of Richmond, Lady Sarah Lennox, but was persuaded instead to marry Charlotte of Mecklenburg-Strelitz, daughter of a German princeling. Domestic respectability settled upon the English court for the first time since Anne's reign. The formidable dullness of life at Windsor is recalled for us by Fanny Burney, but George III's example served to establish an image of propriety which even the excesses of George IV could not entirely destroy. That his sons ranged from the eccentric to the outrageous was poor reward for the conscientious parents; their lavish, loud, embarrassing lives only stressed the value of their parents' simple ways. It may be that his daughters suffered worst. Stifled with heavy affection—George called them "all Cordelias" and was reluctant to let them marry—they wrote gloomy letters from their "nunnery."

The first decade was an unsettled period in domestic politics. After the disintegration of Newcastle's following there was no one dominant group. The elder Pitt's genius did not lie in managing political combinations, and he became autocratic to the point of mania. Until the emergence of North in 1770, there was no man who could be relied upon to carry on the king's government in a way that pleased both the king and the independent country gentlemen; until the precocious maturity of the younger Pitt in 1784, no minister who could justify the king's support by intelligent statecraft. George began with clumsy haste to destroy the partnership of the elder Pitt and Newcastle which had provided such skillful management from 1757 to 1760. His instrument was Bute, "dearest" friend and confidant of the king: in March 1761, he was made Secretary of State. In October of that year Pitt resigned, finding himself thwarted by the cabinet and slighted by the King, who regarded his war as "bloody, expensive, and unnecessary." In 1762 Bute was elevated to First Lord of the Treasury in place of Newcastle. Bute was "a favorite" as no politician had been in that century, but he had neither the ability nor the political following to make good use of the king's favor. George clung to him as he was later to cling to North: his relationship with prime ministers tended to be possessive and framed in terms of personal loyalty. Bute resigned, however, in nervous prostration in 1763 and George had to submit in turn to Grenville, stiff and opinionated, then to Rockingham, who revived the Pelham conception of party and insisted upon his right to choose his cabinet and impose his program. Chatham (1766–68) shared George's abhorrence of faction and promised disinterested reforming government, but was sick and inactive for the best part of two years before yielding to Grafton, who was unequal to the problems which had been exacerbated by years of inconsistency and postponement. Then in North, in 1770, George found a man who could give him peace of mind. Throughout he had been looking for someone whom he could treat as part-servant, part-father. Out of his temperamental weakness, his trembling inner insecurity, came his desire to appear the master, a strict but benevolent patriot-king. North was willing, in his easy way, to be his man. He was a sound parliamentary tactician and a good financier, but unsuited to the critical problems that he encountered in the Wilkes affair, in Ireland, in India, above all in America. The greatest disgrace of George's reign was the loss of America, not only the fact but the manner of it—conciliation, bluff, and aggression in the wrong proportions and at the wrong times. The blame may lie at North's door, but George contributed to the disaster by clinging to North long after it was apparent to everybody, including North, who begged to be released, that he was incapable.

    That George wished to create a tyranny was believed early in his reign and was accepted for a hundred years after his death. The basis of the idea is that George knew the daily business of monarchy as did neither of his predecessors. He did not confine his interest to the army and foreign policy. He was constructively interested in agriculture and became involved in all the political issues of the time. As a monarch he was conscientious, as a politician within his rights, sketchily defined as they were. Unfortunately he was lacking in sense of proportion, he was obstinate in small things (though he tended to give way, until he found the weapon of threatened madness and used it so effectively against Pitt in the matter of Catholic Emancipation), and he was passionately subjective in his judgments. The satire of "Junius," the effrontery of "that

Devil Wilkes," the resistance of the American rebels, the "treason" of the Whigs who applauded the news of Saratoga, touched him personally. We feel from contemporary accounts that he appeared to his perhaps arrogant ministers to be a stupid man. "Farmer George" may have been a pleasing image to unsophisticated provincials. To the worldly, gamey circle of men like Grafton, Fox, Rockingham, to intelligent men like Shelburne and Burke, it verged upon the contemptible.

If George III maddened men, he also suffered. So deeply did he feel the *débâcle* of America and the imminent fall of North that he sat down to compose a message of abdication. With a certain nobility he rose above his sense of failure to express the ideal which he felt was impugned by the colonists and the parliamentary opposition: "His Majesty, during the twenty-one years he has sate on the throne of Great Britain, has had no object so much at heart as the maintenance of the British Constitution, of which the difficulties he has at times met with from his scrupulous attachment to the rights of Parliament are sufficient proofs. His Majesty is convinced that the sudden change of sentiments of one branch of the legislature has totally incapacitated him from either conducting the war with effect, or from obtaining any peace but on conditions which would prove destructive to the commerce as well as essential rights of the British nation." He believed, as he was to believe later in the matter of the Irish Catholics, that he was defending the sacred constitution which he was bound by oath to defend. He held to his course of duty and did not abdicate. Instead he had to endure the growth of radicalism and the efforts by the Rockingham faction, men who in his view were little better than traitors because of their opposition to the American War, to exploit this force for their movement of economical reform: it was designed to reduce the field of patronage and thus the influence of the Crown which, in the words of Dunning's famous motion of 1780, "had increased, is increasing, and ought to be diminished." Rockingham died in July 1782, Shelburne could not sustain his administration, and George was forced to accept the final humiliation of the Fox-North coalition: his former instrument allied to that wicked adventurer who was debauching his son and trumpeting his intention to reduce George to the status of "a kind of slave," in the king's own words. George resisted Fox's demand that the cabinet should appoint junior ministers without consultation—a constitutional novelty—and refused to sign warrants for their appointment. He also handled the ministers with dexterity; for a few months in the winter of 1783–84 he showed himself to be a smarter tactician than Fox. He waited his moment and then intervened personally to destroy Fox's India Bill by authorizing Temple to inform any peer that if he voted for the bill in the Lords he would regard him as an enemy. Now it was his turn to defy constitutional precedent. He dismissed the ministry, asked Pitt to form a government, and supported him against furious opposition and large majorities until the moment was ripe for a general election in which the royal patronage and propaganda proved decisive (1784).

With Pitt, the austere young tribune, invariably deferential but coolly independent in policy, his relations were ideal. He approved his policy, peace, and economy and he trusted his practical, cautious method. He appreciated the discomfiture of the Foxites, but the strains of his life told when he suddenly lost his reason. It had happened briefly before, in 1765. Since then he had borne a burden too taxing for his limited capacities. His eldest son's outrageous conduct may have precipitated this collapse: as heir to the throne he was bound, by the family tradition, to patronize the opposition and he came under the spell of Fox, who encouraged him to gamble, womanize, and prate of liberty. He entered into a secret marriage with Mrs. Fitzherbert and refused to repudiate her. In 1787 the ministry secured the payment of £160,000 to pay his debts and to finance the building of Carlton House. It is not surprising that "the flying gout," as the medical men of the day quaintly called it, went to his head. It is likely too that George would have suffered a breakdown at some point. It seems that he had porphyria, hereditary in the family, a disturbance of the porphyrian metabolism which can lead to the poisoning of the entire nervous system, including the brain. The king gabbled and could not sleep; he tried to strangle his son and had to be put in a straitjacket. Pitt played for time, drafted a Regency Bill which Fox unwisely opposed with the claim that full rights pertained to the prince as soon as the incapacity of the Crown was established; by February 1789 the king had recovered, and Pitt was in a stronger position than ever.

George retreated, thereafter, into a quieter life and tasted respect and even popularity for the first time. This was soon tinged with pity, as it became clear that final insanity was overtaking him. In 1801 he caused the fall of Pitt over Catholic Emancipation by standing by the letter of his Coronation oath with an obsessive frenzy. Thereafter he played little active part. The National Anthem might be played as he descended from a bathing machine to take the waters at his beloved Weymouth; he was seen as "the good King," a useful and lovable symbol of the idea of monarchy in a war fought to preserve England from the bloody threat of Jacobinism; more interest was focused on the lurid behavior of his sons, especially "Prinnie," who eventually became regent and virtual sovereign in 1811. By then George was wandering about his park and farm at Windsor, dropping into cottages to inquire after the health of his tenants, talking to Eton boys or in more vacant mood talking to an oak tree or playing to himself on the harpsichord, a Lear-like figure in purple dressing gown and flowing white hair and beard. To Shelley he was "an old, mad, blind, despised, and dying king," to most people a figure of the past, but one to respect: "the virtuous father of his country."

R. Sedgewick, *Letters of George III to Bute*, 1939.
H. Butterfield, *George III and the Historians*, 1957.
R. Pares, *George III and the Politicians*, 1953.
John Brooke, *King George III*, 1972.

CHARLOTTE SOPHIA, PRINCESS OF MECKLENBURG-STRE-LITZ (1744–1818), was married in 1761 to King George III: it was a prosaic affair. The ardent young king, who had but lately denied himself the imprudent pleasures of a love match with the fifteen-year-old daughter of the Duke of Richmond, gave his ministers to realize, as soon as he was crowned, that he must be married suitably and without delay. While he perused the Almanach de Gotha, his advisers examined the field. The princess must be Protestant, of exemplary life and opinions; preferably German. Charlotte of Mecklenberg-Strelitz, who had lately lectured Frederick the Great upon the evils of war, was thought to be suitable. Zoffany's portrait shows homely features, but not, as Plumb coarsely says of her, "a dim, formidably ugly girl"; the king accepted her without demur and she gave him no cause to regret his choice.

Charlotte had virtues which were more apparent to contemporaries than they have been to historians. Horace Walpole was impressed by her bearing. Fanny Burney, appointed her Keeper of Robes in 1786, found court life exacting and often dull but the queen was "unremittingly sweet and gracious" and she was surprised by the "depth and soundness of her understanding." She was pious and her *régime* was Spartan; the contrast between the life at Windsor and that of many of her richest subjects was indeed conspicuous. From the start she had set up social *ne plus ultra* lines: lapses from sexual propriety and marital fidelity were sternly disapproved.

Some talked of tyranny but the model domestic habits of George and Charlotte may have contributed to the survival of monarchy in the unsettled period of the revolution, building a capital of esteem upon which the Crown could live during the ig nominious reigns of her elder sons. Much of Charlotte's life was given to producing children, fifteen in all; the seven males that survived were in varying degrees embarrassing or unsatisfactory. Of the six daughters, two were married to German princelings; three remained unmarried. She may have been unimaginative and clumsy in her relations with them. But she retained a staid dignity amid worry and crisis. Melbourne, a fastidious judge, did not find her ridiculous in her old age; even her slight German accent he pronounced pretty and he praised her good nature. She was devoted to George, whose mental collapses and final insanity were a stern test of her fortitude. The outrageous conduct of the prince regent, however, clouded her later years. There is pathos in her life at Windsor and Kew, tending an old and mad king. But first to last she was governed by that formidable sense of duty which has characterized so many of her descendants. It is not inappropriate that her name adorns one of our more commonplace puddings.

John Brooke, *King George III*, 1972.

JOHN STUART BUTE, 3rd EARL OF BUTE (1713–92), owed his ascendancy at the start of George III's reign more to the favor and trust of the young king than to his own abilities, for he was more a courtier than a politician. His administration was undermined from the start by his personal unpopularity and his lack of adequate support in Parliament. By his commitment to Bute, George III was placed at an early disadvantage in his search for a stable government acceptable both to Parliament and to himself.

Bute was a representative peer of Scotland from 1737. He might, however, have escaped the notice of history but for a series of fortunate strokes. He appears to have begun a fruitful acquaintance with the court of the Prince of Wales by making a fourth at cards, when rain stopped a cricket match in which Frederick was playing. When the prince died, in 1751, Bute became Groom of the Stole and the leading personality in the household of the widow, a model of adult poise to the young heir apparent. From George's letters we have a rare insight into his mind and especially into his feelings toward Bute, his "dearest friend." He invested the graceful figure of the Earl with the virtues and strength that he felt he lacked himself. As he came to have views upon politics, so Bute grew in his thinking to the stature of a statesman. His role was to be that of the honest minister of a patriotic king, for dishonesty and the spirit of faction were, in George's opinion, the conspicuous features of the political scene. Unsure of his own abilities, he relied upon Bute to help him in the crises of his life. He consulted him about marriage, confided to him his failings, and practiced on him the tentative ideas upon which he proposed to base his rule. Thus Bute was elevated beyond his deserts, the object of a lonely adolescent's trust, the embodiment of his naïve hopes. When George III became king in 1760, Bute came into the center of affairs. Two more deaths further advanced his fortunes. That in 1761 of his relative, the Duke of Argyll, left Bute to assume the leadership of the Scottish members and peers: a solid bloc of parliamentary interest. In the same year his father-in-law, Edward Wortley Montagu, died. He was a millionaire, mostly from property in the new coalfields, and his money went to his daughter, Mary, rather than to his eccentric son. The marriage of his own daughter to Sir James Lowther, another wealthy landowner and boroughmonger, added further to Bute's empire.

In March 1761 he became Secretary of State, the colleague of Pitt and Newcastle. In this year, as the financial burden of the war became increasingly alarming, the issue of the war and the way in which it should be fought took precedence over others. George III, "glorying in the name of Briton," felt that the war in Europe was irrelevant to England's interests. England's war had been won; now peace should be secured. Bute was on strong ground when he represented this view, which fitted with Newcastle's growing concern for the size of the debt and the burden of tax. When Pitt actually proposed an extension of the war by attacking Spain, Newcastle and Bute made common cause and Pitt resigned. Bute therefore became, in October 1761, the senior Secretary of State. But Spain, as Pitt had foreseen, came into the war and the problem of securing a peace commensurate with the victories gained grew accordingly more difficult. When Newcastle failed to convince his colleagues and the king that subsidies to Frederick should be renewed, he too resigned. Bute then became First Lord of the Treasury and Grenville, extreme advocate of economies, the new Secretary of State. Bute's power was less secure than it may have seemed. Characteristically, Devonshire was "surprised to find that they [George III and Bute] knew mankind and the *carte de pays* so little." To set against the king's support, there was the opposition of Pitt, fiercely against any measures which seemed to detract from his own glorious achievement, and Newcastle with his hungry political following. Newcastle saw the position plain: if he declared that he would not oppose, "my lord Bute's next levée would be twice as full as any he had yet had." Bute was weak in cabinet too, for Grenville was an awkward colleague. Inexperienced in the arts of management, Bute tried to draw Newcastle back into the government but it could not be done. So Henry Fox was recruited to strengthen the government in the Commons. He remained paymaster while being given added responsibility as Leader of the House, charged with the delicate business of securing support for the peace.

Meanwhile the Duke of Bedford had completed the negotiations in Paris. Preliminaries were signed in October 1762; in December they were approved by Parliament by the large majority of 319 to 65. In March the Peace of Paris was proclaimed. Britain gained from France the whole province of Canada, all Louisiana east of the Mississippi, Cape Breton and the islands in the St. Lawrence; in the West Indies, Tobago, Dominica, St. Vincent, and the Grenadines; in West Africa, Senegal; in the Mediterranean, Minorca in exchange for Belle Isle. In India, the French had their trading stations back, but they were eliminated from Bengal and made to recognize the British-backed rulers in the Carnatic and Deccan. Spain ceded east and west Florida and the right to cut logwood in the Honduras. This was no mean harvest, but it was open to attack: from those who feared the results of eliminating French rivalry from Canada and expected more trouble with the American colonists as result and those who would have preferred Guadeloupe, saying that there was more money in sugar than in furs.

Most telling, perhaps, was Pitt's attack upon the way in which peace had been made: the alienation of a great ally, the threat which isolation implied to the nation's security. Bute survived, however, with a wide measure of support for the view that the peace was as reasonable as it was essential. The sudden *débâcle* which followed was a personal failure of nerve rather than a political reverse.

Taxes could not be reduced immediately, for war costs to the government persist after the war is over. Rather than continue to increase the debt, Bute saw a new tax upon cider and wine as a logical extension of the beer tax. But the Englishman who was looking forward to easy times was furious at having to pay 4*s.* a hogshead upon his cider. Worse, it was an excise, with all the hated associations of inspection and arbitrary justice. The apple growers in Herefordshire bridled at the prospect. Unfortunately, in Sir Francis Dashwood, the government had a Chancellor of the Exchequer of memorable incompetence. While he fumbled with figures which he appeared not to understand, the opposition made play with Bute's fancied plan to subvert the constitution and bring in the tyrannical *régime* that a Scotsman was supposed to favor. Wilkes fanned anti-Scottish prejudice in the *North Briton*. Riots in the city were followed by a petition to the king to refuse his assent. Inside the cabinet, Grenville was a complete isolationist: in the Commons he appealed for backbench support by moving for an inquiry into the expense of the late war. The ministry rode the storm and the cider tax was pushed through by substantial majorities. But Bute had had enough. He was an honorable man in his way and he was mortified by the gross sallies of the opposition: some went so far as to assert that he owed his position to the favors of the queen mother. He was sensitive to slights and stiff in his approach to the political game. It required readiness in intrigue to keep on terms with men like Fox and Newcastle. In April Bute resigned. He may have hoped to preserve some influence in the closet as adviser and director of royal policy. Grenville clearly thought so, for one of his first actions was to exact a promise from him that he would not interfere. He continued to express his views to the king, but as "minister behind the curtain" his impact was slight despite the existence of a group of "king's friends," watching for the chance to set king against minister. After 1768 his life was mainly spent in the country, where he resumed his studies in botany and science. It should be recalled that he was largely responsible for the development of the royal estate of Kew as a botanical garden. Also he had the discernment to secure for Dr. Johnson the award of a pension. Unfortunate in politics, he was very happy in private life.

K. W. Schweitzer, ed., *Lord Bute: Essays in Reinterpretation*, 1988.
P. D. Brown and K. W. Schweitzer, eds., *The Devonshire Diary*, 1982.
R. Sedgewick, *Letters of George III to Bute*, 1939.

THE HONORABLE GEORGE GRENVILLE (1712–70) owed his political importance at first largely to the connection of his family with Pitt, but later more to his talent for the management of public finance. His training was that of a lawyer. His gifts were largely administrative. There is little evidence of the vision of a statesman.

He entered Parliament in 1741. The activity of his brother, the future Earl Temple, Pitt, his brother-in-law, and their associates of the Stowe House group was then making Walpole uncomfortable in the last year of his administration, during a war which they had helped to force on to the reluctant minister. The Grenvilles were, of all the political connections, the most disliked by George III. To the factious spirit which he thought was prejudicial to the well-being of the country, they added a stiff manner and a pride in acting together that was specially offensive to him. In this he was not alone. Temple and Grenville were both unpopular outside their own circle and found it difficult to secure the wide measure of support that was necessary for an effective administration.

Grenville was Treasurer of the Navy from 1760 to 1762. When Pitt resigned in 1761 he stayed on. Then in May 1762, Newcastle resigned and Grenville, whom the king urged "be narrowly watched and sifted," became Secretary of State. At this time he led that group in the cabinet which stood out for higher terms of peace than Bute thought possible. For his trouble-making Grenville was demoted in October 1762 to the Admiralty. In March 1763 he was asking for an inquiry into the way that money had been spent in the war, a popular move but an embarrassing one for Henry Fox. As paymaster he had made a fortune out of contracts and subsidies; he was now spokesman in the Commons for the ministry and the peace. In April Grenville succeeded Bute as First Lord of the Treasury. In August Sandwich came in as Secretary of State. With the

Duke of Bedford as Lord President of the Council, the administration enjoyed the support of the Russell following. It was Grenville's task to grapple with the economic problems created by the war. He knew that the king had been unwilling to accept him and disliked him for undermining first Newcastle then Bute. For his part, he was not prepared to be a mere stopgap. He therefore devised a novel form of check upon the king and his colleagues. In order to forestall the undermining tactics that he had reason to expect, he insisted that nobody should consult with the king unless he knew about it beforehand. There was to be no second channel of favor: "he must be known to have the patronage or the whole must break." His own secretary, Lloyd, handled this patronage, rather than Jenkinson who had worked for Bute. His fellow-ministers were also to be denied any part in this central activity of political management for they had political interests behind them, whereas Grenville stood alone. He even broke with his family connection. When Lord Temple supported Wilkes in the matter of the *North Briton*, he was deprived of his Lord-Lieutenancy of Buckinghamshire. Grenville could be ruthless. It may be argued, given the weaknesses of governments before and after him, that his method was right. He sought a greater degree of centralization than had been attempted hitherto, even by Walpole. He kept his cabinet small; normally only four or five were present. He sought to meet and punish demagogic opposition before it could damage him. Unfortunately—and this was the prime reason for the failure of his experiment in strong government—his methods were such as to encourage opposition. So far from being the "gentle shepherd" of Pitt's scornful phrase, he was heavily and fussily dictatorial. He was, however, listened to attentively by the country gentlemen to whose interests he appealed by his drastic economies. He was in his way, too, a sound House of Commons man, for his memory was good and he was knowledgeable about procedures. His main hope of survival lay in the approval of the mass of uncommitted members of Parliament who wanted the king's government to be carried on as efficiently and cheaply as possible.

In 1762, with the encouragement of Temple, John Wilkes had launched his paper, the *North Briton*, outspoken, salacious, and hostile to the court. Number 45, in April 1763, stigmatized the phrase in the king's speech about the peace, "honorable to my crown and beneficial to my people," as a falsehood. The ministry chose this point to attack with a General Warrant authorizing the arrest of all concerned in the affair. Wilkes looked beyond the courts to the radical instincts of that almost unknown political force—"the people"; Pratt ruled against the legality of General Warrants and Wilkes secured damages from the Undersecretary of State. In November 1763 the House voted Number 45 a seditious libel. In February 1764 he was outlawed. The government only just survived the subsequent division upon the question of General Warrants. But to show that coercion, not conciliation, was the order of the day, General Conway was dismissed from his posts in the Bedchamber and in the army for voting against the ministry.

Grenville was not alone in being alarmed by the size of the National Debt. The annual charge upon it had risen to £19^1/$_2$ million by 1761, three times the rate before the war. To reduce it became Grenville's object. Within a year of his coming to power, supplies were almost halved. The army was reduced from 120,000 to 30,000; the navy was cut down even more severely. In April 1764 the First Lord was complaining that there were not seventeen ships of the line complete. In the long term the cost of this dismemberment was to be the wretched naval and military performance in the first years of the American War. The cost in human terms could not be calculated. Experienced naval officers moped on half-pay; "the bravest men the world ever saw," as Pitt said of the army cuts, were "sent to starve in country villages and forget their prowess." Grenville's measures nonetheless received wide support. He pegged the Land Tax at 4s. and looked forward to the time when it might be reduced. He added considerably to the list of enumerated goods, those from the colonies which had to be exported via Britain. Finding the molasses duty was being evaded in America he sensibly halved it, to 3d., while tightening up the machinery of enforcement. Unfortunately he decided that the Americans should be made to contribute more to the expenses incurred by the motherland. In equity this was not unreasonable but his Stamp Duty of March 1765, to be levied on papers required in official transactions, raised questions of principle which had hitherto lain dormant; this was a direct tax. There was brouhaha among some of the colonists while, in Parliament, the followers of Rockingham and Pitt opposed the duty in terms that bound them later to repeal it. Thus the first act of the American tragedy was enacted. To Grenville, blinkered, insular, prejudiced, these measures were only part of a large reduction of expenditure in every field. Abroad he refused to countenance a policy which involved the payment of subsidies to foreign monarchs, he extracted payments from France for the upkeep of French prisoners in the war, and he refused to help the Corsican patriots who were in revolt against Genoa. (Later France did; thus the Buonapartes became French subjects.) Inevitably this meant that England drifted into isolation; in 1764 Prussia and Russia came to terms in a treaty which emphasized England's unimportance in Europe.

Sandwich in particular was out of sympathy with Grenville's foreign policy. But the ministers altogether lacked an underlying principle of unity or common interest. Grenville could not, by his personality, supply the deficiency.

"He had no sense that there was more to the government of a great empire than rules and regulations" (Langford). The king fretted under the constraints placed upon him, became ill, and decided to have a Regency Council. Grenville rebuked him for not discussing the matter with him first. He was mortified, too, by being put into a false position over the composition of the council. The ministers urged the king to exclude his mother; then two opposition members moved that she be appointed. The king was made to feel undutiful and ridiculous. He wriggled in several directions to find a successor to Grenville, but for a time it seemed as if the only alternative would be anarchy. Eventually in July 1765 he fell back on Rockingham, with Grafton and Conway Secretaries of State. Grenville remained quite active in opposition but was most effective when riding his old hobby-horse of economies.

D. Lawson, *George Grenville: A Political Life*, 1984.

AUGUSTUS HENRY FITZROY, 3rd DUKE OF GRAFTON (1735–1811), who attained high office at the age of thirty and found himself virtually head of the government in the following year, was a descendant of Charles II and seems to have been both amiable and handsome. He was mediocre, however, both in intellectual and practical attainments and he owed his elevation more to chance than to talents. He might have had a more useful career if he had not come to office before he had had time to learn political business the hard way.

He was one of the keen followers of Newcastle who made his mark in the opposition to Bute and Grenville. But he was always cautious. Although a friend of Wilkes, for instance, he refused to go bail for him in 1763, lest this should arouse the disfavor of the king. He was also a fervent admirer of Pitt and joined the administration of Rockingham, in 1765, on the understanding that Pitt would be brought in as well. This proved impracticable so he became critical of his colleagues, adopted Pitt's policy of lenience toward the American colonists, and, in April 1766, resigned. When Pitt formed a government shortly afterward, he became First Lord of the Treasury, an appointment which shows how isolated Pitt had already become, lacking allies of proven capacity and susceptible to flattering attachment. Grafton's settlement of the Indian problem was a mere time-saving compromise. In June 1767, the East India Company agreed to pay £400,000 a year to the state out of the administrative and trading profits of Bengal. At the same time there was a statutory limitation of the company's dividend to ten percent. No one pretended that this was a solution to any of the deep problems of British involvement in India. But Grafton was not a man for hard thinking or radical solutions. His position was, moreover, unenviable since Chatham withdrew after a few months into gloomy introspection bordering upon insanity and did nothing. When he eventually retired in October 1768, it may be that Grafton would have been wise to follow him. For the next two years he presided over an administration which was as futile as that which preceded it, in which urgent questions, notably America, took second place to Wilkes.

On the ground that Wilkes was an outlaw when he stood, his election for Middlesex was quashed. When he was reelected, the logic of their position drove the ministry into an embarrassing situation. By declaring Colonel Luttrell elected after a poll in which he had secured 216 votes against Wilkes's 1,143, they confronted the "popular party" standing for the rights of the electorate with, as it seemed to their critics, a packed and privileged assembly. Thus radical ideas crystallized into a party with a program of constitutional reform, light was directed toward the corruption of Parliament, and Grafton himself came to epitomize the evils of the system. This was the situation which the pen of Junius was able to exploit. In letters which are all the more wounding because of the polite and stately manner in which he wrote, and with what seemed to be a deadly personal animosity toward Grafton, Junius denounced the government for its weakness and venality. Grafton's reputation has suffered unduly from the attention of this mordant satirist. In Parliament, important business was held up while Wilkes's supporters kept the case alive before a crowded, sometimes exasperated, but fascinated House. Yet it is fair to point out that Grafton was supported, at first by the whole ministry, by the king, by some liberal-minded men like Fox, and by the majority of the House, without whose votes the stand against Wilkes could never have been made. Many believed, with Fox, that the House must have control of its own membership, if it were to be an effective safeguard of the constitution against arbitrary powers, whether of the king or of the people.

Undoubtedly it was because he was laboring for months to combat the moves of the Wilkesites that Grafton was so ineffective in dealing with the American question, about which he did have positive views. The government repealed Townshend's duties, except for that on tea. Grafton would have liked to abolish this as well. But Hillsborough, who drafted the letter to the colonial governors in which the government's intentions were outlined, left out the passages about conciliation, to which the cabinet had assented, and stiffened those which referred to "execution of the laws" and "legislative authority" in a way which was bound to offend the Americans. Grafton would not resign upon this act of indiscipline, because he felt that it would seem that he was surrendering to Wilkes. But the good effect of his policy of friendship was lost and a further step taken to the ultimate disaster.

In fact, Hillsborough's attitude was shared by some others in the cabinet, which fatally lacked common purpose, because it was based upon no recognizable connection. Chatham's ideal of partyless patriotic government simply failed, first because Chatham had collapsed, then because his successor commanded no confidence. Apart from other embarrassments, Grafton lost credit over a legal case—a dispute over estates in Cumberland between the Duke of Portland and Sir James Lowther. The Treasury seemed anxious to find flaws in Portland's claim. Lowther was Bute's son-in-law and was suspected of enjoying favor at court, and Junius was quick to exploit the situation. As Grafton's stock fell, his administration fell apart. Lord Camden, who had supported the policy of conciliation with America, attacked the official policy and was dismissed. Lord Granby followed Camden out of the government, under pressure from Chatham. Charles Yorke, Hardwicke's son, was prevailed upon to accept the Chancellorship but, in an agony of uncertainty about his merits and responsibilities, he cut his throat. After this tragedy Grafton had had enough. He resigned, thankfully perhaps; he may be believed when he says that he had the feeling of "being released from business, and from an office which was peculiarly irksome to me." He was twice in office again, as Lord Privy Seal, from 1771 to 1775 and from 1782 to 1783, but his subsequent political career was uneventful.

R. Pares, *George III and the Politicians*, 1953.
J. Brooke, *The Chatham Administration, 1766–8*, 1956.

JOHN WILKES (1727–97) was a man of no fixed principles who found himself engaged in a series of important constitutional conflicts. His career was active and vivid, but historians dwell on it primarily because of the forces he aroused by his demagogic appeal. In the 1760s, when he was most active, English radicalism acquired a new impetus and direction.

He was the son of a wealthy distiller, educated at Leyden University, and married, to please his parents, to the daughter of Dr. Mead, a wealthy physician. She was ten years older than himself and they separated after she had borne him a daughter. He bought himself both a seat in Parliament (Aylesbury) and the colonelcy of the Buckinghamshire militia. Plausible and reckless, Wilkes lived giddily upon his wits. The devilment of the Hell Fire Club and the somewhat ludicrous blasphemies of the Monks of Medmenham can be evoked today by the curious visitor to the caves above West Wycombe. With Grafton, Dashwood, and Sandwich among others, he set out to scandalize society, always going a little further, with cards and women, than the orthodox could approve. He had entered politics as the supporter of Pitt, but in 1761, encumbered with debts, he sought advancement from Bute. When Bute refused to make him either Ambassador to Constantinople or Governor of Quebec, Wilkes applied himself angrily to political journalism.

In the *North Briton*, whose title ostensibly referred to the sinister encroachment of Scotsmen upon English public life, he attacked the ministry in general and Bute and the Peace of 1763 in particular; he was helped by the raffish poet Churchill and more cautiously by Earl Temple, who used him as a political weapon against the ministry. Before the 27th number of this weekly journal appeared he was threatened with prosecution and had to fight a duel with Lord Talbot. In Number 45 he sailed too close to the wind of royal displeasure, when he described as a falsehood the passage in the king's speech referring to the peace as "honorable to my crown and beneficial to my people." The ministry, Grenville, Halifax and Egremont, issued a General Warrant ordering the arrest of all responsible for the *North Briton*'s publication. Halifax, acting as a magistrate, had Wilkes detained in the Tower and his papers searched. When Temple replied defiantly to the government's order to remove Colonel Wilkes from his post as High Sheriff of the county, he was dismissed from his Lord-Lieutenancy. The government stood on treacherous ground. Wilkes, whose detention in the Tower enabled him to pose as a martyr while enjoying the attentions of his friends, secured his release on the grounds of parliamentary privilege. He then used his trial in the Court of Common Pleas in May 1763 to challenge the legality of the government's actions. The Chief Justice of Common Pleas, Pitt's friend, Pratt, put off decision about the legality of General Warrants, but declared that Wilkes was covered by parliamentary immunity since his offense was neither treason, felony, nor a breach of the peace. In his speech to the judge Wilkes said: "The liberty of all peers and gentlemen and, what touches me more sensibly, that of all the middling and inferior set of people . . . is in my case this day to be finally decided upon." He then accused the Secretaries of State of stealing his possessions and published their reply in the form of a pamphlet. In the Court of Common Pleas Pratt ruled against the legality of General Warrants and Wilkes recovered damages against the Undersecretary of State, Robert Wood. Now he cut himself off from more respectable political associates by his crude appeal to the people.

In November 1763 the House of Commons voted Number 45 a seditious libel and ordered it to be publicly burned. In the House of Lords Sandwich and Warburton, Bishop of Gloucester, brandished an obscene poem, the *Essay on Woman*, which Wilkes had been privately printing and which they had obtained by bribes, and the publication of pornography was added to the charges against him. Parliament was no longer disposed to allow

him the protection of privilege and voted accordingly. Wilkes was
wounded painfully in a duel with a Mr. Martin, which gave him an
excuse for not appearing in Parliament. In December he departed
for France; in January 1764 he was expelled from the House of
Commons. Before the end of the year, as he did not appear to
stand trial, he was outlawed. By his excesses Wilkes had contrived
to spoil a good case. Nevertheless the opposition made a further
issue of the General Warrants and the government won the division on the matter of their legality by only fourteen votes. The majority of members of the counties and the more open boroughs
voted against them. The opposition turned to other game, but in
the country Wilkes was not so quickly forgotten. The "Crown and
Anchor" clubs went on drinking their toasts to "Wilkes and Liberty." The wretch who had been bribed to hand over the *Essay on
Woman* could find no one to employ him and committed suicide.

In 1768 Wilkes returned from exile and presented himself for
election to Parliament. He could not persuade the City of London
to elect him: he secured 1,247 votes, but was bottom of the poll.
The great politicians, the establishment of the city, were no longer
prepared to take him seriously, so he looked for support in the
restless, fringe-of-town population of Middlesex, where the free
holders were unruly and squires were weak. In the radical parson
Horne Tooke, and Mr. Serjeant Glynn, an antiquarian lawyer,
Wilkes had two unorthodox men to work for his election. With a
rowdy troupe of Spitalfields weavers behind him, amid riots and
drunkenness, Wilkes was returned with a majority of 465. He then
had himself arrested, which had the desired result of arousing further excitement. On May 10 a man was killed when a crowd which
had come to take him to Parliament clashed with the troops defending the prison in St. George's Fields. The jury at the inquest
found a Scottish private guilty of murder (a grand jury at Guildford later found him not guilty) and Wilkes's letters made the most
of the theme of "Scottish butchers." He escaped the charge of outlawry when Mansfield found an error in the phrasing of the writ.
In June, however, he was fined and imprisoned on the original
charges. Disorder continued, coming to a climax when his supporter Glynn was elected for the other seat in Middlesex. An ugly
situation was developing in London, where strikes and stoppages
brought workmen out of overcrowded tenements to roam the
streets in protest against the ills of sweated labor. Grafton's min-

istry seems to have been virtually unanimous in its view that Wilkes should be expelled from Parliament. Pratt, now Lord Camden and Lord Chancellor, thought so; as, outside the government, did Fox. In February 1769, on the motion of Barrington, he was expelled, but he aroused support among radical members, was elected as alderman for a city ward, and then reelected for Middlesex unopposed. The government could not now withdraw. As he was explled, reelected, and expelled again, the case narrowed down to an issue of dangerous simplicity: the people *versus* the House of Commons.

The view of "the people" in this case could not be mistaken, for when the ministry, in the fourth election, put up Colonel Luttrell against him, the latter was defeated by 1,143 to 296. The House pronounced, however, that Luttrell had been elected. The justification for this extreme statement of the rights of Parliament was that it was necessary to defend its freedom of action in face of an illegal act of coercion—for so Wilkes's action appeared to his opponents. Others, however, saw his expulsion as a sign of the degenerate submission of the Commons to the executive and the court. On this count Grafton, as the Junius letters show, was especially vulnerable. Wilkes himself could not wait upon the niceties of constitutional debate so, with Horne Tooke to aid him, he appealed again to the people. In February 1768 the Society for the Defense of the Bill of Rights had met for the first time, its object being to get Wilkes into Parliament. It was largely middle class and could raise £16,000 to pay his debts and expenses. A concerted attack of petitions assailed the ministry, none more aggressive than that of the city, which now recognized Wilkes's value as a stick with which to beat the "corrupt" Parliament.

By April 1770, when he came out of prison, Wilkes was representative of a program, if not actually head of a party. Various opposition groups, Rockingham and Burke, Temple and Grenville, for their respective ends, roused public feeling. Apart from inquiries, for instance into the St. George's Fields Massacre, two points may be specially noticed: improvement in the system of trial by jury so as to reduce the power of judges (especially in libel cases) and the right of the public to the whole revenue of India. The aims were too disparate, the organization too weak, for the movement to succeed. The Society of the Bill of Rights split when Wilkes declined to allow its money to be used to pay the expenses of a printer who was jailed for his defiance of Mansfield. Horne

Tooke left the movement; Wilkes, who was more interested in his own cause than in radicalism, turned again to the mob. In 1771, when he was elected Sheriff of London, his platform was unabashedly demagogic. He advocated the abolition of the press gang and controlled bread prices. One more clash with the Commons came when they required three journalists to appear before them on the charge of reporting their proceedings. Again the issue was presented in the name of the people, but the real fight was between city and Parliament; it was as a city magistrate that Wilkes was involved, when the city authorities refused to hand over Mr. Miller of the *Evening Post*. When he, with the Lord Mayor and another city was called to the House to answer for their conduct, he reopened his personal grievances. But the prime minister, now Lord North, saw to it that the summons to Wilkes was made out for a day when Parliament would not be sitting; he was thus deprived of further opportunities of publicity.

In 1774 Wilkes was elected again for Middlesex and allowed to take his seat. He made little use of it, for now the poacher was turned gamekeeper. In 1776 he introduced a bill for parliamentary reform but withdrew it without a division. The initiative passed to other men. Wilkes contented himself with campaigning for the formal expunging of the resolution of February 1769. This was done, and handsomely, in 1782, "as being subversive of the Rights of the whole body of Electors of this Kingdom." Meanwhile he had become Chamberlain of the City in 1774 and he had acted with resolution against the mob in 1780, directing the Guards outside the Bank of England. Wilkes had become a respectable and useful citizen, interesting himself in prison reform and religious toleration. To George III, who found him surprisingly civil, he admitted that he "never was a Wilkite." He had ever been the cool, skeptical, amused spectator of his own career. In scarlet coat and white-powdered wig, living contentedly with his last mistress, Polly, and several bastard children, he survived into an age which scarce remembered the significance of the phrase engraved on his coffin: "The remains of John Wilkes, a Friend to Liberty."

P. Quennell, *Four Portraits*, 1945.
P. Rudé, *Wilkes and Liberty*, 1962.
I. R. Christie, *Wilkes, Wyvill and Reform*, 1962.
J. Brewer, "English Radicalism in the Age of George III," in J. G. A. Pocock, ed., *Three British Revolutions*, 1980.

THOMAS PAINE (1737–1809) wrote *The Rights of Man*, a textbook for the extreme radicals in the England of his day; he was also an international figure held in high repute by American rebels and French revolutionaries alike. Both in France and in America, however, there was a reaction: he was imprisoned by Robespierre and looked at askance by Americans, who found that the extreme views which had been serviceable during the War of Independence were inappropriate to more sober times. In writing and character he was bold and uncompromising to the point of pigheadedness. It was precisely that inability to see more than one side of the question that made him such an effective propagandist. He was not, except in his manner, original, but he was very influential.

Paine was born in the small Norfolk town of Thetford, where his father farmed in a small way and made stays. Thomas was much influenced by the Quakerism of his father, though he was confirmed in the Church of England. Because the Quakers did not approve of the Latin books used at school, he would not learn Latin. Apprenticed stay-maker, he went off to sea at the age of sixteen and served, by his own account, on the privateer *Terrible*, commanded by Captain Death! He soon returned to stay-making, set up his own business, and married; but his business failed, his wife died, and in 1761 he obtained a job on the excise. He was early in trouble for neglect of duty, but he survived in this service until 1774, when he was dismissed for voicing the grievances of the excise men in a tract. In the same year he separated from his second wife and sailed to America. Here he edited a magazine, *Pennsylvania Magazine or American Museum*, wrote articles for it condemning slavery and advocating republicanism and expressed the sentiment, which few as yet dared openly voice, in favor of complete independence for the colonies. In *Common Sense*, which appeared in January 1776, he argued, with a crudely forceful eloquence and logic, his case against the English constitution.

His writings were received with acclaim by the colonists. He was engaged in intelligence and staff work in 1777–78; on one occasion he distinguished himself by carrying a message in an open boat under a cannonade from the British fleet. In January 1779 his indiscretion landed him in trouble, and he had to give up his post as Secretary to the Committee for Foreign Affairs, when he made embarrassing revelations about the French alliance and American profiteering at a time when the French government was anxious to preserve a guise of neutrality. He was more a journalist than a public official and at heart an anarchist with a strong distrust of authority: "Government, like dress, is the badge of lost innocence; the palaces of kings are built on the ruins of the bowers of Paradise." Another sample of his writing gives an idea of his terse style: "Society is produced by our wants, and Government by our wickedness; the former promotes our happiness positively by uniting our affections: the latter negatively, by restraining our vices. The one encourages intercourse, the other creates distinctions. The first is a patron, the last a punisher." In the English government Paine had, of course, admirable material for his superficial and scornful analysis and the occasional trumpet-call to sedition: "Of more worth is one honest man to society, and in the sight of God, than all the crowned ruffians that ever lived." Paine wrote for ordinary men who could not fail to understand his meaning.

Once the war was over, Paine traveled in France and England, chiefly with a view to publicizing and selling plans for an iron bridge. The outbreak of the French Revolution ensured a second career for him. The events were stirring, their implications far-reaching; in Edmund Burke, author of the conservative, romantic *Reflections on the French Revolution*, he had a target who was brilliant, eloquent, and famous. Burke's appeal to the past, his idea of society as an organism and a mystical communion of living, dead, and still unborn, were nonsense and anathema to Paine. Paine was prone to oversimplify, but Burke was simply ignorant of the conditions which had produced the Revolution. Burke's sympathies were therefore, in Paine's view, romantically misplaced: "He is not affected by the reality of distress touching his heart, but by the showy resemblance of it striking his imagination. He pities the plumage, but forgets the dying bird." *The Rights of Man* came out in March 1791. In it Paine argued that the civil rights of man were a natural growth from the rights that men enjoyed as human beings: Burke venerated the English constitution, but what sort of constitution was it that denied the mass of the people the exercise of these rights? Paine's history with stock references to the Norman Conquest and the Glorious Revolution might be vague, but his arguments were sharp-edged. He was able to expose the persistent injustice and inequalities in England and to question hallowed conventions: hereditary monarchy and "mixed" government among them. In some points he was, however, cautious. Republican though he avowed himself, he was no extreme democrat, for he wanted to link the possession of the vote with the payment of taxes.

The first part of *The Rights of Man* was a success, though its vehement attack upon cherished English illusions roused fury. The publication of the second part, in February 1792, forecast, in a somewhat superficial way, that there must be revolutions to sweep away the old order. At the same time there would evolve a new idea: "Government founded on a moral theory, on a system of universal peace, on the indefeasible hereditary Right of Man." Paine was naive in his conception of man standing on the brink of a terrestrial paradise: would his nature change so much that "to be free it is sufficient that he wills it"? But in his enthusiasm for international cooperation, the rule of reason, even Free Trade, he embodies much of what is best in the thought of his time and anticipates the idealism of the Victorians, Mill, Cobden, and Gladstone. He was practical too in his analysis of domestic problems: he wanted graduated taxation, compulsory popular education, provision for the aged, a child allowance, and reform of the Poor Law. "The poor, as well as the rich, will then be interested in the support of the Government, and the cause and apprehension of riots and tumults will cease."

Paine had written a book which was both radical and positive. To his admirers he was an apostle of hope; to his detractors he was a dangerous, subversive traitor. His simple pronouncements appealed dangerously to simple men: no democratic thinker has been more challenging. Even Fox's liberalism was inhibited by the fears of men of property; he thought *The Rights of Man* a seditious libel. Indeed Paine's conduct invited criticism. When the French monarchy fell he was elected a delegate to the first Assembly of the Republic. While his book was being proceeded against in London, he enjoyed the welcome of his constituents in Calais and entered into the debates of the convention. Events were disillusioning. Bravely Paine opposed the spirit of revenge that seemed to prompt the enemies of Louis XVI and voted against the sentence of death. He was temperamentally and ideologically out of tune with Robespierre's Jacobins, and grew isolated; he was imprisoned, threatened with the guillotine. Illness and good luck, not the American ambassador, saved him. Paine emerged from this experience harrowed, with incipient persecution mania, and he worked off his feelings by devising invasion plans against England. Then he published *The Age of*

Reason. Its tone was polemical, popular, mocking. He affirmed a benevolent deism and denounced all churches as enemies of the individual conscience. "My own mind is my own church," he said, a Quaker idea. Revelation he discounted; the Virgin Birth and Resurrection he dismissed in a facile way. For the Bible and revelation he substituted nature. Much of this book is shallow. Paine was a great propagandist, because he was so unsubtle; for the same reason he was incapable of appreciating the complexities and depths of religious feeling. *The Age of Reason* is weak tea, well sugared; but it sustained radicals in their suspicions of the Church establishment. He offered what seemed to be wanted and needed: an undemanding, diluted humanist faith for the common man.

Paine was both enterprising and brave; he met his end with fortitude: "I have lived an honest and useful life to mankind; my time has been spent in doing good, and I die in perfect composure and resignation to the will of my creator." He never indeed underestimated his own worth, nor his services to mankind. In several ways his life was significant. He disseminated hostility toward authorities in church and state, skepticism about institutions and dogmas; he expressed a potent faith in the natural goodness of men; especially he invited the common man to interest himself in politics. In him the inarticulate found a voice and a sense of direction, stirred by his conviction that the happiness of individuals is the only test of the validity of governments.

A. O. Aldridge, *Man of Reason*, 1960.
H. H. Clark, ed., *Paine's Writings*, 1961.
C. Bonwick, *English Radicals and the American Revolution*, 1977.

CHRISTOPHER WYVILL (1740–1822) was an ordained country gentleman of strong personality and original views who led and organized radical opinion in his county, created a short-lived but important instrument of political pressure, and furthered the movement for parliamentary reform.

He came of an old Yorkshire family; after the death of his baronet cousin and brother-in-law in 1774 he came into the family estate of Constable Burton and a rent roll of £4,000 a year. From Queen's College, Cambridge, Wyvill had entered a family living, Black Otley in Essex, which he kept after he went to reside in Yorkshire; he was interested in ecclesiastical affairs but he handed over work and emoluments to a curate. As a clergyman he had qualms over the Thirty-Nine Articles and leaning toward Unitarianism. As a landowner he was not content to grumble about the corruption of court and government but used his influence to make the "county interest" mean something more than a few individual votes against the ministry. In 1779 there was discontent about Lord North's conduct of affairs. High taxation brought only stalemate in America, but public funds and places served, it seemed, to keep Lord North in power with a tame majority and a partisan King: members of Parliament were for sale. One solution, urged by Dr. Jebb, was to extend the popular side of the old constitution, notably the Westminster and Middlesex seats, and Wyvill was later to demand more representation for "those great unrepresented towns and districts of the metropolis." At first, however, he sought to exploit the grievances of the freeholders and to increase the number of county seats so as to balance the minions of the boroughs. In this he was supported by Sir George Savile, a Yorkshire county member. Wyvill was content at first to ride with the county magnates. The Yorkshire Association, mooted in his circular of November 1779, aired at a meeting of Yorkshire freeholders in December, and formed in the following spring, had the support of the Rockingham faction.

There was an impressive show of unanimity from the largest county. Grievances and solutions were alike plainly expressed: taxes were too high, executive power too large; the number of independent men of standing in the House of Commons should be increased. The Yorkshire Association, and others like it, should be instruments of reform "by legal and constitutional means." At the next general election a concerted opposition to opponents of reform would secure a House of Commons well disposed to reform. The movement grew rapidly. Petitions were sent in, committees of action formed in a number of counties; soon an informal central committee was sitting in London. In all this Wyvill led, organized, and inspired. In his private character and public behavior he epitomized the qualities of the independent politician, in whom, he believed, lay the salvation of the country: single-minded and energetic, cautious in tactics but assured and direct in all his dealings. Later in life he avowed that he only took part in politics from "a detestation of corruption, that execrable principle of government; from indignation at direct and open invasion of our rights; and from an honest zeal to defend public liberty."

The words make stirring reading in our century. They were also, however, the stock phrases of those politicians who had less altruistic motives for talking the language of reform. Though Wyvill and Granville Sharp wished their general assembly to be free from party ties and even individual members of Parliament, the latter were admitted; furthermore only twelve counties and four cities were represented. The movement never became truly national; in London, its authority was compromised by the parallel activities of the Westminster Committee, closely linked to Parliament through the patronage of Fox. Inevitably there was a discrepancy of aims: Wyvill was not a doctrinaire radical like Jebb, nor a demagogue like Charles James Fox. His ideas and the lobbying power of his followers lent power to the elbow of Rockingham and Burke and their projects of Economical Reform; they were not interested, however, in franchise reform. Meanwhile the extremism of men like Cartwright, who demanded "equal, annual, and universal representation," alarmed moderates. Wyvill toiled strenuously with petitions, plans and debates in committees but he found the going slow. In 1782–83, after the minor revolution of the Economical Reform measures, the movement reached a climax. He found an intelligent champion in William Pitt, through their mutual friend Lord Mahon. Wyvill's object was to produce a nationwide demonstration in favor of reform in the constituencies. Despite Yorkshire's firm lead, this never gathered enough force to convince Pitt that he must go beyond modest proposals (Wyvill wanted to abolish fifty boroughs). Neither in opposition nor in office did Pitt manage to secure a majority: there was indifference in the country; in Parliament, where two-thirds voted against his second Reform Bill, a stone wall.

Wyvill was active again when the French Revolution aroused popular feeling. He found Jacobinism "wild work" and he deplored the emergence of "a lawless and furious rabble" but he did not lose faith in reform. In 1811 he joined in a Reform Society which contained such varied names as Burdett, Cobbett, and Henry Hunt. He died ten years before the Reform Bill which embodied his ideals. He had done more than any man to educate and prepare public opinion for constitutional reform.

I. R. Christie, *Wilkes, Wyvill and Reform*, 1961.

LORD GEORGE GORDON (1751–93) was the third son of the Duke of Gordon. During the American War the need for soldiers was urgent and it was felt desirable to remove the restrictions which prevented Roman Catholics from serving in the armed forces. In 1778 an act simply required Catholics to take an oath of loyalty to the Crown. In fact, the eighteenth century had been notably tolerant and in Canada Lord North's government had already granted a position to the Catholic Church. Yet Scotland still held out against toleration and the fierce outcry against these measures, which burst out there, inspired some English Protestants to atone for their previous laxity by rising in wrath. An association was formed of which Lord George Gordon became the leader.

He showed himself to be a somewhat feckless critic of institutions and personalities in the eighteenth century "establishment": in a brief career in the navy he made himself thoroughly unpopular for his advocacy of the lower deck. He was as lightly regarded by other opposition leaders as by the ministers themselves, but feeling that the mantle of John Knox had dropped upon him, he began to imitate the Reform Movements that were pouring petitions into Parliament. While they protested against undue growth of royal influence in Parliament, Gordon alleged though with little evidence in support a sinister growth of Catholic influence. In 1780 he attracted more publicity for his petitions by arranging a demonstration at Westminster in favor of his cause. Among the citizens of London many extreme Protestants could be found. In the city some were undergoing difficulties because of the war and its effect upon trade. North's concessions to the Irish seemed to stand in need of revoking and the defeats of the war seemed, as they do to every country, only explicable by the existence of sinister treacherous influences. While Gordon and Lowther, on June 2, presented their petition in the Commons, a large crowd gathered to support them outside. They and the Commons shared in turn the benefit of Lord George's oratory. The crowd at first did little more than impede or hustle M.P.s, but in the absence of any proper constabulary it grew more lawless. Criminals and mobsters began to exploit the situation. The government hesitated to act without the support of the magistrates, and the magistrates of the city were frightened of exposing their persons and their houses to reprisals by calling out the troops. Foreign chapels and private houses were

looted. Lord Mansfield's Bloomsbury house was pillaged, his famous library destroyed. Distilleries in Holborn were attacked and
the mob was swelled by released prisoners from Newgate. At the
Bank of England ink pots were melted down into bullets to keep
away the crazed and drunken crowd: there were but few in whom
more savage instincts had not overborne political or religious feelings. Readers of *Barnaby Rudge* will recall Dickens's memorable account of the riots.

   After four nights and three days of incendiarism and violence
the government, together with Rockingham, the opposition leader,
decided to call out the Guards. The common council of the City of
London, usually chary of having its policy imposed from without,
acquiesced. Lord George Gordon was captured on June 9 and sent
to the Tower, but the troops did not gain complete control of the
situation until the twelfth; 458 people had been killed or wounded
during the outbreak. The riots had unfortunately a more harmful
effect upon the opposition than on the government. Politicians realized how dangerous it was to evoke the masses outside Parliament
and incite them into supporting a parliamentary maneuver. Lord
George was not among the twenty-one who eventually suffered the
death penalty, but his future could only lie in the milder paths of
eccentricity. He became a convert to the Jewish faith and in 1788
he was imprisoned for a libel on the Queen of France (the age of
chivalry not yet being quite dead). Understandably, no one would
go surety for his good behavior, and he continued in prison until
his death from jail fever five years later.

C. Hibbert, *King Mob*, 1958.
G. F. E. Rudé, *Paris and London in the 18th Century*, 1969.

CHARLES JENKINSON, 1st EARL OF LIVERPOOL (1727–1808),
who played a large and controversial role in politics under George
III, was a descendant of Anthony Jenkinson, the Elizabethan explorer who penetrated into Muscovy and Central Asia. Succeeding
generations had been less bold and the family had settled into the
life of Oxfordshire gentry. They provided successive generations of
baronets and parliamentary members and had Jacobite sympathies. Charles came from a younger and relatively poor branch of
the family. His father commanded the Blues at Dettingen. He was

educated at the grammar school at Burford and at Charterhouse; then at University College, Oxford. In the hotly contested Oxfordshire election of 1760 a lively election song which he composed was believed to have carried the day for the wealthy court candidate, Sir Edward Turner. Jenkinson's earlier more serious poetic efforts had found few readers, but he was recommended to the notice of the Earl of Bute, who made him a private secretary and became his close friend. In 1761 he was made an Undersecretary of State and became an M.P. for the borough of Cockermouth.

Under Bute and Grenville, Jenkinson managed much of the electoral work on which the ministries depended for support. With the more frequent changes of minister in the first years of George III's reign, the individual ministers did not always have time to build up large connections in the constituencies where their government departments had posts to offer. In these circumstances the Treasury became more important in keeping in touch with local election agents. Jenkinson, who was made a Secretary at the Treasury, kept up a large correspondence with agents and voters throughout the country. In 1765 when Lord Rockingham's party came to power and interrupted his political ascent, he was given a post in the household of George III's mother, the Dowager Princess of Wales, and George himself came to rely heavily upon him for advice, especially after Bute's retirement from politics. He was referred to as the leader of the king's supporters in the House of Commons and he enjoyed many high positions. In 1766 he was made a Lord of the Admiralty (and was shown the door by Grenville's servants, since this post meant a break with one of his old patrons). In 1767 he became a Lord of the Treasury; under Lord North, Vice-Treasurer for Ireland and a Privy Councillor. In 1775 he secured from Fox a lucrative sinecure, the Clerkships of the Pells, and soon afterward became Master of the Mint. In 1778, while the conflict with the American colonies was in progress, he rose to be Secretary at War and, though he thought North "a weak mind" incapable of facing the dangers that clustered around him, he showed his loyalty to George by defending North's dwindling majorities. He was frequently named by the enemies of the king as one of the secret advisers at court and he was believed to have immense influence.

Accounts of his fawning manner and gestures of humility suggest Uriah Heep. "For God's sake, Mr. Jenkinson," Lady Bute cried out, "do not make those motions." His eyelids twitched and fluttered and his whole appearance lent color to the idea that he was an arch-intriguer. He was methodical and pernickety: the thermometer at his house always stood at 60. Careful compilations of statistics and notes made him a valuable assistant to senior ministers, while his treatise on *Coins of the Realm* was authoritative enough to be reprinted by the Bank of England as late as 1880. "A bureaucrat rather than a politician" (Gash), sometimes his talents were employed in politics, drawing up lists of junior officials who might suffer from a change of power higher up, or calculating the possible votes in a local election or a parliamentary debate. On the fall of North's administration he retired temporarily from the government and made a collection of treaties although he still conducted negotiations for the king.

When George again had a minister to his taste, the younger Pitt, "Jenky" returned, as Lord Hawkesbury, at the head of the Board of Trade, which Burke had abolished but Pitt revived. Pitt was warned that his inclusion in the government would imply too much royal influence, but "Jenky" remained in the background and dealt principally with economic affairs; he supported the policy of "defense" against that of "opulence." In July 1789, when his cousin, Sir Banks Jenkinson, the 6th baronet, died, he succeeded to the family estates. The extent of his influence is shown by the fact that he was able to procure the position of Collector of the Customs Inward, one of the lucrative places which Pitt had declared his intention of abolishing. In 1796 he became Earl of Liverpool and was allowed to quarter the arms of the city with those of his family. The mark of favor was specially requested by the citizens of Liverpool because of his vigorous defense of the slave trade which brought in such a large fortune to the port. His last parliamentary speech was in 1800 on the subject of Ireland and, as one might expect, he took his cue from George III rather than Pitt in the dispute between king and minister. From 1800 onward he suffered from a debility in the knees which prevented him from standing, and the last years of his life were devoted to safeguarding the interests of his son. "Young Jenky" was later to be the prime minister of England during some of the most eventful years in its history.

N. S. Tucker, ed., *The Jenkinson Papers, 1760–1766,* 1949.

EDMUND BURKE (1729–97) was an ineffectual politician in his day; nor did he influence directly the generations that immediately followed him. In the last hundred years, however, he has been more justly valued as the prophet of empiricism in politics, and the lover of liberty within the frame of order, who taught that specific political rights grounded on law are worth more than abstract notions of natural right.

Burke was the son of a Protestant lawyer of Dublin. His mother was Catholic, while he was educated at a Quaker school; all his life he was religious in feeling and practice, open-minded, but a staunch Anglican. In five years at Trinity College, Dublin, he seems to have read widely and broodingly; though he went to London to read law, his mind turned to philosophy and when his father cut off his allowance he made money by writing. In 1756 he published his *Vindication of Natural Society and Inquiry into the Origin of Ideas of the Sublime and Beautiful* and in the same year made a happy marriage with Jane Nugent, a doctor's daughter. He was an early member of the Club, where what Dr. Johnson called his "stream of mind" and his warm, unguarded manner made him friends among intellectuals and artists. In 1759 he became the anonymous editor of Dodsley's *Annual Register*, which brought him a little cash and much knowledge of public men. In 1761 he became secretary to William Gerard Hamilton, who was Chief Secretary for Ireland. "Single-speech" Hamilton may have been selfish, Burke impetuous; they quarreled in 1764, but the connection gave Burke a foothold on the political cliff. It was steep going for one who had neither estate nor birth, but Burke was an agile climber. Rockingham made him his private secretary in 1765 and he entered Parliament with a seat provided by Lord Verney. Rockingham lent Burke money and listened sometimes to his ideas. From the cramped position of this short-lived ministry, nothing but a faction in the king's eyes, and from the disastrous failure of Chatham's "patriotic" government which ensued, Burke evolved a theory of party to which he gave memorable expression in his *Thoughts on the Present Discontents* (1770). He did not lack material, for Chatham had been ill and his successor, Grafton, ineffective, but he rose above personalities to present a vision of the future. Coherence, in his view, could only come from "party," even if this seemed to narrow the field of choice; if policies were to be consistent then "good men must combine."

Philosopher and rhetorician, a commentator ready to tackle any subject in depth, even an economist (Adam Smith said that he was the only man who had independently reached the same conclusions as himself): surely his prospects were brilliant. He had unfortunately a gift for arousing suspicion and hostility. Against his deep insights we must set superficial failings in judgment and taste; against the generosity and largeness of mind which his friends knew, recklessness, bombast, and a display that smelt of corruption to his rivals. How, they asked, did Burke get the money or the fine house at Beaconsfield, Gregories, where he entertained his family and camp followers, known collectively and contemptuously as "the Burkes"? He was probably honest and certainly heavily in debt. Without Rockingham's generosity he might have foundered after the collapse of East India Company stock in 1769: Lord Verney, his patron, was ruined, he and his brother William heavily involved in the ill-advised speculation.

In the House Burke was a leader of the Foxite Whigs. There was plenty to oppose in the government of Lord North and later of Pitt. Indeed, we may wonder if there has ever been, in a comparable period, such a succession of great issues, mingling passion, and principle, as in the two decades 1770–90. America, Ireland, India, the constitutional powers of the king, and the French Revolution— in all these matters Burke's was a loud and insistent voice. We read his majestic sentences and recognize a wonderful gift for phrasing ideas in words which have a validity beyond the events which prompted them: "a great writer," said Hazlitt—and who better to judge? Burke's tragedy was that, in the Commons, where power lay, he was a clumsy performer. His appearance was fine enough, though when he took to wearing spectacles on his long nose he became a cartoonist's delight; but he was so hasty that his friends often had to tug at his coattails to keep him from blurting out some indiscretion. He felt things too deeply, too readily. There were times for deep emotion in that phlegmatic assembly and, as the elder Pitt had shown, times for grave and lofty sentiment, but Burke had neither the right manner nor the saving sense of timing. His speeches were meant to be read, and he delivered them rapidly in a strong brogue with awkward gestures. Though he hardly ever failed to say something important and impressive, his flowered periods were often delivered to empty or yawning benches. The man whom Grafton had thought, in 1768, "the readiest man upon all points perhaps in the whole house" had become before the end of his career "the dinner bell." Young members amused themselves by provoking him, then streamed out to dinner when he rose to speak. His administrative powers were hardly tested, but we may guess that his want of balance, the tendency to exaggeration which turned the trial of Warren Hastings into a sickening charade, would have betrayed him if he had ever had important responsibilities. So committed a party man, so positive a politician, it was Burke's misfortune that for the best years of his life, like Fox, he was confronted by the sedate and immovable North, the formidable Pitt. Even so, he plainly lacked the ordinary political skills. His greatness was in his ideas rather than in his acts, though these reveal again and again integrity and kindness. When Crabbe, a penniless but aspiring poet, came to London, he received money and encouragement which was as generous as it was discerning. All his life Burke remembered what it was to be poor. His public attitudes, his steady sympathy for oppressed minorities, drew upon deep wells of private compassion.

Upon the American question Burke followed the line of his friends Rockingham and Fox, opposed coercion and the subsequent war. He knew little about the American leaders and seems to have believed that proper management would create a bond of sentiment which would be sufficient by itself. We may doubt whether the generous vision of the philosopher would have been interpreted as anything but weakness by the speculators and opportunists of the North American colonies. His memorable words in the speech on conciliation were nonetheless a justifiable rebuke to Lord North's government: "Magnanimity in politics is not seldom the truest wisdom; and a great empire and little minds go ill together."

Party interest inevitably colored Burke's policies and pronouncements. He supported the concessions of Lord North to Ireland and the subsequent grant of legislative independence in 1782, but he opposed Pitt's logical proposals for free trade in Ireland in 1785, following too easily the specious claim of Fox that Pitt was "bartering English trade for Irish slavery." He was prominent in the campaign for "Economical Reform" and inspired the sensible and salutary measures of 1782. Burke was an advocate of honesty in government and genuine in his hatred of corruption, but the aim of the campaign was to reduce the influence exercised by the Crown through that patronage which the Whigs themselves would have liked to use. When, through tactical moves and by the adroit handling of that patronage, Pitt established himself, he was thought by Fox's followers to be most vulnerable on the question of India. Even this cannot, however, excuse the lengths to which Fox and Burke went in their vendetta against Hastings. Burke allowed his sense of fair play to be blinded by his passionate feeling for "the undone millions" of India. Party feeling, personal sense of grievance, and a true concern for oppressed minorities, wherever they might be, were mingled inextricably in his heated mind. The Whigs had lost patronage; the Burkes had lost money in India. Could Burke be objective? Unfortunately he lacked the accurate knowledge which might have strengthened his arguments, put him on his guard against Philip Francis, and restrained his rhetoric. Burke's picture of Hastings as a wild animal, a greedy sadist, was neither great art nor sound politics. Yet he believed that he was appealing to posterity—and posterity, looking back on the trial as the crisis of confidence of an imperial power, can say that he did not appeal in vain. The trial which began with acclaim in February 1788 was, however, an irrelevant bore before the end of the year. Five years later, when Hastings was acquitted, Burke's reputation had suffered more than anybody's; indeed, he was thought by some to be mad.

In fact he was superbly sane. In 1789 liberal-minded men acclaimed the revolutionary events in Paris. Burke looked to the past—and to the future. His *Reflections* on the revolution, published in 1790, were designed to show that the revolution was bad and dangerous because, unlike the ordered constitutional evolution of English history, it was based upon the false assumption that the past could be ignored and its institutions destroyed. Where others could see only enthusiasm or excess, he saw a vision of violence and blood. He was proved right by events and he became an apostle of the new conservatism. His ideas were later travestied by die-hards who saw Jacobinism lurking in every proposal of reform, but he played into their hands by his own impassioned language. While his celebrated eulogy of Marie Antoinette is a breath-taking piece of prose, it trembles, too, on the brink of absurdity: too true that, as Paine said, he "pities the plumage but forgets the dying bird." There were immediate consequences, too, of Burke's apostasy, as his enemies saw it. In May 1791 he broke with Fox in the most public way. To Fox's whispered inquiry he replied so that all could hear: "Yes, there is a loss of friends—I know the price of my conduct—I have done my duty at the price of my friend—our friendship was at an end." With him went Portland and many Whigs. The Foxites whom he had exalted by his theory of party were reduced to a fragment, an insignificant personal following. Burke did not benefit personally from joining the ministerial party. He retired from Parliament in July 1794 and accepted a pension, for which he was scurrilously attacked. He had opposed the removal of disabilities from Unitarians in 1792 but he supported the foundation of Maynooth College for training Catholic priests and he established a school for French refugees at Penn. He was busy to the last denouncing the revolutionaries in letters to the kings and emperors of Europe. His will was weakened by the death of his son Richard in 1794, but he kep his crusade going to the end.

There is no one remotely like Burke in our history. He was a committed politician who happened also to be a man of great intuitive powers and poetic sensibility. His mind, wrote Morley, was "full of the matter of great truths." He can be assessed by what he professed to despise: "sophists, calculators, and economists." Facts and perspectives were indeed blurred in the sentimental mist conjured up by his hot spirit. But let us recall the wonderful reply to Foxite jeers, quoting Paul: "I am not mad, most noble Festus, but speak forth the words of truth and soberness." Then we may assess the positive contributions of a man who, in Cobban's phrase, taught men again "the deeper realities of social life," and whose idea that power and wealth, whether in individuals or in the state, imply a trust, with commensurate responsibilities, has been of supreme value in our history.

Sir P. Magnus, *Edmund Burke*, 1939.
A. Cobban, *Burke and the Revolt against the Eighteenth Century*, 2nd edn., 1960.
Stanley Ayling, *Edmund Burke*, 1988.

CHARLES WATSON WENTWORTH, EARL OF MALTON and **2nd MARQUIS OF ROCKINGHAM** (1730–82), was an important figure in the politics of George III's reign. His large estates, his calm and disinterested approach, and his common sense together placed him in the position of leading a distinct party for nearly twenty years. More brilliant men than he were willing to serve

under him, and the second at least of his two short administrations
was rich in achievement.

He was indeed a characteristic product of the political conditions of the time. If he had not existed, one feels, someone else
would have had a similar career, because of the need for a statesman with the personal gifts to form and lead a connection which
would be close enough to provide a government. With party ties
loose where they existed at all, with men counting before measures, much was asked of a political leader. He must either be conciliatory to the point of negation, like North, or he must be seen to
stand for some principles which would be acceptable to the king as
well as to the mass of independent members. The principles of the
Rockingham Whigs, who were a more stable and coherent body
than any other faction of the time, became increasingly unpalat-
able to the king as the American War proceeded; it was the failure
of this war which gave them, at last, the chance to put their principles into action.

Rockingham's estates, principally in Yorkshire and Ireland,
produced a rental estimated in 1761 at £24,000 a year. Arthur
Young praised the management of his estates, saying that "he
never saw the advantages of a great fortune applied more nobly to
the improvement of a country." His early activities in Parliament
were concerned with promoting the interests of the Yorkshire
woolgrowers. He was a keen racing man, a member of the newly
formed Jockey Club, and active in promoting the meetings at Doncaster and York. Upon such pursuits he might have been prepared
to spend his life—but he inherited, too, a political tradition. His father, who had died in 1750, had owed his advancement in the
peerage to the Pelhams. It was natural that Rockingham should
succeed, in the years after Newcastle's resignation in 1762 and subsequent eclipse, to the leadership of the attenuated Newcastle interest. He was, however, a diffident politician and extraordinarily
inexperienced when he succeeded Grenville as First Lord of the
Treasury in July 1765. He had only been, for short periods, Lord-
Lieutenant of the West Riding and a Lord of the Bedchamber, and
he seems, unlike Bute before him, to have had no illusions about
his fitness for high office: "Howsoever unsuitable I might be for
that office from my health and inexperience in that sort of business, yet I thought it incumbent upon me to acquiesce in the attempting it."

The ministry had certain assets. Rockingham was, in Burke's words, "a man of honor and integrity." He approached his task in a spirit of fairness. The ministry was a party one in that the main posts were filled by his candidates; but he tried, too, to rebuild the Pelham system upon a broad base and was always ready to receive recruits. The crucial figure here was Pitt, who made it plain that he would not serve in any but a dominant capacity. Grafton, who admired him, thus became disaffected, divided from the start. The choice of Grafton and Conway as Secretaries of State underlined the inexperience of this ministry. "An administration of boys" George III called it. Grafton was indeed only thirty, while Conway, the principal spokesman in the Commons, was no match for Pitt or Grenville. After a promising start, the administration fell apart. The unpopular cider tax was abolished and the window tax modified; General Warrants were declared illegal and with them some of the debris of the Wilkes case. The question of American taxation, in which the government stood between the colonists' resentment and the reluctance of English squires to pay for American defense, was resolved by a supple maneuver: the repeal of the Stamp Act was preceded by a Declaratory Act affirming the right of Parliament to tax the colonies. Commercial legislation included a treaty with Russia and the opening of certain ports in the West Indies to stimulate Caribbean trade. The administration drifted, however, toward crisis. The king seemed to regard it as a stop-gap, while the Duke of Cumberland, who was a useful patron and intermediary with the king, died a few months after it was formed. Grafton himself resigned in April 1766; Richmond, his successor, was thirty-one, virtually without political experience. Rockingham allowed his ministry to crumble. Conway was persuaded to stay on and serve under Chatham, whom the king summoned to form a government in July, when the pressure for a stronger head of affairs grew clamorous. Other members remained loyal to Rockingham and in their resignation from office together anticipated the party system of a later age.

Either because of the influence of the views of his secretary, Edmund Burke, upon the necessity of party, developed in his *Thoughts on the Present Discontents* (1770), or because he was anxious not to find himself again in the weak position of his first ministry, Rockingham insisted that, if he returned to office, it should be on his own terms. George was equally adamant for his right to select ministers. As the American War developed, and Rockingham and his associates continued to oppose it, even to the point of deploring British victories on the grounds that they postponed the independence which they regarded as both right and inevitable, George held more firmly to North. In these circumstances the opposition turned to the question of royal influence and planned to reduce it. When the movement for parliamentary reform swelled with county resolutions and petitions, Rockingham made certain contacts with it. His friend Savile was active in Yorkshire, where the freehold franchise was large, but Rockingham's main concern was to increase aristocratic independence, and a better means to this end was to attack the bloated establishment through which the Crown exercised its patronage: this was Burke's program of "Economical Reform." He was chary of popular excitements. As he wrote to a friend in February 1780, "There are so many visionary schemes and expedients by way of reform on float that a general confusion and disagreement will ensue." In that month he introduced his bill for "the better regulation of His Majesty's civil establishments." After keen debate and some success it was rejected, but Rockingham was encouraged to persist in this weapon of opposition, safer, as the Gordon Riots seemed to show, than direct appeal to the people, more damaging as an issue than Ireland.

In March 1782 North resigned and Rockingham took office with a strong hand of cards. He had held back to the point at which George III had virtually surrendered to him: as Richmond put it, "all at your feet in the manner you would wish, and with the full means to do what is right." The king had even considered abdication before accepting Rockingham's conditions, a free hand with regard to American independence, economical reform, and the choice of ministers. In the latter, however, George had one compensation, for to offset Fox, whom he hated, there was Shelburne. Only Rockingham's tact prevented an open breach between the two Secretaries of State. Starting at a dark point of the war, lasting only four months, this was nonetheless a notable ministry. In Ireland he endeavored to counter those critics who said that North's economic concessions were illusory by giving Ireland greater constitutional independence. Following the advice which Burke had expressed often in speeches, his government tried to build upon goodwill at the cost of formal ties. The right of the British Parliament to legislate for Ireland was abrogated, as was the right of the Privy Council to alter Irish legislation. Indeed the constitutional links between Britain and Ireland became very slender. The Lord-Lieutenant of Ireland was a member of the British cabinet and Acts of Parliament required the Great Seal. Otherwise for a brief period Ireland enjoyed virtual independence. At home something was done to answer charges of corruption in public affairs: committees inquired into the methods whereby loans had been raised and contracts granted; salaries were introduced in certain grades of the civil service who had hitherto been paid, or had paid themselves, out of fees. Crewe's Act took away the vote from revenue officers who were supposed to be directly amenable to pressure from the state, their immediate employer. Clark's Act forced government contractors to choose between their contracts and their seats in Parliament.

In the midst of this activity, on July 1, Rockingham, who had never been a robust man, died of influenza. If he had lived, the split which led to the brief administrations first of Shelburne, then of Fox and North, and subsequently the emergence of Pitt, might not have occurred, and Fox, for one, might have had a more constructive career. Rockingham was not the last nor the least of those prime ministers whose task it has been to create a harmonious group in which more brilliant men can work. Langford writes of "his instinct for compromise." For all his limitations, the words of Burke's epitaph ring true: "His virtues were his means."

R. Pares, *George III and the Politicians*, 1953.
P. Langford, *The First Rockingham Administration 1765–6*, 1973.

JOHN DUNNING, 1st BARON ASHBURTON (1731–83), was a spokesman in Parliament for those Whigs who were, or professed to be, alarmed by George III's use of prerogative power. He was a combative barrister who first attracted attention by his defense of the English East India Company against the Dutch in 1762, and became Solicitor-General in Grafton's ministry, 1768–70. He resigned during the Wilkes affair because he thought that Wilkes should be heard in his own defense before his letter about the "massacre" of St. George's fields was voted a libel. He became famous by his resolution of 1780 "that the influence of the Crown has increased, is increasing, and ought to be diminished." Following upon attacks by Burke, Barré, and others, Dunning expressed the view of the Rockingham Whigs that Lord North and George III were engaged in a conspiracy to pervert by place and bribery the independence of members of Parliament. India furnished an important field of patronage, the American War produced rich contracts, and disasters in this war made North unpopular; so the resolution was carried by eighteen votes. After a period of oscillating votes, Dunning attacked again, with a demand reminiscent of the Long Parliament, that Parliament should not dissolve until its grievances were met. This time he was defeated and North survived. Independent country members wished to pare down government expenditure, but they were reluctant to be ruled by the Rockinghamites, and they distrusted the volatile Fox. Dunning possibly went too far in evoking the struggles of the seventeenth century. Whig historians have certainly made too much of his famous resolution. He was also, however, a doughty champion of liberty in the law courts where he defended the rights of juries in libel cases, and Horace Walpole described his *Doctrines Lately Promulgated concerning Juries, Libels, etc.* (1764) as "the finest piece . . . written for liberty since Lord Somers."

P. Brown, *The Chathamites*, 1967.

FREDERICK, 8th LORD NORTH and, two years before his death, **2nd Earl of Guilford** (1732–92), was prime minister, in a limited sense, for twelve years. He owed his power to the support of the king, to his administrative talents, and especially to his hold over members of the House of Commons. He appears, however, to have been inadequate in the face of the grave problems of the later years of office, Ireland, the reform movement, and the American War. He himself felt that he was unsuited to the demands made by war, and posterity has confirmed his estimate.

He was educated at Eton and Trinity College, Oxford. At twenty-two he entered Parliament for Banbury, whose corporation was always amenable to the head of the family at neighboring Wroxton Abbey. In 1759 he became a Lord of the Treasury under Newcastle and remained there through the ministries of Bute and Grenville. Removed by Rockingham, he was further advanced by Chatham, who made him Chancellor of the Exchequer after the death of Townshend in 1767. In 1770 he took on the leadership of the ministry relinquished by Grafton. He spoke well and wittily; he was efficient and sensible about financial matters. In his reluctance to be committed ahead and in his political shrewdness he recalls Walpole, but time was to show that he lacked that minister's energy and ruthlessness. It is fair, too, to suggest that North's rapid rise owed much to luck. Chatham's physical collapse, Grafton's embroilment in the Wilkes case, and Rockingham's party ties, left the field open to a minister who would put the conduct of government before consistency of principle. North had no large personal following, but this enabled him to secure the sympathy of independent backbenchers and to enlist in his ministry men from all connections. The Grenvillites felt free to return to office; one of them, Suffolk, became Secretary of State in 1771. Grafton himself was Privy Seal; Dartmouth, who had been a Rockinghamite, became Secretary of the Colonies; and Sandwich, who had been associated with Bute, went to the Admiralty. North took a modest view of his own role. His executive authority was only that of his department, the Treasury, and in the cabinet he did not press his views. At first the administration basked in the favor of the king, business and city interests, and a majority in Parliament. The prime concern of merchant and landowner was a return to what they saw as normal budgeting, with the reduction of the debt and of rates of taxation swollen by war. That this involved reductions in the army and navy did not concern them, except when some flurry, such as the Spanish attack on Port Egmont in the Falkand Islands in 1770, revealed shortcomings. North sought to avoid entanglements abroad and thus to find a million pounds a year for the reduction of the debt. Eventually this might have led to the reduction of the Land Tax; meantime North pegged it at 3s.

North's talent for the conciliation of interests can be studied in his handling of the complex Indian problem. Here action was called for, because of the boom and subsequent slump of East India stock, caused by widespread buying for influence and patronage in the lucrative affairs of the company. The problem was made more acute by the fact that against the private fortunes of speculators and exploiters there was a serious imbalance of trade which threatened the company's future. Furthermore, the company, which was wading deep in Indian native politics, had to be subjected to some measure of control. Out of this situation, following inquiries which emphasized the corruption of company officials and a vote upon the specific case of Clive (in which North voted against him, but seems to have been relieved that the censure motion was lost), emerged the Regulating Act of 1773. This secured the immediate financial future of the company, by a compulsory loan and by freeing the tea trade from duties payable on re-export. There was to be a supreme court of justice and supreme presidency, Bengal being elevated above Madras and Bombay and placed under a Governor-General and council of four, appointed by Parliament. The scheme represents a typical compromise between the extremes of commercial independence and state control. Because of the value of the patronage and the persistence of problems inherent in the company's expansion, India was to be the subject of further legislation in 1783 and 1784. But North, who showed moderation in the face of the temptation to increase the patronage of the Crown, had achieved his object: the stability of the company and thus of England's position in India.

America offered still more intractable problems. Here North reaped the harvest of earlier and hasty sowings, notably Townshend's duties of 1767. It may be argued that there could be no solution, in the long term, other than independence, but it does seem that North's administration, unimaginative before, feeble during the war, had the worst of both worlds. The unloading of tea in America to help the East India Company's trade balance, and the subsequent dispute with Boston in December 1773, may be laid, moreover, at North's door. The closure of the port of Boston merely served to unite that town with other colonies which had hitherto disapproved of extreme measures. It is ironic too that the colonists' suspicions were increased by a measure which was states manlike in itself. The Quebec Act gave Canada a legislative council and allowed the French to keep their own laws and priests, but it guaranteed also the extension of Canada down to the Ohio and thus barred the expansion westward of the coastal colonies. So New England puritans and property agents convinced themselves that North intended to enslave them. He, myopic and badly advised, believed that he had only to coerce Massachusetts for the disturbances to subside. From the meeting of the pan-colonial congress in 1774 to the skirmish of Lexington in April 1775, the battle of Bunker Hill in June 1775, and the Declaration of Independence in July 1776, North was but a spectator of events. His amiable weaknesses were exposed as the administration drifted from expedient to expedient, discovering too late the cost of military unpreparedness. Gage advised the government to send large forces at once;

but the army was too small for effective land war and the navy was hampered by a shortage of commissioned ships. Since North would not dictate a policy his ministers pursued several policies at once. Lord George Germain wanted swift military blows; Sandwich, afraid of invasion from France, wished to keep the fleet at home. North himself hoped for effective action by the loyalists. He was always obsessed with the problem of National Debt, knowing that his majority depended upon his reputation for economy.

Howe demanded 20,000 troops for 1777, received only 2,500, and felt himself unable to act at a time when the Americans were relatively weak. In October 1777 Burgoyne had to surrender at Saratoga, victim of casual and overoptimistic planning. A big naval and military effort was planned for 1778; at the same time commissioners were sent to treat with congress. But in that year French forces came to tilt the scales. In the following year Spain entered the war and Gibraltar was besieged. The navy was precariously stretched and not yet effective. The recriminations which followed the indecisive battle of Ushant in 1778 between Keppel and Palliser and the former's trial weakened the ministry. By 1779 Howe was defeatist and urged the ministry to come to peace. But George III was convinced that there was principle at stake in what had become a global war. North's political survival became the king's obsession. He begged to resign. "I am not equal in abilities to the station which I ought to hold, as the place next the director of publick affairs at this time," he wrote to the king in November 1779. He was accurate as well as modest in his analysis of the weakness of a government of separate and squabbling departments: "In critical times, it is necessary that there should be one directing minister." He was, however, culpably weak, even negligent. Robinson said in 1779 that he was "the original cause of the bad situation of everything." He could not or would not make a decision, preferring to trust to time to provide a solution. "Nothing can goad him forward," said the Attorney-General Thurlow in January 1780; "He is the very clog that loads everything."

Ireland meanwhile displayed trends uncomfortably close to the American pattern. The American War, moreover, produced a depression in those trades which exported to America or France. The Protestant gentry formed volunteer associations to take over home defense and release regular troops for service abroad. But when Lord North failed to remove some of the restrictions upon Irish trade, as Buckinghamshire, the Lord-Lieutenant, wished, this force became a weapon in the hands of Irish patriots. Flood, Grattan, and their followers called for freedom of Irish trade and greater constitutional independence. Moreover they were encouraged by Fox and his Whig friends to see their challenge in fundamental terms of liberty and oppression. In 1780, too late to assuage Irish discontents, North made concessions: the right to trade freely with the colonies, freedom of wool and glass exports, and the restoration of the bounty of her coarse linen sent into England. Irishmen were left to yearn for legislative security, Englishmen to grumble at North's apparent weakness.

Opposition was given further punch by a revival of radicalism. In the south, Wilkesites led by Jebb were advocating a more popular constitution, with more seats of the Westminster type. In Yorkshire, Christopher Wyvill's Association became the prototype of similar movements for franchise reform all over the country, and propertied men lent their support. To a general disquiet at the handling of the war was added a feeling that the influence of the Crown, through a subservient minister and his handling of the patronage, in the words of Dunning's famous motion, "has increased, is increasing, and ought to be diminished." Old Whig prejudices were reinforced by the discontents of the gentry who wanted America beaten but taxes reduced, and by radicals who urged the need for more independent country members. North, ever at home in the House of Commons, did not lose his grip. The fury of the Gordon Riots in June 1780, irrelevant as they were to the main issues, strengthened arguments for stability. The violence of Fox went further than the squires would accept. North met petitions with bland talk and his majority in the Commons survived all attacks. In April 1780 Dunning was defeated by 254 to 203. In the election of that year, the government actually improved its position. North continued in power throughout 1781, the year of the surrender of Yorktown. "Oh God, it is all over," said North when he heard the news, but he did not resign until March 1782. Then, as Rigby put it, he had "to give the thing up" because peace in America was necessary if England were to defeat her foes in Europe, reinforced now by Holland; and North was disqualified for this task by his commitment to war.   .

Jenkinson, who knew him well, suggested that North was insincere in his constant pleas to resign. The argument that he craved for power, despite the humiliations that this entailed and the additional handicap of failing sight, is strengthened by his conduct in

1783. After the death of Rockingham, and Shelburne's failure to muster enough support, Fox and North came together in a surprising tandem. The king regarded North's defection as an unforgivable piece of treachery and waited for his chance to destroy the coalition. This came, over the vexed position of India. The Regulating Act, which North had always regarded as a provisional measure, had not been working well. Warren Hastings had acquired the odium of many Whigs during his bitter contests with his council. The defense of India against the revenge of France could not be left with safety to a private company. The India Bill of Fox provided for the transfer of the whole territorial responsibilities of the company to a board of seven commissioners. Fox and Burke claimed that public control had been secured, free of executive corruption, but their enemies pointed to an extension of Whig patronage. "Carlo Khan," monstrous and greasy, replaced North as the satirists' butt. With the king's encouragement, the Lords voted against the bill and, in December 1783, Fox and North resigned and Pitt became First Lord of the Treasury.

North had lost reputation by this brief episode; it helps him little to add that he may have conceived that it was his duty to assist in the forming of some government, when all the groups were so much at variance. The cartoonist's portrait—pop eyes, pouting lips, and round belly, the sprawling, somnolent figure on the Treasury Bench, the king's puppet of Whig legend, and the insensate tyrant of American tradition—these figures have obscured the North of history. His reputation might have been secure if he had resigned at the start of the American War. At the height of this war he was able to present budget speeches of a lucid and masterly sort. As a war financier he would have stood higher if he had seen to it that his schemes were not marred by dishonest clerks and contractors, but even here he was unfortunate. In 1779 he had set up the Committee for Examining the Public Accounts: its reports were later to be the basis of Pitt's reforms and North got no credit for them. In his last years he was of no political consequence. He went completely blind and lived only four years to enjoy the earldom that he inherited in 1788 from his aged father.

H. Butterfield, *George III, Lord North and the People*, 1949.
I. R. Christie, *The End of Lord North's Ministry*, 1958.
P. D. G. Thomas, *Lord North*, 1976.

WILLIAM PETTY, 2nd EARL OF SHELBURNE (1737–1805), was one of the most intelligent politicians of the eighteenth century. Intellectual in his tastes, original in his views as in his choice of friends, ambitious to succeed and brave in his policies, it was his fate to arouse widespread suspicion among his associates, to be limited to but two short periods of high office and to see promising plans miscarry or come to fruition under another man's direction.

He was born in Ireland and lived there until he was sixteen, receiving an irregular education in a semifeudal household—a setting in which an original talent may grow more strongly than under conventional schooling. He went to Christ Church in 1755 and joined the army in 1757. He served with enough distinction to be promoted A.D.C. to the king after the battle of Kloster-Kampfen. He sat for a short time as member for High Wycombe and meanwhile took advantage of his position at court to further his career; unfortunately at this time he fell foul of Henry Fox, acquiring a name for deviousness in the process which became a byword in the circle of Fox and his son. As an ally of Bute, however, he was rewarded by the presidency of the Board of Trade which he accepted on the condition that he should have "equal access to the King with other ministers." He resigned in September 1762, but meanwhile played a vital part in the publication of the board's important report which led to the ban upon settlement beyond the headwaters of the Appalachian Mountains.

For the next three years he cultivated the acquaintance of Pitt, whom he admired intensely. This seems to have been a political liaison which never ripened into a friendship, but Pitt respected the younger man's intelligence and rewarded his zeal with the post of Secretary of State for the Southern Department in his adminstration of 1766. He conceived the colonial section of his department to be the most important; again American affairs preoccupied him. Because of Pitt's collapse and virtual withdrawal from responsibility, Shelburne was left to shape his own policies, but he was hampered by the fact that he shared responsibility for the colonies with the Board of Trade. Furthermore he was unable to prevent Charles Townshend from imposing duties upon the colonies which ran counter to his policy. He worked hard for conciliation. He now wished to encourage the westward expansion which had been stopped in 1763. He was unusual too among English politicians in being ready to listen to American views. Franklin, colonial agent for Pennsylvania, was a frequent visitor, so was "omniscient Jackson," former agent for Massachusetts. He also hoped that the financial problem could be solved by taking the quit-rents for new colonies. But his perhaps too optimistic proposals were rejected by the Board of Trade. So Shelburne failed to prevent the growth of tension on this crucial issue.

Though he acquired the name of being the colonists' friend, this was of no assistance to him in domestic politics; he was gradually isolated. As early as June 1767, Grafton was expecting him to go, "considering the little cordiality shown by his lordship toward myself and others of the Cabinet of late." At the end of the year Grafton moved toward an understanding with the Bedford Whigs who were resolved to make no concessions to the colonists. He sensibly proposed dividing the American business from the other functions of the Southern Department. But Shelburne kept the Southern Department, without the "American business," the confidence of his fellow-ministers, or indeed of the king. In October 1768 he resigned, to be followed by Chatham.

He held no office again for fifteen years. He gave up his correspondence with Chatham and watched the American colonists move into positions of defiance without being able to do more than register occasional protests. Burke and Fox would not collaborate with him, while some moderate men came to oppose American claims as a mark of patriotism. Later he went so far as to say that "the right of taxation had, from the first, been chimerical." But he held, like Chatham, to the idea of reconciliation and hoped for "a fair, honest, wise, and honorable connection, in which the constitutional prerogatives of the Crown, the claims of Parliament, and the liberties, properties and lives of all the subjects of the British empire would be equally secured." While military disasters were spoiling the prospect of such generous ideals ever becoming accomplished fact, Shelburne was active in other ways which antagonized politicians otherwise amenable to his ideas. Always somewhat *outré* in his methods and his friends, he used agents in the city, like Alderman Sawbridge, to intrigue for him in London, and he secured influence in the East India Company through purchase of stock by agents. It is not surprising, in view of Shelburne's secretive ways, as well as his grudge against Grafton, that he has been credited with the authorship of the letters of "Junius" (though the evidence is stronger for Philip Francis). More surprisingly he resorted to the dueling sword to settle his differences with a Scottish M.P. In

1780, distrusting the party claque of Rockingham and the wild oratory of Burke and Fox, he employed Price, Priestley, and Jebb to prepare a program of economic and administrative reform. In employing skilled advisers outside the charmed circle of Parliament, he anticipated the methods of some twentieth-century politicians. His ideas were more thorough-going, more in line with the thinking of the "physiocrats," in his anticipation, for instance, of free trade, than those of Burke and his friends who looked back to a parochial tradition. But this free and unprejudiced habit of thought was of no advantage to him in a close political world where personal relationships counted for so much.

Shelburne did, however, have one great asset when, after Yorktown, it became evident that the American War must be decently ended. He was an acknowledged expert in American affairs, he had the trust of a number of Americans who associated his name with the tradition of Chatham, and he was not inhibited, as was North, by his previous actions, from approaching the Americans with a free hand. In March 1782, he became Secretary of State for home, American, and Irish affairs in Rockingham's ministry. His role was to make a separate peace with the Americans while Fox, the other Secretary of State, had charge of the other negotiations with the foreign powers, France, Spain, and Holland. These, naturally, opposed the idea of a separate American peace. Fox and Shelburne worked through separate agents. The situation would have been difficult even without the intense mutual dislike of the two principals. When Rockingham died in July, and Shelburne, upon whom the king now leaned since he was known to oppose full Independence, became First Lord of the Treasury, Fox resigned.

Shelburne was thus left to carry the load of an unpopular treaty himself. In the circumstances he achieved a tolerable settlement, and in a manner which went some way to assuaging old wounds. He had to abandon his cherished dream of a Federal Union. Instead, faithful to his free trade principles, he tried to associate the idea of mutual trade benefit with a peace which otherwise could be none other than a recognition of defeat. In any event Britain recognized American independence and ceded much of the disputed territory in the northwest. The confiscation of loyalists' property was to end, but the request to the individual state legislatures that they should make adequate restitution of properties already confiscated was not given proper sanctions. In the end, perhaps inevitably, the loyalists were sacrificed. France, in the treaty of Versailles, took Goree and Senegal, Tobago and St. Lucia; Spain, Florida and Minorca. But Shelburne was shabbily rewarded for his services. He seems to have believed that George III's influence, together with the basic division of North and Fox, would be enough to ensure his majority. When, improbably, Fox and North combined and the peace terms were debated in the Commons, the ministry was defeated (April 1783). Perhaps Shelburne could have carried on; but he believed, wrongly, that George III had let him down. George in fact accepted the new coalition with revulsion. Fox and North promptly sanctioned the peace which they had formerly rejected; only their dislike of Shelburne had prompted their censure. The defeat of the American Intercourse Bill, in 1784, completed his apparent failure. But the wisdom of the policies that he had tried to implement was seen by the younger Pitt who, like Shelburne, professed himself a disciple of Adam Smith. He had also been Shelburne's Chancellor of the Exchequer and his Free Trade Treaty of 1786 with France might have been Shelburne's work.

In 1784 Shelburne was made Marquess of Lansdowne, but he played no further part in politics. His relative failure remains one of the puzzles of the time. Assessing his influence on the younger Pitt, Disraeli called him one of the "suppressed characters" of history. He could be patient, generous, sympathetic. Yet his was a temperament basically unsuited to the eighteenth-century political game; he was an example, not the last, of the disabilities of an intellectual in politics. He never lived down the taunt of "the Jesuit of Berkeley Square." His manner was unfortunate, sometimes obsequious, sometimes arrogant. Neither the boldness of his ideas, nor his willingness to change his mind, nor his habit of making fine qualifications and distinctions upon matters which seemed plain to less subtle minds, inspired the confidence without which no statesman can do much for long. He found compensation for his departure from political life in his library and pictures at Bowood and Lansdowne House. Besides these two great houses and their treasures, he bequeathed a political tradition: the 3rd and 5th marquesses both became cabinet ministers.

J. Norris, *Shelburne and Reform*, 1963.
R. A. Humphreys, "Lord Shelburne and British Colonial Policy, 1766–8," from *Ec. H.R.*, reprinted in *Essays in Eighteenth-Century History*, 1966.

ADAM SMITH (1723–90), the Scottish economist whose work was extremely influential in the nineteenth century, and who counted the younger Pitt among his disciples, was born in Kirkcaldy in 1723, a few months after the death of his father. As an infant of three he was playing on the doorstep of his uncle's house when he was carried off by a party of tinkers who might have destroyed or abandoned him, had they not been overtaken by the uncle and his friends. At Kirkcaldy school he was taught by a Mr. David Miller, a fine type of the Scottish schoolmaster who teaches his pupils the supreme value of sound learning. After a period at Glasgow University from 1737 to 1740, Adam Smith won an Exhibition to Balliol College, Oxford. As a boy he was remarkable for his passion for reading and for the habit of talking to himself which remained with him all his life. At Oxford he spent a great deal of time translating famous French books in order to improve his own prose style. He showed, however, no marked enthusiasm for any one vocation or employment and he turned away stubbornly from entering the Church of England.

This was an interesting period in the history of Scotland. The ending of religious war and the pacification of the Highlands produced an age of prosperity and culture which made Scotland one of the leading centers of learning in Europe. In Edinburgh, where he went to live in 1748, Smith made the acquaintance of the great philosopher, David Hume. In 1751 he was elected professor of logic at Glasgow University and in the following year succeeded to the professorship of moral philosophy. Like Montesquieu he was preoccupied with the growth of societies and institutions and observed the relationship between economic conditions and political changes. The means of producing a prosperous and powerful state absorbed his attention and much of the exploration which he did in economics and political science at Glasgow found subsequent expression in the "Wealth of Nations." He had a high reputation as a lecturer. He spoke without any great apparatus of notes and put forward his propositions rather hesitantly; then, imagining possibly some disbelief and criticism among his hearers, he lost his diffidence and argued with animation and force. His opinions were discussed widely in literary clubs and among the students, and his turns of speech and mannerisms were much imitated.

In 1759 he published *The Theory of the Moral Sentiments.* David Hume, who despised popularity, was appalled to see how universally well-received it was. Three bishops came to the publishers in one day to buy it. Charles Townshend, of whom Hume dryly observed, "he passes for the cleverest fellow in England," was impressed with Smith's writing and made plans for him to accompany the young Duke of Buccleuch on the Grand Tour of the Continent. In 1764 began the Grand Tour which was to last three years. They visited Paris, Toulouse (where the working of the French system of provincial government was carefully observed), and Geneva. They returned through Paris and Smith was introduced to many of the leading thinkers of France, such as Turgot, Necker, and Helvetius. Unfortunately he kept no journal, wrote few letters, and destroyed before his death many of the materials which would have entertained future biographers. Turgot and the French writers of the period were, like Smith, concerned with discovering the basis of a happy human society and a way of improving it by regulation. Adam Smith was also fascinated by the French theatre and its lively comedies. He was always interested in the art of drama and once began an essay on the subject.

Having returned to Scotland, he lived quietly for almost ten years with his mother in Kirkcaldy. Hume thought a town the best place for a man of letters: "You will cut yourself off from human society to the great loss of both parties," he wrote. The fruit of Smith's withdrawn existence was seen in 1776 when he published the *Inquiry into the Nature and Causes of the Wealth of Nations*. In this book he advocated the benefits of mutual trading between nations and attacked the old "mercantilist" theory that in trading matters all should be competitive and one country could only gain by another's loss. He was thus instrumental in persuading future statesmen such as Pitt and Huskisson to remove many of the old restrictions on trade. "Free Trade" such as he advocated suited England admirably in the industrial revolution, when no country could compete with her rapid output of goods. He also criticized the old belief that the only valuable form of wealth was gold and argued that bullion was merely a token of exchange and that intercourse with other countries should not suffer because one country wished to keep its gold tightly locked up in a national money box. Each part of the world performs certain economic functions more happily than others. It is easy to make wine in France, difficult in Great Britain: Britain should not therefore try to make wine, but should concentrate on her metal industries and exchange hardware for wine. Both countries will then benefit. Underneath the economic argument lies a basic belief, which Adam Smith shared with his French contemporaries, that human nature is capable of choosing a good and unselfish course and that it is wrong for governments to interfere too rigidly in social affairs. Men, if left to themselves, pursue their own good; but they will add greatly to the common happiness by diffusing their prosperity. Just so a millionaire will give employment and prosperity to others if he takes up residence in a poor and derelict village. The arguments of Adam Smith were later quoted by unscupulous employees and business men against governmental control and inspection in industry, but they distorted his views by using them in this way, just as the French revolutionaries distorted the views of the French thinkers with whom Smith had been in sympathy.

The *Wealth of Nations* is not merely a staid statistical study. It has a dry Scottish humor and an elegance that has something in common with those other two products of the age of grace and good sense which also appeared in 1776: Gibbon's *Decline and Fall* and the American Declaration of Independence. For two years after its initial appearance Smith lived in London, but in 1778 the Duke of Buccleuch, grateful to his old tutor-companion, procured for him a position in the Scottish Customs Board and he returned to Edinburgh where he spent the last twelve years of his life. His mother, though of very advanced age, came to live with him in town and his cousin, a Miss Jane Douglas, kept house. He collected a small library and lived the life of a retired scholar, always putting off the collection and publication of his papers. His mother's and cousin's deaths left him very isolated; his own death came in 1790 after a painful illness. A few days before he died he gave orders for the destruction of most of his incomplete work and his early lectures.

In 1787 he had been made rector of Glasgow University. "No man can owe greater obligations to a society than I do to the University of Glasgow," he wrote in his letter of thanks. "They educated me, they sent me to Oxford. Soon after my return to Scotland they elected me one of their own members . . . The period of thirteen years which I spent as a member of that society I remember as by far the happiest and most honorable period of my life, and now after three and twenty years" absence to be remembered in so very agreeable manner by my old friends and protectors gives me a heartfelt joy which I cannot easily express to you."

C. R. Fay, *Adam Smith and the Scotland of his Day*, 1956.
R. Koebner, "Adam Smith and the Industrial Revolution," *Ec. H.R.*, 1959.
I. Hont and M. Ignatieff, *Wealth and Virtue: The Shaping of Political Economy in the Scottish Enlightenment*, 1983.

JOSIAH WEDGWOOD (1730–95) opened his first pottery in 1760 with a capital of about £20. When he died he had created a new artistic tradition and a large business. After a life of great generosity he left a private fortune of half a million pounds. He did not allow the loss of a leg by amputation to restrict him. He was an artist of industry, an entrepreneur of the most admirable sort; yet he was but the youngest of thirteen children of a Staffordshire potter and had little education beyond what he gave himself.

He first gained experience with the Staffordshire pioneer, Thomas Whieldon, one of the first to break away from the production of plain, serviceable ware and to make decorative china. From 1754 to 1759 Wedgwood worked with Whieldon, and he began to envisage the commercial possibilities of good pottery when attention was paid to designs and decoration. Then he branched out himself with a factory at Ivy Burslem. Wedgwood was a founder of factory working; from the start he saw that art and profit must go together. Because raw materials were easy to obtain, the industry had previously been carried on by peasant craftsmen or small family businesses. The same man worked on several processes, and haphazard methods of glazing and firing led to accidents to men and to their wares. Marketing was local and little capital was accumulated to finance improvements. Wedgwood had the imagination to see that the products of Staffordshire might find favor in London, even abroad. Never before, and possibly never since, had so much money been allied to such cultivated taste in the upper classes of Europe. The time was ripe for the mass production of beautiful objects.

Early in his career, Wedgwood employed his brother as a traveler in London. Later he had showrooms in London and Dublin and agents in countries abroad. The eighteenth century admired the patterns and figures of the ancient world. Their houses had classical facades; their halls were filled with sculptures of Greece and Rome. Wedgwood's vases went with the chimneypieces of Robert Adam and the Renaissance paintings that were sent back in crates by the nobleman on his Grand Tour. He sought not only to please the fancy of the private collector but also to produce in quantity from standard designs. Upon the profitable base of ceramics from his large Etruria works (opened in 1769) he financed research into new methods and designs. His workmen exemplified the virtues of the division of labor before Adam Smith erected it into dogma: each worked at one process. He employed the finest modelers, but they did not produce individual masterpieces; rather they acted as a team and the best designs were often the product of several minds. Among the artists who worked for him was John Flaxman; he specialized in copies of the antique, the best of which sold for £50. Wedgwood is, perhaps, best known for his Jasper ware made, after many experiments, from a compound of sulfite of baryta, clay, flint, and carbonate of baryta which mixed into a smooth paste of exquisite texture. It would take a high polish and, when fired in the kiln with certain metallic oxides, could be stained or colored in distinctive hues. Medallions and plaques, tea sets, flower pots, bellpulls, scent bottles, and chessmen, especially ornamental vases, made the name of Wedgwood synonymous with restraint and elegance.

Wedgwood was a careful employer. He raised a village for the workers in Etruria, even instituted an insurance scheme. In 1783, however, when among other disturbances in the country there was a riot at Etruria and one of the ringleaders was hanged, he addressed a stern message to his workpeople, in the form of a pamphlet: "I place my hopes, with some degree of confidence, in the rising generation, being persuaded that they will, by their better conduct, make atonement for this unhappy, this unwise slip of their fathers," he remarked, after observing how much prosperity had been brought into the region by well-directed industrialism.

His interest in selling his goods also stimulated the revolution in communications. Canals like the Grand Trunk Navigation cut the costs of inland transport and were kinder to his fragile goods than carts and rutted roads. Wedgwood could also secure clay by barge; besides the regular supply from Cornwall, he got it from America, and he even used clay from Sydney Cove, brought back by Joseph Banks and Cook. He could, however, be conservative where his industry's future was at stake. It was he who led the English merchants in successful opposition to the proposals of Pitt to admit the Irish to a greater share of English and colonial trade, fearing that cheap Irish labor would enable Irish manufacturers to undercut the English.

Wedgwood married a distant cousin; his eldest daughter, Susannah, married Robert Darwin, father of Charles Darwin. His third son was the first photographer (though he failed to discover a practical process). Over the last century no family has had a more notable record of intellectual achievement and public service.

W. Burton, *Josiah Wedgwood and his Pottery*, 1922.
R. E. Scholfield, *The Lunar Society of Birmingham*, 1963.
L. Weatherill, *The Pottery Trade and North Staffordshire 1660–1760*, 1971.

JOSEPH PRIESTLEY (1733–1804), nonconformist theologian, radical in politics, and tireless experimenter in natural science, was the son of a Yorkshire cloth-dresser, but brought up by an aunt of Calvinist persuasion, whose home was a center for local dissenting ministers. He suffered from poor health as a boy and though he was sent to Batley Grammar School and to the Dissenting Academy at Droitwich, he owed his precocious knowledge of languages, including Hebrew and Arabic, and his interest in science, to his own intensive studies. He early rebelled against some of the strict tenets of Calvinism, but he remained a puritan in his outlook. Plays and novels he deplored; a useful and busy life was his ideal. He is sometimes described as a *philosophe* and his range of intellectual interests may tempt us to align him with Diderot and d'Alembert. His was indeed an original mind and he was impelled in everything by a fervent love of truth; in his political and theological writings alike he would follow where logic led him. He sought for others the liberty of thought which he needed for himself. Though his investigations in chemistry were hampered by his obstinate adherence to the old theory of phlogiston, or "the matter of fire," he did not usually succumb to the temptation to follow in well-worn paths. Rather, he would observe and note from many sources in books and nature, until he had conceived a new synthesis.

In 1755 he became Presbyterian minister at Needham Market, but he soon found himself drawn to rational and liberal views that were inconsistent with conventional theology. He wished to study the scriptures free from the constraining influences of the creeds.

Though he stood firm on evidences for God's existence and power, he denied that Christ's death was a sacrifice, and rejected in turn the Trinity and Atonement. In the end he adopted the Unitarian position after having been at different times a determinist, an Arian, a Socinian, and a materialist. He should be regarded as the author of the modern Unitarianism, which he regarded as the teaching of Christ and the Apostles before the perversions of Hellenistic and Oriental influences. This Unitarianism was a middle-class version of that deism which was already strong in universities; in Priestley it took a very tolerant shape. He could have been embittered by misunderstanding and abuse, for he was branded as an atheist despite the firm arguments of his *Disquisition Relating to Matter and Spirit* (1777). He was a pleasant-natured man, however, and never let his own convictions make him contemptuous of others. He even advocated the toleration of Roman Catholics.

Priestley had many friends. Two notable ones were Benjamin Franklin, whom he met when he came to London on yearly visits from Cheshire, where from 1763 to 1767 he made a living by tutoring at Warrington Academy, and Shelburne, the philosophically inclined politician, whom he accompanied on a Continental tour in the capacity of literary companion and served for a time as librarian. Others were Burke, Banks, Price, and Wedgwood: it is a fair roll call of the genius of the time. Honors accrued at home and abroad: in 1766, Fellow of the Royal Society, later member of both the French Academy of Sciences and the St. Petersburg Academy. In 1780 he became minister of a chapel at Birmingham and he was living there when the French Revolution broke out. He had revived his notoriety among the orthodox with the publication of his *History of Early Opinions* concerning Jesus Christ in 1786, but the "Church and King" rioters who sacked his house, with his library and laboratory, and forced him to seek asylum in the United States, were animated more by political prejudice than theological fervor: he had replied in reasoned terms to Burke's magnificent conservative effusion, *Reflections on the French Revolution*. After the riots he tried to live down his false fame, and he refused the embarrassing honor of election to the National Convention of France. He could not, however, rent a house; cartoonists pilloried him—one saw him as "Dr. Phlogiston," brandishing a political sermon and standing on a tract entitled "Bible explained away"—and his effigy was burned alongside Paine's.

In 1794 Priestley sailed to America, whither his three sons had already migrated while his fellow-Unitarian, Coleridge, denounced "the statesmen bloodstained and priests idolatrous" who had driven him away. Priestley had sympathized with the colonists at the time of their rebellion; now he looked forward to peaceful exile in the rough hinterland of Northumberland, Pennsylvania. He grew lonely, however. His conversation did not entrance his hosts, even his preaching palled. He was involved in controversy, not only with Americans but also with his fellow *émigré*, Cobbett, a very different sort of radical who, among many wild charges, actually declared that he was in league with the Jews. President John Adams, once his friend, came to regard him with contempt: "his influence is not an atom in the world," he wrote, when declining to execute the alien law against him. Adams's successor, Jefferson, however, championed him and he lived out his last years in peace, writing, reading and experimenting. He had been disillusioned in his belief that America might become a pastoral utopia, a land of self-sufficient farmers unconcerned with world power or trade.

The list of Priestley's published works on theology, philology, history, political and moral science fills nearly six columns in the *Dictionary of National Biography*. Two other columns record his scientific writings. The latter suffer from the diversity of his interests: he was also preacher, teacher, philosopher, grammarian, a great talker, and an accomplished player on the flute. But several of his observations in the 1770s and 1780s, those great decades in the history of science, were fruitful. He improved the technique for studying gases. He showed that green plants gave off a respirable gas. He isolated oxygen by heating certain oxides and investigated nitrogen and silicon tetrafluoride. He does not, however, stand quite in the forefront with Cavendish or Black, Scheele or Lavoisier. He would not pursue any single line for long enough for his temperament was restless; moreover he would never believe that natural science was as important as the study of God.

Anne Holt, *A Life of Joseph Priestley*, 1931.
A. Lincoln, *Some Political and Social Ideas of English Dissent 1763–1800*, 1938.
R. E. Scholfield, *The Enlightenment of Joseph Priestly: a Study of his Life and Work, 1733–1773*, 1997.

RICHARD PRICE (1723–91) was a Nonconformist minister and radical whose versatile writings earned him a controversial fame in his lifetime. At the end of his career he had the misfortune to provide a chopping block for Edmund Burke; since his views were either unfashionable or reviled he passed quickly from memory. Today we can see his importance more plainly in the light shed by new studies of the radical and Nonconformist minorities of the reign of George III.

Price was born in Wales, though, like many able Welshmen, he soon left it. The son and grandson of Calvinist ministers, he was perhaps lucky to escape from the cold comforts of his home; his father was a rigid moralist but somewhat concerned, too, about his social position. When he died in 1739, leaving his property to his elder son, Richard came penniless to London, where he met a mellower tradition of dissent in the shape of Samuel Price, his uncle, assistant to Isaac Watts at his chapel in Monk Lane. He was well taught at Hoxton Academy, one of those small dissenting schools like Daventry and Warrington which made such a large contribution to English middle-class culture; there, too, he met John Howard, whose letters about prisons he was later to revise and prepare for the press. Subsequently Price became chaplain to Mr. Streatfield, a wealthy dissenter, who left him some money on his death in 1756; the next year he married and set up a happy but childless home at Newington Green. At a succession of places, notably after 1769 the Grand Pit Meeting House at Hackney, he impressed small but thoughtful congregations with his sincerity and originality. His preaching was the central activity of his life: other interests were diversions to be guarded against. In theology he occupied the middle ground of the moderate rationalists between the scepticism of the deists and the fervor of the new Methodists. In manner, men of his persuasion, mostly substantial and intelligent townspeople like Thomas Rogers, John Aiken, and the American Benjamin Franklin were distinguished by a certain *savoir faire*: restraint rather than rigour, reason rather than fanaticism, above all open-mindedness, set them outside the puritan tradition. They were sober, but they were not saints—nor did they aspire to be.

Price's major contribution to philosophy was his *Review of Principal Questions in Morals* of 1758, which challenged the Lockean theory of ideas, that all thinking was the effect of notice taken by the impact of objects on the senses. Against the idea that the materials of reason and knowledge were limited to experience, which permeated so much of the thought of the time, Price set his belief in the existence of an independent faculty capable of grasping the "universal" ideas which experience could not impart. The ability to judge between right and wrong came from this faculty. Further, Price argued that moral consciousness was a common endowment irrespective of belief or unbelief. In his theology can be seen the same desire to maintain the freedom of maneuver. Politically underprivileged, dissenters like Price were naturally skeptical of any establishment or any system of dogma imposed by an establishment; they valued the more the intellectual freedom which was the envy of *philosophes* across the channel. Price was influenced, too, by an emotional reaction against the Calvinist doctrines of original sin and election. Accepting everything short of the divinity of Christ, he admitted the supernatural element and the possibility of divine intervention. His emphasis, however, was on a Christ who as reformer and teacher did not impinge upon the moral autonomy of the individual.

Price's concern with politics was not inconsistent with his moral and philosophical position. He had a natural sympathy with the claims of the American colonists and with the movement for the reform of Parliament which coincided with the American War. He was patronized first by Shelburne, then by the younger Pitt, though in some measure disappointed by both: the former was devious, the latter cautious; both were imprisoned as much by the political ethos as by the system. Price first made common ground with Shelburne over the Stamp and Declaratory Acts. He was active in the petitioning and lobbying which preceded the Dissenters' Relief Act of 1779. His *Observations on the Nature of Civil Liberty* was more influential than perhaps it deserved to be: its loose definitions and simple arguments appealed to radicals of all sorts and especially to Americans, whose idealism and virtue he certainly exaggerated. A Parliament directly dependent upon popular suffrage was the crux of his political program; here he is nearer to Rousseau than to the property-conscious Locke. There is, however, a saving individualism, a common sense about Price. He touched the political yearnings of an awakening middle class but he never came near to such an abstraction as the general will. His ideas influenced reformers such as the Unitarian Jebb and the Yorkshire squire Wyvill. For political action, however, it was on Shelburne's ministry of 1782–83 that his hopes were focused: its relative failure and the apostasy of Fox disappointed him. He preserved the illusion that Pitt was a reformer for some years. His main link with the young prime ministers was, however, provided by his essays as an economist.

Price was not alone in being alarmed by the size of the National Debt (£72.5 million in 1759, £231.8 million in 1783), but his concern was characteristically a moral one: his view was that of a puritan who deplores the effect upon the family of an indebted and spend-thrift father. He was also fascinated by the actuarial problems. His interest in life insurance went back to 1761 when he first worked out a formula for determining the probability of the recurrence of particular events. He had subsequently supplied the Equitable Assurance Society with calculations, based upon his study of the inhabitants of Northampton (a town that seemed suitably central in position and middling in size), in the form of the *Northampton Tables*, which, using bills of mortality, compared actual with expected deaths, and which remained in general use for half a century. Price's *Observations on Reversionary Payments* was the first published treatise on life insurance: he may well claim to be one of the founders of this service. In his idea for a sinking fund he may have been less original. Walpole had created one for redemption; the idea at least was a familiar one. His observations about the economy owed more to guesswork than to science: he thought he saw evidence for a declining population in window tax returns and seems to have been blind to accumulating evidence of a spectacular growth of wealth and investment. He was not an economist like Adam Smith, or even his Anglican counterpart Dean Tucker, but a moralist. He could claim, however, as author of *An Appeal to the Public on the Subject of the National Debt* in 1772 and subsequently as adviser to Pitt, for whom in 1785 he drew up four alternative schemes, to have influenced that statesman's much-vaunted, and later much-derided, sinking fund.

In 1787 Price became one of the directors of the new academy at Hackney: founded to provide a liberal education for Nonconformists, it failed because of unrealistic management and poor discipline. In 1789, however, Price's attention was drawn to France and the revolution which to men like him announced the dawn of a better age. He was on the committee of the Revolution Society of

London which commemorated 1688 but celebrated its centenary by enunciating principles which were more democratic than Whiggish. Price's celebrated *Sermon* in praise of the Revolution, preached on November 4, was a rallying call to dissenters, the dispossessed, and radicals of all sorts in a society which wanted "the grand security of public liberty." In this political testament all the strands of Price's thought were drawn together. He denounced the luxury and greed and the venal and militarist politics of a selfish and wealthy oligarchy. He stated three principles which he believed the British constitution failed to uphold: the right to liberty of conscience in religion, the right to resist power when abused, and "the right to choose our own governors, to cashier them for a misconduct, and to frame a government for ourselves." In a fine passage he urged the case for liberal government: "enlighten them and you will elevate them. Shew them that they are men, and they will act like men." The words are worthy of the robust old moralist who used to spend some weeks every year by the sea, a pioneer in his enjoyment of sea bathing. In 1790 he took his holiday as usual, at Bridgend. But in the following February he caught a cold while attending a funeral; in April he died.

A. Lincoln, *Some Political and Social Ideas of English Dissent, 1763–1800*, 1938.

C. B. Crune, "Richard Price and Mr. Pitt: Sinking Fund of 1786," *Ec. H. Review*, 2nd series, IV, No. 2.

JAMES WATT (1736–1819) is well described after an encounter with Sir Walter Scott in Edinburgh. He was over eighty, but "the alert, kind, benevolent old man had his attention alive to every one's question, his information at every one's command." Scott dilates upon the range of his interests; he talked with one man about the origin of the alphabet, with others of political economy and literature; he had read all the latest novels. "This potent commander of the elements—this abridger of time and space—this magician, whose cloudy machinery has produced a change on the world, the effects of which, extraordinary as they are, are perhaps only now beginning to be felt—was not only the most profound man of science, the most successful combiner of powers and calculators of numbers as adapted to practical purposes—was not only one of the most generally well-informed—but one of the best and kindest of human beings."

James Watt was the son of a merchant, bailie, and elder of Greenock. He was not a robust boy, nor did he ever enjoy perfect health, though he lived long. From the burgh school he went to work first in London, then in Glasgow, as a maker of mathematical instruments; his father had some skill in this work himself. In 1764, when he was working for the university in this capacity, he was given one of Newcomen's steam engines to repair. At this time, Joseph Black, professor of medicine in Glasgow, was studying steam and enunciating his theory of latent heat. The subject was already one of some interest to Watt; indeed the old story that he had dreamed of the applications of steam while looking at his mother's kettle may be true. By the work of Newcomen and his successors, notably Smeaton, steam had been used for pumping machines since about 1720. The basic idea was simple: a piston at the top of a steam-filled cylinder was weighed down by air when the steam was condensed, and the pump was attached to the piston. By 1769 Smeaton was able to report that a hundred such engines were at work on the northern coalfields alone. The biggest could lift 300 cwt. of water at one stroke, but were slow, making only some dozen strokes per minute and working only on the downward stroke of the piston. Watt's early experiments were only instrumental in saving heat and fuel; this was not of much interest to the coal owners.

In 1769 Watt entered into partnership with Roebuck of the Carron Ironworks and took out a patent for his improvements which proved hard and costly to enforce. These included the separate condenser, air pump, steam jacket for the cylinder, and the double-acting engine which utilized the piston in both strokes. After the failure of Roebuck, Matthew Boulton of the Soho works at Birmingham took Watt into a partnership which was to prove of the greatest importance, a classic alliance of inventor and manufacturer. The manufacture of the new steam engine was begun at Soho and it soon began to replace Newcomen's engines. In the next few years he got successive patents for the sun and planet motion, the expansion principle, the double engine, the parallel motion, a smokeless furnace, and the governor. Boulton was a dynamic partner for Watt, but progress was relatively slow. Between

1775 and 1785 only sixty-six Watt engines were built, all small. Their use for the textile industry was not at first appreciated. Outside the mines and metal plants, Samuel Whitbread was one of the few to appreciate the use of steam; he had an engine installed in his brewery in 1786. In the nineties, however, the steam engine began to challenge water power's supremacy in the manufacturing industries. By 1800, when Watt's patent expired, the steam revolution was a fact. With cheap metal by then in good supply the way was clear for the advance of the iron and textile industries, which were able to make most profitable use of steam. For this alone Watt would have a large place among the pioneers of the industrial revolution. But his fame should have a broader base.

Watt was an engineer of very adaptable skills. It was he who surveyed and planned the Monkland canal from Coatbridge to Glasgow, a money-spinner for the coal owners and industrialists of Lanarkshire. He was also a scientist of distinction who could hold his own with men like Priestley, with whom he shared the discovery that water is a compound of the two elements, and with Lavoisier and Berthollet. He was a Fellow of the Royal Society and a corresponding member of the Institute of France. "I saw a workman, and expected no more; but was surprised to find a philosopher": so a fellow-member of the Lunar Society, John Robison, recalled him. Watt invented the copying press and a way of recording weather in a systematic fashion. He built an organ and would, no doubt, if opportunity had come his way, have been an architect as well. But the heart of his busy life was Birmingham, where he lived until his death, and the happy partnership with Boulton, ended only by the latter's death in 1809. Here he continued to make improvements upon his steam engines, pistons, cylinders, connecting rods, indicators, and boilers. He did not live to see the exciting application of steam engines to railway traction. If he had been born later we may be sure that he would have played a leading part in that advance.

Jeffries, a severe critic, spoke of Watt's "kind of intellectual alchemy" by which he extracted from all subjects what was important and fastened upon it. Von Breder's portrait shows us an interesting sensitive face. Scientist, inventor, *philosophe*, Watt commands our admiration as much for what he was as for what he did.

J. G. Crowther, *Scientist of the Industrial Revolution*, 1962.
L. T. C. Rolt, *James Watt*, 1964.
R. E. Scholfield, *The Lunar Society of Birmingham*, 1963.

JESSE RAMSDEN (1732–1800), optician and inventor, was renowned throughout Europe for the quality of his instruments. He was remarkably versatile. He set up as an engraver in 1762; later he took out patents for important improvements in astronomical and surveying equipment. In 1774 he brought out his Equatorial, by means of which a telescope can be made to follow, by clockwork, the apparent motion of any point in the heavens toward which it is directed. The most modern telescopes still embody this mechanism in some form. He also produced an engine for the mathematical gradation of a circle. The traditional surveyor's instrument for measuring angles, the theodolite, that had been used since the sixteenth century, was transformed by him. His "great instrument," which proved itself capable, in the primary triangulation of England, of measuring angles at a distance of 70 miles to 2 seconds of arc, is the prototype of the modern theodolite. He was devoted to his craft and would never raise his prices, so that from all his inventions he made but a modest fortune.

SIR WILLIAM HERSCHEL (1738–1822), astronomer, was born in Hanover, which was then under the British Crown, but was sent by his parents to England in 1757. He had played the violin and hautboy in the Hanoverian Guards and by patronage of Dr. Edward Miller he found employment as an organist. He turned, however, to astronomy and began to show great skill in making optical instruments. He devoted himself from 1785 to 1789 to designing a "front-view telescope," a forty-foot reflecting instrument which incorporated important technical advances, notably in the casting and polishing of the mirror and in the mechanical apparatus, basically a tube, twelve meters long, mounted on a platform revolving on rollers. With Herschel began an exciting era of observation and discovery. He was much visited by other scientists and sent sixty-nine memoirs to the Royal Society, of which he became a member in 1781. In 1782 he was visited by George III and made Court Astronomer. In 1802 he had an interview with Napoleon who was always fascinated by the stars.

He was concerned primarily with their distribution. He concluded eventually that the starry firmament was of lens shape, diameter about five times its thickness; the sun being not far from the center, the edge formed by the Milky Way. He discovered many hundreds of nebulae, some of which he was able to resolve into star clusters; others he thought were "composed of a shining fluid, of a nature totally unknown to us" (1791). Later he came to the conclusion that such fluids could condense, and stars form at the point of condensation. Since Halley it had been realized that certain stars moved in relation to each other; Herschel went further and noted that many stars were in closely contiguous pairs. From this he proceeded to establish their perspective relations and relative distances. He was nothing if not persistent. By prolonged viewing and meticulous charting over twenty years, he was able to show, in 1805, that some of these stars circulated round each other and thus obey the laws of gravitation.

When Herschel was engaged upon the laborious work of polishing his concave mirrors, he could not be brought to leave his work but existed on food placed in his mouth by his sister. We may guess, however, that he felt rewarded when he was able to announce the discovery of the planet Uranus in 1781, the first addition to the long-established seven.

Lady Lubbock, *Herschel Chronicle*, 1933.

HENRY CORT (1740–1800), inventor, was born in Lancaster, but aged twenty-five he went to London, where he was engaged as an agent, buying guns for the navy. Because the best metal for gun-making had to be imported from abroad, Cort experimented continuously with the object of discovering a superior metal. In 1775 he set up a forge near Fareham and began with success to employ water power. In 1784 he patented a puddling and rolling process which was to allow the production of bar-iron with coal fuel on a large scale. The process consisted essentially of stirring molten pig iron on the bed of a reverberatory furnace. The puddler turned and stirred the mass until it was converted into malleable iron by the decarburizing action of air circulating through the furnace. He also used grooved rollers which were far more effective than forge-hammers or slitting-mills.

The significance of Cort's work was immense. The use of coal fuel ended the dependence on charcoal, limited in supply and costly. It converted native pig iron into bars that were as good as any foreign metal, and made a single process of the hitherto separate actions of puddling, hammering, and rolling. What this meant to

England in the Napoleonic Wars can be estimated from the figures of pig-iron production: 40,000 tons a year in 1780, it was 400,000 by 1820. Cort was unlucky, however, and received scant reward for his patient work. He was ruined by the bankruptcy and suicide of Adam Jellicoe, a naval paymaster, who had used public money to invest in Cort's business and imposed his son Samuel as partner. Cort, a simple, trusting person and no businessman, now made over the patent rights to Samuel, in return for the capital, and these were confiscated by the Admiralty. Eventually his innocence was accepted by the government and he was granted a small pension. He had to keep a wife and large family on £200, while large fortunes were being made by ironmasters who were able to experiment at will with the processes which he had invented.

C. K. Hyde, *Technological Change and the British Iron Industry, 1700–1780*, 1977.

H. W. Dickinson, "Henry Cort's Bicentenary," *Newcomen Society Transactions*, Vol. XXI, 1940–41.

JOHN PALMER (1742–1818) by his vision and good planning achieved almost single-handed a revolution in transport. The son of a well-to-do brewer of Bath, he came to realize the inefficiencies of the post when he helped his father with the management of his theatre at Bath. The Post Office messengers seldom kept time and, being unarmed, were an easy prey to highwaymen. Robberies were frequent and the service was slow. Palmer, who was both self-confident and persistent, worked out a scheme for a fast mail-coach service on the same lines as the stagecoach, with an armed guard and four passengers to defray the expense. Pitt, Chancellor of the Exchequer under Shelburne in 1783, saw the possibilities of the plan. When he became prime minister in 1784, he ordered a trial, against argument and obstruction from the Post Office. Long sunk in bureaucratic sloth, postal officials were driven to advise clients to cut their banknotes in half before sending them by post, and they continued to intrigue against Palmer, despite the success of the new mail coaches. From about three days the journey from London to Bristol was cut to sixteen hours, an hour shorter than the stagecoach. The journey was not comfortable, but it was reliable, except in winter, and safe. Pitt, who was aware of the value to the country of this service, made Palmer surveyor and comptroller-general of the Post Office. Though he was compelled to dismiss him in 1793 because of indiscreet attacks upon his superior, Lord Walsingham, he compensated him with a pension of no less than £3,000 a year.

SIR CHARLES DOUGLAS (?–1789), rear admiral, was responsible for important improvements in gunnery which gave the English fleets of the Napoleonic Wars the edge over their opponents. His life is an obscure one, but it is clear that he was a thoughtful seaman with an inventive mind, one who rose by merit. He led the expedition that relieved Quebec after being checked by ice the previous year, in 1776. In the following year he was created baronet. He served with distinction in the West Indies as captain of the *Duke*, and shortly before the battle of the Saints he was taken on to the flagship. At this decisive battle, in 1782, he was serving as Rodney's Captain of the Fleet, a position comparable with that of chief of staff.

There is no evidence that it was he who planned the maneuver of breaking the French line which was to be so influential on later strategists, but the excellent gunnery of the ships was largely his work. Technical snags were overcome: the clogging of barrels, for example, by the use of flannel instead of silk for cartridge casing, violent recoil by the attachment of steel springs to the rear of the gun. To protect the gunner, a flintlock was released by a lanyard in place of the linstock. Rates of fire were still limited by the heating of the guns. All the more important, therefore, was his contrivance of traversing by a complicated mechanism of blocks and tackles attached to the ship's side. When a traverse of 45 degrees could be obtained, ships could fire obliquely and the need to maneuver into line was correspondingly reduced. When the *Ville de Paris*, de Grasse's flagship, received a broadside from the *Arrogant*, lying at four points (45 degrees) on her bows, the French thought that the English must have wider ports. Douglas had something, too, to do with the development of the carronade, a short piece with a relatively heavy discharge, which was to prove well-suited to the English tactics of fighting at short range. Since battles are won as much by intensity of fire power as by skill of maneuver, Douglas did much to win the war which he did not live to see.

EDMUND CARTWRIGHT (1743–1823), when vicar of Goadby Marwood in Leicestershire, conceived the idea of a power loom which would be of use to friends of his in the weaving business. In 1785 he produced a model and in 1786 an improved version which he then installed in his own factory at Doncester. He solved several problems with devices to stop the loom in case the thread broke, to keep the cloth stretched in width, and to size the warp. He attached the warping to the loom so as to size the threads mechanically before they reached the warp-beam. For the work of an amateur, no trained engineer and outside the industry, the contrivance was marvellous, but it had serious defects and did not at first prove profitable. His machine was worked by a cow; later models, modified by men like Thomas Johnston and powered by steam, were commercially successful. In 1789 Cartwright became bankrupt, but the next year he produced another ingenious machine— for wool-combing. Again, this did not come into general use until after the end of the Napoleonic Wars. Conservatism among mill owners, the defensive attitudes of well-paid wool-combers, and shortage of capital delayed the inevitable advance, but where, as in Bradford, the machine was installed, it quickly made the fortune of the manufacturer, Ramsbottom, and doubled the population of the town in ten years. An advantage of the machine was that it could be minded by children under an overseer; the process was quicker and the wool was finer.

Cartwright seems to have been a most versatile man. For a time agricultural adviser to the Dukes of Bedford, he later farmed on his own account in Kent. He invented, among other things, an alcohol engine. His mechanical genius was poorly rewarded, though in 1809 he received a parliamentary grant. Before his death, however, the textile industry had been transformed. Expanding production and export of cheap textiles were his memorial; so, inevitably, were impoverished hand-loom weavers and the pallid, pitiful children of the mills.

SIR ELIJAH IMPEY (1732–1809) became Chief Justice of Bengal in 1774, earned the threat of impeachment from his association with Warren Hastings and the celebrated verdict of Macaulay: "rich, quiet, and infamous." He was born in London, the son of a merchant from Hammersmith, and educated at Westminster, where he was elected into college at the same time as Hastings. He went to Trinity College, Cambridge, and became a Fellow of the college in 1757. When he was made head of the Supreme Court set up by North the year before, he had a solid reputation among lawyers, and a large family. His friends included Dunning and Thurlow, but his appointment was earned by merit rather than by jobbery. He was knighted and thus placed in a strong position in his dealings with the Council of Bengal, where he ranked second in authority to Hastings himself; but the functions of his court of four were not clearly defined. Was every servant of the company, whatever his race, to be accounted a British subject? Were all revenue cases within the Supreme Court's jurisdiction? What then of the quasi-judicial functions of the Governor's council? Those questions might have led to paralyzing disputes between Hastings and Impey had not Hastings, who was interested in native law, found Impey sympathetic and ready to cooperate.

By 1781 the Supreme Court had given up its claim to decide upon revenue cases and Impey agreed to link the two systems of law by serving in person on Hasting's civil courts for Indians, but the conflict of authority had already been troublesome: for instance, a rajah had been ordered to pay by the Supreme Court— and not to pay by the Supreme Council. Cases like this made rich material for critics of Hastings's *régime* and Impey was represented at home, notably by Francis, as the tool of Hastings. The alacrity with which Impey and his fellow-judges were able to find Nand Kumar, the central figure in Francis's attack upon Hastings, guilty of forgery was also held against him. With more justice he could be accused of jobbery. "Pulbundi" he was called after he had got the "pulbundi"—upkeep of roads and embankments—of Burdwan, worth £15,000 a year, for an impoverished cousin. So he came home in 1783 to find a menacing temper among the Whigs. In 1788 he was impeached and sat under a remarkable display of oratory by Elliot, who moved himself and others to tears with his elegiac upon "the murdered rajah." Impey lacked a winning personality. "If you are in the hanging mood," said Cornwallis, who expressed sympathy for Hastings, "you may tuck up Sir Elijah Impey without giving anybody the smallest concern." Burke put the Whig view with a crude disregard for the conventions: "He [Hastings] murdered Nand Kumar by the hand of Elijah Impey." But Impey defended himself with skill and Pitt and his legal advis-

ers declared their disbelief in the existence of a conspiracy between Hastings and the Chief Justice. The impeachment was not
pressed and he was acquitted honorably. However, he discovered
that the popular view did not die so easily, when he stood for Parliament at Stafford in 1790. He chose his opponent unwisely. The
followers of Sheridan paraded about the streets with the effigy of a
black man hanging from a gibbet, and Impey had to go elsewhere
to find himself a seat.

Sir J. Stephen, *The Story of Nuncomar and the Impeachment of Sir Elijah
Impey*, 2 vols., 1905.

WARREN HASTINGS (1732–1818) was the defendant in the most
prolonged political trial in English history. When he was eventually
acquitted, his fortune was almost expended, his health broken, his
reputation at the mercy of Whig historians like Macaulay. But his
achievement in India survived. More than any man after Clive,
Hastings was the creator of the Indian Empire.

He was born at Churchill in Oxfordshire in 1732. His mother
died in childbirth, his father vanished, and he was left to be nurtured by a village foster mother. His grandfather, rector of Daylesford, taught Hastings to be proud of his ancient but impoverished
family; from him he acquired his lifelong ambition to buy back the
family house. His uncle sent him to Westminster, where he was
school-fellow with two future prime ministers, Shelburne and Portland, and acquired the nickname of "the classical boy" for his taste
for Latin poetry. In his own words, his youth was that of a "solitary,
insulated wanderer." But he did not lack cultivation when he was
sent out to India as a writer in the service of the East India Company; he never fell far below his own high conception of a gentleman. Another clue to his career in India can be found in his
knowledge of Indian life: he learned Urdu and Persian, studied Indian literature, law, and institution and based his conduct on the
principle that India should be ruled for the Indians. To subject Indians to our legal code would, he wrote, be "wanton tyranny"; he
proposed rather to found the authority of British government in
Bengal on its ancient laws. From the start he showed his distrust of
general principles and doctrinaire solutions that took no account
of local traditions; he was in the opposite camp to those who
viewed India in the light of John Locke and the Bill of Rights. His

own faults of temperament, the grievances of servants and rivals, the complex involvement of the affairs of the company with political interests, and the turn of events that made India a crucial issue in the parliamentary struggle, all shaped his stormy career. His were the problems of a man of ambition, who was also an altruist, caught up with the development of a great trading company into a territorial empire, in an area of breathtaking opportunity for profit and power. Inevitably the picture that emerges is one of many shades and subtleties.

In 1756 Hastings was imprisoned when Surajah Dowlah overran the British settlements in Bengal: an early lesson in the flimsiness of the company's position when native rulers turned sour. Clive found him too cautious in his proceedings, more the administrator than the soldier. From 1758 to 1761 he was the British resident in Murshidabad, then a member of the Calcutta Council. He made a fortune of some £30,000, modest by current standards, mostly by private trading, and returned home in 1764, to live for five years the life of a "nabob." He indulged his taste for fine things, had himself painted by Reynolds, met Dr. Johnson, who said that he "had too much pleasure to forget" the occasion, and dealt generously with his relations. In 1769 he returned to India to be second in Council at Madras, and to repair the disorder into which his personal finances had fallen in his absence. The problems he encountered were typical ones: the ill effects of the practice of most of the English company servants of acting as bankers to the nabob, the graft of Benfield and Macpherson, quarrels with Sir Eyre Coote, always the constant threat from Hyder Ali. Against this background he struggled with administration: a new water supply, the extermination of pariah dogs, a new hospital. Then he was appointed to the governorship of Bengal. "A crown of thorns" a friend told him it would be.

Two famines had devastated Bengal in 1770 and 1772; a quarter perhaps of the population had died. The revenues of the company declined accordingly. But military expenditure rose as the English absorbed the Carnatic. A general economic crisis in 1771–72 affected the sales of the company and it was reduced to seeking the support of the government. The atmosphere was rancorous, for money had been lost in rash speculation and the company itself was torn apart by the struggle for influence and patronage between conflicting groups. The government sought to control a situation in which the company had several different policies—those of Calcutta, Madras, and Bombay—in which reforms were checked by the vested interest of company officials in private trading, and loan-mongering. North's Regulating Act created a supreme presidency, Bengal, to be ruled over by a Governor-General and council of four. Under Hastings, whose choice was approved by the company, there were Barwell, another company man and Hastings's ally; Colonel Monson and Philip Francis, appointments from outside the Company; General Clavering, commander-in-chief of Indian forces and the royal nominee. The last three of these men were to be opponents of Hastings, Philip Francis a venomous rival. Hastings had to satisfy two interests which were bound at times to conflict: the company wanted commercial advance, but the government was primarily interested in its stability as a finance house, and peaceful consolidation in India. In 1784, by Pitt's Act, the trading and political functions were cut apart; Hastings had, as he said, "but a delegated and fettered power." If he were not to be powerless, he must use his own judgment and his own followers. By nature autocratic, though gracious in manners, he preferred to work through personal contacts with Indian rulers and merchants rather than through committees where decisions evolved from discussion and compromise. He was a benevolent dictator, but a difficult colleague.

Hastings believed that Clive's Dual System, which he had seen at work in Madras, was unworkable. He wished instead to establish in Bengal an English government, and around it Indian states, friendly to the English but allowed to rule themselves. Inside Bengal he hoped to leave local government to Indians, supervised by committees of senior administrators. Thus he hoped that Englishmen would keep out of the lower levels of government; at the same time he looked for a revival of Indian law and custom. Thus his provincial civil courts administered native law which he himself studied meticulously. Under North's Act a new Supreme Court had been set up, but with uncertain functions; Hastings's solution was typical of his philosophy and of his method. Sir Elijah Impey, fellow-Westminster scholar and President of the Appeal Court, gave up the court's claim to pronounce upon revenue disputes (in 1781); at the same time he associated the two legal systems by serving personally on Hastings's civil courts for Indians. The dispute caused bitterness and Impey was recalled and impeached: his personal agreement with Hastings was assumed to be corrupt. But the impeachment was the product of the long struggle between Hastings and his council, at the heart of which was Hastings's personal clash with Francis. The latter, adept at intrigue, a formidable mixture of politician and doctrinaire, wished England to limit her commitments to the trading ports. Hastings, chary of pushing government interference beyond what would be accepted, felt that the English officials must be allowed their perquisites. His standard was expressed in the verse of the Gita which he liked to quote: "Let the motive be in the deed, not in the event. Be not one whose motive for action is the hope of reward."

The council hindered his every move. He had begun by establishing friendly relations with the state of Oudh; he lent to the vizier, Shuja-ud-doula, troops to use in his defense against the Maratha princes. When he died, in 1775, the council raised the price of company troops, forced the new ruler, Asaf-ud-daula, to give Benares to the Company and to allow the begums (mother and widow of the dead vizier) to keep three-quarters of Shuja's fortune. They abolished the bank which Hastings had created to bring some order into the finances of Oudh, attacked the government monopolies in salt and opium, and charged the Governor-General with corruption in his dealings with zemindars, landed tax-farmers. Indiscreet rather than greedy, Hastings published the amounts that he received and handed them over to the company. Through two seedy agents, Nand Kumar, a money-lender, and Joseph Fowke, a European diamond dealer, armed with evidence scraped up from the bazaars of Calcutta, Francis, Clavering, and Monson pressed charges of corrupt dealings with the Mani Begum. When Hastings made countercharge of conspiracy, Nand Kumar's own enemies were emboldened to have him arrested for forgery. Brought before Impey in the Supreme Court, he was tried by English laws and found guilty. Hastings did not intervene to save him. When Francis worked up an agitation against him he went so far as to offer his resignation, through his agent Macleane. Macleane used his authority to do this in October 1776. But by the time that it was known in India that North had accepted his resignation, Hastings was feeling more secure. He therefore defied Clavering, when he declared himself governor, ordered the troops to stand by him, and secured a ruling from the Supreme Court in his favor. North was embroiled in American affairs and glad to reinstate him; so he resumed his active governorship in the face of the threat posed by the renewal of war with France. Monson died in 1776, Clavering in 1777, and Hastings pressed ahead with his schemes of reform: an inquest into the value of land for tax purposes in Bengal and the institution of local magistrates in place of the provincial councils—forerunners of the modern district commissioner.

The last five years of Hastings's rule saw a fight for survival. Nervous of French friendship with the Maratha princes, Hastings had backed the Council of Bombay which had involved itself, rashly, in a quarrel with the Marathas. When the Bombay army was beaten and forced to capitulate at Wangoon, Hastings sent an expedition across the continent to assist Bombay and himself attacked the enemy from the east. The "key to Hindustan" fell when Captain Popham, with a small force, scaled the high walls of Gwalior. By such feats India was saved at a time when a weakening of nerve on the part of the Governor-General could have been fatal. Peace was negotiated in the name of the Maratha confederacy. But Francis criticized Hastings's conduct of the war. When Hastings called him "void of truth and honor" in an official minute at council, Francis called him out to a duel. Hastings wounded him and he returned to England, to nurse his wounds and his grievances. Hastings faced another crisis when Madras blundered into war with Hyder Ali, having already offended the Nizam of Hyderabad. He acted with speed, bribed Berar to be neutral, suspended the acting governor of Madras, and dispatched Sir Eyre Coote, Clavering's successor on the Bengal Council, to take charge in the Carnatic. By methods which would later be held against him he collected enough money for the cattle, grain, and rice that Coote needed. The fine old soldier did the rest, with victories in 1781 at Porto Novo and 1782 at Arni. The French, under Bussy, assisted Hyder Ali, but neither he nor his ferocious son Tipu made much headway. In 1784 peace was made with Mysore. Hyderabad had already been placated by Hastings's diplomacy so that she played little part in the war. When Hastings sailed home in 1785 he could justly claim that the British, under his inspiration, had held, even improved, their position, while elsewhere they had been beaten.

Fox's India Bill of 1783, which did not become law, and Pitt's of 1784 which did, were designed to deal with the basic problem of the two interests, national and commercial, which North's Act had not solved. Pitt's Act, setting up a Board of Control, did not differ in principle from that of the Whigs. They saw the defeat of 1783 in terms of a conspiracy between the court, its instrument Pitt, and a corrupt set of company directors. Their resentment at political defeat and Burke's ideal of an independent company, purged by its severance from political concerns, were reinforced by the allegations of Francis. In Burke's mind, at once generous, noble, and prejudiced, Hastings embodied the vices of British rule in India. Years of power under stress and the Indian sun had indeed hardened him; he was confident, but he was also vulnerable, for he had helped to prop up a bad system, notably in Madras, where he had been supported by Macpherson, a notorious tycoon.

Burke, Fox, and Sheridan moved that Hastings be impeached. Their first charge, about the Rohilla war, was rejected; on the second and third, ill-treatment of Chait Singh and the begums of Oudh, they obtained a majority. Pitt knew that the Whigs wished to embarrass him by attacking Hastings; at the same time he wished to show the company that the government was in control. On the Benares charge he defended Hastings against the extremer charges, then declared that he must vote against him, because the fine inflicted was too severe. After this the opposition was encouraged to mount a trial which became a gigantic survey of British rule in India, a theatrical display, and social occasion. For the stiff, proud proconsul it was a sustained ordeal which broke him in health and fortune; for London society, at first an unparalleled excitement. The trial began on February 13, 1788. Hastings, dressed in a plain red suit, "pale, ill, and altered" said Fanny Burney, stood up to a torrent of words: hysterically exaggerated in Burke's day-long tirades, eloquent to the point where ladies swooned when Sheridan recounted the fate of the begums of Oudh. The managers defeated their own ends by depicting an autocratic man as a slavering, sadistic tyrant. When, in 1795, after 145 days spread over seven years, Hastings was acquitted of all the charges, his name was vindicated. Meanwhile, in India, Cornwallis, confident that he represented the new attitude, purged the service.

Hastings lingered on, in innocuous old age. He had brought home only £80,000; he spent over £100,000 on his defense. The directors made him a generous grant, however, and he was able to repurchase Daylesford. The House of Commons never acceded to his request that the vote of 1787, which he felt as a stain on his honor, be expunged. He, in turn, refused a peerage. Only a degree of Oxford University and a seat on the Privy Council would he accept. There was a certain grand Cincinnatus-like simplicity about this man, a great servant of the British Raj and benefactor of the native races.

E. P. Moon, *Warren Hastings and British India*, 1947.
K. G. Feiling, *Warren Hastings*, 1954.
P. J. Marshall, *The Impeachment of Warren Hastings*, 1965.

SIR PHILIP FRANCIS (1740–1818) was very likely, but not certainly, the notorious "Junius." Even if he were not, Francis was an unusually interesting person, exceptionally clever, ultimately elusive, for his great gifts were spent largely in intrigue and propaganda.

Like Shelburne he was Irish and like him an intellectual who combined original views with a taste for intrigue. Shelburne is another possible contender for the dubious title of "Junius." Francis began in a smaller way than the future minister and his ambitions were necessarily more modest. He was educated at St. Paul's School. His father put himself in the way of advancement, when he became chaplain to the Fox family. After some diplomatic and clerical experience Philip went to the War Office as first clerk. With Calcraft, a rich place-hunter, he dabbled in the politics of opposition and resigned from his post in 1772. Calcraft left him a legacy, but Francis decided that North's stable *régime* offered more to follower than to foe. He had some reputation for ability and had cultivated a wide acquaintance in the city and press. Among his confidants were Clive and Burke. From the former he learned the proconsul's view of India, and his disparaging opinion of Hastings. Burke was deeply involved in Indian affairs, through his brother, and Francis's Whig principles made some appeal. Agnostic, skeptical, an amateur economist, Francis seems to be posing for the model of an eighteenth-century intellectual. His irony and talent for conversation endeared him to women. Those who believed him to be "Junius" and saw a fierce spirit behind the elegant facade, believed him also to be a man to fear. The king was among these and he was quoted as saying, "Junius will write no more" after his appointment to be councillor in Bengal. Hush money is as good an explanation as any, for no one knew why, in 1773, Francis got the coveted appointment to the council, with £10,000 a year and op-portunities, under the conditions of North's Regulating Act, to control the Governor-General and impose his own view of policy.

From the start Francis was the implacable enemy of Hastings and the leader of a sustained conspiracy against him. With Monson and Clavering, against Hastings and Barwell, he sought to reverse the governor's policy and to undermine his position. Essentially Francis believed in the logical, neat solution, which could be pre-sented in orderly fashion in a minute, debated in committee, and imposed with consistency in the field. It was the way of the home-bred civil servant, steeped in the maxims of the classical writers and imbued with the rational spirit of his time. At the same time he was convinced that all company officials were corrupt. To re-duce their power he advocated a policy of withdrawal; operating simply as traders from established bases, the company men should keep aloof from Indian affairs. As against this, Hastings repre-sented the experience of a man for whom India had been the world since the age of eighteen. He believed, too, that he was act-ing in the interests of the Indians. His altruism was modified by his experience of Indian tax collectors, traders, and lawyers and his choice was seldom as clear-cut as Francis would have it be. He knew that he had to act through the Indians and in traditional ways. Against Francis's dogmatism, his fluency in council, and his talent for lobbying opinion, he opposed his local knowledge, toughness, and pride.

In the end Hastings won. Francis and his allies succeeded in ru-ining good relations with Oudh by tampering with Hastings's policy of client-states. They demoted his agents and created such a vivid picture of mismanagement at home that Hastings felt impelled to offer, and North to accept, his resignation. But Hastings recovered his position and in his main objective Francis failed. Impey, the Chief Justice who played an important part in Hastings's system, quarreled with Hastings, was dismissed, and impeached. But Hast-ings remained governor until 1785. Francis saw his own allies die: Monson in 1776, Clavering in 1777. He himself suffered terribly in the debilitating climate and his desperate and bitter mood is re-flected in his letters, often hysterical in tone. He gambled heavily, making £13,000 at one sitting; he was involved in a scandalous liai-son with another man's wife. He made large sums out of the deals which he condemned in others and sent home altogether £45,000.

He employed shabby instruments, Nand Kumar and Fowke, to prove Hastings guilty of corrupt dealing with the Mani Begum. When Nand Kumar was found guilty of forgery and executed, the attack recoiled upon the heads of those who planned it. When he attacked Hastings's prosecution of the war, in 1780, Hastings denounced him as "void of truth and honor." Francis called him out to a duel, but was wounded, resigned, and went home.

He still saw himself as the champion of an ideal: "the British Empire in India is tottering to its foundation in spite of everything I could do to save it," he wrote in typically grandiloquent vein. Now he sought to carry on the fight in the political field, where he could call on allies to represent the cause. "Pale yellow and a look of diabolical purpose," someone recalled of his appearance. He was still capable of civil conduct; he was a fond father and he loved cats. But he was consumed with rancor, and by pamphlet, letter, and all the means of persuasion at his command, he sought to bring Hastings to account. After the shock they had received over the defeat of their India Bill (the further injury of Pitt's Bill in the following year, 1784) when Francis became a member of Parliament and Fox, Grey, above all Burke were bent on making a political issue out of Hastings's governor-generalship. In 1785 they secured a majority for two of their charges and in 1788 they mounted a trial which was to last for seven years. Hastings was acquitted at the end of it. Philip Francis's hope that the trial would "gibbet" his character "to all eternity" was disappointed. But there was plenty of life in him. If he was cheated of his ambition to become Governor-General of India, he did make progress in good Whig houses. He was devoted to the cause of "the Friends of the People" and he became a close adherent of the prince regent. In 1806 he was made K.C.B. In 1814 he married a second wife, half his age. She was convinced that he was "Junius"—but even she seems to have had no certain proof of the matter. If Francis knew the identity of the author of those letters he took it with him to the grave.

J. Cannon, ed., *The Letters of Junius*, 1978.

SIR WILLIAM JONES (1746–94) was internationally famous for his learning in several fields. At different times he was a Fellow of University College, Oxford, a practicing barrister, reforming politician, and Indian judge; he was a notable classical scholar and his legal treatises were definitive; he was no mean poet and a member of Dr. Johnson's circle. He mastered a number of Oriental languages, began the codification of Hindu law, and helped to popularize the themes and literature of the East by his renderings of them into English verse.

His father was a Welshman, self-taught but a brilliant mathematician, recognized by Newton and befriended by Anson, who appreciated his work on navigation. He died when William was only three; at seven William was sent to Harrow, where he came under the influence of a fine teacher, R. C. Sumner. His friends numbered the future Lord Teignmouth, Governor-General of India and Jones's biographer; Samuel Parr, who was later to destroy his chance of becoming head master of Harrow by voting for Wilkes in the Middlesex election; Bennett, a less colorful scholar, whose hobby was tracing Roman roads in Britain; and Halhed, who was to produce the first Sanskrit grammar. They fostered in each other the precocious scholarship and abstruse interests which may have acquired a special savor as a form of retreat from the hurly-burly of the eighteenth-century public school. They mapped out surrounding fields into the Greek states and transformed their games into Peloponnesian Wars. Greece was a natural magnet; it is interesting, too, to see how they were drawn to the East and especially to India, where the British raj was being so rapidly extended.

At Oxford Jones arrived a finished scholar. At this time University College was second to none in academic standards, and also a nest of lawyers, including Chambers and the brothers Scott. To help keep himself he tutored Lord Althorp, son and heir of Earl Spencer; after three years, in 1769, he went with the child to Harrow: the connection ended when Jones tried to insist upon complete control of his education. The Spencer connection was nonetheless a useful one. Althorp had an energetic career and was First Lord of the Admiralty in Nelson's time. The portrait of Jones by Reynolds can be seen today at Althorp House. Jones used his leisure to widen his knowledge of Eastern languages. He was an exceptionally gifted linguist and is said to have known thirteen languages and to have been acquainted with another twenty-eight. He learned Arabic from one Mirza, a Syrian from Aleppo. At the request of the King of Denmark he translated from the Persian the history of Nadir Shah, a seventeenth-century warrior king. His *Poeseos Asiaticae Commentariorum*, in which he made a metrical comparison between the classical poetry and the East, enhanced his academic fame. In 1771 he produced the Persian grammar which was to prove useful to generations of Indian administrators. Linguistic studies were already fashionable: Horne Tooke, Priestley, and, of course, Dr. Johnson were all formidable grammarians. Now Jones, who corresponded with European scholars like Count Revikski, caught the mood with verses, flowered and fluent. In 1772 he published his very popular *Asiatic Poems*, purporting to be from the original but only flimsily connected if at all. About this time Jones was sometimes to be seen in Persian dress. He enjoyed his cult, but he had sterner ambitions.

He had originally been put off the law by "the crude and barbarous style" of the lawbook Latin but in 1774 he returned to the Bar. He was appointed Commissioner of Bankrupts and was busy on circuit; altogether these were years of intense activity for he wrote treatises, including one, *Essay on Bailments*, which is a classic account of a branch of law almost ignored by Blackstone. To add to a picture of a sprightly, well-balanced character, he was a keen horseman who loved hunting—but despised beagling because, as he said, he liked everything big and disliked everything little—enjoyed swimming, skating, and dancing: the whole man indeed. He also acquired the liberal views which were to become popular during the American War. It may be that he was affected by the scenes of poverty that he witnessed on his journeys. He certainly seems, like Wyvill, to have believed that the liberties of his countrymen were impaired by a corrupt and oligarchic executive and legislature. In 1780 he stood as the popular Whig candidate for Oxford University but withdrew when he found that he could make no dent upon the position of the official Whig and Tory candidates. Since he lost no chance of urging freedom for the American colonies and the suppression of the slave trade, played with the idea of universal franchise, and confessed to being at least a theoretical republican, preferment was delayed; at last, however, in 1783 he became a judge of the Supreme Court at Calcutta. If without financial independence he could make no mark on English politics, there he was superbly equipped for what proved to be his most important work.

When Jones went to India, Hastings was Governor-General; Cornwallis followed him, a great proconsul who devoted himself to the reform of Bengal upon English principles of government. In

1793 Lord Teignmouth succeeded, and carried on the enlightened work. In the conditions created by these outstanding men, imbued with the spirit of service to the native races, Jones's talents blossomed. He worked hard in the courts, projected and supervised the codification of Hindu law, translated Sanskrit works, and elaborated in lectures to the Royal Asiatic Society, of which he was first president, his thesis that Persia was the matrix from which the dispersal of the world's population had begun. His linguistic studies give him some claim to being the founder of comparative philology. As if his central pursuits were not enough, he was an enthusiastic botanist and classified the Indian flora in the terminology of Linnaeus, played skillful chess, and, characteristically, wrote a monograph on the Indian game. From his little wooden house outside Fort William he would walk three miles before dawn to the court, proceed by palanquin to the court house, have a cold bath and breakfast, and work for two hours before his five-hour session on the bench. He made a fortune of fifty thousand pounds by saving rather than by corruption, but he did not return to England to enjoy it. Just after his resignation, and after he had sent his wife home to recover her health, he died. Like so many Englishmen he had given himself to the East: we are left to speculate what the rest of his career might have been. He was better equipped than Bentham to be a legal reformer; he might have been drawn into radical politics, for he certainly aligned himself with Price and against Burke; he might have preferred to work at law and poetry in some country retreat. It became fashionable among utilitarians, like Mill, to decry his work as superficial. Now, as the dust settles upon the British raj and on debates about its government, we are better able to appreciate not only Jones's preeminence as scholar but his value as one of the men who wanted India to be ruled in the interests of its peoples.

Lord Teignmouth, *Memoirs of the Life, Writings and Correspondence of Sir William Jones*, 1804.
P. Brown, *The Chathamites*, 1967.
A. Murray, ed., *Sir William Jones: a Commemoration*, 1998.

JAMES COOK (1728–79), sea captain, was one of the greatest explorers of the eighteenth century. His voyages took him to places which have become a byword for romance, but he was the most pragmatic of men. An accomplished seaman, a natural leader, he was also a meticulous and scientific recorder of journeys, places, and people. His journals are a classic account of adventure, the more stirring because of the modest and unemotional tone of the author. To them the reader should turn if he wishes to know more about Cook.

He was the second of nine children, born in a mud cottage in the North Yorkshire village of Marton-in-Cleveland. His father was an agricultural laborer who learned to read when he was nearly eighty years old in order that "he might gratify a parent's pride by perusing his son's first voyage round the world." It can be guessed from the unadorned style of his first journal, before it was edited, that James Cook also received only the elements of a formal education. But he was not content to remain a farm worker and he soon quarreled with the keeper of the country store in which he worked. He was next bound apprentice to the shipping firm of Walker at Whitby and he learned navigation in the coastal coal trade. In the spring of 1755 Cook, then mate of a collier, volunteered to join the navy, "having a mind to try his fortune that way." He served as an able seaman on the *Eagle*, sixty tons, captain, Sir Hugh Palliser—a valuable patron then and afterwards. He spent the war years in North American waters, his ship was long engaged in charting the St. Lawrence, and he was in command of some of the boats on the night of Wolfe's landing beneath the Heights of Abraham. After the war he continued with his map-making under Palliser, now Governor of Newfoundland. It was Palliser who recommended him for the command of an expedition to be sent to the South Seas in 1768 for the ostensible purpose of observing the transit of the planet Venus.

Cook secured the purchase of a bluff-bowed Whitby collier— the *Endeavour* bark—of 366 tons, square-rigged on three masts. In addition to a complement of eighty-four, she carried eleven civilians, among them Sir Joseph Banks, wealthy young amateur scientist, the artists Parkinson and Buchan, and a botanist, Dr. Solander. The secret and more important purpose of the expedition was to search for a great southern continent, "Terra Australis Incognita." (The voyages of Byron, Wallis, and Carteret had not done more than to outline the problem.) The French were also keenly interested in the discovery of a continent which might compensate them for the loss of North America. There was rivalry between the powers to fill in the details of the map which still left blank vast stretches of the Pacific. According to the charts available to Cook and his rival, Bougainville, which were derived from the discoveries of Quiros and Tasman, an imaginary land mass lay between the west coast of New Zealand and Staten Land (east of Tierra del Fuego). The only known parts of Australia, the north and west coasts, were referred to as New Holland. Cook's secret instructions showed him the way toward the delineation of the New Zealand coast, which was one of the achievements of the voyage. He also demonstrated on this voyage that "New Holland" was bounded on the east by a coast which he called "New South Wales." Cook was given precise instructions and he had the true instinct of the explorer: it was his ambition, not only to go further than any man had ever been, but as far as it was possible for a man to go. In the second voyage (1772–75) he seems to have formulated his own plan. By prosecuting his discoveries "as near to the South Pole as possible," he reduced Terra Australis to the limits of Antarctica. He was provided with two ships and had careful personal attention from Lord Sandwich himself. He had astronomers, botanists, and a landscape artist, Hodges. On his return from an exhaustive search he was able to write: "I have now done with the Southern Pacific ocean and flatter myself that no one will think I have left it unexplored."

On his first voyage Cook contributed further to the conquest of scurvy, which had already been tackled by the East India Company and by Dr. James Lind. Wallis, who sailed round the world in 1766–68, had lost only one man upon a diet of fruit juices and fresh vegetables. Cook stressed the importance of cleanliness and plentiful fresh water. But it was Pelham, Secretary to the Commissioners of Victualling, who was responsible for the stocking of such remedies as sauerkraut. The main part of Cook's first voyage passed without casualties until dysentery was contracted from a long stay in Batavia. The voyages also brought discoveries of great importance to navigators. Cook found, by the use of a chronometer, that he could determine longitude with accuracy. Hitherto log lines had been used. Lunar observations gave him fair results on the first voyage. Harrison's watch, duplicated by Kendall, was Cook's "never failing guide" on his second and third voyages. The accuracy of his charts and positions are perhaps his most impressive achievement.

Cook was equally exact in his accounts of native customs. He was able to record the habits of primitive societies and innocent lives, before they were corrupted by adventurers and tamed by missionaries, in a way that has proved invaluable to anthropologists.

Indeed, certain concepts of this science, totem and taboo, first occur in his pages. His and parallel discoveries made popular the romantic notion of the noble savage. But he was without illusions. He wished the Polynesians and Maoris to have the polish of civilization; he was sufficiently of the eighteenth century for that. At the same time he was not condescending; so he won the trust of the natives. A man too of iron self-control, he would not let himself or his crew indulge much in the easy pleasures provided by the islanders. Tall and strong, he drank little and never swore. Hastytempered when he was crossed, but calm in dangers, stern but fair to his men, Cook was in instinct and conduct a gentleman. His first report to the Admiralty paid tribute to his experts, officers, and seamen, and the "cheerfulness and alertness that will always do honor to British seamen."

Between his voyages Cook was something of a public figure. For his paper on scurvy he was honored by the Royal Society. The narrative of his voyage found avid readers. He was presented to the King and appointed Fourth Captain of Greenwich Hospital. This post, a little sedentary for his tastes, he was never to occupy, for in 1776 he was sent again to the Pacific on the time-honored quest, now renewed, for the Northwest Passage. Cook was to search, with the *Resolution* and the *Discovery*, for the Pacific Entrance which Drake had failed to find. He followed a new diagonal route from Tahiti to America and therefore discovered the Hawaian group— the Sandwich Islands as he called them. He made landfall on the American coast and followed it up to the Bering Strait and reached the latitude of 70° 44' when he was stopped "by an impenetrable body of ice." He returned to winter at Hawaii before resuming the search, but then he was killed, on February 14, like Magellan, covering the retreat of his men. When news of it was received on board, wrote the Swiss seaman Zimmerman, "everybody on the ship was silent and depressed; we all felt that we had lost a father." His body was dismembered by the natives with the grisly honors reserved for chieftains. The *Endeavour* was given safe passage home by the French government with whom England was now at war. When George III heard the news of the great explorer, he wept. His widow, who had seen little of Cook in life, was given a pension and her family a coat of arms.

J. A. Williamson, *Cook and the Opening of the Pacific*, 1948.
J. C. Beaglehole, *The Life of Captain James Cook*, 1974.

JAMES BRUCE (1730–94), explorer, had a singular fate. He was one of the first Europeans to travel extensively in Africa. He made a tremendous journey in parts virtually unknown to the civilized world and he wrote an account of his adventures which was a popular success. Yet he was derided by literary London, treated as a romancer and a charlatan. His early life had been saddened by the death of his young wife; his later years were embittered by the failure to win the respect which he deserved.

A Scotsman, an elder son who was to inherit property which was to make him wealthy and independent, belonging to a family which claimed descent from the ancient Scottish kings, Bruce was sent to Harrow, where he was a promising scholar, and to Edinburgh to study law, which he hated. Immensely tall, six foot four, he seems to have overtaxed his strength. He was ill and spent some years in convalescence, without occupation, before going to London, where he married a wine merchant's daughter and entered her father's firm. She died of consumption in first pregnancy and Bruce retreated into solitary ways, yearning for travel. He made an unusually ambitious Grand Tour and then settled down as British Consul at Algiers, where the ferocious Bey made life dangerous even for diplomats. There he perfected his plan for ascending the Nile and penetrating into the fastness of Abyssinia.

Dressed as a dervish, and accompanied by a young Italian secretary, he set out from Cairo in 1768. He had prepared himself by studies of archaeology and he was a careful draftsman. He was to show self-sufficiency and powers of endurance which were to carry him through all dangers with the air of a laird surveying his estates. His secretary died in 1770 at Gonda, and there is no independent witness, therefore, of his tales. There is evidence that he was inaccurate in his accounts, especially in measurement; he was more the romantic than the scientist. His prejudices sometimes led him astray. Imbued with a fanatical mistrust of Rome and priesthood, he went out of his way to cast doubt on the narration of the Jesuits Paez and Lobo, who had explored Ethiopia in the seventeenth century. But his own journey to the source of the Blue Nile in a swamp under Ghish Mountain was not what he thought it was. He was not the first, for Pedro Paez had been there before him, and the true source of the Nile is in fact a thousand miles away in Lake Victoria. To get so far, to return safely against all hazards, malaria and the guinea worm, in conditions which sent men mad; to drag himself along with suppurating feet, braving sandstorms and the Arabs who guarded the water wells, was nonetheless a superb pioneer effort.

Bruce returned to London and told stories of the sanguinary chaos that was Abyssinian life at this time, and of the strange customs he had seen. Unfortunately he was accepted, not as a serious explorer, but as an entertainer. His tales were not believed; some even professed to doubt whether he had been there at all. Dr. Johnson was enraged by his attack upon Father Lobo, whose *Voyage into Abyssinia* he had once translated. Bruce invited caricature: did he really see Abyssinians cut steaks off a living cow and send it away to grass? Seventeen years after his return, in 1790, he produced his definitive account in five large quarto volumes, but again he was treated as a liar. Meanwhile he had married again, to Mary Dundas, much younger than himself. She bore him several children, but died before him, in 1788. Till then he had been happy enough, enriched by the discovery of coal on his estates, applying himself to astronomy in his own observatory, growing immensely fat. In his last years, however, illusions of grandeur grew upon him. He was always a lavish entertainer. At the end of a dinner party he tripped on his stairs and killed himself. Today we can assess his place more fairly than the people of his day. Much of what he wrote was true and later explorers found him a useful guide. The French took him seriously and his work contributed much to the growth of their interest in North Africa.

James Bruce, *Travels to Discover the Sources of the Nile*, 1790.
Alan Moorehead, *The Blue Nile*, 1962.

ERASMUS DARWIN (1731–1802), zoologist and natural philosopher, is an English representative of the *philosophes*, the intellectual aristocracy of Europe. He was a medical man by training, a botanist by inclination, "extremely speculative" in everything; he corresponded with Rousseau and founded the Philosophical Society at Derby in 1784.

Darwin was the moving spirit of the Lunar Society in Birmingham. He declined the invitation of George III to become his physician, preferring to devote himself to the study of plants. In 1778 he formed a botanical garden near Lichfield. He wrote mostly in verse: the *Botanic Garden*, of which the engaging *Loves of the Plants* is the best-known part (1789), the *Temple of Nature*, and the *Origin of Society* (1803). Something of that gentle, orderly, sober spirit that reminds us of White of Selborne and the poet Gray, a pleasing feature of eighteenth-century culture, pervades Darwin's work. But scientists find particular interest in his prose writing, notably *Zoonomia*, or the *Laws of Organic Life*, in which, carrying further the work of Buffon, the author of the natural history which had prepared the way for the idea of evolution in nature, Darwin set out to show how living things had found their different ways of adapting themselves to their environment. When he collated the various classes of phenomena, changes produced after birth, by artificial cultivation, climate, crossing, or mutilation, with the "similarity of structure in all the warm-blooded animals, including mankind," he was led to the conclusion that all had alike been produced from a similar living filament. How did such changes occur? He believed it was by the transmission of characters acquired, sometimes as an act of will. "All animals undergo perpetual transformations; which are in part produced by their own exertions . . . and many of these acquired forms or propensities are transmitted to their posterity." It remained for Lamarck, and for his own grandson Charles Darwin, to develop this theory and to find scientific evidence to justify general acceptance of the idea of evolution.

Darwin left no uncertain mark on those who met him. As a physician of repute he traveled much. On his carriage, he had a large pail lashed for water, with some oats and hay for the horses. The top of the carriage had a skylight to provide extra light for the doctor, who was in the habit of writing on scraps of paper as he journeyed; most of his books were written in this way. On the floor of the carriage there might be a pile of books up to the height of the window. He was a massive figure, his head almost sunk on his shoulders, and the impression of wisdom that he conveyed was not diminished by a stammer which often made him hard to understand.

Hesketh Pearson, *Dr. Darwin*, 1931.
R. E. Schofield, *The Lunar Society of Birmingham*, 1963.

JOSEPH BANKS (1743–1820), naturalist, was the son of a Lincolnshire gentleman, William Banks of Revesby Abbey, from whom he inherited at the age of eighteen a fortune which gave him an income of £6000 a year. Harrow and Eton may both claim him; the latter properly, since he soon left the hill for the plain. At the age of fourteen he resolved to become a botanist, by his own account almost as if he had seen a vision, in a walk down a lane banked with wild flowers on a summer's evening. He learned his first lessons from old village women who taught him the secrets of their herbal remedies. He was single-minded, with an eagerness that would allow no obstacle. At Christ Church he found that the professor of botany did not lecture in his subject; he therefore went to Cambridge and brought back Israel Lyons, a young Jewish botanist, to be his personal tutor.

In 1766 Banks went with *H.M.S. Niger* to Newfoundland; the navy was concerned with fishery interests, he with plants and the life of the Esquimaux. In this year too he was elected Fellow of the Royal Society, upon the promise of a rich and gifted amateur rather than upon achievement. But he showed that he was no dilettante when he went on Cook's voyage to the South Seas in the *Endeavour*. Cook's object was to observe the transit of Venus. Banks was sponsored by the Royal Society for studying the geography, flora, and fauna of the South Seas. He spared no expense and the already cramped quarters of the ship were altered to find room for a Swedish botanist, Solander, pupil of Linnaeus; an assistant naturalist, also a Swede, Sporing; two painters, Buchan and Parkinson; two servants from Lincolnshire; two negroes; and, of course, two dogs. It is a good picture of the English gentleman preparing himself for the rigors of travel. The negroes, of course, soon died. Cook might have been expected to look askance at this *ménage* and at the botanizing squire with his elaborate equipment. But they became fast friends. Banks's lively interest in everything he saw, his resourcefulness and readiness to tackle anything, his indifference to danger, appealed to the sober seaman who was also a superb navigator and draftsman. Living with men like Banks and Solander for three years spent upon an exciting and novel enterprise must have sharpened his powers of observation. In the development of Cook, the great explorer, Banks played his part. Pictures and accounts of Banks at this time show him to have been pleasant-looking, good-tempered, energetic, a good talker on subjects that interested him—though Fanny Burney found him shy at a tea party. He was also a little vain, cheerfully sensuous, and less diffident than Cook about enjoying the company of the Polynesian women. Above all he was insatiably curious. His journal of the voyage is an entertaining account as well as an invaluable document for naturalists and socioloists. Banks returned from the three-year voyage a celebrity; perhaps this went to his head. Certainly he made unnecessary difficulties about arrangements for the next voyage and seems even to have tried to get a woman on board disguised as a man; he planned altogether to have a staff of thirteen. Cook would probably have liked him, but his pretensions annoyed the Admiralty Board. So Banks went instead to the Hebrides, where he made the beauties of Staffa known to the world, and to Iceland. He was probably the last educated person to see it before it was desolated by the great eruption of Skapta Jokull in 1773.

Banks remained to the end of his life a keen collector and investigator in the field of natural history, but he became increasingly involved in public duties and in social life. In 1779 he married Dorothea Hugessen, from whose letters in the Heber collection we learn much about his busy and fashionable life. Although Banks was keenly interested in other men's work, he published little himself. He was a friend of George III, who gave him a baronetcy in 1781. He repaid the king's interest by developing his estate at Kew and was one of the principal creators of the great botanical gardens. He was President of the Royal Society from 1778 until his death. He founded the African Association and he has some claim to the title of "Father of Australia" through his part in the foundation of New South Wales. His coach was a traveling laboratory, it was so fitted up to receive and examine specimens, and he had kangaroos in an enclosure in his park in Lincolnshire. Indeed, his name is one that one stumbles upon in all sorts of ways. He transferred the breadfruit from Tahiti to the West Indies, the mango from Bengal. When Edward IV's tomb was opened up in 1789, he was of course there, and he presented Horace Walpole with a few hairs from the royal skull. Today his name survives in the beautiful rose that is named after him.

Ed. W. Dawson, *Letters of Sir Joseph Banks*, 1958.

WILLIAM COWPER (1731–1800), poet, was the son of the rector of Berkhamsted. His mother died when he was six and he was sent to a small private school where he was atrociously bullied. This may have been a cause of the mental breakdowns of his adult life.

For the rest of his life he cherished the memory of his mother, safe haven in a forbidding world. At Westminster, however, he was happy both in his work and in his friendships. He learned there to compose good Latin verses, and he went on seemingly to a secure career in law. His great-uncle, Earl Cowper, had been Lord Chancellor; his grandfather a judge. Cowper practiced as a barrister until he was about thirty when, already showing signs of the morbid depression which was to grow on him, he was offered a clerkship in the House of Lords. He broke down under the fear of being found inadequate, tried to commit suicide more than once, and spent eighteen months in a private asylum.

For the rest of his life Cowper was more or less dependent on the kindness of friends and relatives. Even in the periods between his mental breakdowns he suffered from delusions, from fear of relapse, and, underlying all, a conviction that he was damned. He endured indeed the ultimate hell of the Calvinist who believes in predestination: he once said that he spent his night under the sense of God's contempt for him. Cowper's mental stability rested upon precarious foundations. Too exacting work, any sort of criticism, might throw him off balance; and yet this oversensitive soul was subjected to the pressures of evangelical religion in its straitest form. For after his recovery he went to live in Huntingdon, sensibly intending to live quietly. Soon he was adopted into the family of an evangelical minister, Mr. Unwin. After Unwin's death, two years later, he lived with the widow, Mary Unwin. In 1767 they moved to Olney to be under the direction of the noted evangelist John Newton, former slave-trader and now fanatical minister. Cowper was to be his assistant; he preached, composed hymns, and witnessed in his own life to the power of the Bible. Newton, though kind, was unsubtle and his enthusiasm was too much for Cowper, who again became demented. For a year Newton tended him, with Mrs. Unwin; then, happily for Cowper, Newton moved to London and the poet was left to find his own way of life.

There ensued a relatively placid period. Cowper kept pets— hares, cats and dogs, guinea-pigs, a squirrel, many sorts of songbird; his delightful observations of these animals show that he might have been a talented natural historian, another White. He also wrote poetry and translated Homer. He wrote engaging letters, to William Unwin, Mary's son, to Newton, constant in devotion, and to his cousin Lady Hesketh. Cowper was fortunate in having discerning friends. He enjoyed the less demanding forms of social activity and found sufficient exercise in his garden and walking the placid countryside of the Ouse valley. In Lady Austen he found another intimate friend, but when it became evident that she loved him, and Mary Unwin understandably showed signs of jealousy, she had to depart: meanwhile she had suggested the subjects of *The Task* and of *John Gilpin*, both published in 1785. Lady Hesketh then persuaded Cowper to move to Weston, just outside Olney, where he found new friends, the Catholic family of Throckmorton. Another attack struck him: the death of the younger William Unwin or the revival of his morbid fears may have caused it. But when he recovered, he settled to more regular work. His Homer was published by subscription in 1791; he then began to edit Milton. In 1794 he received a Crown pension of £300 a year. Possibly the collapse and paralysis of Mary Unwin, in about 1791, helped to give him a purpose; certainly he returned her care with interest. But their last years were increasingly forlorn. He moved to Norfolk, to the house of a cousin, in 1795, then to East Dereham. After Mary's death in 1796, Cowper slipped into a sort of vacancy, till merciful death brought an end to his impaired powers.

The memorial at Dereham is a pleasing one: "His virtues formed the magic of his song." Charles Lamb, who had reason to understand his condition, said that a simple style "springs spontaneously from the heart." The body of his achievement is not immense, some unpretentious but most engaging letters, some well-loved hymns and poems. But his gentle life was of value for itself and he conferred immortality upon his subjects: the *Royal George*, John Gilpin, his cat, Beau the spaniel, and Puss the hare. Even his own tragic version of religion he turned to a beautiful hymn: "God moves in a mysterious way." In some of his poems such as "Yardley Oak" with a humility and humor all his own, he anticipated some of the freedom of expression of the romantic poets.

Lord David Cecil, *The Stricken Deer*, 1929.
G. Thomas, *William Cowper and the Eighteenth Century*, 1935.

GEORGE CRABBE (1754–1832), poet, stands higher today with critics than at any time since his death. Victorians found his Augustan meter uninspiring and did not respond to his unsentimental view of nature. Now, however, his original quality is appreciated as it was by contemporaries. His realism is as telling in its way as that of Wordsworth, because it is grounded upon minute observation. We may even accept Byron's familiar judgment upon him: "Nature's sternest painter, yet her best."

Crabbe was born at the decayed Suffolk borough of Aldeburgh; only a few streets lay huddled behind the protective shingle, but it still returned two members of Parliament. Smuggling was an important industry as Crabbe would know since his father and grandfather were collectors of the salt tax. After schooling at Stowmarket Crabbe practiced medicine for a time in the borough. Helping his father with the salt barrels on Slaughden quay, ministering without much knowledge to the rough inhabitants, traveling the marshy wastes around the town, Crabbe found solace in wild flowers and poetry. He started to write in the conventional Augustan manner since he had not learned to use his own experience effectively. In 1774 he published, at Ipswich, a poem on the effects of drunkenness, a feeble parody of the *Dunciad*. But he was engaged to the daughter of a tanner, a Miss Elmy, and with this incentive to make his way and the assistance of a generous patron, Mr. Dudley North, in 1780, Crabbe went to London. From chary booksellers and unresponsive patrons he was rescued by Burke, who appreciated him, befriended him, got Dodsley to publish *The Library*, and gave Crabbe the encouragement to start work on *The Village*. The resources of the Church were called to sustain the poet: he took orders and became the Duke of Rutland's domestic chaplain at Belvoir. Crabbe married and *The Village* was acclaimed, by Dr. Johnson among others. The Archbishop of Canterbury conferred a degree upon him, and he entered upon a succession of livings in the gift of the duke or of Lord Chancellor Thurlow, who made amends for earlier slights by two small benefices in Dorsetshire.

Crabbe's mother was a gentle and pious woman and Crabbe was brought up to habits of devotion. He belonged, however, to the dry school of clergy, opposed to enthusiasm, violent against Methodism, but reluctant to reside. Indeed the history of his incumbencies, Frome St. Quintin and Evershot, Muston and Sweffling, is a history in miniature of the shortcomings of the Church in rural England. He did duty for other absentees when he lived at Allington, below Belvoir Castle, and at Glemham in Suffolk. After prolonged evasion he had to be recalled, by the mandate of the Bishop of Lincoln himself, to neglected Muston. By the time of his second stay there (he returned in 1805), his wife was in a decline brought about, perhaps, by the successive loss of five children, and she died there. There was much to sadden Crabbe in his private life. About 1790 too, he began to have recourse to opium on a doctor's advice; this does not seem, however, to have impaired either mind or body. Despondent and unhelpful pastor Crabbe may have been; he was, nevertheless, close to his people in some ways. At Belvoir he was uneasy, oversensitive, perhaps, in the menial position. Thurlow likened him to parson Adams, by which he may have intended only to convey that he was plain, a little rustic in his manners. Burke, however, discerned in him "the mind and feelings of a gentleman." He was straightforward and unaffected. Above all he was without cant. His poems are often bleak in their descriptions, but full of pathos and humor, and they show that he understood the circumstances of humble lives.

In 1807 the *Parish Register* was published, along with earlier poems. Crabbe returned to the theme of *The Village*, but on a larger canvas: the village clergyman relates to a friend incidents of parish history as the register of the parish, open before him, recalls people to his mind. Four editions appeared in a year and a half. Crabbe had found a larger readership than he can have expected for his unvarnished account of country life, so he was encouraged to extend his view. In *The Borough* he culled characters and events out of his early life: Aldeburgh is enlarged to provide a full gallery of persons, mostly faulty, if not downright sordid. In scenes of neglect and vice Crabbe did excel, as his detractors have said, but he conveyed such scenes with a quiet force which gains from restraint. The picture of the Suffolk workhouse is an example of this, where "the day itself is, like the night, asleep." Crabbe was a keen critic of his own writing and destroyed much that he wrote, both poetry and fiction. In consequence he advanced in technique and found a new medium in his *Tales of Verse*, published in 1812. Here his flair for the short moral tale found fulfillment. He continued to use the heroic couplet, but with such flexibility and sprightliness that the meter does not pound the sense into insignificance. He is another Pope in his use of antithesis and balance, but there is no feeling of anachronism. He was writing to men's plain sense, not much to their fancy, but he was ready to explore any subject. When young he had a passion for botany; in his mature verse there is the feeling of a writer peering calmly at humanity through his microscope. Thus he achieves, in stories like *Arabella* and *Peter Grimes*, a pleasing actuality and also sometimes an ironic detachment. Often his verse is no more melodious than a greenfinch's song, but its asperities help to counteract the steady rhythm, save it from monotony. Long before, Burke had remarked the wide range of his knowledge. The tales are indeed prolific in their interest in things and people. Later collections, *Tales of the Hall* (1819) and *Posthumous Tales* (1834), sustained the interest in his writing to the end. Fox had been an early admirer, Jane Austen liked his work (which has some affinities with her own), and Sir Walter Scott's last hours were solaced by readings from *The Borough.*

Crabbe had moved to Trowbridge in 1814. In this Wiltshire market town he spent some agreeable years, tasting his fame in visits to London and Edinburgh, enjoying a social round which must have seemed giddy after the isolation of Muston. He came to be respected by his parishioners and his son and biographer talks of the deepening personal piety of these years. He died regretted by many and these lines from the inscription beneath his monument at Trowbridge do him justice: "He broke through the obscurity of his birth, Yet never ceased to feel for the Less fortunate; Entering [as his work can testify] into The sorrows and deprivations Of the poorest of his parishioners."

E. M. Forster, ed., 1932, *Life*, by his son, G. Crabbe, 1834.
E. M. Forster, "George Crabbe and Peter Grimes," in *Two Cheers for Democracy*, 1951.

WILLIAM MURRAY, 1st EARL OF MANSFIELD (1705–93) was a great Lord Chief Justice; for thirty-two years he sat on the King's Bench. In all that time the court was only twice divided in opinion, and only two of its judgments were reversed in the House of Lords. His wisdom, fairness, and perseverance in difficult cases epitomized the finest qualities of English law.

Murray was a Scotsman by birth, younger son of Lord Stormont and of Margery Scott. He was born at Scone, but went to Westminster School and to Christ Church, where he became known as a consummate and elegant scholar. When he entered the House of Commons in 1742 his legal reputation was already made. He became Solicitor-General and lent weight unquestioningly to successive governments. It was perhaps unseemly that he should have led for the Crown in the Jacobite trials of 1746–47, but his view of his rebel countrymen was not a sentimental one; the ministry had been severely shaken by the '45—and the charge was treason. In the Commons he steadily enhanced his position. "Silver-tongued" Mansfield could speak with sense and style about any matter of law, economics, or politics. After he became Attorney-General in 1754 he was Newcastle's prop and partisan in the Lower House. Two years later he accepted the Chief Justiceship, which was his highest ambition. Offered the Great Seal, he twice refused; he filled briefly the office of Chancellor of the Exchequer, but he took a diminishing part in politics.

Upon Mansfield fell the onus of passing judgments in the several stages of the Wilkes case. These seem to show a bias in favor of prerogative, but when, for instance, he reversed Wilkes's outlawry for the technical reason that the writ was wrongly made out, he was more the cautious lawyer than the supple politician. Indeed, his procedure throughout was influenced by precedents rather than by his instinctive conservatism. Yet Wilkes accused him of subverting the law and "Junius" complained, in his most venomous manner, that he was importing the civilian (Roman) doctrines into English law. He certainly reduced the scope of the jury in libel cases, holding that their only job was to decide the fact of publication; after the special verdict returned in the case of Rex *versus* Woodfall, newspaper editor, he ordered a new trial. Deliberate and wary though he was, Mansfield did not hesitate, when he felt that a principle should come before precedent. No decision was more crucial than that of 1771 in the case of the negro James Somersett, that slavery could not exist in Great Britain. In another important case, Campbell *versus* Hall, he deprived the Crown of its powers of legislation by Order in Council over a colony to which a legislative assembly had been granted. By the sort of ingenious fiction in which Common Lawyers delight, he ruled in Fabrigas *versus* Mostyn that the island of Minorca was for legal purposes deemed to be "within the ward of Chepe."

Lord Mansfield won respect by his manner, for he was "gravitas" personified, and by his magnanimity. During the Gordon Riots a wild Protestant mob wrecked his house and destroyed his precious library, but he subsequently presided with conspicuous fairness over the trial of Lord George Gordon. Judicial manners in those days were not perfect and we are told that, like other judges, he would read a newspaper during counsel's speeches, if he believed that the evidence was closed and that counsel was wasting public time. He made, however, some useful reforms in procedure. He put an end to the practice of allowing any number of counsel on the same side to address the house and thus delay business excessively; he also used to deliver judgment whenever he believed there was no need for reconsideration, where formerly it had been customary to reserve it. His greatest achievement was, however, in the field of commercial law. Before his time commercial cases hardly ever came into the courts; he gradually attracted to the King's Bench a mass of business from the city. He impaneled a special jury of businessmen who attended regularly so that the judge came to know them well; he would talk freely with them in court and some would become habitués.

Mansfield became an earl in 1776, but he did not resign his office until 1788; he spent his later years serenely at his house at Caen Wood, near Hampstead. Boswell spoke of his "air and manner which none who ever saw or heard him can forget." His courtesy, ease of manner, and graceful speech were as impressive as they were unusual in an eighteenth-century lawyer.

C. H. S. Fifoot, *Lord Mansfield*, 1936.

SIR WILLIAM BLACKSTONE (1723–80), jurist, was born in London, the posthumous son of a London silk mercer. He went to the Charterhouse and, aged fifteen, to Pembroke College, Oxford. His early career was worthy, but humdrum. He entered the Inner Temple, was elected a Fellow of All Souls, which was not then such a signal honor as it has since become, and was called to the Bar. He failed to attract notice or practice, but in 1749 he succeeded an uncle as recorder of Wallingford and, in 1753 on the advice of Lord Mansfield, began to deliver lectures at Oxford on the state of English law. In 1758 a Mr. Viner endowed with £12,000 a chair of English law at Oxford, and Blackstone was appointed first Vinerian Professor. In 1765–69 he published his lectures in the form of *Commentaries on the Laws of England;* they brought him £14,000 and lasting fame.

Blackstone supplied an enormous need. English students of his time could only learn by hanging around the courts or by perusing such outworn books as *Coke upon Littleton*, Rolle's *Abridgement*, or Shephard's *Touchstone*. There were only two recognized textbooks: *Doctor and Student* by Saint-Germain had first been published (in Latin) in 1523, though there were subsequent English editions, and Thomas Wood's *Institute of the Law of England* was by general consent unreadable. Academic study of law scarcely existed and Blackstone began by deploring the lack of facilities for teaching and learning it. His *Commentaries*, about 2,000 pages in all, were the more imposing, perhaps, because of the stony ground around him, but nonetheless a massive work. Indeed Blackstone, in his prosaic field, may be compared with Gibbon: there is the same optimism and assurance and a wealth of learning conveyed in pellucid, even elegant style; the same note of complacency too, the critic may add.

The *Commentaries* became a standard textbook for more than a century, but they could be read by the amateur too, for he wrote, as Bentham said, in the "language of the scholar and gentleman." His achievement was to summarize the laws of the country, antique, uncertain, and infinitely complex. As befitted a man of his century he gave due place and importance to the laws of Real Property and its incidents: a quarter of the whole. The conditions of English society explain, too, the faults of omission: together the Law of Contract, the Law of Corporations, and Commercial Law occupy only 100 pages. There are some curiosities. One finds that wager of battle was still legal, that the Saxon wager of law was valid in small debt cases which could be proved by the plaintiff's bringing eleven witnesses to his side. In George II's reign a man was pressed to death by *peine forte et dure* for refusing to plead. Blackstone was robustly conservative and typically condemned the abandonment of Latin in 1730 (it had been reintroduced after the reforms of the Commonwealth in 1660) on the ground that the change impaired the culture of attorneys and their clerks. Some of his assumptions are bland—blind might not be too unkind a word. Writing of the survival of benefit of clergy which had been modified by successive acts declaring small offenses punishable by death, he wrote of the "wisdom of the English legislature having, in the course of a long and laborious process, extracted by a noble alchemy rich medicines out of poisonous ingredients." In an age which was notable abroad for the beginnings of law reform, Cocceji's work in Frederick the Great's Prussia, for instance, we read with surprise of English criminal law, that "it is with justice supposed to be more nearly advanced to perfection than that of any other country." He was insular, little touched by the spirit of the Enlightenment. Of witchcraft, for example, abolished as a crime in 1736, he says: "to deny the possibility, nay the actual existence, of witchcraft is flatly to contradict the revealed word of God." He would find good reasons for manifest absurdities. Instead of focusing attention on the grotesque number of capital offenses which made a mockery of the ultimate deterrent, he wrote with approval of the "pious perjury" by which a jury would undervalue stolen articles so as to place them below the value at which the death sentence applied. Even he could not defend the time-wasting proceedings of the Court of Chancery. But the strength and lucidity of his language, for the most part, confirmed the prejudices of his readers, and put a heavy seal of permanence upon a jumble of laws which was neither rational, humane, nor indeed, in any sense, a system. No wonder that he was anathema to Jeremy Bentham, who looked at law from a more critical and objective standpoint.

Blackstone, a dry personality, though fond of his port, entered Parliament and in 1763 became Solicitor-General to the queen. He became a K.C., his practice grew, and he resigned in 1766 his Oxford appointments. In 1770 he refused to accept the Solicitor-Generalship, but he was knighted and subsequently became a Justice of the Court of Common Pleas. His fame rests, however, upon his exposition rather than his practice of the law. He epitomizes—and he helped to perpetuate—that peculiarly English satisfaction in the excellence of the constitution, "so wisely contrived, so strongly raised and so highly finished that it is hard to speak with that praise which is justly and severely its due."

Sir William Holdsworth, *History of English Law*, 12 vols., 1922–38 (especially last 3 vols.).
D. A. Lockmiller, *Blackstone*, 1938.

EDWARD THURLOW, 1st BARON THURLOW (1731–1806) secured the highest legal places without ever showing himself to be a great lawyer. He benefited from the deference that politicians of his time paid to lawyers as interpreters of the constitution, but his long ascendancy was based upon force of personality. With a strong presence, a good mind, and a cutting tongue, he had the hearty insensitiveness that can carry a man to the fore in politics. Coarse-grained, unsubtle, greedy for place, he was yet able to win the respect of better men, notably North and Pitt. To North he was a tower of strength; Pitt came to detest him, but valued his caustic common sense and his knowledge of men.

He was the son of a Norfolk clergyman, educated at Scarning School and at King's School, Canterbury. Perse Scholar at Caius College, Cambridge, he was sent down for insulting the dean. In a lawyer's office in Holborn he was a fellow-pupil of Cowper. How different his career from that of the gentle poet who shrank and broke before responsibility! Thurlow soon made a name for skillful advocacy. In the celebrated Douglas case he secured a reversal of the decision of the Court of Session—and then fought a duel with the Duke of Hamilton's agent, Andrew Stuart. In 1770 he was appointed Solicitor-General, in 1771 Attorney-General. He overthrew Lord Mansfield's doctrine of perpetual copyright in Donaldsons *versus* Becket (1774) but opposed legislative settlement. By nature he was indolent and attachment to the *status quo* is one of the two principles that can be discerned in his career. The other is a high view of royal prerogative. He won the approval of George III for his inflexible attitude toward the American colonies and became his trusted servant and confidant. Elevated to the woolsack in 1778, he remained there for fourteen years, with only one interval during the coalition of Fox and North in 1783. In the year before, he had been the one minister to survive the fall of North and take office under Rockingham.

'No one," said Fox, "was ever so wise as Lord Thurlow looked." Indeed he dominated the Lords as much by his appearance and manner as by what he said. He was also, however, skillful in debate, with a disconcerting memory, a genial sarcasm, and a sharp eye for the weak points of his opponents. In his judicial capacity he was fair; in all his dealings there was a directness which inspired confidence. Dr. Johnson enjoyed tilting with him: "I honor Thurlow, sir: Thurlow is a fine fellow, he fairly puts his mind to yours." But he might not have approved Thurlow's conduct of November 1788. The Chancellor, who had before acted for the king in a matter so delicate as the notorious intervention to sway the Lords against Fox's India Bill, now, when George III was ill and a Regency was mooted, intrigued behind the backs of his colleagues with the Prince of Wales. George III recovered, Thurlow kept his place, but lost what remained of his reputation. He protested his loyalty in the most shameless way: "If I forget my king, may God forget me," upon which Wilkes muttered, "He will see you damned first," and Burke added, "The best thing that could happen to you." Removed at last in 1792 he at once made his court with the Prince of Wales, but this did him little good. Before all else Thurlow was an authoritarian. He sympathized with Hastings, over whose trial he presided; less justifiably he defended the interests of the slave owners. With all his toughness and shrewdness he lacked the imagination and flexibility to be a great Chancellor.

R. Gore-Brown, *Chancellor Thurlow, the Life and Times of an XVIIIth Century Lawyer*, 1953.

JAMES MACPHERSON (1736–96) was a literary impostor, but not a literary charlatan. He presented his own poems as the work of Ossian; this was a sort of fraud, but his works had an influence and a merit which justifies his fame as an original artist. Dr. Johnson declared that *Fingal* was "as gross an imposition as ever the world was troubled with." Had it been an ancient work, "a true specimen how men thought at that time, it would have been a curiosity of the first rate. As a modern production it is nothing." Dr. Johnson spoke with the indignation of a literary man and a purist in the heat of an argument which now makes pleasant reading in Boswell's account of the *Tour of the Hebrides*. Thousands of less critical readers were attracted by the epic quality of *Fingal*, its notes of romance and sensibility.

Macpherson was born in 1736 at Ruthven near Kingussie, the son of a small farmer. At the University of Aberdeen he acquired literary tastes and ambitions that could not be satisfied by his work as schoolmaster in his native parish. In 1758 he published a poem, *The Highlander*. He became tutor to the son of Graham of Balgowan; when he accompanied him to Moffat he met there John Moore, author of *Douglas* and an ardent fancier of Highland life. Macpherson was already acquainted with the Gaelic fragments of the period of Ossian but believed that he could do better. For his friend he wrote *The Death of Oscar*, then other romantic stories. In 1760 appeared *Fragments of Ancient Poetry Collected in the Highlands of Scotland, and Translated from the Gaelic or Erse Language*. Persuaded by "several people of rank, as well as taste," he traveled around the Highlands and Western Isles: the fruit of his travels, and the patronage of some Highland lairds, was *Fingal: An Ancient Epic Poem in Six Books.* In the following year, *Temora,* another poem, was published, in eight books. Macpherson was borne on by a mixture of conceit, real feeling for the new idiom, and a gale of popular acclaim, and he was undismayed by the heated argument about the authenticity of his poems. He promised to publish the originals but of course never did. He had taken only such expressions and themes from the Gaelic as suited his own epic purpose. Rejecting the Irish Finn in favor of Fingal, conqueror of the Romans and native hero, he slighted Irish scholars as much as he offended the skeptical critics of England. When in 1805 Laing published an edition of Ossian (and of Macpherson's own poems) the extent of his borrowings and of his originality was revealed. By then his Ossian had swept Europe. Goethe and Napoleon read it, and many others who were entranced by the new cult of medievalism and liked his wild, misty melancholy, regretful and somber, couched in a rhythmic language that was as near to the familiar cadences of the Bible as it was to any Celtic bard.

Macpherson wrote a *History of Great Britain* (1660–1714) and an unremarkable translation of the *Iliad.* He was active as a politician, was made surveyor-general of the Floridas in 1764, and sat in Parliament for Camelford from 1780. He lived out his last years at Belleville, the house he built for himself at Badenoch. He did not underestimate his own abilities. It was at his own request and cost that he was buried in Westminster Abbey.

J. S. Smart, *Life of Macpherson,* 1905, and some lively passages in Boswell's *Tour to the Hebrides.*

JAMES BOSWELL (1740–95), diarist and biographer, wrote what many hold to be the finest Life in the language. He also wrote about himself with a combination of honesty and art, and in such detail that we know him more intimately than any man of his time. If his fame rests upon Dr. Johnson, it is also true that to some extent Johnson's rests on Boswell's account. It is a happy chance that a man fitted by temperament for biography should have found a subject as robust and idiosyncratic as Johnson; also that Johnson was so much the center of cultural life in London that a portrait of him is also "a view of literature and literary men in Great Britain" for half a century.

Boswell was born in Edinburgh in October 1740, eldest son of Alexander Boswell, Lord Auchinleck. His father's title was derived from his position as judge in the Court of Session, but he was also a laird whose estates in Ayrshire were granted to an ancestor by James IV. He was a severe and opinionated man, out of sympathy with his more flighty son. His mother was Euphemia Erskine, through whom he claimed kinship with the Earls of Mar and Dundonald; from her Boswell may have derived the gentler elements of his personality. Boswell was educated at Edinburgh, at the high school and university; there he made a friend in William Temple, who was to be his lifelong confidant. In 1759 he was sent to Glasgow University to read law, perhaps because his father was perturbed by the friendships he was forming among theatrical people. In the spring of 1760 he visited London and became a Roman Catholic. The results of this escapade were transitory; it looks like an emotional gesture, and he was reconverted under the tutelage of his father's friend, the Earl of Eglinton. In Edinburgh again, he threw himself into legal studies with the energy that he could always rouse for short spells. In July 1762 he passed the civil law examination and was rewarded by leave to go to London again. There he attempted to secure the commission in the Foot Guards that his father refused to buy for him. During this period he wrote the first long stretch of the journal which was to be his life's companion and confessional. He also met Samuel Johnson, who snubbed him, but was touched by his persistence. Boswell was as eager for patronage as ivy for an old wall. He craved to be a man of the world, to discover "real life," but he also sought a relationship, as of son to father, in which he could serve a great man—and his self-esteem. Outwardly jaunty, conceited, effusive, inwardly prey to doubts, to a hypochondria which grew upon him with age, Boswell was endowed with an abnormal appetite for life, but cursed by an instability of will and purpose which was eventually to destroy his happiness.

In August 1763 he went to Utrecht to acquire knowledge of civil law. The rigors of his life were softened toward the end by an affair with a well-born Dutch girl, Belle de Zuylen. In the following year he went upon a Grand Tour, at first in the company of the veteran Jacobite, later Prussian diplomat, George Keith, Earl Marischal. He did not meet Frederick the Great, Keith's master, but had interviews with both Rousseau and Voltaire. In 1765 he went on to Italy, now traveling with Lord Mountstewart. His adventures at this time read like the plot of a comic opera. He enjoyed an amour with the wife of the mayor of Siena; then in the autumn he visited Corsica, identified himself warmly with their revolt, and befriended the leader, Pasquale de Paoli. He was back in Paris when he heard of the death of his mother. From grief he fell into debauchery; besides occasional affairs he acquired a regular mistress in Mrs. Dodds of Moffat. He also published a Latin thesis on a title of Roman civil law and began to practise busily. In 1767 he took part in a famous case concerning the succession to the estate of Douglas, published an allegorical fiction, *Dorando*, and some pamphlets, and fathered a daughter, Sally, by Mrs. Dodds. In 1768 he made his mark in London by the publication of his *Account of Corsica*. In 1769 he had cause to celebrate in the decision of the House of Lords reversing the Court of Session's decision against young Douglas and led the mob which broke windows in the houses of Edinburgh judges. He became engaged to Marie Montgomery, his cousin, but he was disconcerted when his father also married again and he refused to live under his roof. He had many cases at the bar of the General Assembly and he found increasing employment as defense counsel in criminal cases. Journeys to London brought diversion from work and there it was always Dr. Johnson who provided the calm center of a dissipated existence.

Boswell was a deep drinker; for long periods in Edinburgh he was hardly sober. He had moods of wretchedness, "the spleen," and good resolutions were of no avail against his liking for low life. The picture of the diarist, flushed with wine, wandering the London streets in search of a whore, is no less pathetic for the fact that he is the meticulous chronicler of his own vices and absurdities. Johnson, the rugged and venerable sage, Christian and moralist, was a rock at which he was glad to cast his anchor. Readers of the *Life of Johnson* may think of a steady relationship; in fact, during the two decades of their friendship, there were only some few hundred days on which they actually met, three periods of two years when they were separated. The picture is yet wonderfully complete, because Boswell was acutely observant, had a capacious memory for detail, and was assidodus in filing in the gaps from accounts of mutual friends. He was sometimes humiliated, more often rewarded by the incomparable talk, not only of Johnson but of the friends of "The Literary Club" to which he was elected in 1773—Reynolds and Burke, Garrick and Gibbon, Sheridan, Goldsmith and Doctor Burney. In that year he brought off his greatest stroke when he persuaded Johnson to undertake a trip to the Hebrides. In his subsequent chronicle we see Dr. Johnson against the unlikely setting of mountain and sea, talking with chieftains, being rowed along the coast of Scalpa, inspecting a ruined fortress, or flaunting a Highland bonnet above his bushy wig. No one had quite the effect upon Johnson, who suffered from depressions, that Boswell had. Did he feel that he was called upon to make a special effort in the company of his recorder? More likely Boswell's own enthusiasms were infectious, putting the doctor into "full glow of conversation."

The most important case in Boswell's forensic career occurred in 1774: the trial and condemnation of John Reid, sheep-stealer, whom Boswell had already defended with success on a previous charge. So convinced of his innocence was Boswell that he even hatched an abortive plan to cut him down from the gallows and re-suscitate him. From this experience Boswell's nervous system suffered further shock. His deterioration could not be checked, by his patient wife, by his own moods of contrition, or by pledges against alcohol. He was incurably lecherous, though a fond parent of his seven children. A sudden whim at this time took him to the house of Mrs. Rudd, a notorious forger, who had escaped execution by turning king's evidence; in course she, too, became a mistress. In 1782 his father died and he became laird of Auchinleck, but even from its rocks and pine trees, a proper setting for an avid romantic, the London road was still the finest prospect he could see. The death of Dr. Johnson, however, in 1784, was a catastrophe. Boswell could only work upon his life and it was published with acclaim in 1781. He sought the patronage of Lord Lowther with an eye to Parliament, but was treated contemptuously and secured nothing more than the Recordership of Carlisle. His wife died, in 1789, and he toyed with one marriage project after another with desirable heiresses. It was a miracle that the Life appeared at all; his hand was so unsteady that he could sometimes hardly correct the proof sheets. He suffered, as before, from the effects of venereal disease. Restless to the end, he sought the post of Commissioner to Corsica, recently liberated from the French, but Dundas knew him too well to send him to the island which had first made his fame. In the following year, May 1795, he died at his house in Great Portland Street.

It is almost impossible to convey the flavor of Boswell's personality, but one incident may be cited as typical of the man. Soon after his return from Corsica he went to call upon the elder Pitt, to whom Paoli had requested he bear a message. The gaunt statesman, foot wrapped in flannel on a gout stool, was taken aback when Boswell entered his room dressed as a Corsican chief, with stiletto and pistol, long gaiters, and cap with a plume of cock's feathers. He was a man of exuberant fantasies, and yet an acute analyst of his own conduct. It is an extraordinary thing in this sentimental, sensuous man that his masterpiece was so true to life. Instead of creating a grand impression of his hero by drawing upon his imagination, he built up a true picture of a complex personality by faithfully reporting. Inconsistent, untidy, the Life is a great work because it is so free from varnish. We are allowed to see the doctor as bully or glutton or coarse-mannered eccentric on the occasions when he was these things, just as we are allowed to see Boswell as a toady and an exhibitionist. Anticipating the honesty of self-portrayal which has been more common in subsequent literature, applying the same technique to his subject, Boswell became, more than even he can have guessed, a great creative writer.

F. A. Pottle et al., eds., *Yale Editions of the Private Papers*, 10 vols., 1950–70.
D. B. Wyndham Lewis, *The Hooded Hawk*, 1946.
P. Quennell, *Four Portraits*, 1945.
F. A. Pottle, *Boswell: The Earlier Years*, 1966.

JAMES WOODFORDE (1740–1803), country parson and diarist, made but small stir in his day; when, however, his diary was published in five volumes between 1924 and 1931 he was hailed as a diarist worthy to stand with Pepys and Evelyn. His special claim to distinction is that he was an ordinary man, writing about ordinary country folk. Besides being uncommonly entertaining, Woodforde's placid chronicle is a rich mine for those who want to dig into the unchronicled past. What Gilbert White did for the natural history of Hampshire, Woodforde did for the people of the Norfolk countryside: farmer and laborer, shopkeeper and servant, blacksmith, bishop, parson, and squire—we see them through his observant eye. Nothing was too small for him; so we know what he ate, who came to his church, how his dogs fared, how he suffered from toothache.

The great world impinged upon Woodforde: he dined at Oxford, where he was a fellow of New College; he visited the great houses of Norfolk, recorded the event with satisfaction when Mr. Pitt was delayed at an inn with him for shortage of horses, and registered the victories and crises of successive wars. But the appeal of the diary lies most in its glimpses of rustic life. Woodforde was a curate in Somerset for some years. But the longest part of his diary deals with his life as rector of Weston Longueville in Norfolk from 1776 to his death. He was of his age, no enthusiast; services were unadorned, Communions rare and solemn. His piety was nonetheless constant and unaffected. After being jilted by a girl when he was thirty-four he did not marry, and his life was devoted to the well-being of his parishioners. He did not neglect his own comfort: we see him tucking in with relish to his favorite "plumb pudding," working through meals that would floor most men today. The reader who wants to know about the domestic life of the period, in cottage as well as parsonage, about smallpox and smuggling, country medicine and country churches, prices, partridges, and pigs, should turn to Woodforde. There he will enter into a vanished world: for all its poverty, disease, and toil an Arcadian scene among the elms and oaks, the high hedgerows and flint church towers of inland Norfolk. His account is plain, clear, and light, like the sky of his adopted county, and as full of pleasant surprises as his favorite river Wensum was full of trout and pike.

J. Beresford, ed., *The Diary of a Country Parson*, 5 vols., 1924–31.

JOSEPH WRIGHT (1734–97), painter, is known as "Wright of Derby" because he was one of the few painters of this period to follow his career in the industrial Midlands. He was trained as a portrait painter in London under Thomas Hudson (who had earlier taken Reynolds as a pupil); made the customary journey to Italy; tried to establish himself as a fashionable portrait painter in Bath; exhibited for a time at the Royal Academy. But Derby his birthplace, and the delicious valleys of Dore and Derwent, always drew him back. It was here that he mainly lived and worked; here also that he made his friends—scientists, engineers, and industrialists, presiding over the infancy of the industrial revolution. Among his finest portraits are those of Sir Richard Arkwright of the spinning frame, Samuel Crompton of the spinning mule, Jedediah Strutt, John Whitehurst, Erasmus Darwin (who became Wright's own physician).

But he was more than a good portrait painter of the second rank. All his life he was fascinated by the illustrative effects of light shining in darkness—a domain explored by names as distinguished as Caravaggio and Honthorst (and of course Rembrandt) but yielding to Wright nonetheless a rich crop of moonlit, candlelit, and firelit scenes. What is unique about him is that he harnessed this formula to his own mechanical bent, to create a series of *tableaux* which are the first pictorial records of the dawn of the industrial revolution. "A Philosopher Lecturing on the Orrery" (Derby) and "An Experiment on a Bird in the Air Pump" (Tate Gallery) are only the two best known: paintings of scientific exercises, dramatized by the centrifugal glow illuminating the bodies of the watchers. As industry quickly took root in Derbyshire Wright's imagination was haunted by the incandescence of furnaces, by the blaze of foundries. The paintings which followed are more truly history paintings than most of what passed under that name.

He used the same principle of "light shining in darkness" to make paintings of the eruption of Vesuvius (which he had witnessed), of a somber landscape slashed by a rainbow, of dazzling sunsets, cottages on fire, of "The Earthstopper on the Banks of the Derwent" (Derby), and "An Academy by Lamplight" (Mellon Collection), which are highly dramatic in themselves, and give a foretaste of Romanticism.

It is rare to find a provincial artist who has so many arrows to his bow. Often in a gallery one is startled into saying, "Can that really be by Wright, and was he so various?"

Benedict Nicholson, *Joseph Wright of Derby*, 2 vols., 1968.
Judy Egerton, *Catalogue of Wright of Derby Exhibition*, Tate Gallery Publications, 1990.

JOSEPH NOLLEKENS (1737–1823) was the foremost portrait sculptor of his day; his working life neatly bridged the interval between Roubiliac and Chantrey. His father and grandfather were painters from Antwerp; and he himself was apprenticed at thirteen to the immigrant Antwerp sculptor, Peter Scheemakers, whose statue of Shakespeare for Westminster Abbey (1740) had been uniquely popular. For ten years from 1760 Nollekens labored in Rome, making sketches, "restorations," and copies of ancient statuary, and imbibing that science of the antique which, while it colored his work, has too readily been assumed to be the leading characteristic of it. It was in Rome that Garrick, out of kindness, became his first sitter; but it was the bust of Laurence Sterne, done also in Rome and now to be seen in the N.P.G., which declared his talent. His reputation was published, and he returned to England in 1770 to engross the stage of sculpture. Only two years later he was elected R.A., and married into the Johnson circle. He made it his interest to become a rich man, which he notably achieved. When his tremendously active life closed in a cloud of senile dementia and paralysis in 1823, his estate was found to have reached the mountainous size of some £200,000. In *Nollekens and His Times* is stigmatized the avarice of the sculptor; but the author of that "biography" was disappointed at receiving a mere £100 as Nollekens's executor, and his strictures must be taken with a handful of salt. Undoubtedly Nollekens practiced economy as a virtue; but the scale of his fortune is the scale of his professional success; and it is simply a token of the increasing popularity of portrait sculpture that he was able to charge as much as 150 guineas for a single bust, four or five times what Rysbrack had charged in the 1730s.

More than eighty funeral monuments he has to his credit, a large enough achievement for any sculptor. But these often disappoint: they reiterate motifs which were in any case borrowed from his predecessors—the orthodox pyramid for a background, and in front the lachrymose woman, and the boys who hold up medallion portraits of the deceased. And it is not surprising, in such a number, to find that the modeling has been skimped, or that (especially in the drapery) it is overcomplex in a stylized way.

But that is only a portion of his work: it is as the sculptor of busts that we honor Nollekens. He has been hailed as a neo-classicist; Flaxman said he was the only English sculptor before Banks who had "formed his taste on the Antique and introduced a purer style of art"; but though Nollekens dwelt in the tents of the neo-classicists and carved works (such as the goddesses for Wentworth Woodhouse) which, but for a certain wryness, would decidedly be taken for revivals of the antique, his talent was too various to be neatly labeled, and many of his busts are as unpretentiously realistic as those of Rysbrack or Roubiliac. The bust of Sterne has been mentioned: the bare shoulders and the prominent bonework, the style of the features, are Roman of the Republic; but the face that confronts you is an unidealized, scrupulous study of a humorous and masterful man; and although the eyeballs are incised according to Nollekens's usual practice, there was no need of that to animate the cast of features on which the currents of character had been so unmistakably traced.

Nollekens was known for his skill at taking likenesses, at sifting the essential features from the secondary. Although he made a point of modeling from life, the effect of a Nollekens bust is as if the sculptor had gathered from the painted portraits and concentrated into one head the traits which each painter had separately noticed as the most distinctive in the subject—and this at the time of the zenith of English painted portraiture. Thus—in the case of the king or Rockingham, of Pitt or of Fox—not all the painted portraits look like the bust, but the bust looks like all the painted portraits. Friends must have come upon the busts with the shock of recognition; for us they are the nearest thing to flesh-and-blood acquaintance with the sitters.

JOHANN ZOFFANY (1733–1810), a German-born painter, studied in Italy, and came to England in the 1750s, when Arthur Devis was painting conversation pieces so still as to seem timeless. The conversation piece was an eighteenth-century confection, hit upon first by Hogarth and designed to relieve family groups of the apparatus of shepherds' crooks, clouds, harps, and fillets with which they had been encumbered, and to depict them as they were in their life of everyday. This was Zoffany's *métier*: whether he paints "Lord Willoughby de Broke and His Family" grouped on a rich carpet round the coffee urn, while the fire crackles happily in the background, or "The Garricks with Dr. Johnson Taking Tea on the Lawn in Front of Their Villa at Twickenham," he is perfectly at home among the respectable bourgeois comforts which were the lot of so many families of the time—of which indeed his scrupulously faithful renderings must be borne in mind when Hogarth conducts us down Gin Lane or Gillray introduces us to the Union Club.

Elsewhere he paints his friend Garrick in theatrical roles, and depicts the equally theatrical milieu of the "The Tribune at the Uffizi" or the academy schools. He was in fact a founder-member of the academy, at the king's direction.

SIR HENRY CLINTON (1738–95), soldier, was unfortunate at the height of his career to be given an assignment which all historians have agreed to have been difficult, some have thought impossible. As commander-in-chief in America, he paid the penalty for political blunders and divisions. While he fought against American rebels and American geography, the aims and principles of the war were questioned at home. The loss of supremacy at sea at a crucial time made his difficulties more severe. In the circumstances he fought with skill and energy.

Clinton was born in Newfoundland, where his father was governor. He was for a time captain of the New York militia. Then he came home to serve in the Coldstream Guards. He served with distinction in Germany in the later stages of the Seven Years War. In 1772 he was promoted major-general. In the following year he became a member of Parliament, like so many senior officers, but had little chance to enter political life before he was sent out to America. He fought under Gage at Bunker Hill in 1775; he at least did not thereafter underestimate the enemy. In 1776 he led a naval squadron and a force of 2,000 to conduct a campaign in the south, where the population, it was hoped, was still pro-British. But his attempt to take Carolina failed, because the loyalists were few and poorly organized. Shortly afterwards he took Rhode Island, but as commander in New York, in 1777, he was left without enough troops to go to the help of Burgoyne at Saratoga. In the following year he replaced Howe as commander-in-chief, with orders to try to bring Washington to battle and, if that failed, to limit his activities in North America and try instead to capture the French West Indian island of St. Lucia. This negative course, dictated by the government's reluctance to meet the cost of an all-out war—and their hopes of earning a dividend out of France's entry into the war—merely encouraged the American rebels to reject English terms—the more so when he evacuated Philadelphia.

In 1779, however, prospects were happier: the Americans were suffering from rising prices, disaffection, and mutiny. Clinton concentrated upon recovering the south: Savannah and Georgia were captured. Cooperating closely with the fleet under Rodney, he made a series of expeditions and raids along the coast. He defeated the Americans severely at Charleston in 1780; both North and South Carolina were won back. Meanwhile Cornwallis beat the enemy at Camden and, in 1781, at Guildford Court House. The renegade Benedict Arnold held his own in Virginia. But those successes were sterile. America was now only one theatre of several in a war of survival against a coalition. Losses of men could not be replaced. Victories had no effect once the army had disappeared; farms, villages, and towns returned without hesitation to their old defiance. Then control of the sea was lost, and there ensued a second disaster, comparable with that of Burgoyne at Saratoga. Cornwallis was besieged at Yorktown, Clinton's relief force arrived too late to help and surrendered. This was virtually the end of the war. Neither by Clinton's strategy of invasions in depth, nor by Cornwallis's more prudent idea of conserving strength in well-defended strongholds, could the war have been won. Indeed, as Lord North's government tottered to its fall in February 1782, the struggle took on an air of unreality. The opposed forces remained inactive, but balanced throughout 1782; meanwhile Clinton came home. He lost his seat in Parliament in 1784, regained it in 1790. In 1794 he went out to govern Gibraltar and died there the following year. Both his sons became generals; the younger, Henry, was one of Wellington's favorite officers.

P. Mackesy, *The War for America*, 1964.

SIR WILLIAM HOWE, 5th VISCOUNT HOWE (1729–1814) was the younger brother of Richard Howe, the admiral. Like so many serving officers, he was a member of Parliament: he sat for Nottingham from 1758 to 1790. In 1775 he was promoted lieutenant-general and sent to America to succeed Gage as commander-in-chief, but during the next three years he failed to secure the decisive victory which might have ended the revolt. At the battle of Bunker Hill he pushed the colonists back from their earthworks, but only at a cost of a thousand men killed and wounded, half the force which had labored up the hill, bowed under heavy packs. In 1776 he was forced to evacuate Boston and to establish his base in Halifax, Nova Scotia. At this point he and his brother at sea were provided with a large armament to recover the initiative, and they captured New York. General Howe then pursued the retreating Washington across the mainland beyond the Delaware, but could not bring him to battle. He wintered in New York, with the enemy forlorn, but intact and capable of striking back as Washington showed in December with a foray which cost Howe a thousand Hessians. He had been empowered by the ministry to offer terms, but he now realized that an all-out effort was required. He therefore asked the government to provide 20,000 troops, but was sent 2,000.

Despite Lord North's inability to think in terms of total war, the War Minister Germain's plan of attack for 1777 was an ambitious one: Howe was to move up from New York to meet Burgoyne, marching down the Hudson from Canada, with the result of separating the New England colonists from Washington and his armies in the South. Howe did not, however, wish to stay inactive, until Burgoyne had reached the proposed rendezvous at Albany, while Washington was raising the colonists' morale by his slow reduction of New Jersey and the country around. Germain therefore authorized him to attack Philadelphia. Howe left New York by sea in July, but made slow progress. Eventually he defeated Washington at the battle of Brandywine (August) and took Philadelphia. He was unable, however, to help Burgoyne, when the latter was trapped among the trees and sharpshooters of Saratoga and was compelled to surrender in October. Howe subsequently resigned his command and came home. He became lieutenant-general of the Ordnance but had no further active command.

Howe's apologists stress the inhibitions of the politicians whom he served and the difficulties of terrain and communications. He could only have smashed the revolt by an urgent, perhaps unorthodox, style of campaigning, foreign to him as to most eighteenth-century soldiers. Howe was, moreover, by any standards a torpid and uninspired commander. As Mackesy says: "The weight of the indictment lies in the cumulative impression of his actions and in failures which run through the whole scale of events from the great decisions to the details."

RICHARD HOWE, 4th (IRISH) VISCOUNT, LATER EARL HOWE (1726–99) was a great seaman, in Walpole's phrase "as undaunted as a rock and as silent." It is unfortunate that a fire in an Irish house destroyed a trunk full of papers of Admiral Howe, for otherwise we would know more about him. The son of the second

Viscount Howe, he was only a child when his father died from drinking coconut milk in the Barbados; he went to sea at the age of fourteen and his first experience was on Admiral Anson's voyage of circumnavigation. He was related to the king, for his mother's mother was the German Countess of Darlington, mistress of George I. In 1745 he became post-captain and in that year fought off two French frigates bringing supplies to the Pretender. He was for some time member of Parliament for Dartmouth, but his political duties interfered little with his career at sea.

In the Seven Years War Howe specially distinguished himself; after it, in 1765, he became Treasurer of the Navy. In 1770 he was promoted rear-admiral. In the American War he played a leading part, along with his younger brother, the general. He was sent out in 1776 by Lord North to act with his brother and 20,000 troops, but with authority too to offer peace. When the colonists rejected his overtures, General Howe captured Long Island but failed to destroy Washington's force. In 1777 he was not given the reinforcements he wanted and Sandwich held most of the fleet back in home waters. In 1777 the general managed to beat Washington at Brandywine, but this was small compensation for Burgoyne's surrender at Saratoga. Meanwhile Admiral Howe was unable to do much to answer the destructive activities of American privateers. In 1778, too, he had to restrict his activities. His shortage of frigates was particularly serious and he now had to contend with the French as well, and the need to defend the West Indies was paramount. He came home at the end of the year to report that he did not think that it would be possible to hold America. In 1782 he commanded the expedition which relieved the garrison of Gibraltar; the combined French and Spanish fleet declined to meet his challenge to battle.

From 1783 to 1788 he was First Lord of the Admiralty in Pitt's government and added to his reputation for honest administration. He refused to respond to the requests for promotion which came from political patrons, such as Dundas; he was also unpopular, because of the economies which he had to administer in this postwar period. He grew tired of factious opposition, for he was a rigid man, never at heart a politician. In 1788 he was replaced by Lord Chatham and created an earl. But when war was declared against revolutionary France (1793) he was chosen, at the express request of the king, to command the Channel fleet. He was much admired by the sailors for his honesty, courage, and humanity. During one of his earlier commands he had started the system of leave in turn by watches. His rough compassion was remembered: how he used "to go below after an action and talk to every wounded man, sitting by the side of their cradles, and constantly ordering his livestock and wine to be applied (for them)." Officers knew the gruffer side of his character. Hotham, who served as a midshipman under him, said that he was "cold in his manner and not very accessible." But there was a general acknowledgment of his merit. The navy's signaling system was his work. Moreover his calm, common sense did not conceal his toughness and in the action lasting from May 28 to June 1, 1794, "Black Dick" answered his critics.

The French, under Villaret-Joyeuse, covered the passage of a vital grain convoy from America. For four days the fleets fought a spasmodic battle in a heavy swell. No previous action had been fought so far away from land, 400 miles from Ushant. On Sunday, June 1, Howe passed through the enemy's line and engaged from leeward. He hoped for a series of single ship duels from which the French could not escape. "Now, gentlemen," he had said, "no more book, no more signals. I look to you to do the duty of the Queen Charlotte in engaging the French Admiral. I do not wish the ships to be bilge to bilge, but if you can lock the yard arms, so much the better." Six French battleships were secured; their fleet was terribly mauled. No English ship was lost, but there was much damage and the victory was not followed by the destruction of the convoy. Howe had been brought up to the formalism of the eighteenth century; not for him the great risks involved in an attempt to destroy the enemy utterly. His was the prudence of an admiral who knew, perhaps, like Jellicoe at Jutland, that he could lose the war in a day. His officers valued the victory he had achieved. "Why," said the exhausted admiral after the battle, "You hold me as if I were a child." It was fitting that his last service was to recall the mutinous seamen at Spithead to their duty in 1797. He rowed round from ship to ship with George III's pardon in his hand. The king and he were the only two men whom the sailors would trust.

A. T. Mahan, *Types of Naval Officers*, 1901.
C. Lloyd, *The Glorious First of June*, 1970.

WILLIAM BLIGH (1754–1817) has suffered so much in reputation from legend and film as the captain of the *Bounty* that it is proper to recall that this was not the climax of his career and that he was something other than the brute that the action of the mutineers might suggest. He went as sailing master on Cook's second voyage round the world, 1772–74, and it was he who discovered breadfruit at Otaheite. In 1787, then lieutenant, he commanded the *Bounty*, which was commissioned to fetch breadfruit plants from Otaheite. After an awkward voyage he was confronted by a mutiny, led by Fletcher Christian, in April 1789, and cast adrift in an open boat. The mutineers went on to Tahiti and the sensuous life that attracted them first to mutiny. Bligh landed at Timor and thence reached England, to be exonerated for his conduct and promoted post-captain. He sailed in 1791 to the Society Islands. In 1794 he received the medal of the Society of Arts; in 1801 he became a Fellow of the Royal Society.

When he was Governor of New South Wales in 1805 Bligh again encountered trouble; this community of convicts forcibly deposed him in 1808 and kept him in prison until 1810. He returned to England and again to promotion by a government ill-disposed toward disaffection. Rear-admiral in 1811 and vice-admiral of the Blue in 1814, he was not, however, given any important command. Many of the facts of his life are necessarily obscure. It is likely that Christian was an awkward man, a natural rebel; trouble was only to be expected from the lawless inhabitants of Australia. But there is some evidence that Bligh was clumsy in his management of men. In circumstances of great difficulty, where only the character of a Cook could have held the loyalty of a crew, he failed to assert his authority. It should be remembered, however, that even Cook lost several men by desertion, that Bligh was not unusual in ordering harsh punishments, and that the navy was crippled by a general mutiny only eight years after this affair in the South Seas.

Further Reading

In this necessarily short list appear some of the books which are of general interest or provide essential background to the particular studies and books already suggested.

Linda Colley, *Britons: Forging the Nation, 1707–1837*, 1992.

J. Steven Watson, *The Reign of George III, 1760–1815*, 1960.

W. A. Speck, *Stability and Strife: England, 1714–1760*, 1977.

Paul Langford, *A Polite and Commercial People, England, 1727–83*, 1989.

W. Prest, *Albion Ascendant: English History, 1660–1815*, 1998.

R. Porter, *English Society in the Eighteenth Century*, 1982.

J. Brewer, *Pleasures of the Imagination: English Culture in the Eighteenth Century*, 1997.

L. Namier, *The Structure of Politics at the Accession of George III*, 2nd edn., 1957.

J. C. D. Clark, *English Society: Ideology, Social Structure and Political Practice during the Ancient Regime*, 1985.

J. Black, *A System of Ambition? British Foreign Policy, 1660–1794*, 1991.

P. Mathias, *The First Industrial Nation*, 2nd edn., 1983.

J. Brooke, ed., *Memoirs of the Reign of George II*, 3 vols., 1985.

H. T. Dickinson, *Liberty and Property: Political Ideology in Eighteenth Century Britain*, 1977.

R. Porter, *Enlightenment: Britain and the Creation of the Modern World*, 2000.

K. V. Thomas, *Man and the Natural World: Changing Attitudes in England, 1500–1800*, 1983.

J. Black, *The English Press in the Eighteenth Century*, 1987.

J. Burke, *English Art, 1714–1800*, 1976.

M. D. George, *English Political Caricature to 1792: A Study of Opinion and Propaganda*, 1959.

A. S. Turberville, ed., *Johnson's England*, 1933.

E. G. Rupp, *Religion in England, 1688–1791*, 1986.

L. Stone, *The Family, Sex and Marriage in England, 1500–1800*, 1977.

E. Mingay, *English Landed Society in the Eighteenth Century*, 1963.

J. Cannon, *Aristocratic Century: The Peerage of Eighteenth Century England*, 1984.

D. Hay, P. Linebaugh, and E. P. Thompson, *Albion's Fatal Tree*, 1975.

H. C. B. Rogers, *The British Army of the Eighteenth Century*, 1977.

N. A. M. Rodger, *The Wooden World: An Anatomy of the Georgian Navy*, 1986.

T. W. Moody and W. E. Vaughan, *The New History of Ireland*, vol. IV: 1692–1800, 1986.

P. Morgan, *A New History of Wales: The Eighteenth Century Renaissance*, 1982.

T. C. Smout, *A History of the Scottish People, 1650–1830*, 1970.

P. J. Marshall, ed., *The Oxford History of the British Empire*, vol. II, *The Eighteenth Century*, 1998.

B. W. Labaree, *Empire or Independence, 1760–1776*, 1976.

N. McKendrick, J. Brewer, and J. H. Plumb, *The Birth of a Consumer Society: The Commercialisation of Eighteenth Century England*, new edn., 1983.

J. D. Chambers and G. E. Mingay, *The Agricultural Revolution, 1750–1880*, 1966.

M. D. George, *London Life in the Eighteenth Century*, 1966.

Index